Williamsburg, Virginia:
A City Before the State
1699-1999

Edited by *Robert P. Maccubbin*

Commissioned & Produced by
Martha Hamilton-Phillips
300th Anniversary Commission

City of Williamsburg
2000

Published by the City of Williamsburg
Distributed by The University Press of Virginia

ISBN 0-8139-2011-6

Design by Oller Studios, **www.ollerstudios.com,** 203 Greensprings Rd., Williamsburg,
Virginia, 23185

Printed by Carter Printing Company, Richmond, Virginia

Contents

Special Sections

Acknowledgements

This book, conceived as part of Williamsburg's 300th Anniversary celebration, was developed through discussions in 1996 with two of Williamsburg's most distinguished historians: Dr. Thad Tate, Professor of History Emeritus at the College of William & Mary, and Dr. Cary Carson, Vice President of Research at the Colonial Williamsburg Foundation. We envisioned a volume that would be lively and a pleasure to browse through, but that would, more lastingly, present much new information from archaeological and archival research, and include many unpublished illustrations.

A City Before the State is different from previous publications because it attempts to cover the whole history—even the pre-history—of Williamsburg. The Powhatan Indians, religion, theatre, government, the Greek community, and African-American history over all three centuries are just some examples of subjects that had not been incorporated in earlier histories. Also, in re-examining Williamsburg's rich 300-year history, the book focuses on key themes, not just the chronological succession of events. The city's chronology is incorporated, instead, in an appendix and is more inclusive than any previously attempted.

Such a comprehensive pictorial history had to be collaborative, with essays by many authors, who would provide a multitude of perspectives, fresh insights, and new research. Each chapter, therefore, represents a distinct voice.

The city called on many talents to realize this ambitious project. Dr. Kevin Kelly helped assign the original essays and read a number of early drafts. Mary Anne Williamson prepared some early layouts, a brochure announcing the book and its contents, and suggested the subtitle "A City Before the State." S. Dean Olson, the late Director of Publications at the college, offered much appreciated encouragement and advice.

Our greatest debt is to Dr. Robert Maccubbin, Professor of English at William & Mary: he took on the vast bulk of editorial work in 1999, selected and researched much of the art and many of the captions, and brought the entire book to completion. His rigorous editorial standards, diplomacy in communicating with twenty-five authors, and expertise in design were invaluable. We are also very grateful to David F. Morrill, Managing Editor of the journal *Eighteenth-Century Life*, of which Prof. Maccubbin is the editor. He contributed untold hours to correcting, proofing, and improving the book in its final stages; and his expertise in desk-top publishing was crucial to both the content and layout of the book.

Jack Tuttle, Williamsburg's City Manager, supported the book from its inception, and contributed an excellent chapter on the history of local government. Gerry Walton, Executive Assistant in the city manager's office, deserves special thanks for her expert transcription and formating skills, and countless hours devoted to this book and other tricentennial projects in 1999.

William & Mary and Colonial Williamsburg were partners in assembling images from their archives: special thanks are due Margaret Cook, Curator of Rare Books and Manuscripts at the college; Stacy Gould, Acting University Archivist; Michael Fox in Government and Community Relations; and Ann Madonia at the Muscarelle Museum of Art. Our gratitude extends especially to Marianne Carden Martin, Visual Resources Librarian at the John D. Rockefeller, Jr., Library, for her exemplary help and cooperation. Others at Colonial Williamsburg to whom we owe a great debt are Tim Andrews in Public Relations; Gail Greve in Special Collections; Steve Haller in Archives; Laura Arnette and Catherine Grosfils at the Rockefeller Library for help on picture research and photo orders; and Lael White, Barbara Temple, Kathy Dunn, and Mary Norment for expert and efficient assistance from the Colonial Williamsburg Photo Lab.

For photographs of modern-day Williamsburg people and events, we were fortunate to have had two generous volunteers photograph the city's 300th Anniversary events: Dr. Ellen K. Rudolph and Charles C. Troha. Both of these professional photographers donated their time and pictures. Moreover, the late Thomas L. Williams shared his photographs covering more than fifty years of Williamsburg history, and his daughter Karen Laufer kindly assisted us by lending additional photos from his estate.

Many individuals provided information through interviews or their own research. We are grateful to the Braxton, Gardner, and Tabb families in particular for supplying information for the map inside the cover jacket and for photo captions highlighting the role of African Americans in twentieth-century Williamsburg. Thanks also for the advice of friends and colleagues who read and reviewed some of the chapters, notably Martha McCartney and Philip Burcher. For providing information and assistance in preparing captions for photographs in the final sections of the book, thanks to: Ben Altschuler, Tracy Blevins, Helen Clendenin, Deborah DeMarco, Teri Edmundson, Patrick Golden, Steve Haller, Karen Laufer, Jimmy and Kim Maloney, Marianne Martin, Blanton McLean, and especially Julia Oxrieder and Will Molineux.

The daunting task of formating and doing the final design of the book was assigned to Oller Studios, whose staff had generously designed Williamsburg's 300th

Anniversary web site (www.300th.ontheline.com) *pro bono*. Thanks are due to Bob Oller and Jeané Treviño for their expertise and great patience. We are also grateful to Jimmy Witt for his mastery of all aspects of book printing, and to Carter Printing in Richmond for their excellent production. Thanks also to Richard Stinely for permitting the city to feature on the book cover his award-winning art work, the watercolor renderings of the Wren Building and the capitol; and to George Crawford, whose successful 300th logo design helped generate revenue from commemorative merchandise to underwrite this publication.

Martha Hamilton-Phillips
Executive Director
300th Anniversary Commission

Editor's Note

Wishing to leave a lasting history of Williamsburg behind her when she finished directing the 300th Anniversary of Williamsburg, Martha Hamilton-Phillips envisioned this book. Her experience as university instructor, curator, and art historian gave her the insight to insist on a volume that would stand academic scrutiny but be a pleasure to all in both its written content and its many illustrations. Though she consulted widely, she was the primary mover behind the book, took the main role in the selection of subjects and authors, combed archives, supplied many of the authors with information and suggested art for many of the essays. Although the designation is unusual, she can accurately be thought of as the "Producer" of this book. Without her vision and acumen, this book would never have been born.

In the later stages of this book's production, no one, however, was more necessary than David Morrill, managing conscience of *Eighteenth-Century Life* and experienced page-maker, persistent and meticulous critic, endurer of long and odd hours—witty, quirky, and affable curmudgeon extraordinaire. Without him, this book may never have been finished.

There is no index here, primarily because the essays are relatively short, so that readers looking for most topics or names can easily spot in what range of a few pages to look. The text contains many cross references to illustrations, however, so that when an event, building, person, etc. is first mentioned in an essay, if it is illustrated in another essay the reader will be directed to the illustration.

Although the essays are authoritative, they are not footnoted. At the end of each, however, is a list of "Selected Sources and Suggested Readings" to guide readers to each author's main sources and to further their own pursuits.

❖ ❖ ❖

I hope that because of this volume more residents of Williamsburg will begin to treasure and preserve their family photos and their domestic and institutional memories, participate in the oral history projects now underway, and think of themselves as figures of interest to historians a hundred years from now.

Enjoy the book and Williamsburg's future.

Robert P. Maccubbin
College of William & Mary

Introduction

A City Before The State is a collection of historical essays produced by the City of Williamsburg on the occasion of the 300th anniversary of its founding. In 1699, when Williamsburg came into being, it was in a British colony—one that sanctioned slavery, limited the vote, struggled with native people, and one that was on the path toward creating an identity, a community, and a nation that was new. Today, Williamsburg is perhaps the most important historic city in this nation. It reflects in many meaningful ways the changes that our country has undergone in these last 300 years. It is also a unique and a very special community.

The scope of the volume is broad. It begins with Dennis Blanton's description of the pre-historic natural forces that shaped the landscape of the Virginia Peninsula, creating conditions favorable to native Americans and then the seventeenth-century English settlement. The book concludes with an insightful essay by Jack Edwards reminding us of the major changes that have taken place in the last quarter of the twentieth century. Edwards also outlines the challenges for the future as we work to preserve the special character of the Williamsburg region. Throughout the essays, recurring themes characterize our history and continue to be important today: exceptional institutions, fine architecture and city planning, historic preservation, diversity of population, visionary leadership and an engaged citizenry.

Institutions

From its beginnings, Williamsburg has been the home of some widely respected, outstanding institutions that have also shaped the unique character of the city. Jennifer Agee Jones points out that the establishment of the College of William and Mary and the erection of Bruton Parish Church in Middle Plantation helped persuade Virginia officials to move the capital here and create the city of Williamsburg. According to Mark R. Wenger, that move set the stage for Williamsburg then to become the political, commercial, and social center of America's largest English colony in the eighteenth century. Thus established as an important urban center, even after the removal of the capital to Richmond necessarily diminished Williamsburg's status, antebellum Williamsburg did well because, as Emma L. Powers notes in her essay, four remaining institutions provided its livelihood: the college, a major hospital, the county seat, and a regional market. The active, vibrant religious life of the city is detailed by John Turner. Beginning with the establishment of Bruton Parish in the seventeenth century, houses of worship have grown to more than eighty-five in the Williamsburg area today.

Three institutions deserve special mention for the significance of their contributions to the community and the nation. Blanton McLean looks at the history and development of the pioneering Eastern State Hospital, the first mental health hospital in the country, and chronicles the path-breaking changes in treatment and care provided there

*Williamsburg is
named after King
William III, who
ruled Britain and
its colonies at the
time the new
capital city was
founded in 1699.
William ruled
jointly with Queen
Mary II after the
Glorious
Revolution of
1688-89, and
granted the royal
charter founding
the College of
William & Mary
in 1693. His Great
Seal shows him
enthroned, alone,
after Mary's death
in 1694. The
heraldic beasts
flanking the throne
are the Belgic lion
of William's
native Holland
and the English
unicorn.*

Courtesy,
William H. Cole

for more than two centuries. Thad Tate traces the important relationship between the College of William and Mary and the city, noting that the three-century connection has been dynamic and complex, producing "both discord and harmony"; but it has been beneficial for both, working to strengthen the city and the college. Peter Brown and Hugh DeSamper discuss the success of Colonial Williamsburg, attributing it not only to a wonderfully restored historic site and the wealth of stories it tells, but also to the persistent quest for quality and authenticity established by the foundation's leadership.

Architecture and City Planning

Quality also has been a continuing theme in architecture and city planning through three centuries in Williamsburg. The city was established in the seventeenth century by Virginians eager to create an urban center in the colony that would support the sophisticated environment being developed. A persuasive case is made by Carl Lounsbury that "throughout the eighteenth century the fortunes of a city were frequently measured by its public buildings." Consequently, Virginia's government leaders and the citizens of Williamsburg sought to construct durable brick buildings of architectural significance. The resulting public buildings and early efforts at city planning reinforced a feeling of permanence and were an essential element in the town's success. Ironically, after the Revolution, Thomas Jefferson regarded the town and its fine public buildings as symbols of an old, corrupt order and successfully fought to relocate the capital to Richmond, where new buildings could be constructed.

In his essay, Kevin Kelly chronicles the important events of the Revolution that took place in Williamsburg and details the town's decline with the move of the capital to Richmond in 1780. The decrease in population and the weakened economy brought about by war and the move of the capital, however, allowed the physical structures of the colonial town to survive, provided the basis for the restoration financed by John D. Rockefeller, Jr., and thus created the circumstances for the prosperity the town has enjoyed in the twentieth century.

Historic Preservation

Williamsburg citizens remained proud of their revolutionary heritage long after the battles were won. Carol Dubbs recounts the concerted efforts of townspeople during the Civil War to preserve many of the city's colonial treasures from destruction during that conflict; and Thomas H. Taylor, Jr., shows that the value of the old buildings in the city continued to be recognized by local people in the late-nineteenth and early-twentieth centuries before the Rockefeller restoration began. For example, the Association for the Preservation of Virginia Antiquities purchased the powder magazine in the 1890s, and Bruton Parish was carefully restored in time for the Jamestown Exposition in 1907. Edward Chappell indicates how the designs of John Graham Pollard began to give a distinctive quality to some of the early suburbanization of Williamsburg, reflecting a growing community sense of the need to prevent the historic area's encroachment by ill-planned growth.

The restoration enterprise, a tremendous investment of time and money by Rockefeller over several decades, built upon these early efforts and resulted in the creation of the Colonial Williamsburg Foundation.

Reverse side of the Great Seal, showing King William III in Roman imperial armor astride a war horse, symbolic of his sovereignty and military leadership over Britain and its colonies. The city skyline below his steed represents London. William reigned from 1689 until 1702, when he died as a result of a fall from his horse.

Courtesy, William H. Cole

Diversity of Population

Several authors call our attention to the richly diverse cultures that came together in this community. Thomas E. Davidson notes that the English who arrived here in the seventeenth century entered territory already occupied by Powhatan Indians, "the most powerful and politically sophisticated group of people then living along the Atlantic Coast of North America."

Christy Matthews describes the arrival of the first Africans in Virginia, which began a process that had a deep and long-lasting impact upon subsequent generations of Virginians. Tracing the codification of slavery in Virginia, she also reminds us that by the last quarter of the eighteenth century people of African descent were at least fifty percent of Williamsburg's population, contributing in many ways to the life of the city.

Linda Rowe picks up the story of African Americans in Williamsburg in the late the nineteenth century, noting how life became increasingly difficult with the implementation of Jim Crow laws, denial of voting rights, implementation of strict segregation, and, later, the displacement of homes and businesses by the restoration of the colonial town. However, a strong and cohesive black community was sustained by reliance on family, church, and school, enabling some to own prosperous businesses. Rex Ellis continues the story to the present day, recognizing some of the major individuals and families who struggled to provide educational opportunities and who were the local leadership in the civil rights movement and the expansion of voter registration. He draws our attention to the new, cohesive neighborhoods created by displacement.

Mia Spears reflects on the contributions throughout most of the twentieth century made by Greek immigrants and their descendants in Williamsburg. Playing a major role in the hospitality industry, they developed a network of restaurants that were popular with locals, visitors, and students alike. These business interests later expanded into the hotel industry, and fortunes made were generously shared with the community through donations to many worthy causes.

Visionary Leadership and an Engaged Citizenry

Throughout these essays a portrait of Williamsburg as a city of engaged citizens with visionary leaders emerges. John Page, identified as "the father of Williamsburg," is described as a leader in a group of seventeenth-century men who understood the importance of creating the city and who seized the opportunity to do so. Several essayists acknowledge the contributions in politics, education, and religion of the Reverend James Blair, founder of the College of William and Mary. Partly because they are already so well known, the stories of great patriots who shaped American independence while in Williamsburg are not treated here in great detail. Rather, attention has been drawn to eminent, but now less famous, local leaders—men such as Williamsburg resident Dr. John Galt, well-known for modernizing mental health care. Essayist Julia Oxreider notes that, at the opening of the twentieth century, the African-American merchant Samuel Harris was a leader in business and in civic affairs, and was regarded by a national author as the richest African American in his business in America. Oxreider also calls attention to the accomplishments of Mrs. Cynthia Beverly Coleman in founding the important Association for the Preservation of Virginia Antiquities. The efforts of Dr. W. A. R. Goodwin in stimulating and guiding the restoration of the colonial town during the first half of the twentieth century are addressed from several perspectives in these essays. And it was the stewardship of a series of college presidents in both prosperous and difficult times that built the renowned College of William and Mary that we know today. Another essay documents how Carlisle H. Humelsine led the Colonial Williamsburg Foundation to achieve an international reputation.

On the local level, the civic contributions of leaders such as Steve Sacalis, Angelo Mageras, Mike Kokolis, Dr. James Bland Blayton, Reverend L. L. Wales, Phillip Cooke, and many others are included in this collection; and Jackson Tuttle calls our attention to a group of twentieth-century political leaders, including John Garland Pollard, Channing M. Hall, Sr., and Polly Stryker, whose bold decisions modernized the town while protecting its unique character.

These are only a few of the many leaders whose work for Williamsburg is recognized in this volume. An equally important theme in Williamsburg's history is the active and thoughtful participation of individual citizens and community groups in projects and causes designed to improve the city—including its cultural life, as Wilford Kale notes in his account of the long theatrical tradition in the city. Will Molineux is one of several authors who focus on the contributions of Williamsburg citizens during wartime. The important work of various civic improvement leagues at the beginning of the twentieth century is discussed, as is the African-American struggle for equal opportunity in education, politics, and the economy. The evolution of the city government is traced through the centuries as citizens structured new and better ways to provide necessary services. From each essay in this volume emerges a picture of a community whose residents have been proud of their city, have recognized its special character, and have been committed to preserving its exceptional qualities.

This book is an important contribution to our ever-growing appreciation of our debt to those who came before us and built the city we enjoy today. It also serves to remind us of the continuing importance of an informed, engaged citizenry. Perhaps Jack Edwards says it best:

> The extent to which Williamsburg will be special in the future will depend partly on whether its residents maintain and enhance the large network of service, intellectual, artistic, and social organizations that has characterized Williamsburg.... Such groups not only enrich the lives of members, but also connect citizens to each other and help establish a sense of community.

This thoughtful collection of essays should inspire future generations of Williamsburg citizens to sustain the traditions of civic mindedness, community service, and respect for the past.

Jeanne Zeidler
Mayor of Williamsburg

Williamsburg City Council

Mayor
Jeanne Zeidler

Vice Mayor
Channing M. Hall, III

Council Member
George S. Genakos

Council Member
Gilbert L. Granger

Council Member
Wright B. Houghland

Author Biographies

Dennis B. Blanton is Director of the William & Mary Center for Archaeological Research, where he has worked for eleven years. He was trained in anthropology at the University of Georgia and Brown. His research interests have always been focused on the eastern United States, and his areas of specialty are prehistoric archaeology and historical climatology.

Peter A. G. Brown attended Yale University and served during World War II in the Pacific theater as an officer with the combat engineers. He joined Colonial Williamsburg in 1953, and served as assistant to the president, director of the Abby Aldrich Rockefeller Folk Art Collection, and as vice president responsible for all programs in the Historic Area, the craft shops, exhibition buildings, student programs, and the Information Center. He retired in 1988.

Edward Chappell is Director of Architectural Research at Colonial Williamsburg, where he is responsible for the study and interpretation of historic buildings and is an advocate for the visual environment. He has directed restoration and re-creation of the Peyton Randolph and James Anderson complexes, the 1770 Courthouse, and the late colonial slave quarter at Carter's Grove. Outside Williamsburg, he has been involved in restoration of the plantation houses at Prestwould, Blandfield, and Jefferson's Poplar Forest.

Thomas E. Davidson is Senior Curator for the Jamestown-Yorktown Foundation, which operates two area history museums, Jamestown Settlement and the Yorktown Victory Center. An archaeologist by training, Dr. Davidson received his Ph.D. from the University of Edinburgh. His main research interests are English-Indian relations in the colonial Chesapeake and 17th-c. material culture.

Hugh DeSamper is a graduate of William & Mary and Navy veteran of WW II and the Korean War. In a 36-year career with Colonial Williamsburg, he prepared travel articles, news, and other information for nationwide distribution in all media. He also wrote and edited a variety of publications. Since his retirement, he has continued to write, most notably a historical booklet about Bruton Parish Church and two travel books.

Carol Kettenburg Dubbs, a native of San Diego, received her M.A. degree from the College of William & Mary in 1980 with a thesis entitled, "The Battle of Williamsburg." Since then she has expanded her research and completed a manuscript on Williamsburg during 1861-1865.

Jack D. Edwards received a B.A. from Macalester College, a J.D. from Harvard Law, and a Ph.D. in political science from Vanderbilt. He taught Government at William & Mary from 1962 to 1996 and was a civic leader as well, being elected to the James City Board of Supervisors from 1971 through 1999. He served as president of the Virginia Association of Counties and the Virginia Municipal League and has been a member of several commissions, including one on population growth.

Rex M. Ellis has an Ed. D. degree from Wiliam & Mary and is presently Curator and Chair of the Division of Cultural History at the National Museum of American History. Before that, he directed the Department of African American Interpretation and Presentations at Colonial Williamsburg. He has essays in several journals and a book, *Beneath the Blazing Sun: Stories from the African-American Journal*. He is working on a book on black banjo players. His lectures, work-

shops, and consultancies focus on museum studies, public programing, diversity, interpretation, and education.

Jennifer Agee Jones is a historian in the Department of Historical Research at Colonial Williamsburg, where she directs the Digital Library project. She previously worked for the Department of Archaeological Research as both an excavator and researcher. She is a doctoral candidate in American History at William & Mary.

Wilford Kale spent his last 25 years in the newspaper business as a reporter and bureau chief with the *Richmond Times-Dispatch.* He is now Senior Staff Adviser at the Virginia Marine Resources Commission. His first book was *Hark Upon the Gale, an Illustrated History of William and Mary* (1985); and in 1993 he co-authored *Traditions, Myths and Memories*, published on the occasion of the college's 300th anniversary. Kale has edited and been co-author of several books in the past decade.

Kevin Kelly has been a historian in the Department of Historical Research at Colonial Williamsburg since 1977. He took a B.A. from Michigan State and Ph.D. at the University of Washington. He has taught at William & Mary, Bowdoin College, and was a Fellow at the Institute of Early American History and Culture. Dr. Kelly researches the social history of Williamsburg, helps instruct the interpreter corps, and assists in interpretive planning.

Carl Lounsbury took a B.A. at the University of North Carolina and Ph.D. in American Studies in the Smithsonian Program at George Washington University. In the Architectural Research Department at Colonial Williamsburg, he has been engaged in research and restoration of a number of buildings. His many writings include *Architects and Builders in North Carolina: A History of the Practice of Building, The Charleston County Courthouse,* and *An Illustrated Glossary of Early Southern Architecture and Landscape.* He has also taught at several Virginia institutions.

Christy S. Matthews grew up in York County and earned a B.A. and M.A. at Hampton University. She began her career at Colonial Williamsburg in the former Company of Colonial Performers. In 1986-89, she was Assistant Educator for the Baltimore City Life Museums. Returning to Williamsburg, she published on museum interpretation. She is also a playwright and performer. She directed African American Programs at CW from 1994 to 1999, before leaving to become Director of the Museum of African-American History in Detroit.

R. Blanton McLean, educated at William & Mary and Vanderbilt, has been since 1988 Library Director at Eastern State Hospital. He is most proud of his discovery, in 1981, of the 2,200-item collection of John Galt papers, and of his appointment as Assistant Professor of Psychology at William & Mary. He became the first since Galt's 1862 death to reunite the two libraries founded by Dr. Galt in 1843.

Will Molineux, a 1956 graduate of William & Mary, is a retired journalist who, for 35 years, wrote for the *Daily Press* of Newport News. He was a reporter, manager of the Williamsburg Bureau, and editor of the editorial page.

Julia Woodbridge Oxrieder took a degree in mathematics from William & Mary and then applied that background at NACA (forerunner of NASA), the Aberdeen Bombing Mission, and Occidental Life Insurance. In recent years she has become a folklore and local history buff, publishing articles and two books—*Kiss the Doorknob: Folkways and Folklore of Floyd County, Virginia* and *Rich, Black, and Southern: The Harris Family of Williamsburg (and Boston).*

Emma L. Powers, a native of Virginia, has conducted historical research at Colonial Williamsburg for more than twenty years. She holds a B.A. in history and an M.A. in American Studies from William & Mary.

Linda Rowe is a historian for Colonial Williamsburg. Her research interests include colonial religion, the history of Williamsburg's First Baptist Church, 18th-c. women, and education in colonial times. She also has done extensive work in local county records. In 1996–97 she wrote a history of Bruton Heights School and helped design the permanent exhibit about the school now on display in the lobby of the renovated building.

Mia Stratis Spears is a local historian who was born and raised in Williamsburg. She earned a B.A. from the University of Virginia and a M.Ed. from William & Mary. She is also a graduate of the Ahepa Greek School in Williamsburg. She currently teaches in the Richmond Public School system's Gifted and Talented program and is developing educational material for publication.

Thaddeus W. Tate, Jr., Murden Professor Emeritus of History at William & Mary, was, until 1961, on the research staff of Colonial Williamsburg. He served as research historian for the 1957 film, *Williamsburg: The Story of a Patriot.* After joining the college faculty, he became book review editor and editor of the *William and Mary Quarterly.* From 1972 to 1989 he was director of the Institute of Early American History and Culture and later was director of the Commonwealth Center for the Study of American Culture. Tate is author of *The Negro in Eighteenth-Century Williamsburg,* co-author of *Colonial Virginia: A History,* co-editor of and contributing author to *The Chesapeake in the Seventeenth Century,* and co-editor of *An Uncivil War: The Southern Backcountry in the American Revolution.*

Thomas H. Taylor, Jr. is chief architectural conservator for Colonial Williamsburg and manager of the architectural collection. He has a Bachelor of Architectural History and a Master of Architectural History from the University of Virginia and a Ph.D. in American Studies from George Washington University. In 1998 he received the Harley J. McKee Award for his work in bridging the gap between objects conservation and architectural conservation for museums in historic buildings. He is a Fellow of the Association for Preservation Technology International.

John W. Turner has headed the Religious Studies Program at Colonial Williamsburg since its inception in 1990, and has been associated with CW since 1968. Ordained in 1976, Rev. Turner is a minister of the Presbyterian Church, U.S.A., and since 1986 has served as Pastor at Gilboa Christian Church in Cuckoo, Virginia. Dr. Turner received a B.A. from William & Mary, a Doctor of Ministry from Union Theological Seminary in Virginia, an M.A. from the Presbyterian School of Christian Education, and a Ph.D. from Virginia Commonwealth University.

Jackson C. Tuttle, II, has been Williamsburg City Manager since February 1991. Formerly, he was City Manager in Gulf Breeze, Florida, and Assistant City Manager in Pensacola. He holds a B.A. in history from the University of North Carolina, and an M.P.A. from the University of West Florida. He is a native Marylander and Navy veteran.

Mark R. Wenger holds a Bachelor of Architecture from the School of Design at North Carolina State University, and a Master of Architectural History from the University of Virginia. Since 1980 he has worked as an architectural historian at Colonial Williamsburg, where he writes, teaches, and assists in the restoration of the historic buildings. His publications include two books and numerous articles on Virginia's architectural past.

1

*Indian burial showing copper beads in place,
Paspahegh Site. Such beads were important
indicators of high status among the Powhatans.
(See text on pp. 10-11 & 23.)*

Courtesy, Thomas E. Davidson

2

Colonel John Page, *from the circle of Sir Peter Lely (English,
1618-1680). The founder of Williamsburg donated the
land for Bruton Parish Church and helped establish the
College of William & Mary. His lifelong promotion of
Middle Plantation facilitated the relocation of the capital to
this site in 1699. (See text on pp. 15-18).*

Courtesy, Muscarelle Museum of Art,
College of William & Mary;
gift of Dr. R. C. M. Page

3

*The heart cartouche was built into the brickwork just above the door of Page's
house at Middle Plantation. It was probably a religious symbol for Page rather
than a sentimental one, and it hints of Page's attitude toward his Middle
Plantation home and neighborhood. (See ill. on p. 18 & text on p. 23.)*

Courtesy, Colonial Williamsburg Foundation

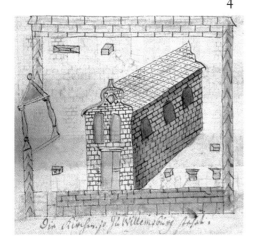

4

In 1702, Francis Louis Michel traveled to Virginia, recording in words and sketches what he saw. This crude drawing showing the first brick church built in Bruton Parish leaves out the brick footings for the buttresses, which were later discovered during archaeological investigations of the church. The corners of this church are marked in the present churchyard. (See text on p. 26.)

Courtesy, State Library of Switzerland, Berne

5

Rev. James Blair, *by Charles Bridges (English, active in Virginia, 1735-1743). In 1692, the General Assembly asked the youthful head of the Anglican church in Virginia to prepare a petition for chartering a college in Middle Plantation and to present the petition to William III and Mary II. He did so successfully. (See ills. on pp. 107 & 108 and text on pp. 108 & 137-139.)*

Courtesy, Muscarelle Museum of Art,
College of William & Mary

6

Indian students were housed and educated in the Brafferton building at William & Mary. Descendants of some of Virginia's recognized tribes stand in front of the Indian School of 1723: Chief Arthur L. Adkins of the Chicahominy Tribe, Shirley "Little Dove" Custalow MacGowan of the Mattaponi Tribe (on his rt); and members of a Powhatan Indian family (l-rt) Tashina, baby Meno, and Jamie Ware. Income from the Yorkshire estate, "Brafferton," of the great English scientist Robert Boyle helped fund the college under terms of Boyle's will.

Courtesy, Ellen K. Rudolph

7

The colonial capitol building is the preeminent symbol of Williamsburg. The building was planned in 1699 immediately after the capital city was founded and was completed in 1705. Although the original structure was destroyed in 1747 by fire (as were successive buildings), it was reconstructed in the early 1930s as part of the restoration of the colonial city (see text on pp. 31-32).

Courtesy, Ellen K. Rudolph

8

The formal gardens behind the Governor's Palace are part of ninety acres of gardens and greens that comprise a significant portion of the 174 acres in the historic area of Colonial Williamsburg. The 1930's reconstruction of the 18th-c. home of the royal governor was based on the Bodleian plate (see p. 41), as was the reconstruction of the walled formal garden, with its diamond-shaped boxwood parterres.

Courtesy, Colonial Williamsburg Foundation

9

Drawing from the manuscript Journal of Georg Daniel Flohr (1756-1826), a German soldier serving in the French regiment Royal Deux-Ponts during the Revolution. In 1781 Flohr visited Williamsburg after fighting in the Battle of Yorktown and sketched the plan of the city in a charming folk-art style with fanciful architectural details. The key public buildings are recognizable from their position or Flohr's inscriptions: the college (bottom) flanked by the President's House and the Brafferton; the capitol (top) at the eastern end of Duke of Gloucester St., the Governor's Palace and Bruton Parish church along the north side; and the arcaded market hall on the south side (upper rt).

Courtesy, Robert A. Selig and the City of Strasbourg, France

10

The Old Plantation, *anon. (ca. 1795). To relieve their hardship, slaves gathered in their quarters and amused themselves with storytelling, singing, and dancing. (See text on pp. 51-52.)*

Courtesy, John D. Rockefeller, Jr., Library,
Colonial Williamsburg Foundation

12

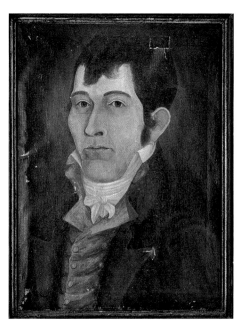

11

Virginian Luxuries *(ca. 1810), with a portrait of a gentleman on the other side. The double-sided image vividly depicts the enigmatic nature of the slave society, and the ironically titled* Virginian Luxuries *makes clear the range of control a slaveowner had over his slaves. (See text on p. 53.)*

Courtesy, John D. Rockefeller, Jr., Library,
Colonial Williamsburg Foundation

13

The Death of Major Peirson, *6 January 1781, by John Singleton Copley (1783). African Americans fought on both sides in the American Revolution. This is a rare image of a black soldier who has the rank of sergeant. (See text on pp. 57-58.)*

Courtesy, Tate Gallery, London/Art Resource, NY

14

Generals at Yorktown *by James Peale. Peale's painting shows Washington and Rochambeau with staff officers Lt. Tench Tilghman, Brig. Gen. Henry Knox, and Lt. Col. Alexander Hamilton during the siege of Yorktown. Washington and Rochambeau arrived in Williamsburg on 14 September 1781 in advance of the allied armies. When the armies finally assembled around, they marched on Yorktown on 28 September. (See text on p. 70.)*

Courtesy, John D. Rockefeller, Jr., Library, Colonial Williamsburg Foundation

15

Federal artist Robert K. Sneden, attached to the III Corps, copied the official map of the 5 May 1862 Battle of Williamsburg and added details of terrain and troop dispositions. These are rather accurately depicted on the left of the central Fort Magruder ("No. 6"), where Joe Hooker's and Phil Kearny's III Corps divisions faced James Longstreet's Confederate division. Sneden mislocated ponds, creeks, roads, and redoubts on the far right flank, however, as this territory was unfamiliar to him. It was the scene of a climactic late-day assault by Jubal Early's gray brigade against Redoubt No. 11 defended by Winfield Hancock's brigade. (See Dubbs' essay.)

Courtesy, Virginia Historical Society

16

Thomas Charles Millington, a member of the science faculty at William & Mary, painted this watercolor of Bruton Parish Church and its surroundings in 1840.

Courtesy, Swem Library, College of William and Mary

Its yard littered with broken wagons and weapons, William & Mary suffers the further indignity of having the stars and stripes flutter from one of its towers in this watercolor by Federal artist Robert K. Sneden. The college was seized by Union troops on 6 May 1862, the day after the Battle of Williamsburg. According to Sneden, Gen. Hooker turned out the four hundred Confederate wounded found in its halls to make room for his own. (See Dubbs' essay.)

Courtesy, Virginia Historical Society

18

17

Cynthia Beverley Tucker Coleman (1832-1908), painted by Joseph Wood in the 1850s. Daughter of Nathaniel Beverley Tucker (see p. 75), she wrote sketches of colonial-era personalities and incidents, recorded her experiences during the Civil War, and was a co-founder of the Association for the Preservation of Virginia Antiquities. Two of the APVA's earliest purchases were the "Powder Horn" (magazine) and the site of the capitol. Continuing in the family tradition, Mrs. Coleman's granddaughter, Dr. Janet Kimbrough, helped establish the local historical records association. Through several generations, Tucker descendants helped to highlight and preserve Williamsburg's history.

Courtesy, Cynthia K. Barlowe

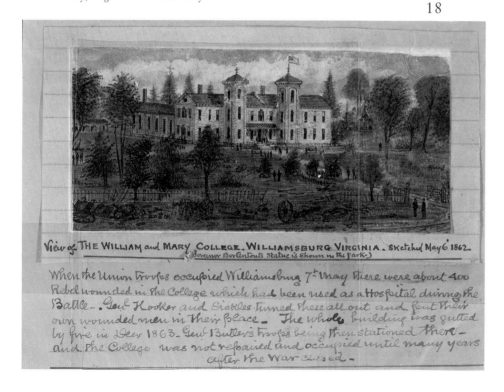

In May 1983 heads of state converged on Colonial Williamsburg for their annual Summit of Industrialized Nations. Shown leaving the capitol are, from left: President Fanfani of Italy, President Thorn of the Commission of the European Communities, Prime Minister Nakasone of Japan, President Mitterand of France, Chancellor Kohl of West Germany, Prime Minister Trudeau of Canada, Prime Minister Thatcher of Great Britain, and President Reagan of the United States.

Courtesy, John D. Rockefeller, Jr., Library,
Colonial Williamsburg Foundation

20

Emperor Hirohito came to Williamsburg with Empress Nagato in 1975 on their first trip away from Japan since World War II. Their son, now Emperor Akihito, preceded them to Williamsburg by twenty-two years.

Courtesy, John D. Rockefeller, Jr., Library,
Colonial Williamsburg Foundation

The Wren Building, fronted by Lord Botetourt, remains the most enduring symbol of William & Mary, linking the campus to the town, as it has since its first construction. Weathering badly and having enduring nearly two hundred years of vandalism, the original marble statue of Botetourt was installed inside Earl Gregg Swem Library in 1965. A bronze recreation sculpted by Gordon Kray ('73) was placed in the Wren Yard on the occasion of the college's tercentenary in 1993.

Courtesy, Ellen K. Rudolph

21

22

To celebrate Williamsburg's 300th anniversary on 1 May 1999, William & Mary hosted a ceremony commemorating the pivotal role of the college and its students in the founding of the city. Five students recreated the student orations of May Day 1699 in front of the Wren Building. Shown here on the staircase of the President's House are the five orators (rt, top to bottom): Elizabeth Burling, Mayur R. Patel, Kristin A. Zech, Jason D. Sibley, and Sharon M. Sauder. Accompanying them are faculty mentors (l, top to bottom): James P. Whittenburg, Clay Clemens, Rhys Isaac, and Clyde Haulman. In front, along the landing (l-rt) are Mayor Jeanne Zeidler, 300th Anniversary chairman Trist McConnell, Rector A. Marshall Acuff, Jr., President Timothy J. Sullivan, and Student Assembly President Marcus Hicks.

Courtesy, Charles A. Troha

23

For May Day 1999, a spectacular 300th-Birthday cake was decorated with models of the Wren Building, Bruton Parish Church, the capitol, and the 1699 Bland survey map (see p. 137). The cake was prepared under the direction of Colonial Williamsburg executive pastry chef Joe Sciegaj and a team including Roberta Lipford, Judy Hornby, and Michelle Brown. At least 3,600 citizens and visitors feasted on the cake while enjoying 1699-style games and amusements.

Courtesy, Charles A. Troha

24

The Fife and Drum Corps led crowds celebrating Williamsburg's 300th anniversary on May Day between the three host sites, emphasizing the interconnectedness of the college, the city, and the Colonial Williamsburg Foundation. Here, they perform at the picnic and community block party in the municipal center, heralding the ribbon-cutting and dedication of the new Community Building.

Courtesy, Dianne Nea Spence

Ancient Seas, Ice Ages, and Indians:
Williamsburg before History

by: Dennis B. Blanton

Appreciation of the natural conditions and the peoples of earliest Williamsburg is possible only with the greatest powers of imagination. What existed here before Williamsburg, before Jamestown, even before the Powhatan Indians, is so remote from modern experience as to be truly alien. Williamsburg now is vastly different from what it was even a decade ago, but this is a mere blink of time. The scene portrayed in Colonial Williamsburg's eighteenth century is even more foreign, yet this is but two blinks. Here is a considerable challenge: conjure up images across the gulf of time...since people first arrived here...and even before.

Look far enough back to discover a time before humans when only natural forces sculpted the landscape. This inquiry leads into the realms of geology and earth history—a foray that ultimately connects with the planet's formation. The emphasis here, however, is only to paint in broad strokes the scenes from relatively recent geological history that have culminated in the physical character of today's Williamsburg.

Hollywood has nothing on Williamsburg and the Tidewater when it comes to natural catastrophes. Would anyone believe that an enormous asteroid crashed into the present-day Chesapeake Bay basin and affected the area? The western rim of the seventh-largest impact crater on earth lies just east of Williamsburg. The crater is no longer evident from the surface but geological studies have established that it measures some fifty-five miles in diameter. The depression made between forty and fifty million years ago has long since filled with sediment left by ancient seas, leaving the rim buried roughly fifty feet below the present land surface. The maximum depth of the crater is estimated to be at least 150 feet.

Ancient oceans, however, are responsible for the fundamental character of the Lower Peninsula upon which Williamsburg is centered. The sea has risen and fallen across our area more than once over the last seventy million years. Each time it has deposited new sediment and shaped some of the old. This recurrent cycle has blan-

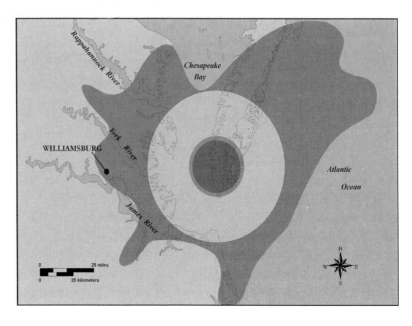

Chesapeake asteroid crater location.

Courtesy, Dennis B. Blanton

Typical Chesapeake region marine fossils of extinct whales, sharks, and shellfish.

Courtesy, Dennis B. Blanton

keted the area in scores of feet of sand, silt, and clay to form a coastal plain that extends from the present Atlantic shore westward to the fall line at Richmond. This means that a shallow sea once covered that entire expanse. Doubters need only examine eroding ravines or fresh construction trenches around Williamsburg to discover telltale evidence of marine history, where fossil shells, whale bones, and sharks' teeth abound. Indeed, Virginia's official state fossil, a scallop-shaped shell known as *Chesapecten jeffersonius,* commonly occurs in area deposits. It achieved recognition through the efforts of William and Mary geologist Gerald Johnson and his students.

Seawater last drowned the Williamsburg area about two million years ago. Gradually, the water receded well to the east. Sea level fell, as it had each time the global climate cooled to the point at which vast glaciers formed and covered the northern latitudes of North America. The moisture that fell to form the glaciers ultimately derived from the world's oceans; consequently, ocean levels fell dramatically. At the height of the last glaciation, about eighteen thousand years ago, sea level in the Atlantic Ocean was depressed about three hundred feet below today's level. If this suddenly happened today, vacations at the beach would require another hour's drive to reach the shore some sixty miles farther east! The closest that glaciers extended toward Williamsburg was New York. Nearer home, the character of streams like the James and York rivers would have been considerably different. Rather than broad, tidal, brackish streams, these rivers would have been free-flowing, narrow, and fresh. The same would be true of tributaries like College and Queens creeks, now characterized by tidal marshes and mud flats.

Those familiar with Williamsburg know about the ups and downs created by abrupt ravines. Over several hundred thousand years, erosion has created this topography. The deposit of sand and mud left by the last shallow sea probably had a generally level surface originally. In fact, Williamsburg sits on a portion of what geologists call the "Lackey Plain." The erosive action of water, mainly in small streams finding their way to larger rivers, is apparent in the pattern of local ravines, especially where lakes like Matoaka fill narrow valleys.

The cycle of global climate turned again about fifteen thousand years ago with the beginning of another warming trend, which still continues. At the outset of this period, temperatures warmed to the extent that the enormous continental glaciers began to melt and retreat, thus returning huge volumes of water to the oceans. Sea level has been rising ever since, with periodic changes in rate. This process has changed local streams from fresh water to brackish, and from narrow and free-flowing to broad and tidal. In fact, area sea levels have risen about three feet just since Jamestown was settled in 1607.

The deep mud, sand, and silt that fill local stream valleys store a wealth of information about Williamsburg's climate since the last ice age. Archaeologists are eager to understand these past conditions so that they can better understand the habitat of the area's earliest people. This interest has prompted explorations of local swamps for climatic clues, including a study sponsored by the state highway department just west of Williamsburg prior to Route 199 construction at Chisel Run, near Longhill Road.

Evidence from the Chisel Run swamp came in core samples extracted from the sediments. The cores were obtained from plastic drainpipe driven into the swamp and then pulled to extract a sample of what lies in the layers below the modern surface. Once split, teaspoon-sized bites were taken every two inches from the core's contents. The incremental samples were examined for pollen and other traces of past conditions. The longer cores reached ten to twelve feet down.

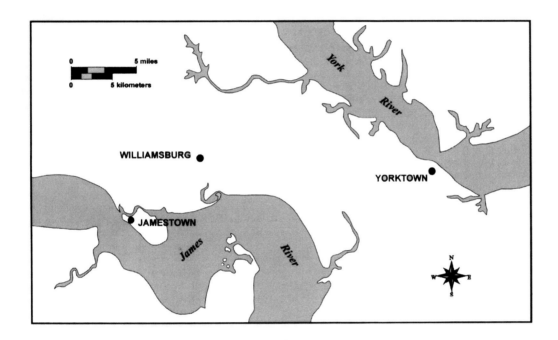

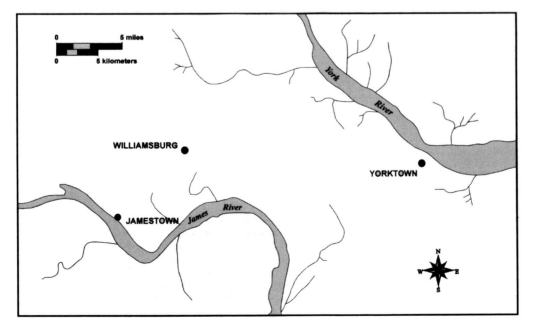

Illustrated Effects of Sea level Changes, a) sea level today, b) sea level ca. 12,000 years ago.

Courtesy, Dennis B. Blanton

From those lowly mud-filled plastic pipes comes an impressive record of the area's conditions over the last fifteen to twenty thousand years! The oldest sections, corresponding to the end of the last ice age, contained pollen from plants in a forest starkly different from today's, one more akin to what thrives now in northern Ontario, Canada, or northern Maine. Telltale pollen from spruce and northern varieties of pine trees verifies cooler, moister conditions here until about ten thousand years ago. More familiar forest cover began to dominate the area after this time, first consisting mainly of oak, hickory, and other hardwoods, but then becoming the more mixed forest of today, with an abundance of pine occurring with the deciduous types.

The samples also reveal evidence of increasing human activity. Certain types of stone spear tips exposed at the shore of nearby rivers or plowed up in area fields indicate that prehistoric Indians first entered the Williamsburg area about eleven thousand years ago. This matches the earliest confirmed human occupation along the Atlantic seaboard. But populations were sparse, and the mobile hunting-and-gathering lifestyle of these groups meant stays in the area were brief. It is true that numbers increased exponentially over the ensuing millennia, but archaeological evidence speaks clearly of a continuation of the initial pattern of use. Thousands of stone tools were lost in the soil of present-day Williamsburg and James City County over the course of some nine thousand years, but their numbers are not impressive given the span of time and quantities found in other Tidewater locales. Until about two thousand years ago, human groups favored locations along the margins of the Great Dismal Swamp and along the fall line near Richmond. The availability of native foods influenced these settlement patterns.

This picture changed dramatically about two millennia ago when the area experienced its first "real estate" rush. Suddenly, at least in archaeological terms, small campsites dotted the area landscape. These were occupied for the period of a few days or as long as a season by parties of pottery-using hunter-gatherers. Scientific excavations of these places reveal concentrations of heated stone that mark hearth locations. Around these hearths, a scatter of campsite debris includes everything from traces of table scraps like bone to perfectly functional lost tools to broken cooking pots. Nuclear or extended family groups probably used these places in their yearly rounds. Particularly impressive numbers of these campsites are known along the full reach of Powhatan, College, and Queens creeks. Almost invariably they correspond to the very places where Williamsburg residents still choose to live.

Recognition of this activity naturally begs the questions of why it started and where and when it began. The answer is not altogether obvious, but parts of the explanation seem clear. One factor is simply the effect of a net increase in population density over time. By two thousand years ago the landscape was beginning to fill up, relatively speaking, so that people were less free to pick and choose from the choicest places to call home. A second reason has to do with the changing river system. During this period, local rivers became brackish,

Representative prehistoric Indian artifacts.

Courtesy, Dennis B. Blanton

and extensive tidal marshes formed along them. Alteration of the river environment likely required adjustments, including a shift to other sources of drinking water. A natural place to turn would be the interior tributaries, which would still flow with potable water.

Evidence in the Chisel Run cores confirms this new, intensive use of the area. The tip-off to a significant human presence after a couple of thousand years ago is provided by pollen from weeds and tiny pieces of charcoal. At precisely the time an unprecedented number of prehistoric camps appears, the occurrence of ragweed pollen jumps, as does the amount of burned wood in the sand and mud. What these peculiar clues indicate is that these larger numbers of people were beginning—for the first time—to clear the forest in small patches. Plants like ragweed thrive in newly opened clearings, and fire is a popular method of clearing land the world over. Just to complete this story, it is important to add that the very top of the swamp sequence is even more distinctive, corresponding to the historic period (after 1607). After that time, enormous amounts of sand and silt washed into the stream valleys as the forest was cleared extensively for farming.

Between five hundred and nine hundred years ago, local Indian societies developed an unprecedented way of making a living and organizing themselves. The long-standing, conservative way of life, based on natural resources, was altered to include a serious commitment to small-scale farming and a relatively permanent, village-oriented lifestyle. Shortly before the English arrival in 1607, this further developed into an organization that recognized a paramount chief, who commanded tribute and allegiance from native groups over most of the Virginia Coastal Plain.

Rivers tended to be a magnet for the villages of this time. Large streams offered the convenience of water travel as well as an abundance of food. The nearest known examples occur at the junction of the Chickahominy and James rivers and along the York River between Williamsburg and Yorktown. Captain John Smith's map of the Chesapeake identifies these settlements and many others in the region.

No prominent villages from the late prehistoric period were located on the divide between these rivers where Williamsburg now sits. Instead, scattered small camps, occupied by hunters or others pursuing food away from the villages, dotted the area. Early descriptions by the English tell of a system of trails that connected villages and other important places. The major thoroughfares tended to follow drainage divides where possible. Such a trail may have passed through what became Williamsburg, connecting points on the Chickahominy, James, and York rivers.

Seldom do we consider how events preceding Williamsburg's colonial settlement influenced the character of what was to come. Natural forces sculpted the land to create conditions colonizing Europeans would find advantageous at the end of the seventeenth century: an elevated divide served conveniently by two natural ports surrounded by arable soils. The lifestyles of Native Americans before them favored settlement elsewhere for the most part; but here again, changing natural conditions strongly influenced their patterns. Williamsburg's environment is changing still, always slowly with respect to the ongoing natural cycle, but also very rapidly now due to our own modern alterations. While we can never go back, it does pay to understand what came before so as to appreciate what has happened since and anticipate what lies ahead.

Selected Sources and Suggested Readings

Blanton, Dennis B., Wayne Walker, and Charles M. Downing. *Preserving Our Hidden Heritage: An Archaeological Assessment of James City County, Virginia* (Williamsburg: Prepared for James City Co. and the Virginia Department of Historic Resources by the William and Mary Center for Archaeological Research, 1997).

Dent, Richard J., Jr. *Chesapeake Prehistory: Old Traditions, New Directions* (N.Y.: Plenum, 1995).

Egloff, Keith, and Deborah Woodward. *First People: The Early Indians of Virginia* (Richmond: Virginia Department of Historic Resources, 1992).

Frye, Keith. *Roadside Geology of Virginia* (Missoula.: Mountain Press Publishing Co., 1986).

Poag, C. Wylie. "Structural Outer Rim of Chesapeake Bay Impact Crater: Seismic and Bore Hole Evidence," *Meteoritics & Planetary Science* 31 (1996): 218–26.

Poag, C. Wylie, D. S. Powars, L. J. Poppe, and R. B. Mixon. "Meteoroid Mayhem in Ole Virginny: Source of the North American Tektite Strewn Field," *Geology* 22 (1994): 691–94.

The People of Tsenacommacah:
Powhatan Indians in the
Williamsburg Area

by: Thomas E. Davidson

When the first English settlers came ashore at Jamestown in 1607 they did not expect to find an uninhabited wilderness. From the accounts of earlier European visitors to North America, the organizers of the colony knew that this land, like other parts of the New World, would be occupied by an indigenous American people whom Europeans had already named "Indians." What the colonists and their English backers did not know, however, was that by deciding to settle in the Virginia coastal plain they were entering the world of the Powhatan Indians, the most powerful and politically sophisticated group of people then living along the Atlantic coast of North America. The site that one day would become Williamsburg lay near the heart of the Powhatans' domain, one geographically as large as some European nations.

Map showing the approximate extent of the Powhatan paramount chiefdom.

Courtesy, Jamestown-Yorktown Foundation

The Powhatan chiefdom took in all of Virginia's coastal plain from the Potomac River to well south of the James River. This huge area was split up into more than thirty separate territories, each with its own chief. These chiefs, however, all acknowledged the supreme authority of a single paramount chief, a remarkable man named Wahunsenacawh whom we know today as Powhatan. Wahunsenacawh was called Powhatan after the name of the village on the James River where he was born. "Powhatan" later became the collective term the English used for all of the various peoples Wahunsenacawh incorporated into his paramount chiefdom, even though the Indians of the Virginia coastal plain never completely lost their separate tribal identities and loyalties.

In the days of Powhatan, the Williamsburg area probably fell between two of the more than thirty territories or districts under his control. These two districts were named Paspahegh and Chiskiack. The principal village of the Paspahegh Indians was lo-

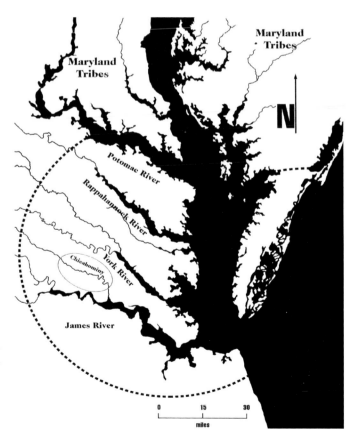

Maryland Tribes

Maryland Tribes

Potomac River

Rappahannock River

Chickahominy

York River

James River

N

0   15   30

miles

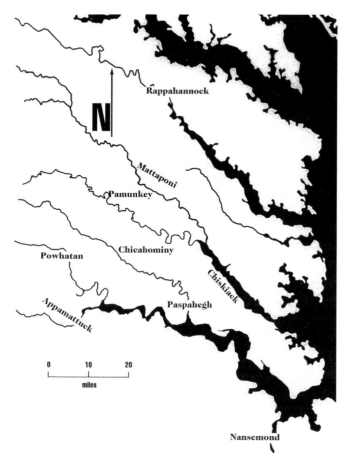

N

Rappahannock

Mattaponi

Pamunkey

Powhatan

Chicahominy

Chiskiack

Appamattuck

Paspahegh

Nansemond

0   10   20
miles

*Map showing
Powhatan tribes and
territories.*

Courtesy, Jamestown-
Yorktown Foundation

cated on the western side of the Chickahominy River where it flows into the James River. Paspahegh territory extended down the north bank of the James as far as Jamestown Island and inland probably as far as the center of the Peninsula. On the adjacent northern side of the Peninsula was the territory of Chiskiack, whose principal village was located on the York River. Williamsburg, centered as it is between the two rivers, probably was not located entirely within the boundaries of either of the chiefdoms, and the resources of the Williamsburg area were likely used by both. Farther up the Peninsula from Williamsburg was the territory of the powerful Chickahominy tribe, and, beyond the Chickahominy, the original homeland of Powhatan himself. The Williamsburg area, therefore, had considerable strategic significance in the long conflict between the Powhatans and the English for control of Tidewater Virginia.

Separate chiefs ruled the two Powhatan groups closest to Williamsburg, the Paspaheghs and the Chiskiacks, and each group probably maintained a strong sense of its individual identity within the larger framework of Powhatan society. In most aspects of day-to-day life, however, the Chiskiacks and Paspaheghs probably were very similar. All of the tribes brought together by Powhatan shared a common cultural heritage, which linked them not only to each other but to other Indian groups living to the north and south of Virginia, like the Piscataway of Maryland and the Roanokes of coastal North Carolina. The various Indian tribes of the Virginia coastal plain were often at odds with each other, but their reasons for conflict were political and economic; they were not the result of important differences in language, culture, or way of life. In times of peace, Indians frequently traveled from one territory to another for trading and other purposes, and Powhatan Indians typically married people from other Powhatan tribes. Strong social forces tended to bring the Indians together and to mitigate the effects of intertribal rivalries.

Although the Powhatan paramount chiefdom emerged only in the mid to late sixteenth century and did not reach its largest and most developed form until after 1600, the Powhatan way of life was rooted in a tradition that had developed over many centuries. The Powhatans called the Virginia coastal plain "Tsenacommacah," a term that meant "the densely inhabited land." This name testifies to the Powhatans' well-developed skill at living on the land and making use of its many resources. Evidence suggests that some thirteen thousand Powhatans lived in Virginia in the early seventeenth century, a figure more likely to be an underestimate than an overestimate of the total Powhatan population. In comparison to other surrounding Indian groups, the Powhatans supported quite a large population within their territories.

The Powhatans were a sophisticated agricultural people, and their most important food was the corn they grew in fields surrounding their villages. Other familiar Powhatan crops included beans and squash, but the Powhatans also cultivated and harvested some plants that farmers do not grow today. One of these plants was little barley, which still grows wild in Virginia. The English colonists never attempted to grow this native American plant, which is not related to domesticated barley. The English soon acquired a taste for Indian corn, however, and came to depend on this grain almost as much as the Powhatans did.

Corn and other cultivated plants did not meet all of the Indians' food needs. The Powhatans depended very heavily on wild plant and animal foods throughout much of the year. In the spring they gathered and ate a great deal of tuckahoe, a wild tuberous plant that grows in marshy areas. In the summer, a wide range of berries and fruits was available, and, in the fall, nuts of various kinds were an important part of their diet.

The Indians ate fish, oysters, and other kinds of shellfish mainly in the spring and early summer, and they hunted animals and birds throughout the year. The Powhatans had no domesticated animals except the dog, so the meat they ate came from wild sources. The most important animal to them was the white-tailed deer, which provided both food and clothes. The Virginia Indians did not have woven cloth and depended on deerskin garments instead. Indian men hunted year-round, usually alone or in small groups. Sometimes in the fall or winter, large numbers of men might join together in communal hunts with the aim of driving many animals together into a restricted area where they could be killed more easily. In 1607, Captain John Smith encountered such a group. This hunting party comprised some three hundred men from the Paspahegh and Chiskiack districts and four other Powhatan territories in the region.

The importance of wild plant and animal resources to the Indian way of life meant that Indian men and women spent a considerable amount of time away from their home villages each year hunting, fishing, and gathering wild plants. Most people returned to the villages in the fall, when the corn was ready for harvesting; but particularly in the spring, many people would be away from their villages for weeks or months at a time. Each of the territories within Powhatan's domain had a principal village where the district chief or "werowance" lived, and there probably would be other villages in that territory as well. The Paspahegh Indians seem to have had at least five villages in addition to the chief's village.

Fortunately, we know a great deal about one of the Paspaheghs' villages because the site of the village has been excavated by archaeologists. The site, on the Governor's Land tract in James City County, just east of the Chickahominy River, was almost certainly occupied in 1607 when the English first encountered the Paspaheghs. Archaeological evidence shows that the houses of this settlement were similar to those at several other late prehistoric sites throughout the Virginia Tidewater. A typical house had an oval ground plan and probably contained only a single room. The framework of the house consisted of two lines of saplings driven into the ground, then bent toward each other and tied together at the top to form a series of arches. The Indians covered this arched framework with woven reed mats or sheets of tree bark. Although lightly built, these houses remained warm and dry even in winter. English chroniclers like Captain Smith found the houses comfortable but very smoky from the fire kept burning in the center.

At the Paspahegh site the remains of more than forty such houses have been found.

Aerial view of the Paspahegh archaeological site today.

Courtesy, Jamestown-Yorktown Foundation

Most of the houses were small, averaging about twelve feet by twenty feet, but clustered within one part of the Paspahegh settlement were three larger buildings, each of which was close to thirty feet long. The archaeologists who excavated the site think that these may be the houses used by the chief or werowance of the village. Early English accounts of Powhatan houses indicate that chiefs' houses were built in the same way as ordinary houses but were broader, longer, and likely to be divided into separate rooms by partitions made of mats. Archaeologists found evidence of such internal features in two of the large houses at Paspahegh.

View of the reconstructed Powhatan village at Jamestown Settlement Museum.

Courtesy, Jamestown-Yorktown Foundation

Defensive palisades made of vertical wooden posts or saplings set into the ground surrounded some Powhatan villages. The excavated Paspahegh settlement did not appear to have this architectural feature, however. Perhaps the Paspaheghs, living as they did near the heart of the Powhatan chiefdom, did not greatly fear attack, although we do know that they had some trouble with another Powhatan group, the Weyanocks, before the coming of the English.

Most Powhatan houses probably were occupied by single families consisting of a husband, a wife, and their children. When Powhatans married, a new house was built in the husband's village and the wife came to live with him there. Chiefs and other important members of the tribe could marry more than one wife if they could afford to pay the price of more than one bride to their brides' families. Most Powhatan men did not have the wealth to do this, however, so they had only one wife. When a man had more than one wife it is not clear whether the women occupied the same house, or whether they lived in separate houses. It may be that chiefs had larger houses because they had to accommodate the larger families that resulted from polygamy.

Chiefs were wealthier than other Powhatans and could afford more than one wife because they had the right to collect tribute from the other inhabitants of the districts they ruled. The chiefs then redistributed much of this tribute within the district to reward their supporters and enhance their authority. Each district also paid tribute to Powhatan, who was the paramount chief ruling over all the district chiefs. Powhatan redistributed tribute like the subordinate chiefs did, but on a much grander scale.

Tribute items included corn and other foods, deer hides, and copper and shell beads. The last two items, beads of copper and shell, were especially important indicators of status within Powhatan society and were used extensively as grave goods in the burials of high-status individuals (see color plate 1). Powhatan's ability to give copper beads, as well as shell beads and other ceremonial items, to his subordinates was an important mechanism for asserting and reinforcing his dominant place in the social and political hierarchy. Powhatan placed so much importance on copper that he tried to maintain a monopoly over all copper coming into the Virginia coastal plain.

In Powhatan society the positions of werowance (chief) and mamanatowick (paramount chief) were hereditary. Not just the chiefs themselves but also their families were considered to be of a higher status than ordinary Powhatans. Religious practices and burial customs clearly show this difference in status. Chiefs maintained special mortuary houses, guarded by priests, where the remains of the chiefs' ancestors were kept and where special ceremonies were conducted. Members of chiefly families believed that their spirits would move on to a comfortable afterlife. Ordinary people, on the other hand, were not thought to have an afterlife at all.

The majority of Powhatans seem to have been buried in ossuaries, which are collective burial sites that may include dozens of individuals. Most ossuaries contain few or no grave goods, even though items like copper and shell beads had significance to higher status Powhatans for the afterlife and were placed in the chief's mortuary houses or temples. Some Powhatans were buried in individual graves with east-west orientations. The head of the corpse typically was placed at the east end of the grave, perhaps so that he or she could gaze westward, the direction in which many Powhatans believed the spirit land was located.

At the excavated Paspahegh site near the mouth of the Chickahominy River, ossuary burials and single inhumation burials were found. Archaeological evidence from the site indicates that both kinds of burials were in use when the English first contacted the Paspahegh Indians. Copper beads were found in two of the ossuary burials and one single inhumation burial, but most of the Paspahegh burials contained no valuable grave goods. After they had been studied, the human remains and grave goods discovered at the Governor's Land archaeological site were re-interred near their original burial sites in a ceremony conducted by modern-day Powhatan Indians.

Although the Powhatans made some use of copper for beads and other ornamental or ceremonial objects, they did not know how to smelt or forge metal. Copper artifacts were made from naturally occurring nodules of pure copper that were hammered into shape. Tools and weapons were made of stone, bone, and wood. Powhatans had clay pots for cooking food, and they wove baskets and mats from a variety of plant materials. The baskets were important for transporting and storing food, and the mats not only covered Powhatan houses but also served as bedding inside the houses. Canoes, probably the largest artifacts the Powhatans made, were formed by hollowing out logs and could be up to fifty feet long.

The arrival of the English in Virginia and their competition for control of the land seriously disrupted the Powhatan way of life. No group was more profoundly affected than the Paspahegh Indians, whose territory included Jamestown Island, where the English chose to build their fort. At first, contacts between the English and Paspahegh were guarded but friendly. Wowinchopunck, their werowance, visited Jamestown and gave the settlers there gifts of food. Only a few weeks after the English came, however, the Paspaheghs joined several other Powhatan tribes in an attack on Jamestown. Powhatan intervened and reestablished peace between the English and the Paspaheghs, but it did not last. Because the Paspaheghs were the closest Indian group to Jamestown, many opportunities for disagreements arose between the English and the Indians. The English blamed the Paspaheghs whenever tools or other valuable goods were stolen, and Captain Smith and other English leaders retaliated by raiding Paspahegh villages and kidnapping or killing individual Paspaheghs.

Finally, in 1610, the English staged a full-scale attack on the principal Paspahegh village, killing several people and capturing and then murdering chief Wowinchopunck's wife and children. Wowinchopunck himself was killed early in 1611 in a raid on Jamestown. Thereafter, the Paspaheghs abandoned their territory and probably joined with other Indian groups living farther away from the English settlement at Jamestown.

The historical evidence suggests that the Paspahegh village found and excavated by archaeologists on the Governor's Land tract probably was abandoned by the Indians within a few years of initial English settlement in Virginia. The Paspahegh site, therefore, offers a valuable picture of Indian life when the Powhatan chiefdom first came into conflict with the incoming English. Interestingly, almost the only English-made artifacts recovered from the Paspahegh site are copper beads and pendants. These copper items look very much like the copper beads and ornaments that the Indians made for themselves, but scientific analysis shows that many of them probably were manufactured by the English at Jamestown. The beads symbolize the complex nature of the relationship between the English and the Indians, a relationship in which trade and warfare could go hand in hand.

A little more than a decade after the departure of the Paspaheghs, the only other Indian group living near Williamsburg, the Chiskiacks, abandoned their land on the York River. For some time afterward the Williamsburg area became a no man's land separating the English- and the Indian-controlled parts of the Peninsula. The boundary was made clear in 1633 when a wooden palisade was built between College Creek and Queens Creek to keep Indians out of the lands claimed by the English. With the defeat of the Indians in the 1644–1646 Anglo-Powhatan War, the whole of the Peninsula, as far as the fall line, became English territory. Indians were not allowed even to enter the Peninsula without official permission. While in English territory they had to wear special clothing and, later, to carry metal badges issued by the Virginia government to prove that they had such permission.

Although an important treaty was signed between the Powhatans and the English at Middle Plantation in 1677, not until the end of the seventeenth century did the Williamsburg area begin again to play an important part in the lives of Indians. In 1699, Williamsburg became the seat of government for the Virginia colony; and the Virginia Indians, who were no longer independent, self-governing peoples, had to come there to pay tribute to the governor for their reservation lands and to conduct various legal business. Williamsburg was also the site of the College of William and Mary, which maintained a school for Indians paid for by a bequest from the English scientist Robert Boyle. At first the Indians were taught in the Wren Building, but in 1723 the Brafferton building was constructed to house the school (see color plate 6).

During the 1700s, Indian tribes who had treaty relationships with the Virginia government sent some of their sons to the school in return for a remission of the tribute that the tribes owed to the colony. Although the stated purpose of the school was to teach Christianity and useful skills to the Indians, its real purpose was to convince the Indians to abandon their traditional way of life. However, most graduates chose to return to their tribes and live as Indians, not as Englishmen. The school did teach a number of Indian boys to speak, read, and write English, skills valuable in dealing with the English authorities. In 1734, the Virginia government stopped employing official interpreters in dealings with the Indians since, in the words of a government official, "tributary Indians understand and can speak the English language very well."

The Indian school at William and Mary closed with the coming of the American Revolution, and soon thereafter the capital of Virginia moved to Richmond. Since education and essential government business were the two main factors that drew Indians to Williamsburg, the town had considerably less involvement with the Virginia tribes once the colonial era ended. Even though the town of Williamsburg ceased to play an important official role in the lives of Virginia Indians after the eighteenth century, Powhatans had not left the region. Indians continued to live in all parts of Virginia, whether on officially recognized reservations like those of the Mattaponi and Pamunkey, in other non-reservation Indian communities, or as individuals and families mixed into the general population of the state. The Chiskiacks and the Paspaheghs may no longer exist as separate tribes on the Peninsula, but their descendants undoubtedly are with us today, represented by the seven Powhatan-descended tribes: the Chickahominy, the Eastern Chickahominy, the Mattaponi, the Nansemond, the Pamunkey, the Rappahannock, and the Upper Mattaponi. Like Williamsburg itself, the Virginia Indians remember and honor their past, but look forward to and prepare for what they may accomplish in the future.

Metal peace badge issued to the Appamattuck Indians in 1662.

Courtesy, Jamestown-Yorktown Educational Trust

Selected Sources and Suggested Readings

Beverley, Robert. *The History and Present State of Virginia*, ed. by Louis B. Wright (Chapel Hill: for the Institute of Early American History and Culture by Univ. of North Carolina, 1947).

Egloff, Keith, and Deborah Woodward. *First People: The Early Indians of Virginia* (Richmond: Virginia Department of Historic Resources, 1992).

Luccketti, Nicholas M., Mary Ellen N. Hodges, Charles T. Hodges, et al. "Paspahegh Archaeology: Data Recovery Investigations of Site 44JC308 at The Governor's Land at Two Rivers." Williamsburg: James River Institute for Archaeology, 1994.

Potter, Stephen R. *Commoners, Tribute, and Chiefs: The Development of Algonquian Culture in the Potomac Valley* (Charlottesville: Univ. Press of Virginia, 1993).

Rountree, Helen C. *The Powhatan Indians of Virginia: Their Traditional Culture* (Norman: Univ. of Oklahoma, 1989)

_____. *Pocahontas's People: The Powhatan Indians of Virginia Through Four Centuries* (Norman: Univ. of Oklahoma, 1990).

Smith, John. *The Complete Works of Captain John Smith (1580-1631)*, ed. by Philip L. Barbour. 3 vols. (Chapel Hill: for the Institute of Early American History and Culture by Univ. of North Carolina, 1986).

Turner, E. Randolph, III. "Native American Protohistoric Interactions in the Powhatan Core Area," in *Powhatan Foreign Relations, 1500-1722*, ed. by Helen C. Rountree (Charlottesville: Univ. Press of Virginia, 1993).

"The Very Heart and Centre of the Country": From Middle Plantation to Williamsburg

by: Jennifer Agee Jones

In 1660, John Page (see color plate 2) visited England and had his portrait painted by a prominent artist. Page gazes directly out from the canvas, aristocratic in his demeanor and his dress. He might have been any well-to-do English merchant of the mid-seventeenth century, but Page was a Virginian who had lived in the colony for more than a decade. Indeed, he was one of the wealthiest, most powerful Virginians of his day. The portrait that Page took back to Virginia with him probably hung in a substantial brick house in a small settlement called Middle Plantation.

Throughout his life, Page sought to elevate both himself and his small village. When, at the end of the seventeenth century, Virginians decided to rebuild the capital of Virginia in Middle Plantation and rename it Williamsburg, they were taking advantage of the area's natural merits. But the move was in no small measure due to the work of John Page and his Middle Plantation neighbors. Page, James Bray, Otho Thorpe, Thomas Ludwell, and Philip Ludwell achieved political power in the colony, gave Middle Plantation a distinctive, wealthy appearance by building fine homes and public buildings, and ultimately influenced the decision to move the capital there in 1699. Page was in many ways Williamsburg's founding father. He was the force behind the transformation of the place from a small, unlikely inland site into the capital of England's largest mainland colony in North America.

It would take many decades for others in Virginia to see Middle Plantation's possibilities. In 1660, when Page went to England, Jamestown was still the most important settlement in the colony; it was virtually the only place in Virginia large enough to be called a town. Throughout its tenure as Virginia's capital, Jamestown was plagued with problems ranging from bad water to susceptibility to fire. Virginians, however, were loyal to the place where their countrymen had first made a foothold in the colony and were unwilling to move the capital away from this traditional and accustomed place.

Seventeenth-century settlers in Virginia naturally assumed that the colony's chief town would be located on the James River. The tidal waters that flowed miles into Virginia's interior were the lifeblood of Virginia's commerce and culture, especially in the burgeoning tobacco economy. From the time that John Rolfe discovered that sweet-scented tobacco would grow prolifically in Virginia's climate, men cultivated tobacco to the exclusion of virtually all other crops. Tobacco cultivation in seventeenth-century Virginia encouraged people to spread out along the rivers in the land-rich colony because successful crops required considerable acreage. As soon as the soil on one tract was depleted, usually in as little as four years, planters would simply move to another tract. After a few decades, the need for large tracts of land and the ease with which it could be acquired, combined with a growing number of settlers led the richer planters to claim the land along the rivers up to the fall line that marked the boundary beyond which ocean-going vessels could not travel. Large planters depended on the rivers to bring ship captains directly to their private wharves for the loading of tobacco and the unloading of goods from home.

Although Virginians of Page's standing profited from this system of river commerce, the lack of towns, they believed, could lead to cultural degeneration. Virginians associated towns with civility and the preservation of their Christian heritage. Legislation in the seventeenth century succesively prescribed the development of port towns at various places along the colony's rivers. The legislation reveals the extent to which some Virginians deplored their lack of urban areas and the assumption that any towns that developed should be located along the rivers. Yet despite the passage of five town acts promoting sites such as Tindall's Point in Gloucester County, Jamestown was the only town in Virginia until the 1690s.

The small settlement that eventually replaced Jamestown as the colony's capital was located several miles from the shores of the tidal rivers. Middle Plantation, as its name sug-

Augustus Herrman's map of Virginia and Maryland in 1670, showing the rivers and Jamestown and Middle Plantation. Virginia's seventeenth-century economy was based on river transport. The tidal rivers allowed ship captains direct access to planter's wharves. Virginians had little incentive to establish ports, and towns were slow to develop in the colony.

Courtesy, Geography and Map Division, Library of Congress.

gests, was situated midway between the settlements on the James and York rivers. The small cluster of buildings and farms that made up the settlement sat on a high ridge on the peninsula, between two navigable tidal creeks. Unlike other areas in the colony, the emergence and growth of Middle Plantation was not due to its potential as a port town. Instead, a massive public works project that began in 1633 brought the settlement to the attention of the colony's leaders.

After two decades of settlement, Virginians still faced the threat of Indians. The Indian uprising of 1622 that nearly destroyed the colony quashed the early optimism that Indians might be assimilated into English communities through conversion to Christianity and education in English customs. By 1634, the numbers of Indians on the peninsula had greatly declined from the first years of settlement. That they remained at all, however, kept the spectre of violence in the minds of the English men and women living in the colony. The palisade of 1634 was built to quell concerns about the proximity of the Indians by drawing an unmistakable boundary between the English and the natives. The pales also served the practical purpose of protecting the cattle and hogs from Indians and wolves. In the act authorizing the construction of a palisade, the legislators directed that every fortieth man in the colony was to report to Middle Plantation and begin the work of "securinge that Tract of Land lyinge betweene the sayd Creekes."

By 1644, a second Indian uprising had claimed numerous settlers' lives. The palisade at Middle Plantation had either been torn down or was in such a state of decay that the colony's leaders decided to build another one. Planter Richard Higgenson was employed by the colony to create the pale across the peninsula. This second palisade was either a restoration of the first one or a replacement built in the same location. While the Indian threat gradually diminished throughout the century, men and women living in Virginia in the 1640s probably felt safer knowing that the land to the southwest of the pale had been marked out and claimed by the English.

By mid-century, Middle Plantation's only distinction was that it had been the site for the palisade. Throughout the seventeenth century, however, the settlement attracted wealthy planters who recognized good land for their homes and tobacco fields. The early settlers likely found Middle Plantation's high ridge to be pleasing terrain, preferable to lower, wetter land near the rivers. The legislative act that founded the town referred to Middle Plantation's "serene and temperate air" and noted that its residents had found it to be "healthy, and agreeable to their constitutions." Compared to swampy Jamestown, Middle Plantation evidently seemed to have a dry, healthy, and pleasing environment. Certainly, Jamestown had easier river access, something seventeenth-century planters needed to be successful in the tobacco market, but Middle Plantation residents could make use of the two small streams—Queens Creek and Archer's Hope (today College) Creek—that wended seaward into the York and James rivers. Smaller sloops could travel to the settlement's landings on the creeks to load tobacco and then deliver the hogsheads to the larger vessels that could navigate only the tidal waters.

John Page was one of the first planters to recognize Middle Plantation's advantages early on. He arrived in the colony in 1650, settling briefly in what became Gloucester County before deciding to make York County his permanent home. In 1662, he built a large brick house in Middle Plantation for himself, his wife, Alice, and their children. He worked his way up in the colony government, serving in a series of offices with, first, local influence and, later, colony-wide prestige. He was the high sheriff for York County in 1677 and served as a member of the Bruton Parish vestry from 1674 to 1684. By the 1680s he had become a member of the Governor's Council, Virginia's upper house of government.

Other influential men also made Middle Plantation their home in the middle of the century. James Bray and Otho Thorpe, members of the council in the third quarter of the seventeenth century, lived near Middle Plantation. A few years after John Page arrived, Thomas Ludwell came to Virginia to serve as the secretary of the colony. He settled on a plantation that had belonged to his predecessor in the office, a tract of land at the head of Archer's Hope Creek, and brought his temperamental and ambitious brother, Philip, to live with him. The Ludwells lived relatively close to Page.

The Ludwell brothers set out to transform their plantation into a richer place than the homes of their countrymen in the colony. Rich Neck became the largest, most luxurious private home in Virginia short of Green Spring, Governor William Berkeley's James City County mansion. The two brick dwelling houses at Rich Neck, adorned with elegant details, such as expensive delft tiles surrounding the fireplaces, easily dwarfed the comfortable brick house that Page constructed about the same time. All three men capped their houses with clay roofing tiles instead of more readily available shingles. Like Page, the Ludwells were men on the make in the new colony, eager to reap the rewards that government service offered in Virginia. While their plantation was more distant from the core of Middle Plantation's settlement than was Page's, they also served as vestrymen for Bruton Parish, which was named in honor of the English town that the Ludwells had called home.

By the 1670s, the building activity of Page and the Ludwells gave Middle Plantation a distinctive appearance. Most seventeenth-century Virginians built only small, impermanent houses. Twentieth-century archaeologists have called these buildings post-in-the-ground structures and have identified their remains throughout the Chesapeake region. The typical seventeenth-century house would have been a modest wooden building

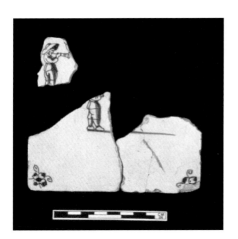

These delft tiles bordered the fireplace in one of the buildings at Rich Neck. These artifacts and others hint at the wealth of the powerful Ludwell brothers.

Courtesy, Department of Archaeological Research, Colonial Williamsburg Foundation

Conjectural drawing of the Page house. Page's brick house was one of a number of brick houses in Virginia. While other planters built less substantial buildings at the site of their plantations, Page and others of his rank erected well-designed, English-style homes.

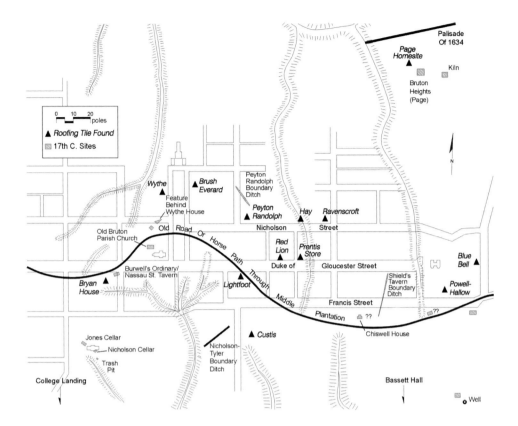

By the last quarter of the 17th c., Middle Plantation's landscape was marked by a cluster of well-built brick buildings. A rider traveling from Jamestown to Yorktown along the horse path in the 1690s would have passed by a fine brick church, a brick ordinary, Page's cross-plan house, and several other brick homes.

Courtesy, Department of Archaeological Research, Colonial Williamsburg Foundation

without sills to support floorboards. Indeed, some of Virginia's most prosperous planters would have lived out their lives in small clapboard buildings, some with dirt floors. But a 1680s visitor to Middle Plantation would have seen very different structures. John Page's brick house and the buildings that made up the Ludwell complex were large, substantial buildings with ornate brick decorations.

With men of prominence and wealth clustered in Middle Plantation, it is not surprising that, by 1676, the settlement was considered a place of importance by men in the colony. The events surrounding a rebellion that broke out in that year demonstrate just how significant Middle Plantation had become. When a conflict with the Indians on Virginia's northern and western frontiers ignited a colony-wide rebellion within a few months, Middle Plantation's residents became players in the battle of control between Governor Berkeley and the rebel leader, Nathaniel Bacon.

When he arrived in Virginia in 1674, Bacon already had connections and wealth. By marriage, he was a cousin of Governor Berkeley; and an older cousin, also named Nathaniel Bacon, already sat on the council. The younger Bacon soon became owner of a plantation in Henrico County and, though newly arrived and only twenty-nine, had already been appointed to the council.

Despite all his connections and wealth, the young Nathaniel Bacon still felt aggrieved by his circumstances in Virginia. Bacon and his countrymen who lived close to the frontier were concerned about the close proximity of their homes to the Indians. An attack upon his own plantation and a skirmish on Virginia's northern border in July 1675, between settlers and the

Susquehannock Indians, convinced him that something must be done. Bacon rode to Jamestown to demand a commission from Governor Berkeley to raise an attack against the Indians. Berkeley refused to grant the commission and punished Bacon by removing him from the Council.

Berkeley probably resisted Bacon's demands for a commission to fight the Indians out of a concern that such action would upset a tenuous peace and lucrative trading situation between English traders and friendly Indians. In June 1676, Bacon traveled to Jamestown, threatened the assembled legislators and the governor with harm, and received his commission by force. By the time he got it, however, the focus of his ire had begun to shift from the Indians to the governor and the wealthy men of the colony. Bacon had been joined in his plans to march against the Indians by a large number of former indentured servants, who readily cast their allegiance with Bacon and against Berkeley and his supporters. On 30 July, Bacon arrived at Middle Plantation and published a declaration denouncing Berkeley and his councilors. Bacon's Declaration listed grievances against the powerful men in the colony, including John Page, the Ludwells, and Page's neighbor Otho Thorpe. Why Bacon chose to publish his declaration while in Middle Plantation cannot be known for sure; but, by 1676, the settlement was known as the "the very Heart and Centre of the Country." With Berkeley in control of Jamestown, Bacon evidently traveled to the second most significant place in the colony.

The tides turned quickly during Bacon's Rebellion. In the fall of 1676, Bacon died unexpectedly of dysentery, leaving the rebellion without a dynamic leader. Berkeley, already on the offensive after having taken refuge briefly on the Eastern Shore, restored control and order quickly. Traveling through the countryside to Green Spring, his James City County plantation, Berkeley accepted apologies and renewed allegiance from some of Bacon's supporters; but he reserved a more brutal response for a few. In the last days before arriving at his own plundered plantation, Berkeley stayed at Middle Plantation, first at the house of James Bray and then at John Page's home. While in Middle Plantation, he ordered the execution of rebel William Drummond.

Two months before Berkeley managed to return to power, Nathaniel Bacon had burned Jamestown to the ground. Berkeley briefly took up the reins of the government, but the government had no place to meet in Jamestown; and without a statehouse, the council and the House of Burgesses were forced to meet in other locations. Several times in the years following the rebellion, the government convened at Middle Plantation. The council assembled at Middle Plantation in 1682 and 1690. On 10 October 1677, the entire assembly met Otho at Thorpe's house. Middle Plantation also served as the site for certain ceremonial functions. Middle Plantation was twice designated as the site for negotiating with Indians. In 1677 and 1680, peace conferences between leaders of several Indian tribes and representatives from the colony were held at Middle Plantation, and in 1698 Indian leaders met the governor there.

That such important functions took place so near their homes and farms made public life easy and convenient for men like John Page. Such men were eager to have the capital nearby. Moreover, their positions of authority enabled them to exercise their influence when talk among the councilors and burgesses turned to founding towns and selecting a new capital.

Page may have been at the center of an effort by Middle Plantation residents to move the capital to their settlement in 1677. At that time, Middle Plantation residents petitioned the commissioners sent by the king to investigate the rebellion to move the capital of the colony to Middle Plantation. The commissioners' reply reveals how important the rivers were to the colony. To move the capital of the colony away from the James River was about as sensible as if "Middlesex should have desired, that London might have beene new built on Highgat Hill, and removed from the grand River that brings them in their Trade." In 1677, few people were willing to consider the inland site of Middle Plantation as a capital for the colony. Virginians were not ready to move the seat of government away from Jamestown, the "most ancient and convenient place" for the capital. Moreover, many government officials owned property there.

While the commissioners refused to consider the Middle Plantation plea, the end of the rebellion offered the settlement another distinction. The outbreak of the civil conflict caused alarm in London, and, along with instructions recalling Governor Berkeley to England, the king sent one thousand troops whose purpose was to put down the uprising in the colony. Altough their military service was not required when they arrived, the troops remained in Virginia for a number of years; and Middle Plantation was designated a garrison for the troops and the location of a magazine for arms and munitions. Prominent Middle Plantation residents collected and distributed food for the troops and managed the store of weapons in the settlement. In February 1677, the House of Burgesses set aside a parcel of land near Middle Plantation so that the idle troops could plant and tend their own corn.

Excavations of the first brick church at Bruton Parish in 1992 revealed the brick foundations and evidence of the buttresses.

Courtesy, Department of Archaeological Research, Colonial Williamsburg Foundation

Middle Plantation continued to grow during the two decades that followed Bacon's Rebellion. In 1683, members of the Bruton Parish vestry built a new parish church, large and grandly designed to match their impressive and attractive homes. John Page donated money to the project and pledged "to give lande sufficient for the Church and Church Yard." In 1702, a Swiss traveler in the colony sketched the church, an impressive brick building and one of the largest churches in the colony (see color plate 4).

The church was one of a growing number of brick buildings in a colony that was characterized by much flimsier building standards. In addition to the Page and Ludwell mansions, a number of other brick structures was found in the settlement. The prosperous Bray family may have had a brick dwelling near modern-day Bassett Hall. John Page built not only his manor house of brick, he also constructed a number of brick outbuildings, which had to be pulled down in 1705 to clear the way for Duke of Gloucester Street. In 1693, the College of William and Mary was founded, and its main building was constructed in brick a short time later.

In 1698, the state house and jail at Jamestown burned again. Middle Plantation was now a much more likely candidate to become the capital of the colony. By this time, Middle Plantation residents had a new ally, the ambitious young minister who was highly instrumental in founding the College of William and Mary, James Blair (see color plate 5 and pp. 107 & 152). Blair wanted Middle Plantation to become the capital of the colony as much as the settlement's longtime residents did. Blair brought to the cause his authority in the colony (he had been appointed the bishop of London's representative in Virginia), strong personality, and determined nature. Blair was well-connected politically and in the early years of the college was a friend and ally of Governon Francis Nicholson., and he secured a seat on the council. Blair became the necessary catalyst that finally made Middle Plantation the capital of England's largest mainland colony.

Blair arrived in Virginia in 1685, settled on a piece of land once owned by the Ludwells, and solidified his position among the Virginia elite by marrying Sarah Harrison, daughter of a prominent Surry County planter. Blair and Governor Francis Nicholson gave Middle Plantation a power base from which to argue for the move of the capital. In 1699 May Day exercises orchestrated by Blair and Nicholson, Blair put five carefully prepared students before a combined meeting of the legislature to argue for the move of the capital from Jamestown to Middle Plantation. (See color plate 22.) The third speaker summarized Middle Plantation's merits: "Here is good neighborhood of as many substantial Housekeepers that could give great help towards the supplying and maintaining of a constant Market." The student acknowledged the important men whose homes lay near or in the settlement. Moreover, he told the audience, great strides had been taken "towards the beginning of a Town, a Church, an ordinary, several stores, two Mills, a smiths shop a Grammar School, and above all the Colledge." The student offered this as evidence that Middle Plantation was a growing and substantial hamlet.

The student speeches were designed to counter considerable ambivalence and opposition to the choice of Middle Plantation from property owners at Jamestown and residents of other locations in the colony. Even as late as 1699, some Virginians saw Middle Plantation as little more than an attractive piece of real estate on a geographically pleasing ridge of land high between the rivers. The fourth speaker, in fact, felt obliged to acknowledge the major objection present "in many mens minds" to Middle Plantation as the site of a capital, namely, that access to it was "reduced to two Creeks navigable only by small craft that draw 6 or 7 foot [of] water." Although the student argued that the many other merits of location outweighed its inconvenient river access, his speech indicated the extent to which the settlement's inland location was still a source of concern.

This May Day performance convinced enough of the assembled legislators that the move of the capital was able to go forward: the General Assembly agreed on 7 June to build a new statehouse in Middle Plantation. Middle Plantation received a new name, and acts were passed directing the laying out of the streets and building of the new government structures. By the end of the century, the colony was well established and had been pushed so far west that it scarcely concerned colonists living on the Peninsula. Middle Plantation seemed an increasingly likely site for a town despite its inland location, and Blair's students helped the remaining doubters see that it was, in fact, "the very heart and center of the country."

John Page had been dead for seven years by the time the May Day exercises took place, but he too had a hand in the events of 1699. The fourth student speaker credited Page with initiating the idea for the college at Middle Plantation during a meeting in Jamestown in 1690. The student said, "The person that had the chief honour to be the first to move in procuring such a meeting was the Honble Colonell Page: to whom and his family this great work has been exceedingly beholding." Throughout his years in Middle Plantation, Page supported the growth and development of the town. Although the names of the petitioners who asked the king's commissioners to move the capital to Middle Plantation in 1677 have not survived, Page, as one of the county's leading men, certainly must have signed his name to the petition, if not authored it himself.

Page's motivation for encouraging the growth of a town so near his fields was typical. Some prominent seventeenth-century Virginians were concerned with the lack of towns, and the legislature tried to remedy the situation by passing the town acts. However, planters generally were unenthusiastic. In the 1680s, the pastor of the church at Jamestown, the Reverend John Clayton, complained that every influential man in the colony tried to secure a town in his own backyard. Page, by the 1680s, would have been in a position to do just this as one of the most powerful men in the country. Blair and Nicholson could claim the final victory in 1699, but much of the groundwork had been laid by Page in the preceding decades.

Recently, Colonial Williamsburg's archaeologists discovered evidence that suggests that the move of the capital was not just a convenience to Page; it was the fulfillment of his view of the world. In 1995, archaeologists excavating the remains of his house discovered pieces of a brick cartouche in the rubble (see color plate 3). The cartouche was built into the wall above the front door of the brick cross plan house. On its surface were the raised initials "P" and "A" (for "Page" and "Alice"; the initial for "John" was never found), the date 1662, and, at the bottom, with faint smudges of red paint still visible, a heart. Page evidently thought a great deal about the meaning of hearts. In a 1687 religious tract he prepared for his son Matthew, he wrote, "All the faculties of man follow the heart, as servants the mistress. ... So the heart leads, directs, moves the parts of the body and powers of the soul ... and the mouth speaketh, hand worketh, eye looketh." Page brought together the notion of the heart as a symbol of centricity in its broadest sense and the idea of the heart as a core religious symbol. God placed the heart "in the midst of the body, as a general in the midst of his army." Page also told his son that if "your body be the temple of God, sure your heart is the holy of holies."

For Page and other seventeenth-century men, the heart was the center of the body and the metaphorical center of God's relationship with man. Through a symbol on his house and his decades-long effort to promote Middle Plantation, Page told the world that the settlement was at the heart and center of his world. During the last two decades of his life he elevated the importance of the small settlement through his influence and prestige in the colony. By 1699, most people in the colony had come to agree that Middle Plantation was the very heart and center of Virginia, the most appropriate place to build a new capital town.

Selected Sources & Suggested Readings

Goodwin, Rutherfoord. *A Brief & True Report Concerning Williamsburg in Virginia* (1941; rep. Richmond: Dietz, 1980).

Kulikoff, Allan. *Tobacco and Slaves: The Development of Southern Cultures in the Chesapeake, 1680-1800* (Chapel Hill: for the Institute of Early American History and Culture by Univ. of North Carolina, 1986).

Metz, John, Jennifer Jones, Dwayne Pickett, and David Muraca. *"Upon the Palisado" and Other Stories of Place from Bruton Heights* (Richmond: Dietz, 1998).

Morgan, Edmund S. *American Slavery, American Freedom: The Ordeal of Colonial Virginia* (N.Y.: Norton, 1975).

Reps, John. *Tidewater Towns: City Planning in Colonial Virginia and Maryland* (Charlottesville: Univ. Press of Virginia for the Colonial Williamsburg Foundation, 1972).

Rouse, Parke, Jr. *James Blair of Virginia* (Chapel Hill: Univ. of North Carolina, 1971).

Washburn, Wilcomb E. *The Governor and the Rebel: A History of Bacon's Rebellion in Virginia* (Chapel Hill: for the Institute of Early American History and Culture by Univ. of North Carolina, 1957).

Ornaments of Civic Aspiration:
The Public Buildings of Williamsburg

by: Carl Lounsbury

Throughout the eighteenth century, the fortunes of a city were frequently measured by its public buildings. Indifferent or, even worse, non-existent churches, courthouses, and marketplaces spoke of a place of no consequence. William Byrd, a man who spent much time in Williamsburg, played no small part in shaping its public structures. He was quick to disparage Edenton, North Carolina, by noting that its courthouse had "much the Air of a Common

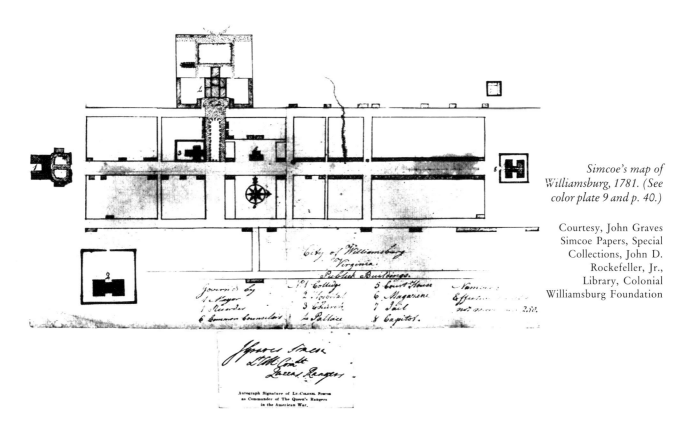

Simcoe's map of Williamsburg, 1781. (See color plate 9 and p. 40.)

Courtesy, John Graves Simcoe Papers, Special Collections, John D. Rockefeller, Jr., Library, Colonial Williamsburg Foundation

Tobacco-House. I believe this is the only Metropolis in the Christian or Mahometan World, where there is neither Church, Chappel, Mosque, Synagogue, or any other Place of Publick Worship of any Sect or Religion whatsoever." Even if Byrd would not admit it, Virginia's government and the citizens of Williamsburg often struggled mightily to erect structures of durable quality and lasting significance. It was not an easy task to undertake massive projects such as the College of William and Mary, the capitol, or the Governor's Palace in a colony whose architectural achievements through most of the seventeenth century had been extremely meager. Those who envisioned lasting monuments in Williamsburg had only to look at the shabby failure of Jamestown to realize what obstacles they had to overcome.

In the absence of a convenient supply of stone, brick became the symbol of permanence in Williamsburg, and every public building of consequence was constructed of this material. Yet, it was no guarantor of permanence, as the repeated destruction of the city's public buildings demonstrated. Sometimes the scale, form, and quality of the buildings matched the ambitions of men like Byrd, Francis Nicholson, and Alexander Spotswood. In other instances, bad workmanship and ill proportions earned them strong epithets. Thomas Jefferson, no friend of Williamsburg's architecture, likened the college and public hospital to "rude, misshapen piles, which, but that they have roofs, would be taken for brick-kilns." Given the small amounts of money often allotted to major undertakings and the difficulty of coordinating workmen and the supply of materials, it is something of a surprise to observe how much was accomplished in the century from the construction of the first Bruton Parish Church at Middle Plantation to the removal of the state government from Williamsburg in 1780.

By the 1670s, a few well-established parish vestries had initiated a program of transforming earlier impermanent wooden structures into the first brick churches in the colony. A couple of years later, the vestry of Bruton Parish asserted its building aspirations, and ordered that "a New Church should be built with brick, at Middle Plantation." Once levies were raised and donations from wealthier parishioners were in hand, the vestry committed itself to a church equal in size and quality to those new ones in Jamestown and Isle of Wight County, and in 1681 turned to Francis Page to build it. Page was ideally suited to the undertaking since he had the financial wherewithal to carry the project through and had considerable experience in the construction of brick structures. His own cruciform brick house erected in 1662 stood a few hundred yards northeast of the proposed building site that he had donated to the parish in 1678; and Page's brick- and tile-making kilns located near his house had supplied materials for buildings in Jamestown and on neighboring plantations. Within two years, Bruton Parish had its first substantial building.

Standing a few dozen yards northwest of the present church, it measured sixty-five by twenty-eight-and-a-half feet. Like all Episcopal churches, it was oriented toward the communion table at the east end. Above the principal entrance in the center of the west facade, two windows lighted a gallery. Benches and tall pews lined a central aisle, and at the east end a raised and railed area for the communion table was lit by a large window. Typical of other Virginia churches of the period, Bruton had a small chancel door, probably in the last bay of the south wall, for exiting the church after the Eucharist service.

The most striking features of Bruton Church were the curvilinear gables capping the west and east walls and the series of buttresses that accentuated the longer north and south walls. Michel's crude, inaccurate sketch of the church in 1702 (see color plate 4) depicts three arched or compass-headed windows on the south wall and omits the buttresses, which are evident in the archaeological footprint. The shaped gables, molded bricks, decorative windows and doorways, and buttresses are indicative of brickwork that had begun to flourish in Virginia in the last half of the seventeenth century.

As the new capital grew, the church became too small. In 1711, Governor Alexander Spotswood provided a plan for a much larger structure, a cruciform church measuring seventy-five by twenty-eight feet, with two wings, each twenty-two feet wide by nineteen long. There was no liturgical significance to the cruciform plan: the wings simply provided more space for the new capital's population of artisans, merchants, and officials. Rather than creating a wider building of boxier proportions, the plan followed regional predilections for narrow roof spans, eschewing those of more than thirty-five feet.

Because members of the provincial government would be using the church, Spotswood agreed to provide public funds to construct the two wings, but Spotswood's plan was revised, the wings being trimmed from nineteen to fourteen-and-a-half feet long. Although the new structure probably had some type of decorative parapeted gables like the first church, the walls and apertures featured elements that were becoming the standard form of late colonial brickwork with glazed, Flemish-bond headers and rubbed arches. The new church opened for services in 1715.

Entrance was through three doorways: the principal western one and two subsidiary ones into the wings. Each doorway may have been reserved for particular groups of parishioners, as was customary in many communities, and would have been in keeping with the fact that architectural divisions inside the church reflected social distinctions. Whereas pews were set aside for the governor, councilmen, members of the General Assembly, and other important provincial officers, ordinary parishioners were seated according to their rank, sex, and age. In 1716, the vestry ordered the men of the parish to sit on the north side, the women on the south side—although the more influential families probably continued to sit together. From the beginning, students from the college were seated in the west gallery, eventually taking over the entire area for themselves. It seems unlikely that any special space was allotted to slaves, in part because of the ambivalence many slaveholders felt toward Christianizing them. The few who did attend church must have been relegated to standing or sitting in the aisles or on a back bench. Although it has been asserted that an enclosed outside stairway that once ascended along the north wall of the church may have provided an entrance for slaves to a gallery in the north wing, this seems unlikely since the north gallery was erected as a private pew in the early 1760s.

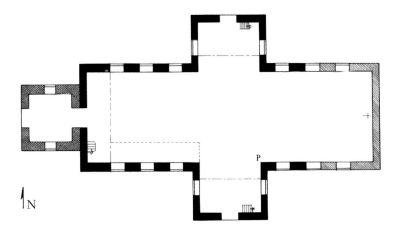

Plan of Bruton Parish Church, with additions of ca. 1715 and the tower of 1769. Dotted lines locate the galleries.

Courtesy, Special Collections, John D. Rockefeller, Jr., Library, Colonial Williamsburg Foundation

The church continued to be enlarged, reworked, and rearranged. Among the more important changes, in the 1750s the churchyard wall was constructed and the church was lengthened twenty-two feet eastward. The last major addition was made in 1769, when Benjamin Powell erected a brick tower and wooden steeple at the west end of the church. Throughout the century its cruciform design was copied throughout the region.

Middle Plantation's centrality to the growing population of Virginia's tobacco planters in the early 1690s became evident when the House of Burgesses debated the location of the new College of William and Mary; and among the benefits of siting the college here was the presence of a substantial brick church that would serve the spiritual needs of the new institution. The statute passed by the burgesses stipulated that the college was to be "built as neare the church now standing in *Middle Plantation* old fields as convenience will permitt."

Setting a precedent that would haunt almost every major public building project in the later colonial period, construction was plagued by a host of problems. First was the enormity of the undertaking. Following the example of English colleges at Cambridge and Oxford, the men who designed the plan of the college envisioned an enclosed, three-story brick quadrangle containing rooms and apartments for the students and professors as well as a communal hall and chapel. A front block facing east and measuring one hundred and thirty-eight by forty-six feet was to be connected to smaller blocks sixty-four feet long and thirty-two wide on the north and south sides, the north containing the hall and the south, the chapel. At the west end would be another range similar in size to the front. Although Virginians had undertaken a few large brick structures earlier, nothing close to this size had been contemplated, and members of the building committee were wary of straining the public purse.

Bruton Parish Church, late 19th-c. view.

Courtesy, Colonial Williamsburg Foundation

Nonetheless, begun in August 1695, enough of the college was finished by 1699 for it to be put to use. A massive brick building extended thirteen bays, a smaller wing containing the hall being attached at right angles on the north end. The importance of the hall to the communal life of the college was emphasized by the set of five large compass-headed windows lighting the north and south walls of the wing. Two balconies projected from the center bay, one at the second story, the other at the dormer level; and the building was capped by a two-story cupola. The windows contained sliding sashes rather than pivoting casements, heralding the use of these new forms in the colony. Perhaps the most novel element in the entire design was a covered arcade or "piazza" extending across the rear of the main block as the principal connector between key parts of the building. The arcade had been an integral part of English public-building design for more than a century. Perhaps most pertinent were the several colonnaded arcades built by Cambridge and Oxford colleges during the seventeenth century. Within a decade, the college arcade had been copied at the new capitol at the east end of the new Duke of Gloucester Street; and, from these two examples, the arcade passed into the building vocabulary in several Virginia county courthouses.

The responsibility for the design of the college building has been a matter of contentious speculation since the structure was restored in the late 1920s by the firm of Perry, Shaw & Hepburn (see p. 181). At this time, it was given the name "Wren Building" in honor of the English architect Sir Christopher Wren who was thought to have been its original designer. The attribution dates back to 1724, when Hugh Jones, a resident of Williamsburg, observed that the building was "first modelled by Christopher Wren, adapted to the Nature of the Country by the Gentlemen there…and is not altogether unlike Chelsea Hospital." Despite the clarity of Jones' statement, the meaning is fraught with ambiguities. Did Wren or someone in his Office of the King's Works supply the actual design drawings; or were his public buildings, such as Chelsea Hospital, models altered to fit the needs of a fledgling institution and the abilities of the local building trades?

The college scarcely had time to adjust to the growing presence of the town before a fire in October 1705 left only a burned-out shell. This was the first of a number of fires that would ultimately destroy most of the major public buildings of Williamsburg. The response of college officials to this disaster was like that of later public officials: they debated whether a new building should be erected or the ruined walls salvaged. Finally, in 1709, officials decided to build on the footprint of the old building, incorporating as much of the earlier walls as were structurally sound. The principal change was the reduction of the main east facade, the third story being incorporated into a garret lit by a series of dormer windows.

Given the slowness of rebuilding, the spurt of sustained building activity during the next decade is remarkable. Starting around 1723 and drawing to a conclusion in the mid-1730s, three new

The College of William and Mary, 1702. Drawing by Franz Ludwig Michel.

Courtesy, Burgerbibliothek Bern, Bern Switzerland

Hall (left) and Chapel (right), College of William and Mary, from the Bodleian copper plate, ca. 1735–1740.

Courtesy, Colonial Williamsburg Foundation

The Brafferton (left), College, and President's House 1732 (right), from the Bodleian copper plate, ca. 1735–1740.

Courtesy, Colonial Williamsburg Foundation

projects were successfully projected and completed. First, in 1723, the college constructed a substantial brick school for Indians a few dozen yards southeast of the main building and on an axis, not with it, but with Duke of Gloucester Street. The two-storied Brafferton measured fifty-two by thirty-four feet, and was crowned by a tall, hipped roof (see color plate 6). At a time when most government officials, artisans, and freeholders in town and the surrounding countryside resided in much smaller, one-story, wooden dwellings, this brick pile was another remarkable achievement, far surpassing in detail and planning the accommodations of most citizens. Rather novel, and seen in only a few recently built houses, such as the Brush and Levingston houses on the east side of Palace Street, the Brafferton had a central passage running through the house, separating the schoolroom on the west from what was probably the two-room apartment of the Indian master on the east. Above stairs were a library and rooms for the students.

Second, at the end of the decade the college moved a step closer to completing its original design. To house the chapel, in 1729 Henry Cary, Jr., began constructing a two-story wing located at right angles to the west end of the main block and mirroring in outward form the hall to the north.

Third, a little over a month after the chapel was opened for service, on 31 July 1732, the college laid the foundations for the residence of its president. Cary built a two-story brick dwelling whose foundations were laid at right angles to the main building and nearly opposite the Brafferton. The dwelling was nearly a copy of the Indian school though slightly larger. Like the Brafferton and most houses of any pretension, the dwelling had a broad center stair passage. The principal ground-floor rooms, two on either side of the passage, probably contained a dining room and a parlor in the front and two smaller private rooms at the rear— possibly a chamber and a study. This arrangement would have been in keeping with the plans of many of the fashionable new gentry houses of Tidewater Virginia. Despite a fire in 1781 that forced extensive rebuilding, the President's House still serves its original purpose.

The completion of the Brafferton and the President's House completely reoriented the campus of the College of William and Mary eastward toward the new capital. Instead of closing in around itself in the original quadrangular plan, the open-ended campus became an integral part of the grand baroque plan of the city, anchoring one of the major vistas at the end of Duke of Gloucester Street and reflecting the desire of the college to be a part of the community and to partake in its social and cultural activities. The layout of the main building, with its two detached flanking buildings, replicated the form of the governor's house and its two primary outbuildings at the end of Palace Street and might be reckoned to follow the pattern of plantation architecture where the principal subsidiary structures were sited symmetrically within an open courtyard. It heralded a break from English collegiate forms and signaled the willingness of Virginians to adapt their European inheritance to the needs and preferences of a maturing colonial society.

The destruction of the statehouse by fire at Jamestown in 1698 provided the opportunity for Governor Francis Nicholson to remove the capital from Jamestown to a new and healthier location. Throughout his tenure in Maryland, Virginia, and later South Carolina, Nicholson did everything he could to promote tighter bonds between the colonies and England by strengthening the authority and trappings of imperial governance and the Church of England. On his return to Virginia from Maryland in 1698, he soon had a chance to refine his ideas about the symbolic importance of church and state in English America; but he had to take into account the location of established institutions such as the college and the church. Had there been no Bruton Parish Church, it seems quite likely that the state church would have anchored one of the important terminal points of his new city plan.

Nicholson and the provincial government proceeded to plan and construct the most important public building in the city—the capitol—at the east end of Duke of Gloucester Street. The name "capitol" must have been a deliberate attempt on the part of Nicholson, the probable designer, and his councilmen to attach prestige to the structure. After all, the old statehouse in Jamestown, which had burned and been patched a number of times, probably had few architectural at-

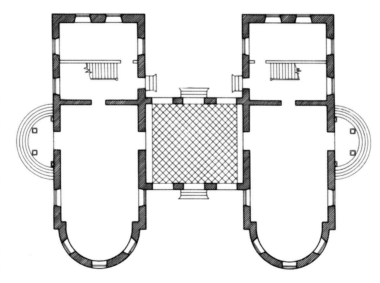

Reconstructed plan of the first capitol, drawing by author.

Courtesy, Colonial Williamsburg Foundation

tributes to distinguish it from the collection of neighboring taverns, storehouses, and dwellings. Placing the capitol at a prominent location and giving it a name with classical allusions provided the appropriate setting and aura for the architectural composition.

The design integrated novel ideas with traditional forms. For the first time in more than a quarter of a century, all of the most important provincial bodies were to be housed within the same building. In Jamestown, the Governor's Council had abandoned the statehouse for private dwellings and taverns and returned only to hold general court. The lower house of the assembly met upstairs in a small chamber while provincial secretaries and archives were wedged into any available spaces. The capitol was to contain two, two-story buildings connected by an open arcade and provided a neat and equitable division of space for its various functions. The west building, facing onto Duke of Gloucester Street, housed the general court and the secretary of the colony's office on the first floor, while above was the chamber for the governor and council. The east building contained the House of Burgesses, offices for its clerk, and other apartments for provincial officials. The long room above the arcade served as a committee room and provided enclosed circulation between the two parts of the capitol. An important adjunct of the capitol, the public gaol, used to hold prisoners awaiting trial before the general court, was built a few dozen yards to the north. Constructed by Henry Cary, Sr., in 1703–1704, the brick structure measured thirty by twenty feet with communal rooms for the incarcerated. Already slightly larger than most county prisons, it was enlarged in 1711 as an addition was made for the reception of debtors.

Part of the design of the capitol derived from a familiar form—the rectangluar county courthouse with an entrance on each long side and jury rooms either at one end of the courtroom or above stairs. However, other elements of the design varied significantly from this prototype. Foremost was the curvilinear apse at the south end of each wing. The form expressed the physical arrangement of the curved magistrates' bench in the general court-room and was replicated in the House of Burgesses, where it provided the backdrop for the Speaker's Chair. Such curved benches had become fashionable in English courtrooms in the late seventeenth century. The compass-headed windows on the ground floor, the cupola sitting atop the connecting gallery, the semicircular porch that opened off the courtroom entrance onto Duke of Gloucester Street, and the coped brick wall that encompassed the grounds set the building apart from familiar forms. (Unfortunately, the design for the recon-structed capitol by the firm of Perry, Shaw & Hepburn in the early 1930s seriously misjudged the original configuration of the building. By ignoring archaeological and documentary evi-dence in favor of a more harmonious design, the architects mislocated the main doorways, failed to build the semicircular porch on the west facade, added an interior set of arcade arches, and created a far more elaborate decorative scheme of paneling in the courtroom and council chamber than was warranted.) Imitation marbling in the courtroom and councilroom, paintings of the monarchs, and a representation of the royal coat of arms enhanced the symbolic aspect of the capitol as the locus of imperial authority and seat of government of a prominent colony. After some modification of the 1699 plan, the capitol was completed in 1705; and the elements that made it such a novelty gradually began to be imitated in a number of county courthouses.

Destroyed by fire in 1747, the capitol was reconstructed in 1751-1753 by James Shelton (see color plate 7). The walls of the old building were razed to the ground and a new structure erected upon the foundations, including a two-story pedimented portico facing Duke of Gloucester Street. In the tympanum of the pediment hung the carved and gilt royal arms of George II. This second building, which witnessed the dramatic events associated with the Revolution, like its predecessor, came to a fiery end. It burned to the ground in 1832.

The threat of the destruction of records and other important public items in the first capitol fire led to the construction of a fireproof building for the storage of provincial documents in 1748 on a lot just to the northwest of the capitol. The Secretary's Office, as it became known, had a large central room heated at both ends by fireplaces. On either side of this room, were two rooms where the colony's papers were stored. Here young men learned their clerical craft under the secretary before they were assigned clerkships in the various county courts. To ensure the safety and preservation of the records, the floors were paved with stones; and fires in the hearths vitiated the effects of Virginia's notorious humidity during summer months.

The immediacy felt in 1699 about designing a structure to house the government was not shared when discussing how to house the governor. Although urged by English officials to plan a residence, Governor Nicholson and members of the assembly felt that such an undertaking could not be sustained given the enormous cost of the capitol. Not until Governor Edward Nott succeeded Nicholson in 1706 were the first steps taken: the assembly set aside three thousand pounds for a two-story brick structure at the north end of the cross-axial street that became known as Palace Street. Specifications called for a fifty-four- by forty-eight-foot house with sash windows, a vaulted space and other rooms in the cellar, slate roof, and detached kitchen and stable. Henry Cary, Sr., who had just completed the capitol and gaol (see p. 181), was once again the overseer. Scarcely had work begun when Nott died suddenly, and his successor was taken prisoner on the high seas by the French. With no resident governor in Williamsburg to press the work, Cary labored less diligently and, by 1709, had spent all the money allotted to him without finishing the house. The walls were up, the roof covered, and a kitchen, flanking the front of the building, had been erected; but it was left to Alexander Spotswood, who assumed office the following year, to see the building to completion after making a number of alterations to the plan of the house and accompanying gardens.

When finished, the house had five bays across the front with an iron balcony over the front doorway, and a

Plan of the Governor's Palace, ca. 1779, drawing by Thomas Jefferson.

Courtesy, Massachusetts Historical Society

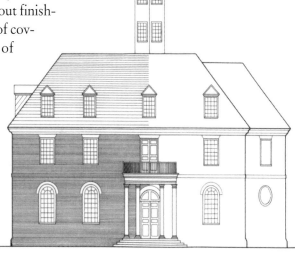

Governor's Palace, ca.1730s.

Courtesy, Special Collections, John D. Rockefeller, Jr., Library, Colonial Williamsburg Foundation

steep hipped roof punctuated by dormers and capped by a balustrade enclosing a two-story cupola. In a manner reminiscent of small English country houses of the period, the "Governor's House," as it was first known, contained a formal entrance forecourt, separated from the street by a tall brick wall with a ceremonial gate crowned with decorative sculpture atop the piers. On either side, one-story brick service buildings sat at right angles to the house. A wall running parallel to the front wall of the mansion enclosed this ceremonial yet functional forecourt. At the back of the house, formal parterres were laid out and other service buildings constructed.

The house was both a home and a public building where domestic and official business were intertwined in the layout of the house and grounds. The front door opened into a large reception hall where visitors of various ranks and purposes were welcomed and examined. In this room, a large symbolic display of weaponry reminded visitors of the governor's military preeminence as leader of His Majesty's forces in Virginia. Those of sufficient rank and status were led through the hall, up the grand staircase at the back of the house, and through a center passage on the second floor to the "great Room in the second Story." This was the most elaborately furnished room of the house and "its position in the center of the front of the house on the superior level and at the terminus of a parade of rooms that began with the otherwise major space of the hall signaled its appointment as a room of state reception." Besides these official rooms, there were semi-official state rooms, which were used for public and private purposes. On the ground floor were a parlor and dining room; above stairs, the governor and his family had their private bedchambers and study. The garret rooms served as additional bedchambers for the extended family of children, relatives, and servants. A growing fashion for large public entertaining spaces led to the construction of a large one-story addition to the back of the house in the early 1750s. This wing contained a larger ballroom and smaller supper room where governors could entertain in a manner characteristic of the spaces provided in assembly rooms in English public buildings and taverns. It was in these rooms that honored guests toasted the health of the king on his birthday or celebrated British victories over the French.

This was not the first large residence in the colonies. Seventeenth-century houses, such as Arlington on the Eastern Shore and Green Spring near Jamestown, were impressive. Yet, the Governor's House set the architectural precedent for Virginians who wanted to take their places in society. Before now, few of the wealthy lived in dwellings distinguished by size or refinement; but no aspiring planter after the 1720s could ignore the cultural significance of a well-appointed brick house replete with formal entertaining spaces and pleasure gardens (see color plate 8). Thomas Jefferson, the last resident of the house, observed that it was "not spacious without: but it is spacious and commodious within, is prettily situated, and, with the grounds annexed to it, is capable of being made an elegant seat." Rather than a promising future, however, the palace suffered a quick demise: the movement of the government to Richmond in 1780 made it redundant; and in the fall of 1781, French and American troops occupied it following the battle of Yorktown. At the end of that year, it burned to the ground.

Governor Spotswood took an active part in transforming Francis Nicholson's two-dimensional plan for the capital into a physical reality. In the midst of his architectural interests in Bruton Parish Church and the Governor's House, Spotswood directed the design and construction of a brick magazine on the market square. In 1714 a shipment of arms and ammunition received from England required secure storage. There had been a magazine in Middle Plantation; however, it must have been in bad condition by the time of the English gift, and Spotswood took the lead in raising the money and consulting in the design and construction of a new one. John Tyler, the builder of the north and south wings of Bruton Parish Church, oversaw the construction of a two-story, octagonal brick building more than thirty feet across. In the mid-1750s, a brick wall was erected around the building to further secure its contents.

The magazine, early 20th c. (see pp. 41 & 136)

Courtesy, Colonial Williamsburg Foundation

The wooden floors, glazed windows, framed roof, and an armorer's workshop violated all bomb- and fire-proofing measures found in similar structures. Despite this, the building managed to survive the catastrophes that beset other public buildings. By the late eighteenth century, however, it had been transformed into a markethouse; and during the nineteenth century it served as a Baptist meetinghouse and later, a dance hall.

Prior to the construction of a public institution dedicated to their care and treatment, those deemed insane were either confined at home, locked in county prisons, or, by the 1760s, sent to Philadelphia to receive care at the Pennsylvania Hospital. It was to Philadelphia, the

Floor and elevation plans for the Public Hospital. Drawing ca. 1825 (see pp. 47 & 89-92).

Courtesy, Library of Virginia

leading city in the study of medicine in North America, that Virginia's officials turned when seeking a more suitable way of housing the mentally ill. In April 1770, Robert Smith, Philadelphia's leading architect, produced drawings and specifications for a two-story brick, pedimented, three-bay center section. The rectangular box with projecting center bays had become a common plan for public buildings in the colonies; but Smith did cap his rather prosaic design with a one-story cupola over the shallow hipped roof. In June, an act authorized the construction of a hospital for the "Support of Ideots, Lunatics, and other Persons of unsound Minds."

If not distinctive on the exterior, the interior was somewhat unusual for a hospital. Flanking an articulated public space in the three central bays were lateral passages lined on either side with individual cells for patients, rather than the usual open wards. This plan was adopted possibly to control the movements, behavior, and interactions of patients undergoing rehabilitation. Although it has been argued that "security, rather than medical treatment, played the greatest role in affecting the purpose, function, and details of specialized accommodations for the insane," rather than allow the hospital to become a place to incarcerate the incurable, the directors established a policy of taking only those patients whom they thought could be cured.

Whatever the underlying assumptions of its architect and directors, the hospital continued to serve the colony and state well into the next century. By the time the original building burned in 1885, another story had been added along with flanking wings. It had become the centerpiece of Eastern State Hospital's large campus, which rivaled in sheer physical presence its northern neighbor, the College of William and Mary.

The capitol, Governor's Palace, and other major provincial structures may have dominated the colonial capital, but a handful of other public buildings also took their place in the city, including a courthouse and market hall. In 1715, the county voted to abandon its old courthouse at Jamestown and to erect a new one at the southwest corner of England and Francis Streets. Little is known about the form of this building because all of the county record books, which may have contained specifications for its construction and orders for its repair, were destroyed in a fire in Richmond in April 1865. No doubt the building was similar to other courthouses of the period, which were modest, one-story structures with an unheated courtroom and a pair of small jury rooms. Each month for a day or two, a handful of magistrates, composed of the most prominent planters and

Courthouse, ca. 1870s (see p. 41).

Courtesy, Colonial Williamsburg Foundation

merchants of the county, gathered in the courtroom to preside over the administrative and judicial affairs of the county.

In 1723 Williamsburg was incorporated as a city, which gave it powers similar to those granted to the county courts. It is unclear where the city council met or where the mayor and aldermen convened the hustings court during the first twenty years of the city's existence. More than likely, they either held their sessions in a room at one of the many taverns, as was the custom in a number of English towns, or shared the county courthouse. In 1745 the city government found a permanent home in William Levingston's old theatre on the palace green. Within this two-story frame structure, the mayor and aldermen presided over the affairs of the city for twenty-five years.

Finally, in 1770, the city and county governments joined together to build a new courthouse on the market square. The designer and undertaker of the courthouse are unknown, but whoever it was showed great skill in handling the proportions of the plan and its constituent elements. Though it appears as a one-story structure, the walls are nearly twenty feet high, and the apertures are enlarged proportionally to accommodate the increased scale. The form derived from two sources. In plan, the T-shaped building contained a central courtroom flanked by a pair of jury and storage rooms. Except for the addition of smaller unheated storage spaces, the T-configuration had been standard for Virginia courthouses since the 1730s; and although the compass-headed windows were unusual, they were not unknown in courthouse architecture. What set this building apart from others of its type was the Ionic pediment across the front. Whereas earlier courthouses used the arcade to distinguish their civic function, the new courthouse was inspired by the second capitol's two-story portico. Unfortunately, the columns that were to go with the pedimented portico were either soon destroyed or were never in place: in 1796 architect Benjamin Henry Latrobe observed their absence. Although the building burned in 1911, preservation-minded citizens fought a movement to tear down the ruins and build a larger building. The courthouse was repaired and functioned until 1932, when a new structure was erected on the site of the 1715 courthouse.

Until the 1750s, the weekly market on the south side of the market square probably consisted of several temporary stalls and stands set up by hucksters, merchants, and "country people"—that is, farmers selling produce, firewood, and small items of manufacture. In 1757 the city authorized the construction of a market hall. The absence of city records and inconclusive archaeological evidence make the precise size and location of this structure uncertain; however, it is clear from other sources that it stood on the south side of Duke of Gloucester Street, east of the magazine.

The market does not appear to have flourished as well as those in larger cities because of ready access to foodstuffs and other provisions from neighboring farms. Despite its vulnerability, the market continued to function through the Revolution. When the market hall disappeared is uncertain; but by the end of the century, the magazine was used for market functions, and in the 1830s a new market house, perhaps bordering on the southeast side of the square, was erected to served a community bereft of its exalted status as capital of the commonwealth.

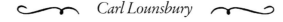
Selected Sources & Suggested Readings

Byrd, William. *Histories of the Dividing Line betwixt Virginia and North Carolina*, ed. William K. Boyd (1929; rep. N.Y.: Dover, 1967).

Chappell, Edward A., and Travis C. McDonald. "The Architecture of the Public Hospital: Containing Madness," *Colonial Williamsburg* 7 (Spring 1985): 26–29.

Goodwin, Rev. W. A. R. *The Record of Bruton Parish Church*, ed. Mary Frances Goodwin (Richmond: Dietz, 1941).

Hening, William Waller. *The Statutes at Large; Being a Collection of All the Laws of Virginia, from the First Session of the Legislature in the Year 1619* (Philadelphia: Thomas Desilver, 1819–1823).

Hood, Graham. *The Governor's Palace in Williamsburg: A Cultural Study* (Williamsburg: Colonial Williamsburg Foundation, 1991).

Jefferson, Thomas. *Notes on the State of Virginia*, ed. William Peden (New York: W. W. Norton, 1982).

Jones, Hugh. *The Present State of Virginia* (London: J. Clarke[?], 1724).

Kocher, A. Lawrence, and Howard Dearstyne. "Discovery of Foundations for Jefferson's Addition to the Wren Building," *Journal of the Society of Architectural Historians* 10. 3 (1951): 28–31.

Kornwolf, James D. *"So Good a Design": The Colonial Campus of the College of William and Mary: Its History, Background, and Legacy* (Williamsburg: Muscarelle Museum of Art, College of William and Mary, 1989).

Lounsbury, Carl. "Beaux-Arts Ideals and Colonial Reality: The Reconstruction of Williamsburg's Capitol, 1928–1934," *Journal of the Society of Architectural Historians* 49 (Dec. 1990): 373–89
_____. "Take a seat, But Not Just Any Seat: The Accommodation of Slaves in Early Virginia Churches," *The Interpreter* 12 (Nov. 1991): 4-5,10.

Turner, Paul. *Campus: An American Planning Tradition* (Cambridge: MIT, 1984).

Upton, Dell. *Holy Things and Profane: Anglican Parish Churches in Colonial Virginia.* 2nd edn. (New Haven: Yale Univ., 1997).

Whiffen, Marcus. *The Public Buildings of Williamsburg* (Williamsburg: Colonial Williamsburg Foundation, 1958).

Boomtown: Williamsburg in the Eighteenth Century

by: Mark R. Wenger

Nowadays people regard Williamsburg as a kind of snapshot, a moment in history captured for the delight and instruction of future generations. Most forget that this town has existed in a state of constant flux since the day of its founding, three hundred years ago. To be sure, Williamsburg is a place, but it is also a process—a parade of change that continues forward even today.

The first question one might ask about this process is, "Why?" What did the authorities hope to achieve by bringing a new town into being? Created in 1699, Williamsburg was the centerpiece of efforts to imprint English culture on Virginia's undeveloped landscape. Two years earlier, Henry Hartwell, James Blair (see color plate 5 and pp. 107 & 152), and Edward Chilton had undertaken to survey the colony's progress and reported their findings in a slender volume titled *The Present State of Virginia and the College*. The verdict was not favorable; Hartwell, Blair, and Chilton censured the colony for its failure to make the land recognizably English:

> As to the natural advantages of a Country, it is one of the best, but as to the improved ones it is one of the worst of all the English plantations in America...if we inquire for well built Towns, for convenient Ports and Markets, for Ships and Seamen, for well improv'd Trade and Manufactures, for well educated Children, for an industrious and thriving People, or for a happy Government in Church and State, in short, for all the other advantages of Human Improvements, it is certainly, for all these Things, one of the poorest, miserable, and worse Countries in all America...As to the outward Appearance, it looks all like a Desart; the High-Lands overgrown with Trees, and the Low-Lands sunk with Water, Marsh and Swamp: the few Plantations and Clear'd Grounds bearing no Proportion to the rough and uncultivated.

After nearly a century of English settlement, Virginia was still a vast wilderness, relieved only by a cluster of buildings at Jamestown, and by myriad tobacco plantations that occupied the necks of land between innumerable creeks. The second half of the seventeenth century had seen repeated attempts to legislate towns into existence, but with few exceptions these efforts ended in failure. Williamsburg, with its broad avenues and massive public buildings, was a new beginning, then, a new center of gravity around which the colony might gather itself and thrive. The orderly arrangement and sheer bulk of its public architecture exuded an aura of permanence and thus elevated prospects for the town's success. Even privately constructed buildings were to be of such scale and substance as would enhance the monumental quality of Virginia's new main street; all were required to stand six feet back from the right-of-way, and to be "ten foot pitch," that is, ten feet from floor to ceiling.

Public architecture gave a new, awe-inspiring presence to the administrative machinery of the British Empire. To fully appreciate the effect of this architectural ensemble, we must remember that all but a handful of Virginians still occupied rude wooden houses at the time—houses having no foundation, no raised floor, no interior plaster, and no glazed windows—houses in which a wooden or "Welsh" chimney was frequently the only source of heat. In a landscape of clapboard houses and wooden chimneys, the new constellation of public buildings served to buttress British rule and the social institutions it upheld.

Because Williamsburg was a new beginning, all boundaries and thoroughfares were laid off in conformity with a single, grand conception. Governor Francis Nicholson appears to have provided the plan. Just a few years earlier, Nicholson had created a new capital for the Maryland colony—the city of Annapolis. At first glance, the two towns appear to have little in common, but a closer look reveals two important similarities:

First, each plan responded directly to the topography of its site. In Annapolis, major streets radiate outward from the summits of two major hills, while in Williamsburg, the main thoroughfare runs east and west along a ridge separating the drainage systems of the York and James rivers. Second, each plan emphasized the importance of secular and religious institutions by maximizing their visibility. In Williamsburg, the capitol and college staked down both ends of the main street, while other public buildings terminated or marked the intersections of major thoroughfares and vistas. Similarly, the church and statehouse in Annapolis occupied the two foci of the town's bipolar layout. Just as public institutions were the foundation of social order in Maryland and Virginia, public buildings were the basis of spatial order in Annapolis and Williamsburg. In each case, Francis Nicholson affirmed the importance of religious and secular order while capitalizing on the physical properties of the site.

Because Nicholson was forced to leave Virginia before his plan could be fully realized, it was left to a later governor, Alexander Spotswood, to "finish" and expand the Nicholson plan. Through

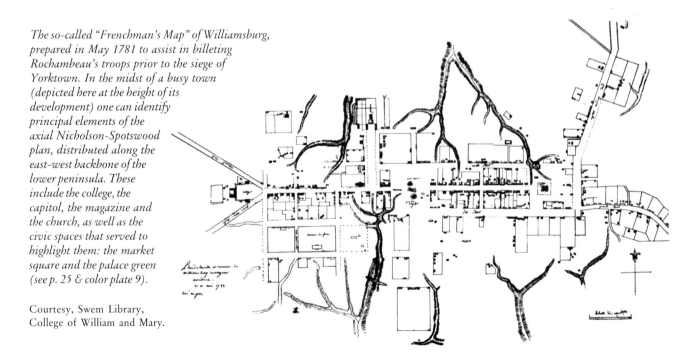

The so-called "Frenchman's Map" of Williamsburg, prepared in May 1781 to assist in billeting Rochambeau's troops prior to the siege of Yorktown. In the midst of a busy town (depicted here at the height of its development) one can identify principal elements of the axial Nicholson-Spotswood plan, distributed along the east-west backbone of the lower peninsula. These include the college, the capitol, the magazine and the church, as well as the civic spaces that served to highlight them: the market square and the palace green (see p. 25 & color plate 9).

Courtesy, Swem Library,
College of William and Mary.

his efforts, Williamsburg witnessed the construction of a new powder magazine, the building of a new church for Bruton Parish, and the completion of a new house for the governor. Like Nicholson, Spotswood recognized the importance of landscapes as expressions of social ideas and manipulated the layout of Williamsburg to this end.

The governor's residence, for example, stood at the end of an impressive green, terminating the town plan's major north-south axis. This house and its symmetrical entourage of subordinate buildings were connected into a continuous frontage broader than the green itself. The grandeur of this compound was intended to elevate and dignify the man who stood at its center.

Detail from the Bodleian plate, an engraving of ca. 1735–1740, possibly executed by John Carwitham or Eleazar Albin to illustrate a projected history of the American colonies by William Byrd II.

Courtesy, Colonial Williamsburg Foundation

The powder magazine, on the other hand, stood along the secondary cross-axis of England Street, giving a stern aspect to the force of arms that ensured order within the colony and guarded against foes from without. According to historian Peter Martin, however, the octagonal form of this structure was less a matter of military necessity than an allusion to French gardening tradition. Comparing the market square to the *rond point* of a French garden, Martin argues that the magazine functioned like the polygonal garden structures situated in these open spaces where the networks of allees and paths converged. Just as the garden structure presented a suitable face to every path, so too, the magazine could be seen to advantage from virtually any part of the town.

Finally, the new church occupied another conspicuous location, standing at the junction of palace green and the main street. The prominence of Bruton Parish Church in the scheme of the town underscored the inextricable link between secular and ecclesiastical authority, and so identi-

Watercolor of the magazine and courthouse, by Dwight Williams, 1892.

Courtesy, Colonial Williamsburg Foundation

fied the church as an agent of both. At the same time, its generous size reflected the need to accommodate large numbers of worshippers during sessions of the General Assembly.

Gradually, the town began to fill in around this framework of public buildings. Historian Cathleene Hellier explains that Virginians were initially reluctant to purchase property in the new town. Between 1699 and 1710, only a handful of lots were deeded to private owners by the city trustees, mostly in the vicinity of the capitol. Not surprisingly, little in the way of private construction survives from this earliest period of the town's existence, the Nelson-Galt house being a possible exception. This structure may pre-date the town but did not occupy its present site until about 1718.

The 1705 fire that consumed all but the brick walls of the new college presented a significant obstacle to the town's development. In the decade that followed 1710, though, Spotswood's continuing work on the governor's house, his completion of the Nicholson plan, his rebuilding of the college, and the General Assembly's resumption of regular sessions at the capitol, all served to accelerate the pace of lot transfers. By the mid-1720s nearly all the lots had been taken up by the artisans, merchants, or professionals—those with compelling reasons to live in a town. Initially, the gentry stayed away. Those gentlemen who did purchase lots were often government officials who found it convenient to live near the seat of government. In these early years, Williamsburg was more a center for government and commerce than a place of resort for gentlemen and their families. For the time being, it remained a socially mixed community, commingling different sorts of people and activities.

Bruton Parish Church. The easternmost bay of the chancel (nearest the photographer) was added in 1752; the tower followed in 1769.

Courtesy, Colonial Williamsburg Foundation

Although diarist William Byrd mentioned a "Governor's Avenue" as early as 1711, Hellier points out that the first lot transfers around the palace green did not occur until about 1716. From the time of the founding, then, nearly twenty years elapsed before development began to highlight the importance of open spaces like the palace green and the market square. By the early 1720s, the city trustees levied taxes for filling and leveling the streets, a project that required the construction of an extensive system of brick culverts.

Only a handful of the town's domestic buildings date to these formative years between 1710 and 1725. Through the efforts of Dr. Herman J. Heikkenen, dendrochronology has provided construction dates for many of the town's surviving houses—Timson (1715), Peyton Randolph (1716), Brush-Everard (1718), St. George Tucker (1718) (see p. 99), and John Blair (1722). From

Dendrochronology, the science of dating wooden components by the historical pattern of their annual growth rings, reveals that the William Timson house was erected soon after 1715. The central core constitutes the original construction phase, the shed at the left being a mid-18th-c. addition. The right-hand extension appears to date from the first half of the 19th c. Prior to this time, the front door stood between the two main windows.

Courtesy, Colonial Williamsburg Foundation

these buildings emerges a picture of early Williamsburg differing significantly from the genteel town that came to exist by the eve of the Revolution. In some cases, early dwellings were covered, roof and walls, with riven clapboards, rather than sawn and planed weatherboards. The interiors of several, such as Timson and Brush, remained wholly or partially unplastered until mid- century and had unpainted interior trim. Where interior finishes did exist, they were rather modest by later standards. At the Brush-Everard house, which stood in the very shadow of the governor's residence, there were originally no chairboards or cornices in the principal rooms. In the back rooms, even baseboards were omitted, the plaster running from floor to ceiling without interruption.

The quarter-century between 1725 and 1750 witnessed profound changes in the character of these and other Williamsburg houses. Many structures were rebuilt, expanded, or simply refinished, changing their internal organization, outward form, and interior embellishment. Hellier tells us that the social complexion of Williamsburg also changed during this time. Artisans, merchants and professionals, once the dominant groups, now owned scarcely a third of the property in town. The remainder had been purchased by gentlemen for rental purposes or residential use. Once acquired, these properties tended to remain under gentry ownership, and such lots as did come up for sale were often too intensively developed to be within the reach of less affluent buyers. Over time, artisans lost ground as owners of property, becoming renters instead. Gradually, Williamsburg came to resemble provincial towns in England where landowners from the surrounding region gathered at certain times of the year.

In 1749, growing demand for additional lots pushed the town beyond its original boundaries. Having purchased a piece of land on the edge of town, just east of the capitol, Benjamin Waller parceled this tract into lots, which he then offered for sale. Significantly, most of the buyers were artisans—those who had been pushed out of the market by rising prices.

Williamsburg had changed in other ways. While various kinds of activity continued to co-exist in every part of town, the intensive development of certain lots had created a commercial district in the vicinity of the capitol, where the throngs of people present during sessions of the General Assembly required food, lodging, and diversion. Taverns and shop crowded both sides of the street as lots were repeatedly subdivided and developed.

Meanwhile, the area around the market square was becoming more diffuse and residen
tial in character, the result of a general trend toward consolidation, rather than subdivision. George
Wythe's residential compound now occupied two lots, as did those of several other gentlemen.
Some bought up entire blocks, eight lots in all, to create spacious settings for their houses and
gardens. This was particularly true along Francis Street, where such gentlemen as John Custis had
assembled large holdings on the south side of the town.

Williamsburg had become a town—the thriving center of a newly awakened colony—but it
was never urban in the way that Charleston and Philadelphia were. Those port cities created
wealth at a pace Williamsburg could not hope to equal. Unlike Virginians, well-to-do residents of
Charleston and Philadelphia tended to maintain their primary residences in town. The resulting
concentration of energy and wealth invested these cities with a special sophistication, as compared
with Williamsburg, where very few of the wealthy class maintained even a secondary dwelling.

For this reason, Williamsburg always retained the quality of a village, looking more like a
collection of rural houses than a real city. Two factors important in defining the town's spacious,
rural character were the generous frontages of individual lots (eighty feet) and the practice of
consolidating several lots into larger properties. Further emphasizing the open character of
Williamsburg were a handful of narrow, side-passage houses built on undivided lots. Having first
appeared around mid-century, this dwelling type created broad spaces between adjacent buildings.
The Tayloe house on Nicholson Street is the best example of a house that had this luxuriant,
greening effect.

By any measure, Williamsburg was a flourishing enterprise, but events soon cast a shadow
over its future. On the night of 30 January 1747, a devastating fire destroyed the old capitol,
leaving it a charred masonry shell. Almost immediately, the House of Burgesses entertained
proposals for moving the seat of government to some new location. Historian Patricia Gibbs was

*The Tayloe house probably dates from the third quarter of the 18th c. Contrary to expectation, the side-passage plan of this
and similar dwellings served to diminish the density of the street front. The gambrel roof provided full-height chambers on
the upper floor, an indication of the upper story's growing importance in the daily routine of the family.*

the first to note the effect of this fire and its aftermath on the local population. For months residents of the town held their breath as members of the General Assembly debated its future. All the while, tavernkeeeper James Shields was literally counting the cost. His will, drawn during this period, stipulated that each daughter receive £100 from his estate if the capital remained in Williamsburg, only half that if the capital moved.

Finally, in the closing weeks of 1748, the General Assembly voted to rebuild the burned-out statehouse, thereby retaining Williamsburg as the capital of Virginia. Assured that the government would stay, Williamsburg embarked on a frenzy of construction as numerous property owners erected new houses or renovated existing ones. Most of the larger brick dwellings in town date from this period, including the Wythe house on the palace green, the Palmer house next door to the capitol, and the Ludwell-Paradise house near the market square. Previously existing houses such as Peyton Randolph's, together with taverns such as Wetherburn's and the Raleigh were updated by the addition of fashionable new rooms for public entertainment. Even the palace received a new extension, comprising a ball-room and a supper room. This proliferation of new entertaining spaces reflected the growing importance of Williamsburg as a meeting place for the gentry. Consequently, even the church was enlarged and the churchyard enclosed by a genteel brick wall. The infrastructure of public life was rapidly coming into existence.

Dendrochronology indicates that the Ludwell-Paradise house was erected shortly after 1752, making it one of three important brick dwellings dating from the period immediately after reconstruction of the capitol.

Courtesy, Colonial Williamsburg Foundation

Granted the role of the capitol fire in sparking this phenomenon, it is important to note that the new importance of public entertaining spaces was not unique to Williamsburg. Between 1730 and 1750 public assembly rooms had been constructed in provincial cities throughout England, those at York and Bath being only the best-known of numerous examples. Evidently, private houses echoed the trend. In 1756, scarcely a year after completion of the governor's public rooms, one English author complained, "In houses which have been some time built, it is common practice to build a great room to them. This always hangs from one end, or sticks to one side of the house and shows to the most careless eye that, though fastened to the walls it does not belong to the building." The large entertaining rooms that appeared in Williamsburg after 1750 were almost certainly related to the construction of similar spaces throughout England—all to accommodate a growing interest in public life or "polite society" as historian Mark Girouard has called it. For a half-century Williamsburg had been the political and commercial center of the colony. By the end of the 1750s it had become Virginia's social capital as well.

It was during this pre-evolutionary period that Williamsburg assumed something like its present appearance. We have seen that many of the town's smartest dwellings date to the early 1750s, and several of the town's earlier ones were remodeled during this time, as well. In 1752 apothecary George Gilmer, owner of an early house on the palace green, wrote to his London

The "Blue Room," St. George Tucker house (see pp. 99 & 169).
This space served Tucker as a study from 1788 to 1826.
Originally it had been a dining room, created by apothecary
George Gilmer in 1752.

Courtesy, Colonial Williamsburg Foundation

factor, "I am wainscoting my dining room, which will make a tolerable room for an apothecary." He might have added that he was rebuilding the stair as well.

Gilmer was only one in a cadre of upwardly-mobile tradesmen and shopkeepers who sought to create genteel houses in the years before the Revolution. Like their more affluent neighbors in town, these people rode high on a wave of prosperity after mid-century. Among those residing in Benjamin Waller's suburb were tailor Robert Nicolson and wheelwright Benjamin Powell. In the 1760s both men expanded their houses, while silversmith James Geddy pulled down his father's old house adjoining the palace green and erected a genteel new dwelling. Gradually, this transformation of individual properties began to affect the overall character of the town. By the 1770s, the market square had become an important and desirable address. Peyton Randolph had expanded an early house and re-oriented it to face the green, while Robert Carter Nicholas and possibly Grissell Hay had completed new houses, also adjoining the square.

In the midst of the square, moreover, stood a new brick courthouse, shared by James City County and the city of Williamsburg. At first glance, the cock-eyed relationship of this building to the magazine appears to violate the regularity of the town, but there was a certain logic behind the

This frame addition probably dates to the period around 1763 when house carpenter and joiner Benjamin Powell purchased an existing brick house on this lot and enlarged it substantially. His addition provided an elegant new dining area and a broad passage for independent access to each of the ground-floor rooms as well as the upstairs.

Courtesy, Colonial Williamsburg Foundation

choice of its site: the magazine stands on the original central axis of the market square while the courthouse stands at the center of the diminished square resulting from encroachment by Market Square Tavern and Chowning's Tavern to the east.

Within a few years, the last of the town's major public buildings, a new hospital for care of the insane, was rising from its foundations on the south side of Francis Street. Williamsburg was looking like a capital, complete with monumental architecture and even an episode of suburban sprawl.

Good times and expanding credit provided the means with which Virginians increasingly sought to emulate the manners and tastes of their peers in England. Ironically, as Virginia drew closer to Britain in cultural matters, political ties were approaching the point of rupture. With the coming of the Revolution, the status of Williamsburg as Virginia's capital was jeopardized, only this time, Governor Thomas Jefferson led the proponents of change. Regarding the town and its public buildings as symbols of an old and corrupt order, Jefferson sought to relocate the government so that new buildings expressive of a new political order could be erected. Ultimately, he succeeded, and the state of Virginia built its new capitol in Richmond, on a hill overlooking the falls of the James River. More than any of his contemporaries, Jefferson understood the symbolic import of public architecture, and it was in this symbolic dimension that the public buildings of the old capital had become obsolete.

Construction of the hospital was under way by 1773.

Courtesy, Colonial Williamsburg Foundation

Selected Sources and Suggested Readings

Carson, Cary, et al. "The Impermanent Architecture of the Southern Colonies," *Winterthur Portfolio* 16: 2/3 (Summer/Autumn 1981): 135-96.

Girouard, Mark. *The English Town: A History of Urban Life* (New Haven: Yale Univ., 1990).

Goodwin, Rutherfoord. *Brief and True Report Concerning Williamsburg in Virginia* (Williamsburg: Colonial Williamsburg Foundation, 1957).

Hartwell, Henry, James Blair, and Edward Chilton. *The Present State of Virginia and the College*, ed. Hunter Farish (Williamsburg: Colonial Williamsburg Foundation, 1940).

Hellier, Cathleene. *"Private Land Development in Williamsburg, 1699-1748: Building a Community,"* M.A. thesis (College of William and Mary, 1989).

Jones, Hugh. *The Present State of Virginia*, ed. Richard L. Morton (Chapel Hill: Univ. of North Carolina, 1956).

Kornwolf, James D. *So Good a Design: The Colonial Campus of the College of William and Mary: Its History, Background, and Legacy* (Williamsburg: College of William and Mary, 1989).

Martin, Peter. *The Pleasure Gardens of Early Virginia* (Princeton: Princeton Univ., 1991).

Reps, John. *Tidewater Towns* (Williamsburg: Colonial Williamsburg Foundation, 1972).

Wenger, Mark R. "Thomas Jefferson and the Virginia State Capitol," *Virginia Magazine of History and Biography* 101:1 (January, 1993): 77-102.

Whiffen, Marcus. *The Eighteenth-Century Houses of Williamsburg*, rev.edn. (Williamsburg: Colonial Williamsburg Foundation, 1984).

Whiffen, Marcus. *The Public Buildings of Williamsburg* (Williamsburg: Colonial Williamsburg Foundation, 1958).

In Search of Freedom:
Eighteenth-Century Williamsburg's African-American Experience

by: Christy S. Matthews

The arrival of Africans into Virginia in 1619 was a seminal event that profoundly shaped the way succeeding generations of Americans of various ethnicities would view themselves and others. The story of Williamsburg and its African-American populace increases our understanding of the strength of the human spirit and the never-ending struggle for justice and the preservation of human dignity. The story also poignantly reminds us of our shortcomings as we continue to struggle with slavery's pernicious legacy: racism.

As the ship anchored off the shore at Yorktown, young Kofi and the others were brought to the upper deck. This was the first time in several days that he had seen the sun or smelled air that was not thick with the foul scents of the slaving vessel that had held him for at least ten weeks. His right shoulder still ached from the hot iron that burned a mark into his skin. With heavy iron shackles still binding his wrists, ankles, and neck, Kofi could only wonder what fate now awaited him in this strange land among even stranger peoples.

When Africans first landed at Olde Point Comfort, Virginia, in 1619, chattel slavery was neither practiced nor legislated in Great Britain and its North American colonies. However, it was not a concept foreign to them. Other European nations had been exploiting African labor since the mid-sixteenth century in the Caribbean and Central and South America with

Traite des Negres, *engraving after George Morland (1790-91). It is estimated that 11.5 million Africans were sold into slavery, making the transatlantic slave trade the largest forced migration in history. The subject is typical of Morland, an English painter whose works in the 1790s expressed sensitivity towards human suffering and promoted benevolence as a necessary social action. The Mansfield Act of 1772 outlawed the importatation of slaves into Britain; and though largely ineffectual, it marked a shift in British attitudes towards slavery. In 1807 Britain ended its role in the slave trade and in 1833-38 emancipated its West Indian slaves.*

Courtesy, Colonial Williamsburg Foundation

great success. Additionally, throughout Britain disenfranchisement and various restrictions on freedom were common for the poor, who often faced extended indentures or lived on manor estates in conditions reminiscent of early feudal systems. The British began systematically purchasing Africans and regarding them as slaves as early as the 1640s. Hampton Roads, and the James and York rivers, became entry points for landing an increasing number of creole Africans (persons of African descent born in the West Indies). Many of the Creole Africans were accustomed to the language and culture of the English, often intermingled with them, and found ways to assert themselves and gain personal freedoms that became more elusive for later generations. A smaller number of Africans were brought in directly from Senegambia, the Congo, and the Ivory and Gold coasts in western Africa.

Drawing by Benjamin Latrobe of an overseer and field hands (1798). Most plantations and farms operated with fewer than twenty slaves. Many, however, employed overseers whose function included disciplining slaves and ensuring that production was done at acceptable levels.

Courtesy, Maryland Historical Society

For the British, the use of African labor meant fewer problems than those associated with the indigenous Algonquin peoples in Virginia whom they had attempted to enslave with only limited success in the colony's early years. Unlike the Native Americans, most West Africans did not regard field labor as women's work. Also, many of the creolized Africans from the Caribbean were accustomed to the labor required of them in the colonies. The enslavement of Africans also meant that planters did not have to replace workers every three to seven years as they had to with European apprentices and indentured servants. The increasing demand for labor throughout the seventeenth century led to greater numbers of Africans' being imported directly from western Africa, especially toward the end of the century. The use of enslaved African labor in Virginia had become standard practice, and Africans quickly replaced white indentured servants as the preferred work force. Virginia planters found using African labor allowed for higher long-term profits while the non-Christian customs of Africans made their exploitation and inhumane treatment easier to justify. Whether captured and enslaved by Europeans or by other Africans, these men, women, and children were unwilling immigrants in a strange land. White Virginians subjected them to greater restrictions, cruelty, and prejudices than their creole predecessors. The enslaved Africans struggled to adapt to the environment, English customs, creolized Africans, and each other.

Throughout the mid- to late-seventeenth century, various county governments allowed a number of slave practices to develop; and they were often contradictory even within a particular region. In 1705, these inconsistencies led the House of Burgesses and the Governor's Council, meeting at the new capital, Williamsburg, to standardize, clarify, and enact new laws regarding enslaved Africans, free blacks, and the few Indians who had not relocated to areas further west. Known as the 1705 Slave Code, these measures not only defined who was to be enslaved (regardless of conversion to Christianity) but also restricted the Africans' actions, established separate court protocols, and determined the nature of punishment to be administered if a slave were found guilty of a crime. More important, these laws helped to fuel the growth of slavery in Virginia.

> Kofi had been on the Carter plantation outside of Williamsburg for many years. He worked tobacco fields in the spring and summer and harvested in the fall. During the winter months, he was trained as a cooper by an Irishman named Bailey. There were twenty or so workers at Carter's place, a few whites who stayed on after their indentures were complete, two young mulatto boys, and a number of slaves. Some of the slaves had been born in Virginia or Jamaica, but Kofi also saw the faces and markings of the Coramantees, Akans, Mendes, and others he did not know. When the work was done, all the workers sat and talked in English of places that were quickly becoming distant or painful memories for most. But there was one who could ease his troubles …a woman named Sukey who called him Cuffy.

By the mid-eighteenth century, Africans and their descendants accounted for forty percent of Virginia's population, the majority living in the Chesapeake region. In many urban and long-settled areas, such as Williamsburg and Norfolk, the percentage approached fifty percent or more. Rural areas tended to have a higher percentage of African-born slaves, whereas urban areas had more slaves born in Virginia or the Caribbean. Regardless of birthplace, many slaves managed to retain a few West African customs while altering others to address their spiritual and cultural needs within the institution of slavery. Despite the diversity of West African peoples and their descendants in Virginia, commonalities in their customs provided a unifying force. Their beliefs in a supreme God and their traditions of personified storytelling, polyrhythmic music, and highly physical dance continued as important aspects of life (see color plate 10). Stories that were once told to teach customs, rituals, morals, and values of the tribes were transformed. The slaves' stories usually taught survival techniques and mocked slave holders or whites in general.

Music continued to be a part of the slaves' lives. Some whites recognized the Africans' musical talents even if they did not fully understand the style; but others found their music harsh, too loud, and high pitched. Africans also began experimenting with and mastering European instruments. Free black Sy Gilliat became so accomplished that in the 1760s and 1770s he was often called upon to perform at the Governor's Palace and in the homes of Williamsburg's wealthiest families. Other

The Virginia Planters Best Tobacco, *label from a packet of Virginia tobacco (ca. 1740s). Tobacco was Virginia's primary cash crop. Being both a source of great wealth and labor-intensive, its cultivation increasingly demanded more slaves.*

Courtesy, Colonial Williamsburg Foundation

blacks displayed their talents at gatherings created to bring about a sense of community among enslaved and free peoples. An English observer noted that a slave "travelled . . . six or seven miles . . . to a negroe dance, in which he performs with astonishing agility, and the most vigorous exertions . . . until he exhausts himself, and scarcely has time, or strength, to return home before the hour is called forth to toil next morning." Phillip Vickers Fithian, a tutor to the Robert Carter family in the 1770s, noted that "This Evening the Negroes collected themselves into the School-Room & began to play the Fiddle & dance." These gatherings helped to ease the burdens of daily life, maintain family connections, and nurture the young. Without these activities, cultural and spiritual survival would have been doubtful.

The slaves also engaged in enterprising activities because their survival often depended on it. An adult's rations usually included only a peck of corn, a pint of salt, a little salted pork, and molasses, so they had to obtain any other foodstuffs on their own. Obtaining food became a collective effort. Fithian observed, "in several parts of the plantation they are digging up their small Lots of ground allow'd by their Master for Potatoes, peas & c.; all such work for themselves they constantly do on Sundays, as they are otherwise employed on every other Day." Preparing for winter was also an important activity. Most rural slave dwellings were crude log structures that required frequent repair and the daubing of gaps between the logs with a mortar-like substance made of straw, limestone, clay, and manure to keep out the cold. On an evening walk, Fithian observed "a number of Negroes very busy at framing together a small House—Sunday they commonly spend in fishing making Potatoes &c., building & patching their Quarters or rather Cabins." Some slaves were also able to sell goods or hire themselves out in an attempt to earn money for personal effects or perhaps to gain freedom by purchasing themselves.

The loading of tobacco into barrels for shipping, from A Map of the most Inhabited part of Virginia, containing the whole Province of Maryland (1775) *by Joshua Fry and Peter Jefferson. Its being featured in the title cartouche indicates tobacco's economic importance in the lands along the Chesapeake Bay. Slaves cultivated, cured, and shipped the tobacco.*

Courtesy, Swem Library, College of William & Mary

Community gatherings and family activities helped blacks escape the trials of their enslavement. In fact, most found various ways to cope with the customs and laws. Although slaves had little control over where they lived or with whom, they often left their owners' property without permission to visit with friends and loved ones regardless of the consequences. They formed families and often performed their own marriage ceremonies, even though marriages among enslaved people were not sanctioned by the church or recognized by the law. When Fithian questioned the practice of denying slaves the right to marry, he learned that "the slaves in this colony are never married, their lords thinking them improper subjects for so valuable an Institution." The law may have stipulated that children of enslaved Africans were property from the moment of birth, but it did not prevent parents from nurturing those children and trying to arm them for survival until freedom came. Throughout their lives, enslaved people resisted the many indignities that defined slavery in subtle as well as overt ways throughout their lives (see color plate 11).

Benjamin Latrobe drawing of Norfolk slaves shaving in preparation for a fine Sunday (1797). Sundays were usually the one day that slaves had time off from assigned tasks. They used it to cultivate their own crops, and also to visit with loved ones.

Courtesy, Maryland Historical Society

Cuffy wailed in despair as the driver rode away with Sukey and their children, Little Cuffy and Sal. He was told that they had been given to Mr. Carter's nephew in a place called Fairfax, more than 150 miles away. Tears streamed down his face, despite promises he and Sukey made to each other. He knew he would never see them again unless. . . . in one swift moment, he ran toward them, only to be chased down by the overseer who struck him repeatedly about the head and back. The pain his body endured could not compare with that in his heart.

Some blacks took a more assertive stance by running away or lashing out at their oppressors. Isaac and David, two slaves who belonged to James and Katherine Hubbard of Williamsburg, were charged in 1770 with deliberately burning down their house. In the ensuing trial, Isaac was found guilty and put to death. Although acquitted, David was held in the jail as a dangerous person for several months. A few slaves became desperate and distraught enough to commit suicide or to commit infanticide to keep their children from a life of slavery.

Despite the harsh realities of slavery, a few African Americans–usually descended from indentured Africans or Europeans—managed to maintain a modicum of legal freedom within the emerging slave society. Their mere presence was an affront to the premise of racial slavery. Simply put, free blacks blurred societal lines. The growth of this segment of the population benefited from a mid-seventeenth century Virginia law stating that the legal status of the mother determined that of the child. A few free black families actually prospered within the Williamsburg community. One of the most notable, the Ashby family, emerged in the eighteenth century. Matthew, the eldest son of white servant Mary Ashby and an unknown African man, was a carter. He not only earned a considerable living for himself, but also acquired enough money to purchase his enslaved wife and children. In November 1769, he successfully petitioned the Governor's Council to free them. Earlier that year, a number of free blacks, which may have included Ashby, petitioned and won from the General Assembly the same

Benjamin Latrobe drawing of blacks working boats on the James River near Richmond (1798-99). Enslaved and free blacks worked as oystermen, fishermen, boatswains, and pilots on the James River. Their knowledge of the Chesapeake and contributory waterways proved valuable to both American and British forces during the Revolution.

Courtesy, The Library of Virginia

exemption from taxes on their wives and daughters that was enjoyed by white men. Another free black, John Rollinson, a successful shoemaker, often wrangled in civil court with other tradesmen and shopkeepers. Adam Waterford worked as a cooper, providing needed wooden barrels, buckets, and other containers to the community. At one point, he was the only cooper in town and regularly sold his wares to the palace. Betty Wallace and Elizabeth DeRosario, both Williamsburg seamstresses, managed to hold their growing families together despite being separated from their enslaved husbands. These and hundreds of other free black families lived in a society that devalued persons of African descent, but in their daily lives they challenged negative perceptions and maintained close affiliations with their enslaved brethren. Although free, the men in these law-abiding and self-sustaining families were still denied many rights, among them the landowning white man's right to vote. By 1790, forty-six free blacks lived in Williamsburg and 521 lived in the surrounding area, representing five percent of the area's population.

In the last quarter of the eighteenth century, persons of African descent made up at least fifty percent of Williamsburg's population. All engaged in a variety of trades and domestic occupations. Women worked as cooks, laundresses, maidservants, spinners, fieldhands, seamstresses, wetnurses, and domestics; men were coopers, carpenters, joiners, blacksmiths, silversmiths, cabinetmakers, fieldhands, manservants, and general laborers. Some of the largest slave holders in the city were tavernkeepers who often owned ten to fifteen slaves and used slave labor for every facet of their operations. Often privy to the latest news of the day and having reasonable mobility about the town, this group of slaves could capitalize on their advantages. For example, Nanny, a scullery maid at the King's Arms Tavern, owned by Jane Vobe, ran away with the theater company that came through town. Another young Vobe slave named Gowan became a Baptist preacher. After Vobe's heir granted him freedom, Gowan established the First Baptist Church of Williamsburg.

Other households also had a large number of slaves. For example, Peyton and Elizabeth Randolph required twenty-seven, most of whom were adults, to operate their household. Their tasks varied. Eve (or Betty) may have been a maidservant or cook; Charlotte probably served as personal maidservant to Elizabeth Randolph; Johnny was the personal manservant to Peyton Randolph and traveled with him to Philadelphia when the First Continental Congress met. Similarly, the home of Thomas Everard, a widower with two young daughters, included nineteen slaves, eleven adults and eight children. Although female relatives presumably helped care for Everard's daughters after their mother died, it is likely that Beck and Kate assisted in their upbringing. These enslaved women also saw their own children given to Everard's daughters. Several other Everard slaves were hired out to other households in town: Bristol and Sarah, for example, served Governor Botetourt at the palace for two years.

Among the fourteen slaves at the home of George Wythe on the palace green (see p. 180), the most notable was Lydia Broadnax, who served Wythe for several decades and was eventually freed by him. Once free, Lydia continued to work for Wythe in Richmond, and she acquired her own home while receiving a salary from him. She is best known, however, as the survivor of the 1806 poisoning that killed George Wythe and a young slave named Michael Brown. The alleged culprit—although never convicted—was Wythe's nephew, George Sweeney, a forger and known gambler who did not want his inheritance shared with slaves. When she was no longer able to provide for herself because of age and blindness, Lydia appealed for and received financial assistance from one of Wythe's most famous students, Thomas Jefferson. Many enslaved people who lived in Williamsburg are known only by name—often only by their first name—but their stories are no less important.

> Cuffy had grown too old and weak to work. He now spent his days looking after his grandchildren and other young ones about the slave quarter. Although he had taken another wife and had more children, two of which had been sold to families in Williamsburg, he still longed to be rejoined with Little Cuffy and Sal and to talk with Sukey once more. As the summer breeze blew across his face, he leaned back in his chair, closed his eyes and went to sleep.

The American Revolution was a period of great paradox. While white Americans proclaimed their independence and asserted their "inalienable rights," more than twenty percent of the total colonial population was enslaved. Fully aware of this paradox, many slaves, often aided by free blacks, took decisive steps to secure their own liberty. In many colonies, African Ameri-

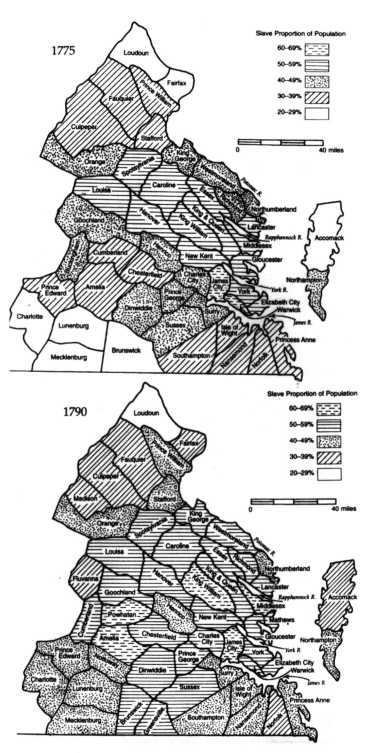

Maps of eastern Virginia showing the proportions of the population that were slaves in 1775 and 1790.

Courtesy, Philip D. Morgan and the University of North Carolina Press

cans petitioned the legislatures to abolish slavery, arguing that it was inconsistent with the goals of the cause for freedom. Others took even more direct courses of action.

In November 1775, Virginia's royal governor, John Murray, fourth earl of Dunmore, issued a proclamation that offered freedom to slaves and bonded servants belonging to patriot sympathizers. Issued in response to the increase in armed and organized rebel forces throughout Virginia, the proclamation was intended to end quickly what Dunmore considered traitorous activity. The fervor it created among the populace has led some historians to argue that it actually helped align white Virginians of all classes against the British government. Nevertheless, more than eight hundred slaves immediately fled to the British, while thousands simply took advantage of the chaos and ran away to points unknown. Several slaves from Williamsburg attempted to get to Dunmore's forces. At least eight of Peyton Randolph's slaves, among them Eve, Billy, and Aggy were reported to have "gone to the enemy." At least three of James Moir's female slaves reached British lines and, eventually, were relocated to Nova Scotia at the end of the war. Similarly, John Jones, formerly owned by Richard Jones; Isaac from the household of John Henderson; Nancy Dixon, Mayor John Dixon's slave; and Hannah Jackson and her daughter Hanah from the household of William Holt all found the freedom they struggled so hard to get. Historian Benjamin Quarles has observed that the slaves "reserved allegiance for whoever made them the best and most concrete offer. Robert Brent of Northern Neck noted that the long premeditated escape by one of his slaves "was from no cause of complaint...but from a determined resolution to get liberty, as he conceived, by flying to lord Dunmore." Reporting on the strength of British forces, Robert Carter Nicholas, president of the Virginia Convention, informed the Virginia delegates in Congress that "great Numbers of Slaves from different Quarters have graced their Corps" and that "every Art" had been used "to seduce the Negroes." Writing to the delegates about Dunmore, Richard Lee reported that "slaves flock to him in abundance; but I hope it is

Drawing of slaves being marched from Staunton, Augusta County, Virginia, to Tennessee, from Lewis Miller's sketchbook (1853). After the American Revolution, many planters moved large numbers of slaves to western Virginia to cultivate newly available land. Virginia law allowed them to be moved to other states also, as shown here. Miller commented sympathetically on the hardship of the march on the slaves.

Courtesy, Abby Aldrich Rockefeller Folk Art Museum, Williamsburg, Va.

magnified." Even George Washington warned that "Dunmore should be crushed . . . otherwise like a snowball rolling, his army will get size."

The decision to join the British cause created tremendous debate and concern throughout the enslaved and free black communities. What factors would influence whether a slave's allegiance was given to the British or the colonists? There are a variety of possible answers. For some slaves, the desire for freedom was so overwhelming that they seized the first viable offer, but it is also possible that these slaves wanted to show that they were worthy of respect and the rights of citizenry by remaining faithful to the authority of the British government. Others struggled with the dilemma of leaving behind loved ones who might never be seen again and who would have to face the wrath of an angry owner. Conversely, how does one explain the numbers of blacks such as Salem Poor, Oliver Cromwell, and Peter Salem, who wholeheartedly supported the colonists? Were their reasons based on the same criteria? Possibly. The death of the free black Crispus Attucks in the Boston Massacre of 1770 moved some colonists to revere him for having lost his life for liberty; but slaves surely must have asked, "whose liberty?"

Full rights of citizenry were denied to free African Americans; and for those slaves who stayed with their owners, conditions worsened exponentially. Many were suspected of aiding and abetting runaways, especially if the runaway was a relative. The scant freedoms afforded slaves before the conflict were revoked. In 1775 and 1776, slave patrols in and around Williamsburg were dramatically increased. As a result, Saturday night and Sunday gatherings were probably forbidden to limit the slaves' contact with each other; and minor infractions that would once have caused a raised brow or gruff comment, were no longer overlooked. Punishments could include beatings, whippings, dismemberment, or death. As fear and discontent mounted among the white populace, slaves had to endure the wrath of not only their owners but whites in general.

In this modern Colonial Williamsburg reenactment, the slave patrol stops Moses, a black Baptist preacher, from illegally preaching to the crowd.

Courtesy, Colonial Williamsburg Foundation

In the meantime, many wealthy slave owners continued to seek solutions to the runaway problem, but legislative efforts proved only minimally effective. As more and more slaves joined the British throughout the war (see color plate 13), slave holders placed increasing pressure on political and military leaders. Some owners wanted the leadership to reconsider their decision to disallow blacks from serving in the Continental Army, believing that Washington's initial decision, in early 1755, to turn away free blacks who wanted to enlist (and in some cases re-enlist) had convinced them to join the British. That many free black men had served valiantly during the Seven Years' War (the French and Indian War) had little effect on Washington's decision to prohibit them from becoming Continentals. Most whites feared the prospect of arming blacks, making the possibility of blacks in the military a dilemma that struck at the very core of the new nation. As Virginians, who most forcefully of all colonists articulated the patriotic ideology of liberty and equality, struggled with losing their own slaves to the British, they found themselves in the middle of a dangerously compromising position.

They needed more soldiers, but did not want black soldiers, so they offered captured run-aways to white enlistees as bonuses for signing. As the war dragged on and recruitment lagged, blacks were allowed to join the Continental Army; and in Virginia, some slave holders were allowed to substitute a slave rather than go into the army. During the course of the war, it is estimated that almost 100,000 African Americans–one out of six!–tried to escape slavery, with perhaps 15,000 joining British forces, compared to the 5,000 who fought with the colonists. A telling anecdote of the period concerns Prince Whipple, a slave of Captain William Whipple in New Hampshire. Asked by his master why he looked so dejected, Prince replied, "Master, you are going to fight for your liberty, but I have none to fight for." Apparently, the truth in the slave's words so struck Captain Whipple that he immediately set Prince free. Prince Whipple subsequently became one of the Continental Army's most decorated soldiers.

Cuffy gathered his small bundle and headed off into the woods. He came upon a familiar clearing near the tall oak tree with a rusting cup and spoon at its base. It was at this place that he and Sal, along with his other brothers and sisters, laid their father, the African known as Kofi to rest. He knelt down on one knee and whispered quietly, "Poppa, the time's come, I intend on getting me free." He didn't know where he was headed, but for the first time in his life, he felt his fate in his own hands, for better or worse.

Selected Sources and Suggested Readings

Curtin, Philip D., ed. *Africa Remembered: Narratives by West Africans from the Era of the Slave Trade.* (Madison: Univ. of Wisconsin, 1967).

Kulikoff, Allan. *Tobacco and Slaves: The Development of Southern Cultures in the Chesapeake, 1680-1800.* (Chapel Hill: for the Institute of Early American History and Culture by Univ. of North Carolina, 1986).

Morgan, Phillip D. *Slave Counterpoint: Black Culture in the Eighteenth-Century Chesapeake and Lowcountry.* (Chapel Hill: for the Omohundro Institute of Early American History and Culture by Univ. of North Carolina, 1998).

Nicolls, Michael L. "Aspects of the African-American Experience in Eighteenth-Century Williamsburg and Norfolk." Research report. (Williamsburg: Colonial Williamsburg Foundation, 1990).

Tate, Thaddeus W., Jr. *The Negro in Eighteenth-Century Williamsburg.* (Williamsburg: Colonial Williamsburg Foundation, 1965).

Walsh, Lorena S. *From Calabar to Carter's Grove: The History of a Virginia Slave Community* (Charlottesville: Univ. Press of Virginia, 1997).

James Armistead Lafayette

The Continental Army initially declined to enlist slaves: Washington issued an order in November 1775 forbidding the recruitment of "Negroes, boys unable to bear Arms and Old Men unfit to endure the fatigues of the Campaign." As the need for recruits in the patriot army increased, however, the pressure from free African Americans in the north and the promise of freedom by joining the British Army forced General Washington to permit slaves to enlist. By the end of the war, over five thousand slaves had fought in the Revolution on the patriot side. One of these was the slave named James Armistead, who lived on the farm of William Armistead in New Kent County near Williamsburg.

Lafayette painted in military dress, by John B. Martin.

Courtesy, The Valentine Museum

When Lafayette arrived in the area of Williamsburg in 1781, he badly needed information concerning the strength and movements of the enemy. The spy who carried out the dangerous assignment of collecting information from the British camps and passing it on to other spies for delivery to the patriot army was James Armistead. *The Writer's Program of the Works Project Administration. The Negro in Virginia* (1940) gives this account: "So successful was Armistead in winning Cornwallis' confidence that the British general sent him back to the Colonial camp to spy on Lafayette. Whereas Armistead carried to Lafayette correct information, he carried to Cornwallis what information the French General chose to send. On one occasion when Cornwallis appeared on the verge of making good his boast of capturing Lafayette, a ruse staved off the superior British forces. Lafayette gave the Negro spy a piece of paper, torn carelessly in half, ostensibly an order to General Daniel Morgan to take up his station in support of Lafayette's right flank. Armistead strolled into Cornwallis' camp with the paper and Cornwallis promptly demanded it. The spy explained that it was but a scrap he had picked up and brought along not knowing what it said, since he could not read. Piecing the scraps together, Cornwallis was astonished to learn of General Morgan's arrival in support of Lafayette, when the Colonial general was supposed to be several days' marching distance away. Just as Lafayette had hoped, Cornwallis decided not to attack."

Armistead was emancipated by an act of the Virginia Legislature in 1786. The act stated that "Armistead kept open a channel of the most useful information to the army of the state." When the War for Independence ended, James Armistead returned to his home in New Kent County, where in 1816 he puchased a farm of forty acres of land. In 1819 the Virginia Assembly granted him a pension of forty dollars per year as well as an award of one hundred dollars. Armistead later changed his name to Lafayette, after his famous former French commander.

by: E. Harris-Bernard

The World Turned Upside Down: Williamsburg During the War for Independence

by: Kevin Kelly

By 10:00 o'clock on the morning of 15 July 1779, the free citizens and inhabitants of Williamsburg had finally gathered in front of the James City County/Williamsburg courthouse. They were in a sullen and angry mood. Several concerned residents, not the town's officials, had called this extraordinary town meeting. At issue was the frightful state of the economy. After nearly four years of war, imported goods were costly and in short supply, and the demands of the Continental Congress to provide the army with food and clothing had driven the price of those necessities to new heights. Moreover, Virginia's paper currency was rapidly depreciating. During the meeting, merchants were roundly condemned for hoarding scarce goods; others blamed the greed of unpatriotic citizens; and all in attendance agreed that unless something was done to reverse the situation, inevitable ruin would ensue. A committee of five men, headed by Colonel James Innes, was elected to draft the necessary address and resolutions.

Fifteen-dollar bill, Virginia. To fund the colony's initial war effort, the Third Virginia Convention, in August 1775, authorized the printing of £350,000 in paper currency. The new commonwealth government thereafter printed even more paper money. From the very first issue, the paper was worth less than its face value.

Courtesy, Colonial Williamsburg Foundation

At the same hour the next morning, the townspeople once again assembled at the courthouse to hear the draft proposal. It began by praising the sacrifice of patriotic Virginians both on the battlefield and on the home front. It went on to state that the only hope Great Britain (and those enemies within) had for victory was the economic collapse of the commonwealth. This possibility was so real that drastic measures were necessary to confront the threat. The

Patrick Henry, by Thomas Sully. The Fifth Virginia Convention elected Patrick Henry to be the commonwealth's first governor on 29 June 1776. Henry was sworn in on 6 July and served until 1 June 1779.

Courtesy, Colonial Williamsburg Foundation

proposal's key measures were a set of fixed, "fair and just" prices for farm produce, imported goods such as rum and pepper, and everyday necessities such as shoes, firewood, and soap. To enforce these prices, a committee of inspection and observation was to be elected. Anyone caught demanding more, or even willingly paying more, than the set price was to be publicly named as "inimical to the rights and liberties of America." After the drafting committee's address and resolutions were read twice and debated, they were unanimously accepted and the committee of inspection and observation was elected. Nothing more was heard of this committee, and Williamsburg's action did little to stop the collapse of Virginia's paper money. By 1781, when the legislature finally repudiated it, the scale of depreciation of the virtually worthless paper stood at a thousand paper dollars to one silver dollar.

The mood of Williamsburg's citizens two years earlier, on 30 October 1777, had been much different. For several days, rumors circulated in the city that the Continental Army had scored a great victory at Saragota, New York. At three o'clock in the afternoon of the 30th, confirmation of General John Burgoyne's defeat and the surrender of his entire army of nine thousand was received at military headquarters in Williamsburg. Word quickly spread throughout the town as the regular soldiers formed up in Benjamin Powell's woods. As their parade reached the capitol, the city's militia joined it. Together the two forces marched down Duke of Gloucester Street, which was lined with cheering men, women, and children, to the market square. There, General Thomas Nelson, the speakers of the lower and upper houses of the General Assembly, and the city fathers reviewed them. After the review, there were thirteen discharges of cannon, three volleys from the infantry, and three huzzahs from all present. The importance of this victory was not lost on those in the crowd who closely followed the news of the war, for it was widely hoped that France would now form an open alliance with the new United States. Later that evening, the city was illuminated and the news of the victory was celebrated with ringing bells, drinking, and gunfire. On 13 December, in accordance with Governor Patrick Henry's proclamation, the town's citizens again celebrated the victory at a sober thanksgiving service at Bruton Parish church. If there was a high-water mark in the townspeople's experience of the war, this was it. By the war's end, Williamsburg and the lives of its citizens would be profoundly changed.

The war began for Williamsburg in the predawn hours of 21 April 1775. Under cover of darkness, Lieutenant Henry Collins, a British naval officer acting on orders from Governor Dunmore, sent a detachment of men to Williamsburg to remove fifteen half barrels of gunpowder from the magazine. Their movement out of town was discovered and an alarm was sounded. As men rushed onto the streets, their fear that the city was on fire gave way to anger. Williamsburg's independent company assembled and many urged it to march on the Governor's Palace and demand the return of the powder. However, Peyton Randolph and other town leaders counseled moderation and their words were heeded. No sooner had a tense calm been restored than word reached Williamsburg that British troops and Massachusetts militiamen had fired on each other at Lexington and Concord. Events quickly swirled out of control. Independent companies mobilized and the palace was fortified. In the early hours of 8 June, Lord Dunmore, in fear of his life, abandoned the palace and sought refuge on a British war ship on the York River. In slightly more than a month's time, life as Williamsburg's residents had known it came to an end. Old friendships were strained and families divided as former loyalties were questioned and new ones were demanded.

By July, Williamsburg had become an armed camp with more than two hundred independent militiamen stationed in and around the city. During the summer and fall, the presence of armed soldiers, flushed with initial enthusiasm for the patriot cause, precipitated a number of unfortunate incidents that disturbed the peace. Petty pilfering was a constant irritant; fence rails disappeared into campfires; and the trees in Benjamin Powell's woodlot were used for target practice. Furthermore, troops eagerly intimidated those they judged as poorly committed to the rebellion. Armed members of Williamsburg's independent company confronted the Reverend Thomas Gwatkin in his lodgings at the College of William and Mary because they objected to his outspoken support of the governor. Joshua Hardcastle, after uttering some intemperate remarks at a tavern, was dragged before a mock court martial that threatened to give him a "coat of thickset." Soldiers demanded that Robert Prentis, clerk to the receiver general; Deputy Auditor General John Blair; and Postmaster John Dixon swear not to release any royal revenue without the soldiers' approval. In the face of this intimidation, a number of other townsfolk, such as Dr. George Pitt and Attorney General John Randolph, who could not bring themselves to be disloyal to their king, felt compelled to go into exile in Great Britain.

As the tense stand off of the summer and early fall of 1775 gave way to open warfare in late autumn, tensions increased in Williamsburg. A steady stream of prisoners of war and Tories arrested because of their political views were carted through the city to the public jail. While some, such as the elderly William Aitcheson, a Norfolk merchant, were paroled, most were not. Those thought to hold the most dangerous views were kept in close confinement for months or even years and were a vivid reminder of the price to be paid for loyalty to the crown. Even acts of kindness toward prisoners, such as that Dr. Alexander Middleton provided to Lieutenant Andrew McCan of the Queen's Rangers in spring 1776, were viewed with deep suspicion by townspeople.

The Alternative of Williamsburg, *published for R. Sayer and J. Bennett (16 February 1775). The Continental Association, which prohibited the purchase of imported British goods, went into effect on 1 December 1774. Virginians who continued to trade with Great Britain were often threatened with tar and feathers to force their compliance with the association.*

Courtesy, Colonial Williamsburg Foundation

THE ALTERNATIVE OF WILLIAMS BURG.

On 15 May 1776, the Fifth Virginia Convention instructed its delegates at the Continental Congress to introduce a resolution declaring the colonies independent. After that the convention turned to the business of writing a constitution. On 12 June 1776 the convention adopted the Declaration of Rights and on 29 June adopted Virginia's first constitution.

Courtesy, Colonial Williamsburg Foundation

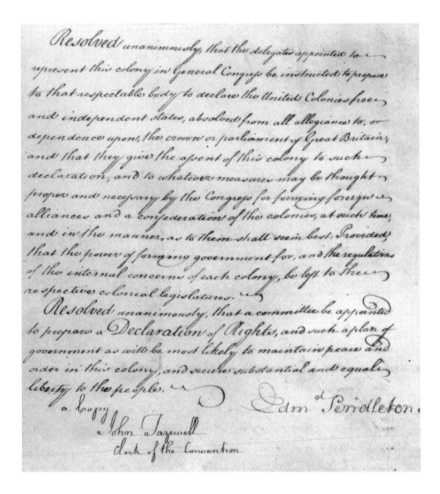

Neutrality had quickly become virtually impossible. Yet, at the very same time that Tories were being imprisoned, an unknown number of Williamsburg slaves escaped their rebel masters and sought the freedom Dunmore held out to them if they joined his army. The spring and summer of 1776 were seasons of high excitement in Williamsburg. The fifth Virginia Convention, meeting at the capitol, declared the colony independent on 15 May and approved a declaration of rights and a state constitution in June. The excitement peaked on 25 July. In the afternoon, amidst military parades, the discharge of cannons, and the firing of small arms, the Declaration of Independence was "solemnly" proclaimed to the cheers of the townspeople at the capitol, the courthouse, and the palace. The celebration continued into the evening with the town's illumination. Undoubtedly, toasts were given and drunk by revelers at the Eagle (formerly King's Arms) Tavern.

With Lord Dunmore's departure from the Chesapeake Bay on 5 August, excitement subsided, and citizens soon settled into a new routine. Governor Henry and his staff were in residence at the palace, and the rhythm of the new central government asserted itself. The courts soon resumed sitting, and the General Assembly of the new commonwealth met for the first time in Williamsburg in October 1776. Thereafter, it reassembled regularly in May and October. Added to this was the general bustle of a military headquarters. Wagons rumbled to and from the two public storehouses in and near town. Newly enlisted and furloughed soldiers awaiting assignment bivouacked near the city. The jail continued to house military prisoners along with the usual criminals. The most notorious prisoner was Lieutenant Governor Henry Hamilton of Detroit. Known as the "Hair Buyer" because of his aggressive use of Indian allies, Hamilton had been captured by George Rogers Clark at Vincennes on 24 February 1779. Clark sent Hamilton and his garrison under guard to Williamsburg. At word of Hamilton's arrival on the evening of 17 July, a crowd of townspeople quickly gathered and taunted him as he was escorted to jail. However, not everyone in Williamsburg heaped scorn on Hamilton, who later recalled that, had it not been for the kindness of James and Frances Hubbard, his suffering would have been

Detail of 1756 map of eastern North America. Some of the sharpest fighting of the Revolution occurred on Virginia's western frontier. Virginia militiamen under George Rogers Clark fought with Shawnee and other Indian groups, backed by British Lieutenant Governor Henry Hamilton, stationed at Detroit, for control of Kentucky.

Courtesy, Colonial Williamsburg Foundation

far worse. Many of the men of Williamsburg answered the call to war. Blacksmith James Anderson was appointed captain of the commonwealth's Company of Artificers. His duties took him to Richmond to be closer to the supply center at Point of Fork. Edmund Dickenson, a cabinetmaker and member of the local Masonic lodge, received an officer's commission in the First Virginia Regiment. Henry Nicholson, who as a fourteen-year-old commanded a group of boys who played at soldiering in 1775, volunteered to join Virginia's Corps of Horse in 1778. On the recommendation of General Nelson, a number of the town's citizens raised the money to equip Nicholson and three other young men of the city. John J. Carter, a local publican, and James Purdie, the eldest son of Alexander Purdie, both served in the Continental line.

Not surprisingly, Williamsburg residents closely followed the course of the war as it was reported in the newspapers; but news from the front lines was slow to arrive and was often misleading. At times it was better to get information from returning veterans. After his enlistment was up, John Carter returned to Williamsburg and regaled his customers with tales of the Battle of Trenton. Unfortunately, news from the battlefields was sometimes all too true. Word reached Williamsburg by 4 August 1778 that Major Dickenson had been killed at the Battle of Monmouth on 28 June. The 2 August 1780 issue of the *Virginia Gazette* reported that young James Purdie died on board a British prison ship in New York harbor. Perhaps it was fortunate his father had died in April 1779 without knowing his son's fate.

Through the late 1770s, the failing economy rivaled the war as the major concern. When the city's residents met on 17 July 1779 to tackle the problem of inflation, they had an additional reason to worry about their economic future. The General Assembly, which had adjourned less than a month earlier, had voted to move the capital to Richmond in the spring of 1780. There had been periodic efforts to relocate the capital since mid-century, but the strength of the Tidewater councilors in the upper house had blocked those attempts. The new constitutional government, put in place in 1776, seriously weakened the influence of the Tidewater interests because the new Senate, unlike the colonial upper house, included members from the western parts of the state. Furthermore, the new General Assembly reversed Great Britain's late colonial policy of not creating new counties in Virginia. By May 1779, delegates from eleven new western counties sat in the House of Delegates. Friends of Williamsburg also lost two votes when Jamestown and the college were denied representation in the new assembly. The appearance of a British fleet in the bay, in early May 1779, probably spurred the western delegates to action. Citing the need for a more centrally located capital, as well as Williamsburg's exposure to an attack, they carried the day.

When the last General Assembly that would meet in Williamsburg convened on 4 October 1779, rumors that it might reverse the previous decision gave faint hope to some townsfolk. But those hopes died as it became clear the decision to move the capital would go forward. When the assembly finally adjourned on Christmas Eve, the holiday spirit was absent from many Williamsburg homes. There was little anyone could do but wait for the inevitable to happen. On 25 March 1780, formal notice was published that the business of the executive branch of government would cease in Williamsburg on 7 April and would resume in Richmond on the 24th.

As if the capital's relocation was not bad enough, Williamsburg was to face even more wartime troubles. Until 1780, Williamsburg had avoided the full brunt of the war; but that seemed about to change. In August 1777, when a British fleet carrying General William Howe's army to Head of Elk entered the Chesapeake Bay. Six hundred soldiers, including a company of college students, quickly mustered at Williamsburg; and by the end of August, four thousand soldiers were encamped around the capital. They were soon sent home, however, when the British threat diminished. Then, on 8 May 1779, a British expeditionary force sailed into the bay and captured Portsmouth and Norfolk. Again, the city militia and the college company mustered and joined the 1,800 soldiers stationed near Yorktown. Not intending to stay, the British withdrew on 24 May. Later, on 20 October 1780, General Alexander Leslie led an invasion force of 2,200 hundred into Virginia: British troops were landed at Newport News, and British cavalry units patrolled within fifteen miles of Williamsburg. Again the British stay was brief. Leslie departed the region on 22 November in response to urgent orders sending him to Charleston, South Carolina. Although alarming, these brief intrusions caused only minor disruption in Williamsburg.

That changed in late December 1780, when newly commissioned British General Benedict Arnold led another invasion force of 1,800 troops into Virginia. Unlike the earlier British armies, this one planned to stay. To make his intentions clear, Arnold led a lightning strike up the James River, capturing Richmond before settling into his winter quarters at Portsmouth on 19 January. In response, 3,700 Virginia militiamen were stationed near Fredericksburg, Cabin Point, and Williamsburg. On 26 March, General William Phillips reinforced Arnold with

2,600 more troops. The presence of a large British force nearby heartened the spirits of several Williamsburg residents who had become disillusioned with the patriot cause. In March, William Hunter, a former printer, was able to slip in and out of Portsmouth to provide the British with important intelligence; and on 18 April 1781, Phillips and Arnold began their spring offensive. Encountering little resistance, the British occupied Williamsburg two days later. With the willing guidance of the veteran John J. Carter, they captured and burned the shipyard on the Chickahominy River. After remaining in town for two days, Phillips and Arnold continued on to Petersburg where, on 20 May, Major General Charles, Earl Cornwallis joined them with his southern army and took command of a combined army of approximately seven thousand soldiers.

Arnold's invasion caught Virginia off guard and Cornwallis' arrival compounded the problem for Virginians. A widespread panic set in across the commonwealth, reaching a peak in early June, when Lieutenant Colonel John Graves Simcoe captured Point of Fork (and Captain James Anderson) and Lieutenant Colonel Banastre Tarleton nearly caught the entire General Assembly napping at Charlottesville. After these raids, Cornwallis pulled his troops back toward the Tidewater. General Marquis de Lafayette, at the head of a small band of Continental troops, cautiously followed him. On 25 June, Cornwallis' army reached Williamsburg: the city was occupied for the second time.

Skirmish at Richmond Jan. 5th 1781. Benedict Arnold's raid on 5 January, led by Lieutenant Colonel John Graves Simcoe and the Queen Rangers, argued that the new capital had not been moved to a safer location.

Courtesy, John Graves Simcoe Papers, Special Collections, John D. Rockefeller, Jr., Library, Colonial Williamsburg Foundation

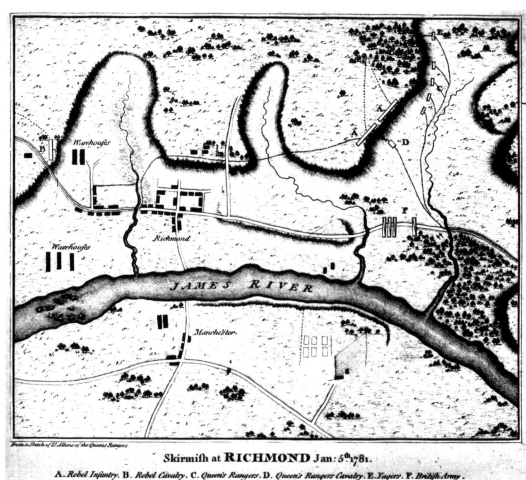

Skirmish at **RICHMOND** Jan: 5th 1781.

A. *Rebel Infantry.* B. *Rebel Cavalry.* C. *Queen's Rangers.* D. *Queen's Rangers Cavalry.* E. *Yagers.* F. *British Army.*

Conclusion De La Campagne de 1781 en Virginie. The Marquis De Lafayette, a young French nobleman, came to America in 1777 and volunteered to serve in the Continental Army. He was commissioned a major general. In April 1781 Washington ordered Lafayette with 1,200 light infantrymen south to counter the British army in Virginia.

Courtesy, Colonial Williamsburg Foundation

Cornwallis established his headquarters at the President's House at the college. President Reverend James Madison and his wife, Sally, were forced to lodge in the main building of the college. Other senior officers secured housing elsewhere in town, while the army of seven thousand camped in and around the city. With the army were several hundred run-away slaves who sought freedom with the British, as well as a small number of loyalist refugees with their families. The army spent ten days in Williamsburg resting and replenishing its supplies. Cattle drivers soon herded nearly one hundred cattle and two hundred sheep into town. Army carters brought in wagonloads of shelled corn, hundreds of pounds of bacon, and 150 gallons of rum. William Plum lost a valuable inventory of tanned leather. On 4 July the British marched off toward Jamestown and, eventually, Portsmouth, leaving behind several soldiers ill with smallpox and what St. George Tucker called a "plague" of stinging flies. Before the townspeople could recover from the occupation, Cornwallis returned; and on 2 August, his advance guard landed at Yorktown only twelve miles from Williamsburg.

Cornwallis' occupation of Williamsburg brought to a head the ambivalence many of the city's residents felt toward the patriot cause even after, or because of, six years of war. Slaves of Dr. James McClung and James Cocke ran away with the British. Other slaves may have as well. Convinced the British would win the war, William Hunter openly joined them in June. So, too, did James Hubbard, who had refused to take the oath of allegiance to Virginia in 1777. That action resulted in a brief imprisonment and the destruction of his law practice. By 1781, the Hubbard family, which was divided over the father's action, lived in greatly reduced circumstances. Hubbard may have joined the British simply as a way out of an intolerable situation. Others also willingly assisted the occupying troops. As an excuse not to muster with the city's militia, some probably used the parole Cornwallis insisted all men of military age take, which allowed them to remain free on their promise not to take up arms against the British. Their actions earned them the censure of their neighbors. Two were arrested for "disaffection," and the Common Council urged the commonwealth to punish the rest.

Decisions made in the West Indies and New York soon ended the uneasy stand off between Cornwallis and Lafayette. When word reached Washington that the French fleet in the West Indies was sailing to the Chesapeake Bay, he marched the allied army south in hopes of trapping Cornwallis. The fleet reached Virginia on 31 August 1781; and on 5 September, a French army of three thousand landed at Jamestown Island. On 7 September, Lafayette moved his troops into position just east of Williamsburg. When Washington and French General Rochambeau (see color plate 14) reached Williamsburg on 14 September, Washington established his headquarters at George Wythe's house, while Rochambeau settled in at Betty Randolph's. The first element of the American army landed at College Landing on 20 September. Within six days, a combined allied army of 16,000 was encamped all around the city. Once again the town was engulfed by the war.

The next three weeks saw a whirlwind of activity in Williamsburg. As a secure rear area, the city served as an important supply depot and evacuation point. Refugees from Yorktown made their way here. Both the Americans and the French established their main hospitals in Williamsburg; the French housed their sick and wounded at the college, while the Americans housed their disabled soldiers at the palace. The total number of sick and wounded carried to Williamsburg is not known, but at least four hundred were still hospitalized there when the siege of Yorktown ended.

On 19 October 1781 Cornwallis formally surrendered. After a few days rest, the defeated British soldiers marched through Williamsburg on their way to prison camps in western Virginia and Maryland. Undoubtedly, many Williamsburg residents relished the changed condition of these once proud soldiers who, just a few months earlier, had been masters of the city. On 6 November the victorious American army marched through on the way back to New York. Shortly thereafter, Rochambeau's French army took up its winter quarters in fields east and west of town and its commander set up his headquarters at George Wythe's home.

Although fire was a great hazard of urban life in wartime, Williamsburg had, until 1781, managed to escape its worst terrors. In April 1779, a fire had broken out on the roof of a house near Market Square, but it was quickly extinguished and caused little damage. On 23 November 1781, the President's House at the college caught fire; but although the house was gutted, the twenty-three hospitalized French officers were safely evacuated, and the French kept the fire from spreading to the main college building. A month later, at eleven o'clock on the night of 22 December, a fire was discovered in the basement of the palace. The sick and wounded Americans were carried to safety with the loss of only one life, but the fire burned with such intensity that the palace was completely consumed within three hours. Flaming embers from the fire rained down on all the houses along the palace green; but again, the alert French prevented further destruction, climbing out onto roofs to smother the hot coals. In the morning, the American invalids were moved to the empty capitol. To comprehend the loss of these two buildings so soon after Cornwallis' surrender, townsfolk rumored that either slaves or Virginians still harboring Tory sentiments must have set the fire.

When the French army finally departed in late July 1782, the war went with them, but its impact remained. As the townspeople went about their daily business, they passed many vacant houses and deserted shops. Except for an occasional admiralty court, the capitol stood locked and empty. A few people were salvaging bricks from the rubble that once was the palace. Repair work had begun at the college, but it was some time before the president and his wife could move back in. The vestry of Bruton Parish had to cope with the loss of public taxes that had supported the church before the war; and with fewer visitors coming to town, the number of taverns declined. A city that was once a thriving center for nearly forty rival merchants could boast of less than half that number in 1782. By 1782, Williamsburg had lost more than a quarter of its pre-war population and would lose even more in the following decades.

When word came announcing the general peace between Great Britain and the United States, the citizens of Williamsburg, despite their loses and an uncertain future, put on a celebration that equaled any they had ever done. On 1 May 1783, they gathered at the courthouse and, after reading Congress' proclamation, formed a parade, led by four flag bearers and a mounted herald. Next came the city sergeant carrying the city mace, followed by the mayor, the recorder with the charter, and the city clerk with the plan of the city. Behind these officials marched the aldermen and common councilors two by two. Bringing up the rear were the rest of the town's citizens, who also marched two by two. To the pealing of the college, church, and capitol bells, the parade moved to the college, where the proclamation was read again. It then reversed course and proceeded to the capitol, where the proclamation was read a final time. The war-weary but jubilant citizens spent the rest of the day toasting the independence that had been so hopefully declared in the old capitol in May 1776 and remembering the hand they had played in making the Revolution happen.

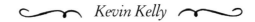
Selected Sources and Suggested Readings

Buel, Richard. *In Irons: Britain's Naval Supremacy and the American Revolutionary Economy* (New Haven: Yale Univ., 1998).

Davis, Burke. *Yorktown: The Winning of American Independence* (N.Y.: Harper and Row, 1969).

Goodwin, Rutherfoord. *A Brief and True Report Concerning Williamsburg in Virginia* (Richmond: Dietz, 1980).

Johnston, Henry P. *The Yorktown Campaign and the Surrender of Cornwallis, 1781* (1881; rep. Eastern National Park and Monument Assoc., 1975).

Lumpkin, Henry. *From Savannah to Yorktown: The American Revolution in the South* (Columbia: Univ. of South Carolina, 1981).

Selby, John E. *The Revolution in Virginia, 1775-1783* (Williamsburg: Colonial Williamsburg Foundation, 1988).

Virginia Gazette 1775-1780. Microfilm. John D. Rockefeller, Jr., Library, Colonial Williamsburg Foundation.

York Co., Virginia. *County Court Records*. Microfilm. John D. Rockefeller, Jr., Library, Colonial Williamsburg Foundation.

"No mean city":
Antebellum Williamsburg

by: Emma L. Powers

In 1824, forty-three years after the Siege of Yorktown, the decisive victory in the American Revolution, Congress invited Marie Joseph Paul Yves Roch Gilbert du Motier, the Marquis de Lafayette, to this country. As the "Nation's Guest" he spent more than a year touring, speaking, and shaking hands.

He spent 19 October 1824, the anniversary of Cornwallis' surrender, in Yorktown. Following their afternoon meal the next day, he and his large entourage left for Williamsburg. The marquis traveled in a barouche, while the others rode in carriages. The illustrious party included Governor James Pleasants and his council, the commonwealth's chief justice and secretary of war, and a variety of high-ranking military officers. Escorted by a military battalion, they arrived in Williamsburg "amidst merry peals of bells and the congratulations of its citizens." Sentimental embraces and the very best the little town had to offer the "boy general" were given on his return.

This portrait of the Marquis de Lafayette by the American artist Samuel Lovett Waldo dates from 1824, the year of Lafayette's return to America. It was formerly owned by President James Monroe.

Courtesy, Colonial Williamsburg Foundation

Mayor William T. Galt and other municipal authorities received him; and Galt gave "an eloquent address," apparently making the distinguished visitor an honorary citizen. The marquis responded as follows:

Your affectionate welcome, and the honorable expressions of your esteem, are the more gratifying to me, as I remember my old personal obligation to this seminary, the parent of so many enlightened patriots who have illustrated the Virginian name. Here, sir, were formed in great part, the generous minds whose early resolutions came forth in support of their heroic Boston brethren, and encouraged the immortal Declaration of Independence, so much indebted, itself, to an illustrious Virginian pen. Those, and many other recollections, such as the efforts made by a colonial assembly of Virginia, in time still more remote, to obtain from the British Government the abolition of the slave trade, inspire a great respect for the college, where such sentiments have been cherished. I am sensible of the honor conferred on me by the adoption you have been pleased so kindly to announce, and I beg you, sir, and the other gentlemen of the college, to accept my most grateful thanks.

Local hostesses vied for the opportunity to entertain the general. Mrs. Mary Monroe Peachy was the lucky one and made room for Lafayette at her residence (now known as the Peyton Randolph house), which had served as Rochambeau's headquarters before the Siege of Yorktown. On Friday morning, the 21st, the general left Williamsburg. He and his escorts traveled to Jamestown where they were met by a deputation from Norfolk, their next port of call. All boarded the steamboat *Petersburg* and before sailing enjoyed a "sumptuous collation" to music provided by a band playing from the *U.S.S. North Carolina*.

Lafayette's return was one of the high points for Williamsburg in the nineteenth century. In hosting the "Nation's Guest," Virginia's colonial capital had temporarily rekindled memories of grand victories and selfless patriots; and André-Nicolas Levasseur, secretary to Lafayette on his journey, noted happily that the general was received with great feeling, and had the pleasure of greeting a considerable number of ancient friends, with whom he passed the day. A vestige—literally, footprint—best describes Williamsburg between 1800 and the onset of the Civil War. Numerous travelers during the period recorded their impressions of the place, every account remarking on the dwindling population, the dilapidated state of colonial buildings, and the place's "decaying grandeur." Even Lavassuer remarked that Williamsburg was a

> small town retaining very little of its ancient importance. Its college which was founded under the reign of William and Mary, and bears their name, was celebrated for the excellence of its learning until within about a half century, since when it appears to have partaken of the sad destiny of the town, to which it belongs....the population of Williamsburg is not more than 14 or 1500 souls.

A visitor earlier in 1824 also found Williamsburg to be ramshackle: "the houses are small and old...some of [them] are fallen down and the whole village bears the marks of poverty." Another exclaimed that it was "a paltry village without even a venerable ruin to rescue its decay from insignificance!" Summing up the disappointment of expectant visitors, another traveler in the year of Lafayette's return lamented that "this poor town had very little to recommend it to a stranger except the memory of its ancient importance."

Thomas Jefferson had never been particularly fond of the city where he attended college, read law, wooed, lost in love, and served as legislator and later as the second governor of the commonwealth. "Devilsburg," he called it; and as chief executive he managed to shift the seat of government to Richmond in April 1780. On the other hand, St. George Tucker (1752-1827), Jefferson's friend, longtime correspondent, and fellow student of George Wythe, called Williamsburg "no mean city" in 1795 to refute the negative assessment of the town published by the New England geographer, Jedidiah Morse. Tucker—jurist, poet, family man, immigrant from Bermuda, and resident of Williamsburg for most of his adult life— was fond of his chosen home, that same place others saw as a crumbling ghost town: "Few villages can boast a more pleasant situation, more respectable inhabitants, or a more agreeable and friendly society." In 1834 his son, Nathaniel Beverley Tucker (1784-1851), inherited the family home and, feeling as his father did about the town, returned to take up the law professorship at William and Mary.

Given these conflicting impressions, what was antebellum Williamsburg? A college, a county seat, a market town, and a major hospital—these four institutions provided Williamsburg's considerable livelihood between 1800 and 1860. Although not a bustling port or industrial city, Williamsburg held its own fairly well. No longer, however, could visitors expect to encounter royal governors with trains of lackeys, hear fiery patriots' orations, or eavesdrop on events of national significance. Williamsburg had become a provincial town, important to twelve or fifteen hundred town dwellers and to residents of a sizeable hinterland of farmers, tradesmen, and laborers—both black and white.

Naturally, the population of Williamsburg dropped quickly between 1775 and 1782, when its legislative purpose ceased and war raged in the vicinity, but for the first half of the nineteenth century, the number of townspeople remained fairly steady at about 1,200. The 1860 census for Williamsburg is more detailed than most and indicates a growth to 1,895. It also categorizes the population by race and status: 742 whites and 121 free blacks, as well as 743 slaves. Additionally, 270 whites and nineteen blacks were patients at the Eastern Lunatic Asylum.

This census also gives occupations for 288 of the town's heads of households. The largest single category was washerwoman, all twenty-nine of whom were black. Twenty-six "mechanics," a catchall phrase for semi-skilled white workmen, formed the next largest group. The twenty-four servants (one white man, eight black men, and fifteen black women) constituted the third largest category. Eighteen merchants, all but one of whom was male, comprised another large group in the work force. The hospital employed a sizeable staff of superintendent, matron, steward, and various officers; and the nine local physicians probably attended hospital inmates. The presence of ten lawyers in such a small place indicates how important the James City County Court remained. Clothing production in its various aspects engaged the largest occupational force—thirty-five, ranging from mantuamakers and dressmakers, to seamstresses, tailoresses, and tailors. The shades of distinction between these jobs are no longer clear in our ready-to-wear era, but the differences were important then.

St. George Tucker's cousin, also named George Tucker, summarized the three major functions of the town in the phrase, "the College, the court, and the lunatics." There was as much truth as wit in his remark. The first of these, the college, struggled through the years of transition

St. George Tucker, by C. B. J. Fevret de Saint-Memin (1807). Member of a prominent Bermuda family, Tucker came to Williamsburg in 1771 to enroll at the College of William & Mary. He never left, becoming one of the most prominent and devoted citizens of the town in the early 19th c. A friend and ally of Thomas Jefferson, Tucker was jurist, law professor at the college, and editor of the first American edition of the famous legal treatise, the Commentaries of Sir William Blackstone.

Courtesy, Colonial Williamsburg Foundation

Nathaniel Beverley Tucker (1784-1851), by Joseph Wood (1828). After being trained in law by his father, he moved for a time to Missouri but returned to Williamsburg in 1843 to take up his father's old position as professor of law at the college and to continue to make the family home a center of the social and cultural life of the town. He become a novelist, an essayist, and, as the sectional crisis deepened, a noted defender of slavery and advocate of southern independence.

Courtesy, Mr. Erich Kimbrough

from colony to new nation. Reverend James Madison, cousin of the U. S. president of the same name, served as head of the college from 1777 until his death in 1812. From 1790, he was also Virginia's first Episcopal bishop. Highly respected as a scientist and teacher, Madison perhaps paid more attention to the college than to his diocese. In some circles it was even whispered that he was a freethinker. Madison's slightly younger contemporary, Bishop William Meade, who knew him well, hoped to quell such rumors:

> It has been asserted that Bishop Madison became an unbeliever in the latter part of his life....I am confident that the imputation is unjust. His political principles, which in that day were so identified...with those of infidel France may have subjected him to such suspicion. His secular studies, and occupations as President of the College and Professor of Natural Philosophy, may have led him to philosophize too much on the subject of religion...but that he, either secretly, or to his most intimate friends, renounced the Christian faith, I do not believe, but am confident of the contrary.

The French, who had played so vital a role in the American Revolution, came in for particular reproach. Meade considered them responsible for the college's dismal state.

Infidelity, indeed, was then rife in the state, and the College of William and Mary was regarded as the hotbed of French politics and religion: "I can truly say, that then [1811], and for some years after, in every educated young man of Virginia whom I met, I expected to

Wood engraving of the college before 1850.

Courtesy, Colonial Williamsburg Foundation

find a skeptic, if not an avowed unbeliever." French sympathies still held sway in 1824, as Lafayette's visit proved.

Bishop Madison died in 1812, at the age of sixty-three, having served as president of the college more than half his life. Some expected the institution itself to die with him, but William and Mary survived, though in a much reduced state. In 1813, for instance, during John Bracken's brief tenure as president, the main building was put to use as "Barracks for the Militia," interrupting its use by students and faculty. Bracken, who apparently had a drinking problem and was perhaps appropriately deemed a "simpleton" by Jefferson, was totally inept and in 1814 was asked to resign.

Bracken was replaced by John Augustine Smith, the first layman to be president. Finding "the whole establishment tending rapidly to ruin"—partly from student vandalism—Smith set to work. Lecture rooms were put "in complete order," a chemistry laboratory was built, leaking roofs mended, and interiors throughout the main building repaired and replastered by 1823. An insurance appraisal indicates the amount of improvement between 1815 and 1821: the Wren Building's value increased from $30,000 to $70,000. No wonder Smith encouraged Lafayette's visit to his renovated and ostensibly sound college—a very wise public relations ploy!

Despite his intelligence, however, Smith was, in historian Ludwell Johnson's words, "a man almost pathologically tenacious in opinion and purpose, an egocentric, self-righteous, insensitive authoritarian," whose offensive temperament prevented him from achieving many financial and personnel goals he recognized as necessary to the success of the college. Smith was perceptive enough to realize that after Jefferson's university opened in Charlottesville in 1825, William and Mary's future would be more secure if the college were moved to Richmond. Removal was vigorously opposed by Jefferson, however, who saw it as a threat to his university's success. Jefferson held the day, and a disappointed Smith departed for New York.

After the short presidency of William Holland Wilmer, 1826-1827, Adam Empie took the job. He succeeded in increasing enrollment to over a hundred students in the grammar school and college in 1829 and 1830; and in 1831 there were still over ninety. In 1833 and 1834, when the law professor left and law courses were temporarily suspended, enrollment dropped off. Beverley Tucker's appointment to the law chair in 1834 reversed the trend, and students again numbered over ninety. In 1836, President Empie resigned, however, to become the minister of a church in Richmond.

Thomas Roderick Dew, president of William & Mary 1836-1846, by William Garl Browne, Jr. Dew made the college the intellectual center of southern economic and moral thought in the 1830s and '40s, and has been called by modern historians "The Philosopher of the Old South." After the Nat Turner slave revolt in Virginia in August 1831, the Virginia House of Delegates debated abolishing slavery. Dew's Review of the Debates *took the south by storm, providing a complex view of the problem that was recognized as cogent even in the north. In his writings over a fifteen-year period, Dew argued that the Commonwealth of Virginia needed to fund the expansion of roads, canals, and railroads as a way to build an economic system that would eventually result in the abolition of slavery. Like many southerners, however, Dew increasingly felt compelled to defend slavery because of the threat of northern dominance and northern impatience with a southern plan for ending slavery.*

Courtesy, Muscarelle Museum of Art, College of William and Mary, purchased from the artist

The next president of the college was Thomas Roderick Dew, who served from 1836 to 1846. A brilliant arguer for state-funded roads, canals, and railroads, and author of the *Review of the Debates of the Virginia Legislature of 1831-1832,* Dew was the only president of the college ever to achieve a national reputation. A popular teacher earlier at the college, Dew became a popular president; and although enrollments fluctuated under his leadership, in one year they reached the highest they were to be again for decades to come.

After Dew died unexpectedly in 1846, the college selected Williamsburg native Robert Saunders, who can hardly be called a success. In May 1848, a faculty member wrote of the serious problems at the college: "Since the death of our late esteem[ed] president Mr. Dew, a great change in the affairs of our College—acts of Nepotism have disturbed our former peace—a schism exists between the Faculty & the Visitors and as a means of checking this, the Visitors have requested the whole Faculty to resign." All college activities except the law class were suspended for a year. Quite naturally a more genial and effective president was sought. Benjamin Stoddart Ewell, who accepted the position for in 1848, helped the college survive the Civil War and the economic difficulties that plagued the entire south in the postwar era. (For more on the college, see Thaddeus W. Tate's essay.)

While the college had its ups and downs in the early nineteenth century, Williamsburg remained the county seat. The courthouse on Duke of Gloucester Street had been built in 1770, and that handsome brick building became the focus of the town (see pp. 36 & 41). Besides its obvious legal function, the courthouse served as a communications center and local gathering place. Across the street from it still stood the magazine (see pp. 35, 41, & 136), converted into a Baptist church. Another Baptist church on Nassau Street (see p. 113) served the black congregation.

The third in Tucker's list of the town's major institutions, the hospital for "disordered minds," completed in 1773, had become gradually more important since it first opened its doors. Under the guidance of three generations of physicians in the Galt family—John Minson Galt from 1795 to1808, his son Alexander Dickie Galt (1800-1841), and grandson John Minson Galt II (1841-1862)—the hospital improved its services, added new facilities, and admitted more and more patients, 289 by 1860.

The treatment of the insane changed drastically in the nineteenth century. Whereas earlier patients had been subjected to harsh and intimidating treatments in a prison-like atmosphere, under John Galt II a new regime of "moral management" prevailed. This system emphasized the personal relationship between doctor and patient. It was optimistic and sought cures, rather than merely providing long-term custodial care. Galt encouraged patients to perform music, spin thread, garden, and play sports as well as cards, dominoes, and other indoor games. Many responded well to this new therapeutic approach and were released. When Dr. Galt died in 1862, he was the end of the line in two ways—the last of his family to be associated with the hospital and the last of its long-term chief physicians. (For more on the hospital, see Blanton McLean's essay.)

Bruton Parish Church remained active and was a major landmark, although disestablishment had taken a heavy toll. Episcopal churches were no longer favored and protected by the government, nor supported by taxes. Under Virginia's first bishop, James Madison, the diocese of Virginia got off to a lackadaisical start. Money was scarce and other denominations plentiful. The number of communicants shrank to only twenty-five in 1821; and in 1827 there were "about thirty, ten of whom have been added lately."

Like Madison, the Reverend Adam Empie was simultaneously president of the college and rector of Bruton Parish. In 1829, he began modernizing the old church building by "cutting down and repainting the high-backed pews" and "rearranging the stairways" to the galleries. The next year he sold the old organ. Empie's successor, the Reverend William Hodges, continued the modernization. In 1839 it was resolved that "all the interior of the Church not necessary for further use be sold." The interior was thoroughly remodeled, while the exterior remained unchanged (see color plate 16). (For more on religion, see John Turner's essay.)

Another building important in the colonial period had been reduced to rubble—the Governor's Palace. During Lafayette's initial visit in 1781, it and several other public buildings had been used as military hospitals. A fire on 22 December 1781, however, destroyed the main palace building; and afterwards the remnants were pulled down and the bricks sold. Luckily, the fire was kept away from neighboring buildings, and the two "advance buildings" to the south of the main entrance were modified as homes for a series of Williamsburgers (see pp. 95, 104, & 136). In 1835, fresh from Oxford, Sir Charles Augustus Murray, grandson of the colonial governor Lord Dunmore, was in the midst of a two-year tour of America. Murray visited the palace site and found it an emotional experience, which he recounted in his travel journal:

> The center of the palace where the governor resided has long since fallen down, and even the traces of its ruins are no more to be seen. Two small wings, which formed part of the range of offices, are still standing: they have been bought and fitted up by Mr. B— [Samuel Bright], their present possessor, in a neat cottage style. I did not scruple to enter, and ask permission to cast my eye round the apartments and adjoining garden, which was politely granted. It may be imagined with what mingled and undefinable feelings I viewed this spot, as a stranger and a foreigner, where my grandfather had lived, surrounded by the pomp and pageantry of vice-royalty!

The original Raleigh Tavern still stood in 1824, although it had been somewhat altered and added on to over the years. In 1848, a traveling journalist and artist captured the Raleigh

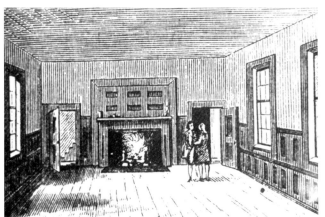

Benson John Lossing drew the Raleigh Tavern in December 1848. His interior view of the large public area, called the Apollo Room, is particularly detailed and greatly aided in the reconstruction of the town's most famous tavern. From The Pictorial Field Book of the Revolution *(New York: Harper and Brothers, 1859-1860).*

The Williamsburg Female Academy was built on the site of the capitol. Lithograph on paper by an unidentified artist, ca. 1855.

Courtesy, Colonial Williamsburg Foundation

with his pen as it teetered on the verge of destruction. Benson John Lossing's engravings show the interior and exterior of the Raleigh at the time of his one-day visit. The establishment still rented rooms, for Lossing says that is where he stayed. Fortunately, the Raleigh had escaped the huge fire of 1842, which wiped out the block across the street and just to the west. Reminiscing about his childhood, John S. Charles recalled that there were "immense brick gable ends of houses" still standing in 1860 and that the foundations"often filled with water that afforded the small boys rare sport–boating in the summer and skating in the winter." The Raleigh accommodated a girls' school and a public house simultaneously from 1854 until it too burned to the ground on 11 December 1859. A notable American institution had gone up in smoke.

The capitol had long been neglected. Deserted after the Revolution, the structure gradually went to ruin. In 1793, the eastern section had to be pulled down for reasons of safety. What remained nearly forty years later was destroyed by fire. In 1849, the Virginia General Assembly gave the property for the Williamsburg Female Academy. Until its closing in 1861 when the Civil War began, it was an exclusive school catering to the well-to-do and ambitious. The structure seems to have been both commodious and handsome if a contemporary print can be believed.

To sentimental nineteenth-century visitors, the capitol, Governor's Palace, and Raleigh Tavern had to be eloquent in their absence. In search of the glory and finery of the colonial capital city, visitors had no eyes for the everyday, workaday town about them. Residents, however, took a decidedly different attitude. Williamsburg was a very pleasant place to live among excellent company. Some townspeople kept up fine Georgian homes that they loved and respected. Others renovated their colonial-era buildings to make them more efficient and comfortable. A few built in the fashionable Greek Revival style. Not one of Williamsburg's proud residents wondered that their town should be honored by Lafayette, the "Nation's Guest."

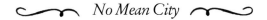

Selected Sources and Suggested Readings

Carson, Jane D., comp. *We Were There: Descriptions of Williamsburg, 1699-1859.* (Williamsburg: Colonial Williamsburg Foundation, 1965).

Charles, John S. "Recollections of Williamsburg: As it appeared at the beginning of the Civil War and just previously thereto, with some incidents in the life of its citizens." Manuscript, in the John D. Rockefeller, Jr., Library, Colonial Williamsburg Foundation.

Faculty Minutes, 20 Oct 1824, cited in Mary R. M. Goodwin, "The President's House and the Presidents of the College of William and Mary, 1732-1975," unpublished research report, Colonial Williamsburg Foundation, 1975.

Goodwin, W.A.R. *Historical Sketch of Bruton Church....* (Petersburg: Franklin Press, 1903).

Levasseur, André-Nicolas. *Lafayette in America in 1824 and 1825; or, Journal of a Voyage to the United States*, trans. John D. Godman. 2 vols. (Philadelphia: Carey and Lea, 1829).

Meade, Bishop William. *Old Church, Ministers, and Families of Virginia*, 2 vols., (1857; rep. Baltimore: Genealogical Publishing, 1966).

Ward, Robert D., comp. *An Account of General LaFayette's Visit to Virginia, 1824-25.* (Richmond: West, Johnston, 1881).

"Williamsburg, Va.: South View," pencil drawing done between 1859-1862 by James Austin Graham (1814/15-1878). From the left are a cluster of houses; the College of William & Mary's main building with its 1859 towers, Brafferton building, and President's House (just to the left of the "A" in the caption); the Griffin house; behind its walls, Eastern Asylum's Gothic and main buildings (right of the "S"); Bruton Parish Church (above the "U"); the Greenhow-Repiton brick office; the courthouse of 1770 and magazine (just to the left and right of the "G"); and the Robert Carter Nicholas house (since razed), Tazewell Hall (since moved), and the Chiswell house.

Graham did the drawing while a patient at the asylum. The time needed to complete the drawing and the distance of its vanishing point from the asylum walls argue that he must have been given extended liberty. Graham apparently had developed head trauma from a fall, as thereafter he suffered from seizures as well as erratic paranoid behavior. In March 1855, he opened fire in a hotel bar, wounding several men and killing William H. Spiller, a merchant. He killed Spiller because he loved his daughter and thought Spiller had insulted him. In modern parlance, Graham was found not guilty by reason of insanity. Admitted to the asylum in November, he lived there the rest of his life.

Courtesy, Abby Aldrich Rockefeller Folk Art Museum, Williamsburg, Va.

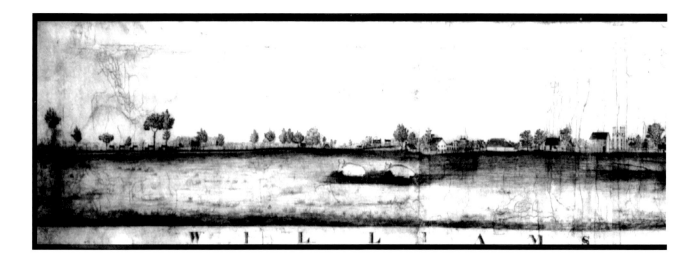

Eastern Asylum and the Third Revolution in Psychiatry: Dr. John Galt's Advanced Therapeutic Community, 1841-1862

by: Blanton McLean

The facility now called Eastern State Hospital, founded in 1773 as the first public psychiatric hospital in North America, was one of the last gifts of the European Enlightenment to colonial Virginia. Although the original twenty-four bed building was noticeably cleaner than contemporary European facilities, patient care was, as in Europe, uninformed by concepts of human dignity or effective treatment. Referred to informally as the "Public Hospital for Persons of Insane and Disordered Minds," the hospital's purpose was unusual for 1773: to be an acute care facility, admitting only those who could be "cured" and discharged.

Twenty years later, an important letter provides an eyewitness account of a visit by a citizen of Williamsburg to London's Bethlehem Hospital (the source of our word "bedlam"). Medical student Alexander Galt described the scene thus:

> Aug. 11th 1793...They have for breakfast every day water gruel–They have meat for dinner three times a week on the intermediate days porridge–on Saturday they have for dinner Rice Milk–The keeper could give me little information concerning their Medical treatment, only that they were

purged once a week, frequently bled, and sometimes blistered on the head– Saw only two men in Strait Waistcoats. What particularly engaged my attention was a contrivance before the fire-place of one of the Wards made of iron in the form of half a bird-cage to prevent the madmen from doing any mischief–The poker was chained within this fender if I may so call it. I saw several who had been in this Hospital 20 years. There was a Dr of Divinity whose name was Bailey that had been confined 50 years–from his appearance one would be led to suppose that he was upwards of 100 years of age....At the front of the Hospital there was a garden on each side of the Walk leading to the door–& on each side of the Hospital a yard in which some of the Madmen were allowed to amuse themselves at the game of nine-pins, cards, & any other games.

These remarks about the relative lack of restraint and the presence of some few recreational activities at Bethlehem show the influence of a new way of looking at mental illness.

As late as the 1830s, however, care in Williamsburg was not substantially changed from what was offered at Bethlehem Hospital over forty years earlier. It was in fact even less advanced, for there were hardly any therapeutic activities and strait jackets were used regularly. Patients ate with their hands in solitary; and their gardening looked suspiciously like serfdom, as it occurred only on the farm of Dr. Alexander Galt, the last of a line of part-time "visiting physicians" with which the hospital always had made do. The hospital was not well-served by the medically conservative and unimaginative Alexander, nor by its governing Court of Directors who knew little of current trends in mental health care. An 1835 report from an investigative committee of the House of Delegates had found the hospital a "well-regulated prison" where the patients were "excluded from all rational employment and amusement."

This was soon to change. After Alexander Galt's death in 1841, the hospital, renamed Eastern Asylum and housing 109 "inmates," came under the supervision of his son, Dr. John Galt, a brilliant and sensitive physician who brought a full-fledged program of "Moral Management" treatment to Williamsburg. Galt explained this new treatment:

A primary principle of moral management, consists in the endeavor to withdraw the mind of the lunatic from its delusive fancies and diseased feelings, by presenting new and varied objects, and by arousing the feelings and mental operations which remain undiseased...each faculty of the mind is increased in power by action and lessened by remaining inactive.... morbid ideas and feelings shall...be thus gradually enfeebled or effaced....the insane can engage in most of the active operations, and are able to participate, and with pleasure, in most of the amusements of the sane....Another principle of the highest importance...is the law of kindness. If we are unkind [and]...employ any unnecessary harshness the consequence is that we increase the...tendency to fancy themselves injured and persecuted by those around them.

The non-medical cornerstones of treatment were therapeutic activities, talk therapy and socialization, and reduction of restraint. Galt's mid-nineteenth century modes of treatment were a forerunner of the psychosocial rehabilitation program currently in use at the hospital today, where positive social interaction is the principal focus. Now as then, the inability of the mentally ill to interact in society is what brings them to and keeps them in psychiatric hospitals. By rewarding appropriate actions and interactions, and not attending more than is necessary to the inappropriate, the patient is brought closer to discharge.

Although the directors decided admissions, hired, and approved expenditures, Galt immediately became one of the town's most prominent citizens and in 1852 was elected mayor on the Democratic ticket—though he did not serve. Altogether there were as many as one hundred persons employed at the hospital, forty-five of them slaves, and from 150 to

280 patients. Except for The College of William and Mary, then quite small, there were no other significant public or commercial institutions, so the hospital's need for provisions and services contributed much to the economy of the town. So tempting was the profit that families tried to pass employment on from one generation to the next, as had the Galts, or to friends or other relations. Frequently attached to those positions were extensive perquisites, including housing and various provisions. From such examples Williamsburg came to be characterized as a place where "the lazy lived off the crazy." Chronic corruption was attached to the bidding for hospital contracts for products and services, particularly in the 1850s. Frequently, the directors engineered the awarding of what were not the lowest bids to themselves, and the town's citizens sought to replace corrupt directors in order to advance themselves. One of the privileges of W. W. Vest, as treasurer, was the personal use of hospital bank deposits, interest free. Those who appointed the directors also got their hands in the till by offering the appointments as patronage plums, contingent on election victories. If one excepts his family connections, Dr. Galt was one of the few not to profit personally from the asylum: he three times turned down raises, although Francis Stribling, his rival superintendent at Western Asylum in Staunton, made $5,000 annually, to Galt's $1,300. Regardless how he first achieved his position, through experience and self-education Galt acquired such clinical skill and effective therapeutic manner and displayed such a scientific imagination, that it is doubtful whether any of his fellow founders of the American Psychiatric Association could have far surpassed him.

Dr. Galt, like other asylum superintendents of the time, encouraged patients to work for both therapeutic and economic reasons, and Eastern surpassed most other facilities in the proportion of patients so engaged. Patients' needlework, leather, and garden produce were sold in the community and supplemented the asylum's state support. Perhaps, however, the town's strongest and most continuous relationship with the hospital has been community volunteerism. In the mid-nineteenth century the townsfolks' gifts of time, handiwork, property, and money were so much a part of the social round that Galt hardly mentions them in his annual reports. He wrote in a notebook that "The fair alluded to...was held and the usual articles...were sold; about $200, being salvaged, from which an addition was made to the library, musical instruments were purchased, and a Good Green House was erected." Patients were invited to private homes, offered boat rides and excursions to plantations, and were entertained on the grounds by song, drama, devotionals, and simple companionship. Though she and Dr. John shared a strained relationship, he frosty and she critical, the patroness of volunteerism, Dorothea Dix, visited frequently, accompanied by the ladies of the town in a swirl of charity and crinoline.

What we now refer to as deinstitutionalization and community-based mental health care were referred to by Galt as Williamsburg's "Third Revolution in Psychiatry" (the first and second being the hospital's founding as a publicly-supported facility exclusively for the care of the mentally ill, and the introduction of the moral management system). In the American Journal of Insanity, he wrote in 1855, "I am satisfied that the insane, generally, are susceptible of much more extended liberty than they are now allowed." Earlier, when his revolution was

Marble bust of Dr. John Galt by his cousin, Alexander Galt of Norfolk (1857).

Courtesy, Eastern State Hospital

Report

In accordance with my appointment at the last meeting of the "Association" to report at the present session of this Body, on "reading, recreation, and amusements for the Insane," I beg leave to submit the following remarks.

Here, as on most points of treatment, we are led into great error, if we entirely abstract the insane from the sane, if we look upon the former class as altogether different in their psychological manifestations from the latter. Hence in making a just and proper basis, upon which to originate alike our theoretical ideas and our practical operations, we must consider these two divisions though evidently differing in many particulars, as in the main holding the same position objectively with regard to reading, amusements, and recreation. Therefore it is, that if it be desirable to penetrate beneath the mere crust of the subject under consideration, it is requisite to take such a scope of inquiry as includes not only the insane but also those who have the mind in an unimpaired condition. The same general remark applies to reading, as to the two accompanying heads of our article, so far as regards the principle upon which it is employed as a moral means in the treatment of insanity — we adopt it as a measure

Presentation copy of "Reading, Recreation and Amusements for the Insane" (1848), penned by Dr. John Galt for a meeting of the American Psychiatric Association, and later published in Essays on Asylums for Persons of Unsound Mind, *second series (1853). This is an early work dealing with therapy via occupation, recreation, music, and reading. It may be one of the earliest writings to discuss systematically the use of reading with the mentally ill. Galt's patients spent the majority of their time engaged in therapeutic activities. Galt's policy when possible was to encourage patients to engage in the same work and leisure activities that they had performed when in the community, and to prescribe certain activities, both solitary and social, to promote an attitude that was active rather than passive, and would tend to remove attention from "morbid fancies."*

Courtesy, Eastern State Hospital

in full swing in 1847, he had said that it was "fully as important...after a while to separate a maniac from the associations of the hospital as of those at home." Galt drew inspiration from the experimental farm of St. Anne at the French asylum of Bicêtre and the Belgian village of Gheel. He envisioned the mentally ill living in supervised group homes, boarding with community members, or living independently and even working. In particular, Galt wished to remove harmless chronic patients from the asylum: "A large number of the insane, instead of *rusting* out their lives in some vast asylum, should be placed...in the neighboring community....Were any other class of persons than the insane collected together in such large numbers as in some asylums...the greatest disorder would be likely to ensue."

This proposal excited controversy among members of the American Psychiatric Association, founded in 1843 as the Association of Medical Superintendents of American Institutions for the Insane. Matters were not helped when founding member Galt reflected upon other American asylums and found them to be prison-like, nor did his characterization of his fellow superintendents as "tinkering with gas-pipes and studying architecture" improve the

Visitor's pass, after 1854, printed by the Virginia Gazette. *Since 1841 Williamsburg residents had been not only welcome, but had been encouraged by Dr. Galt, to visit the patients without restriction. An 1851 ruling by Judge Beverly Tucker required all patients who had formerly had the freedom of the town now to be escorted when leaving the grounds. Although only partially effective, his ruling began a slow slide into an increasing separation of townsfolk and patients. After 11 October 1854, any citizen who did not have a pass was denied entrance to the asylum.*

Courtesy, Eastern State Hospital

situation. Thomas Kirkbride of the Pennsylvania Hospital for the Insane in particular felt himself a target and retaliated: he argued that Galt had "little idea of the restraint really necessary for recent cases" and carped that "so much liberty permitted between townspeople and the patients...is not seen in any other institutions." Kirkbride's sharp rebuke refers to Dr. Galt's experiment, in which from 1841 until 1851 almost all male and many female patients at the facility were able to go "unattended and at will about the neighborhood," while many others went out with escorts. The townspeople were encouraged to visit and socialize with the patients still confined to the grounds. Although Galt believed restraint necessary when patients were a danger to themselves or others, it was seldom applied. In 1846, in fact, Galt restrained no one. This unusual record was due in part to Galt's use of what we would now term chemical restraints. To reduce agitation and violence he prescribed the opium derivative, laudanum, quite liberally—so much so that townspeople said the hospital was often "wreathed in smoke." This ten-year experiment in what amounted to deinstitutionalization is an extraordinary chapter in Williamsburg's history, and reflects great credit on the enlightenment (or at least tolerance) of the citizens, the good behavior of the patients, and Galt's inspired expectations. What town today would support such an experiment?

Inevitably there were conflicts, some handled better than others. One patient "bothered so many persons in town by talking pertinaciously" that Galt confined him to the grounds. Another incident, wonderfully related in the letters of patient Richard Miller and William and

Mary law professor, Judge Beverly Tucker, reflects Miller's confused attempt to enlist the professor's help in forcing a student to duel or otherwise fight. Miller evidently felt in some way offended and in need of satisfaction. In his last letter of 6 November 1845, Miller retracts the patient-abuse charge against Dr. Galt, stating that the charge was an attention-getting device employed to force the unresponsive judge to acknowledge his concerns. Examination of Tucker's letter indicates he may have mishandled the affair by consistently refusing to dignify Miller's concerns with any response; and his suggestion that Galt restrain Miller and deny him mailing privileges indicates the attitudes of some community members with which Galt was contending, a prejudiced wish to put the patients "out of sight, out of mind." Miller was by no means unsophisticated; aside from skill in writing, he well knew the next step in his struggle with the judge was to go to the media.

Richard F. Miller begs leave most respectfully again, for the third time to obtain the attention and intercession of Judge Tucker, and when he informs his Honor, as he now does, that he has, this morning, had palpable evidence of a most cruel design on the part of the Superintendent of the Asylum, through agency of a subordinate, to destroy his life! he hopes and prays this last appeal will not be disregarded, as it mortifies and pains him to find have been the two first.

Should it please Judge Tucker, however, to leave me to my fate with my inhuman persecutors, I have to beg the retrieval of this paper as well as the two previously sent (and which I have most positive evidence were opened and read by his Honor) by the going down of the sun on this day.

Most respectfully submitted
Richard Floyd Miller
Eastern Asylum
Williamsburg Va   Thursday, 10 O'Clock A.M.

+++

My dear Sir [Dr. Galt]

This letter is a specimen of the means used by this poor fellow to keep himself excited. A day or two ago he got up a quarrel with one of my class & sent him a challenge. You see how mightily his indignation is moved at my neglect of his former letters. To make sure of this he brought it himself–strutted into my lecture room–handed the letter and strutted out again. I suggest the expediency of debarring him from the means of thus keeping up the…[?] of his mind, restraining him, and forbidding the servants to take letters from him.

Yours
B. Tucker   Thursday morning

+++

[to Dr. Galt]
Eastern Asylum, Nov. 6th 1845   Thursday morning. Eleven O'clock A.M.

Although I have this morning written and delivered to Judge Tucker a note charging the Superintendent of the Asylum with the cruel and inhuman design of destroying my life I do not believe that Dr Galt has any such design and would go as far as any friend I have to prevent such a thing, but such has been the silent contempt with which Judge Tucker has thought proper to treat me that I have adopted that as the means by which to avenge myself, for, in the event of his failing to attend to my third note I shall most certainly hold him upthro' the medium of the public press as an unfit person to preside over the Law department of Wm & Mary College

R. F. Miller

Witness,
Richard Demmit Clark
Wm Christian

In 1851 Judge Tucker, at least officially, put an end to Galt's "Third Revolution." The judge ruled after an incident that "no patient was safe without someone attending him." There was, however, no great change, and Galt merely told his employees that if patients went "beyond the premises...[the employees] must be...responsible, and the same hold good as to patients employed by persons in town." There was a gradual loss of openness, though, and in 1854 townsfolk had to obtain passes to visit. By 1860 the asylum became for the first time completely enclosed by walls: no one could leave without permission of the superintendent; and no one excepting staff could enter the gates without consent of either the superintendent, the mayor, or the president of the Court of Directors.

As Virginia's other state mental health facility in Staunton was from its opening in 1828 for whites only, Galt could easily have followed the path of least resistance and segregated the Williamsburg facility. Instead, he enforced the founders' policy of admitting blacks and, going well beyond what he felt was required, even trained slaves to provide talk therapy to white patients (much to the displeasure of the otherwise enlightened Dorothea Dix). Integration stigmatized the hospital in the eyes of some whites. Galt found this sufficiently worrisome that he never published a patient census categorized by race, and emphasized in advertisement brochures that paying white patients could be assured of a strict "separation of the classes." That this was not in fact quite true would not have been discovered until after a white patient had been admitted.

Salt-treated process photograph of the Main Building from before 1855, probably for a stereopticon. The 1840 Greek Revival portico, third floor, and new cupola entirely altered the structure's 1773 appearance. Although it had twenty-four "cells" for patients in 1773, the building shown here contained offices and employee housing.

Courtesy, Eastern State Hospital.
Collected by Thomas L. Williams

Galt claimed to treat all patients "without regard to race." In 1846 he wrote and helped pass in the Virginia legislature an act to admit slaves as patients, and in the same year had appropriated $7,000 to construct a "building for colored," which became known as the Gothic Building for its tall towers. It was from there that the ladies of the town viewed Civil War action, and it was from there that Dr. Galt was falsely rumored to have spied out Union troop movements.

Four years after the war, there were thirty blacks remaining out of the less than 190 patients. Paradoxically, Eastern became a segregated facility only when the Union Commander of Virginia in 1869 forced the discharge of those thirty patients, who were transferred to Howard's Grove near Petersburg, where they became inmates at another segregated hospital, this one for blacks, which became Central State Hospital. When one considers that during the Civil War years the policy was to discharge first slaves, then free blacks, so that there might be room for whites, one can surmise that the pre-war number of blacks might have been significant.

Although blacks were not entirely segregated, sometimes participated in the freedom of the town in the 1840s, and were offered the same time and kindness Galt offered whites, they were restricted to more limited and menial-appearing activities, approximating their duties before admission, and did not partake as much in the family-like atmosphere promoted for whites. Unlike his Pennsylvania University anatomy professor Dr. Morton, who after filling a small number of black and white skulls with gunshot concluded that whites were superior in intelligence because their skulls held more pellets, Galt did not believe in inherent racial inequality. His policies and refusal, in opposition to many among the APA, to advocate separate psychiatric hospitals for the races, mark him as somewhat ahead of his era in his thinking.

Neither is there evidence that Galt subscribed to the views of racist nineteenth-century psychiatrists that blacks' mental illness could be subsumed under two diagnoses, the tendency to run away and the tendency to avoid labor. He did, however, theorize that slaves would be expected to experience fewer symptoms of mental illness, as their dependent status freed them of some anxieties caused by the necessity of decision-making. That Galt was compas-

The Doric Building, after 1862. In Dr. John Galt's time this 1850 structure was for paying white patients. The statue is of Lord Botetourt, Virginia's royal governor 1768-1770. He strongly supported the hospital's establishment and arranged to send mentally-ill criminals to Philadelphia for psychiatric care at public expense. One of 19th-c. Williamsburg's most beloved icons, the statue was transferred to Eastern Asylum from the college in 1862 to protect it from vandalism by Union soldiers, who had succeeded in burning the college on their second attempt that year. (See color plate 21 and pp. 102, 141, 149, & 152.)

Courtesy, Colonial Williamsburg Foundation

sionate, if not bold, as regards to blacks outside the hospital, is exemplified by episodes such as the following: Williamsburg slaveholder Parker Holis, learning that Galt was "anxious that the two negro women belonging to Mr. Hunt, should not be sent away from Williamsburg, as they are related to your servants," agreed to Galt's deception that "if you will say to me in a letter that the girl shall not bring less than one thousand dollars [more than anyone would pay] I will not send her away."

The Civil War found the asylum first on one side, then another, of the battle lines, although it is fair to say that both Confederate and Union forces usually took great care for it, almost competing to see who might treat the venerated hospital with more respect and less disruption. After Galt died in May of 1862, however, a most difficult period began. Federal troops had marched into Williamsburg on the 6th, and at the end of the month the Union commander appointed a Northern surgeon, Dr. Clinton Thompson, acting superintendent; but Court of Directors President Henry Bowden and the new mayor, his brother Lemuel Bowden–both pro-Unionist locals–actually held sway. They attempted to purge the hospital of those thought to be "extreme Rebels"; and when they would not take the loyalty oath usually required of defeated southerners, many of the employees were fired. There is no evidence that the Union commander was unwilling to grant the hospital's staff an exemption from the oath, rather it suited the Bowdens' purposes so that they might thereby install their own supporters and perhaps gain control of the asylum's resources. Things went from bad to worse: often the patients had food only because the expelled employees and others shared their slender rations. General McClellan's reversal at Richmond, however, caused the Bowden faction to suffer a loss of nerve: on 20 August they collected wagons loaded with previously hoarded hospital food and provisions (and $12,000 in cash as well) and fled, leaving the 252 patients locked in without food or water. Only the black staff remained to care for the

Eastern Asylum, view from South Henry St., ca. 1855, lithograph by L. A. Ramm. From the left are a corner of the Doric Building, the columned West Covered Way, the West Building, and the Gothic Building. The Doric Building, completed in 1850, was alternatively called the White House, but whether because of its color or the color of its patients is not known. The Doric Building was an "elite preserve" where paying white patients received treatment. The Gothic Building, finished around 1850, was originally built for all African-American patients, but actually housed only African-American men and patients considered demented or incurable. Four years previous, the asylum had begun to admit slaves. The cathedral-like towers of the Gothic Building were routinely used by townsfolk to take the view, and when the Civil War reached Williamsburg, to observe the fighting as well. It alone among the asylum's major structures survived the 1885 fire, but in 1902 it too burned down.

Courtesy, Colonial Williamsburg Foundation

patients. The keys were returned the next day, and Union forces were called in to rescue the patients, bringing in supplies to replace those looted by the pro-Unionists.

While rumors circulated that Dorothea Dix was to become acting superintendent, that position in fact went to Captain Peter Wager, a hard-drinking Union surgeon who, when not incapacitated by his addiction, did a fine job—as even Galt's sister, the southern firebrand Sally, affirmed. During that late spring and summer of 1862, to know who had control of the hospital was often difficult. When the South periodically controlled Williamsburg, Captain Wager's position became unclear. On one occasion the Confederate commander left him in

Eastern State Hospital's Main Building, 1973 colored reproduction of a 1846 lithograph by Thomas Millington. Dr. Galt used Millington's image on several printed documents, often with subtle variations in the details: the weathervane's direction, the variety and location of persons, animals, implements and trees in front of the East and West Buildings. This version is from a brochure advertising for out-of-state paying patients who are represented by the fashionable couple promenading down the walk toward the Main Building, surrounded by Arcadian delights: Rhett and Scarlett or their Northern cousins "taking the cure." One visitor who actually saw the building described it as "large and imposing, but not beautiful."

Courtesy, Eastern State Hospital

control, although he was to consider himself under house arrest and was on his honor not to spy. Wager sometimes begged credit in town or even used his own personal funds to keep the patients fed. Mirroring the abusive behavior of the Bowden faction in late August, retreating Confederates also looted the hospital and kidnaped its slaves as well, it being said that "the Rebels cared no more for lunatics than the Yankees [who had burnt The College of William and Mary] cared for the Collegians" (see p. xxx). When he was more firmly in control, Wager released the former employees of the hospital from the hated loyalty oath requirement, if they would return to care for the patients. He fairly and efficiently administered the hospital until late 1865, when it and the 180 remaining patients were returned to civilian control.

Dr. Galt himself, so a romantic story goes, had appeared for work the day after Federal troops first entered Williamsburg, but was barred by a bayonet-wielding Union soldier and turned away. He returned home and died something more than a week later of a "broken heart." More reliable evidence suggests that overwork, extreme worry, and the experience of the hospital's capture increased the pressures of his chronic depression to such an extent that Galt took his own life by an overdose of the laudanum he so liberally dispensed to his patients. As his medical records indicate a great meticulousness in his dosage of the opium derivative, suicide is the likely cause of his early death at the age of forty-three.

After the war's end, the formerly optimistic view that the mentally ill could return to their communities was replaced by attitudes reflecting the new, but atavistic, "Age of Custodial Care." The tide of Moral Management had ebbed long before, and a warehouse mentality now prevailed. Eastern State Hospital was broke, desolate, and dilapidated, its staff demoralized. Without Galt's animating spirit, the continuance of the therapeutic activities he had

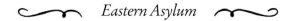
introduced became simply a matter of going through the motions, while their purpose—discharge and optimal social functioning—had been forgotten. Increasingly, the nation's mentally ill were to be kept "out of sight, out of mind," as there was a reversion to the view that they were fundamentally different from the mentally healthy, deserving only decent maintenance and a lifetime of isolation.

Almost a century and a half after Dr. John Galt's "Third Revolution in Psychiatry," Eastern State Hospital in the last half of the 1990s has made his dream live again; and this time with the help of more effective medications and stronger community support the dream is coming true. In 1995 the hospital accomplished its first deinstitutionalization since Galt's experiment ended in 1851. The hospital's current director is once again John—social worker John Favret–whose profession specializes in relating and returning the patient to the community. Once again, the hospital's current adult population is 275, about what it was in Galt's time. Here are the words of Leonora Oliva, a patient in the Psychosocial Rehabilitation Program. Dr. John Galt himself would have used and understood her words:

Leonora: We...are out in the active treatment program for many hours....I am very active in my classes. In the morning I have psychotherapy, I have Clubhouse, I have symptom management.

Interviewer: You mentioned Clubhouse. What do they do there?

Leonora: I was assigned to the clerical unit, and compiled patient treatment statistics, and put together newsletters. All the members of the Clubhouse go to the other Clubhouse [in the community] in order to associate with other Clubhouse...members and staff members and learn what they are doing...I used to be a waitress and help them prepare the cooking...we are not just being isolated, but are associated and being socialized, too. We learn where the Community Services Boards are, to be acquainted with us, where to get our medicine. We've been to our supervised apartments too, and though we're not discharged yet, we understand what are the regulations.

Interviewer: So you're very excited to be discharged fairly soon?

Leonora: (SMILES): Yeah.

Selected Sources and Suggested Readings

Those who are interested in learning more about the history of Eastern State Hospital may visit its site on the World Wide Web at *www.easternstatehospital.org.* There is also an experimental search engine at *www.esh.tni.net/searchgp.html* where the abstracts of Dr. Galt's papers in the Eastern State Library may be accessed.

Dain, Norman: *Disordered Minds; The First Century of Eastern State Hospital in Williamsburg, Virginia 1766-1866* (Williamsburg: Colonial Williamsburg Foundation, 1971).

Galt Family Papers, manuscripts. Swem Library, College of William and Mary.

Galt Papers, manuscripts. Library, Eastern State Hospital.

Zwelling, Shomer: *Quest for a Cure; The Public Hospital in Williamsburg, Virginia 1773-1885* (Williamsburg: Colonial Williamsburg Foundation, 1985).

Fortress Williamsburg:
Treasure through Four Years of War

by: Carol Kettenburg Dubbs

To the casual observer, much of Williamsburg's colonial grandeur was no longer visible by 1861. The impressive capitol and Governor's Palace had long since fallen victim to fire, though the palace advance buildings had survived and been converted into private homes. The College of William and Mary, although reconstructed after an 1859 fire, no longer had its stately pedimented portico and traditional cupolas. Dwellings dating to the eighteenth century had likewise undergone such transformations as modernized front porches and additional stories. Nevertheless, nineteenth-century families still treasured these homes for their prominent roles in the nation's origins and their associations with the founding fathers.

Thus, when rumors of war became reality in April 1861, some inhabitants feared for their historic property as much as for their personal safety. Williamsburg, a staunchly Confederate community, lay midway between Federal-held Fort Monroe at the tip of the Peninsula and the South's capital at Richmond, exposing it to almost certain involvement in the conflict. In May, William and Mary president Benjamin Ewell, a graduate of the U.S. Military Academy at West Point, was commissioned a Major of Volunteers and ordered to construct a line of earthworks across the Peninsula just east of Williamsburg to defend Richmond. Soon, hired

L.J. Cranstone's 1850 painting looks north on the palace green and shows the Robert Saunders house (now called Robert Carter house) on the left, with the palace's two advance buildings (see p. 136) expanded for use as private residences.

Courtesy, Colonial
Williamsburg Foundation

slaves and free blacks wielded picks and shovels side by side with soldiers of the Williamsburg Junior Guards military company. The Fifteenth Virginia Regiment joined them at the end of May, followed in June by the Tenth Georgia commanded by Colonel Lafayette McLaws. Most Williamsburg ladies gladly opened their homes to their defenders, providing room and board to officers, throwing parties for the men, nursing the sick, and sewing tents, uniforms, and hospital bedding. Not all Tenth Georgians felt so welcome, however. The superintendent of Williamsburg's Eastern Asylum, Dr. John Minson Galt II (see p. 85) , wrote in July that "a Georgia soldier talking to the Ladies, wept, because he said, of the treatment experienced by the Georgia troops from Virginians, some lady for example declaring, he asserted, that she was more apprehensive of them than the enemy."

That lady's apprehensions were shared by many others the following month when the force working on the Williamsburg line was augmented by the Tenth Louisiana Volunteers. They bore, remarked McLaws, the "reputaton of being the most lawless set in existence." Upon their arrival, Dr. Galt noted, "persons were warned...to be on their guard against depredations from them." Actually, several regiments from the Pelican State were in the area. These included a colorful battalion of soldiers wearing "baggy red breeches, leggings, a blue jacket, and red cap of a kind of stocking effect," imitating the admired French army Zouaves and representing various nationalities recruited from the tougher segments of Louisiana society. The Second Louisiana and another unit called the Dreux Battalion, on the other hand, were composed of the cream of New Orleans society and spent much of their time in Williamsburg romancing the local belles. All Louisiana soldiers kept the town entertained through the summer and into the fall, hosting two balls for the townspeople in October, "giving parties and picnics, singing and serenading," observed McLaws. The Zouaves were also purloining chickens, shooting hogs, and pulling planks off of Williamsburg houses. One October night Dr. Galt learned that historic old Tazewell Hall had been broken into–partly, no doubt, because its owner, John D. Munford, was away serving as a colonel with the Confederate army in western Virginia. Locals suspected the Zouaves, who were "frequenting the homes of the neighboring...free-coloured people, who would wash for them."

Zouaves were not the only threat to Williamsburg homes. In early August, General John Bankhead Magruder, commander on the Peninsula, ordered Hampton burned to prevent its occupation by Federal troops from Fort Monroe. At the end of the month Dr. Galt heard a "Report that Williamsburg was to be burnt" as well, presumably for the same purpose. Whatever consternation that false rumor created subsided as attention was diverted to multitudes of sick soldiers, mostly typhoid cases, who filled the town at the commencement of the late summer to autumn "sickly season." Soon every available building from the college to the Female Academy on the site of the old capitol and all the churches in between were crowded with sick. Many private homes were likewise opened to the fever's victims; Dr. Galt's Superintendent's House sheltered seventeen altogether. Bruton Church became so overrun that Dr. Galt's maiden sister Sally and the superintendent of hospitals for the entire town, Mrs. Letitia Tyler Semple (daughter of President John Tyler), requested in November that the churchyard be "railed in, to guard against an excess of desecration."

As winter approached, typhoid cases diminished, and a Louisiana colonel "greatly encouraged playing ball, and other games amongst his men" to distract their wayward energies. The seasonal change brought about new "vandalism." Soldiers in winter quarters pulled down fences to use as firewood; "one gentleman it was stated, had lost ten miles of fencing from this source." A massive Federal landing at Fort Monroe near the end of March 1862 brought more rumors "about the probability of Williamsburg, being burnt." Dr. Galt was skeptical: "Some persons seem to present this pleasing idea, simply by way of seeing what effect is induced in the hearer." The approach in April of General George B. McClellan's army of more than 100,000 elicited "great panic in Williamsburg; many persons moving, or preparing to move off with their families & servants." Several houses retained at least one trusted servant to guard them, but others were totally abandoned.

After the two armies spent a month taking potshots at each other across a fortified line at Yorktown, the Confederates, including the Williamsburg Guards, retreated west toward Richmond under their commander, General Joseph E. Johnston. The Federals caught up with them at the Williamsburg line–fourteen earthen forts called redoubts anchored in the center by massive Fort Magruder. The initial clash occurred on the afternoon of Sunday, 4 May, when an artillery duel and two cavalry charges resulted in dramatic hand-to-hand combat and a few casualties on both sides. One Mississippi regiment marching westward through Williamsburg during this skirmish was amused by a patriotic young lass dashing out of her house with two pistols buckled around her waist, imploring the men to turn back and "defend this old town, the Cradle of American freedom!" Defend it they did the following day in a pouring rain that impeded the Confederates' retrograde movement to Richmond. Two gray divisions led by James Longstreet and D. H. Hill held back Joe Hooker, Phil Kearny, and parts of three other blue divisions in a fierce rearguard action that came to be known as the Battle of Williamsburg (see color plates 15 & 18). No Williamsburg structure reportedly suffered damage during the fight, but many of the wounded among the more than four thousand casualties ended up in the college and the churches as well as in Williamsburg homes.

Throughout the night of 5 May, the Confederates evacuated the earthworks and continued their march to Richmond; and early the next morning, McClellan's hordes took possession of Williamsburg, striking terror into the hearts of townspeople, who refused to relinquish their homes and expected the worst. Instead, they were shocked by the sight outside their windows. "At our front gate stood a sentinel placed there by order of McClellan to protect us in our homes, though we did not understand that at the time," remembered Cynthia Beverley Tucker Coleman (see color plate 17). She was staying with her mother, Lucy Smith Tucker, widow of Judge Nathaniel Beverley Tucker, in the Tucker House on the market square. Mrs. Tucker insisted on "standing her ground in order to save, at least some of her property," perhaps in more jeopardy than most because of her late husband's contribution to the secession movement.

Dr. Galt also refused to surrender his responsibilities in the asylum and, at the entry of Federal troops, requested of the commanding officer "that this house...be included in the protection." His sister was relieved to find the obligatory search for wounded and contraband less onerous than expected. "So far from tearing the house to pieces as I had thought they would they were very polite & agreeable," Miss Sally confessed, "& some very elegant officers amongst them not withstanding our prejudice to them." Miss Harriette Cary living in the Charlton House with her grandmother, Harriette Henley, had a similar experience as "a fine looking Officer with two men very respectfully announced this morning their orders to search, which was but nominal–a glance at each room seemed only necessary–all houses were

Only the western (right) half of the Palmer house (shown here ca. 1907) was built in the mid-18th c. Eighty years later, merchant W. W. Vest bought it and in 1858 nearly doubled its size by adding the east wing and third-floor dormers. Furnished with costly carpets, cushioned easy-chairs, cut glass chandeliers, pier and mantel mirrors, this spacious home at the eastern end of Duke of Gloucester Street was abandoned by the Vest family at the approach of the Federal army. During the Battle of Williamsburg, it made ideal headquarters for Confederate General Joseph Johnston, and, the next day, for Union General George McClellan. Sometime after McClellan departed, James City County planter John Coupland and his family lived in the mansion until Federal guns in Fort Magruder opened fire on Williamsburg the morning of Wise's raid. "While hitching the horse a shell burst directly over our heads, but doing no damage; two fell in the garden and 3 within a few feet of the house under our chamber window," Coupland wrote. The house was subsequently occupied until the close of the war by a succession of Federal provost marshals governing the town. One, Lieutenant W. W. Disoway, while sitting at the top of the front steps, was shot and killed by one of his own men. After the war, Vest returned to Williamsburg and found his house had "escaped wonderfully." He and his youngest daughter resided in its luxury for another three decades.

Courtesy, Tucker-Coleman Collection, Swem Library, College of William and Mary

Tazewell Hall (shown here ca. 1907) was the site of an elegant ball hosted by Louisiana officers in 1861. Vandalized by both gray and blue soldiers, as well as runaway slaves, the house survived the war, only to be dismantled by Colonial Williamsburg to make room for the Williamsburg Lodge.

Courtesy, Tucker-Coleman Collection, Swem Library, College of William and Mary

During the war, Mrs. Lucy Tucker ably defended the Tucker house (shown here c. 1890-1907, and see p. 136), which sheltered seven generations of this distinguished family. Lucy's eldest daughter, Cynthia Tucker Coleman (see color plate 17) also stayed in the house until July 1862, then "refugeed into Dixie" to join her husband, a Confederate army doctor.

Courtesy, Colonial Williamsburg
Foundation

The Coke-Garrett house (shown here ca. 1907) has changed little since Dr. Robert Garrett treated Confederate and Federal wounded alike on his expansive front lawn on the day of the battle. Though his barn burned during the war, Dr. Garrett and his family preserved this residence, which is used today by Colonial Williamsburg's president.

Courtesy, Tucker-Coleman Collection, Swem Library, College of William and Mary

subjected to the same with more or less scrutiny." Though McClellan posted sentinels at all occupied abodes, those abandoned had already "been more or less despoiled," according to an observer. "The presence of even one servant would almost certainly save a dwelling from intrusion by predatory soldiers."

McClellan allowed his bloodied army to rest in Williamsburg a few days before continuing up the Peninsula after the Confederates. He left the town under a guard instructed to maintain order and ship north all wounded. Dr. Galt's sudden death in mid-May compelled the Federals to take over management of the asylum and forced Miss Sally to move out of the Superintendent's House back to her old family home, the Nelson-Galt house, at the eastern end of town. Williamsburg guard duty had just been assumed by the Fifth Pennsylvania Cavalry, "more replete with the vulgar 'devices of the human heart' than any Regiment of the enemy that has yet cursed our Southern shores," grumbled one resident. Its colonel, David Campbell, became the town's military governor. He appropriated the college's Brafferton building for his headquarters, and his troops immediately took possession of all vacant domiciles, as their predecessors had done. Soon, reports of depredations began filtering out of Williamsburg. Cynthia Coleman's in-laws had to flee their home, one of the palace advance buildings. She wrote to them that "their house & lots were nearly destroyed, the furniture ruined, & every thing that had been left locked was broken open." The other palace advance building, owned but abandoned by Letitia Semple, "was filled with Negroes of the *lowest* order, but...the Gov. intended to make them leave." The nearby Robert Carter House, left by owner Robert Saunders in the care of his faithful butler, Edmund Parsons, was converted into headquarters for the Federal provost marshal overseeing the town's security. In July, Harriette Cary recorded in her diary, "constant complaints of the Citizens have induced the posting of sentinels at various houses for the protection of property." The month of July ended with a series of fires in and around town, consuming sundry barns and the clerk's office for the courts, the latter blamed on slaves hoping to destroy their ownership papers.

Meanwhile, despite the prolonged Seven Days Battle at the end of June into July, McClellan failed to capture Richmond and retreated down the Peninsula through Williamsburg. As these Federal troops began arriving in town, about mid-August, a new rash of nocturnal fires broke out in barns, storehouses, and the college's Old Steward's House, the only frame structure on campus. The night that Dr. Robert Garrett's barn, stable, and cornhouse burned at the present-day Coke-Garrett house (leaving him only the corn he was storing in his library), his neighbor Dr. Samuel Griffin in the Tayloe house was protecting his home by entertaining three Fifth Pennsylvania officers. "Our fellow citizens are in such apprehension about fire," Dr. Griffin's son, James, related in his journal, "that there is no little watching among them at night." He was gratified to learn that patrols of soldiers were being sent out "with a view to prevent fires, to arrest suspicious characters."

Upon the blue army's exit from the Peninsula, calm again descended on the town, still held by the Fifth Pennsylvania. But the evening of 8 September, "the cry of fire" once more reverberated through Williamsburg streets. The main college building, so recently rebuilt, was in flames. Miss Mary Southall, living with her family in the President's House on campus, quickly recruited a bucket brigade of onlookers whose efforts extinguished the blaze before major damage was done. Federal soldiers appeared unsympathetic; Mary later remembered one telling her "if the College was not burned that day it would be the next." Sure enough, early the next morning, 9 September, a Confederate cavalry raid led by Colonel William Shingler dashed into town, captured stores, ammunition, and several prisoners, including Colonel Campbell, and vanished before any resistance could be organized. Incensed over this humiliation and emboldened by a supply of whiskey left unguarded in the confusion, some Pennsylvania troopers set fire to the college again and made sure it would burn down this time by forming a cordon of drawn sabers around the building to discourage another bucket brigade. All but the outer wall and part of one tower was consumed. A nearby barn was also destroyed, as a Northern soldier boasted: "I burned that d--d College, and I intend to burn this d--d town." Few could sleep in Williamsburg that night.

Though the town as a whole did not burn, isolated fires continued to break out. One October night, farmer Robert Cole's kitchen, barn, and stables ignited behind his home across the street from Bruton Church. Flames spread to Williamsburg's former post office next door, while the church's nearby parsonage, though threatened, escaped. "This fire was beyond doubt, the work of an incendiary or of incendiaries!!" declared James Griffin. Not only flames but souvenir hunters endangered Williamsburg's treasures. Later in October, Mrs. Tucker watched helplessly as furniture and invaluable books from Robert Saunders' library were carried by the wagonload to Fort Magruder. Her entreaties to Edmund Parsons to bring the books to her for safekeeping were futile. Mrs. Virginia Bucktrout Smith in the Brush-Everard house across the palace green managed to salvage some strewn on the trampled lawn. The Wythe house, George Washington's headquarters during the Revolution, was also plundered after its abandonment. Soldiers found "a large lot of old letters from many distinguished persons of the revolutionary time" in its attic. Pieces of the community continued to disappear through the winter in a combination of mysterious fires and lootings. Tazewell Hall's mistress, Mrs. Margaret Munford, reported runaway slaves "destroying for fuel many unoccupied houses, fences, and shade trees."

Frequent attacks by Confederate cavalry on the Federal lines drawn just west of the college ruins on both Jamestown and Richmond roads punctuated winter's monotony. Near the end of March 1863, New York lawyer and politician General Richard Busteed, temporarily in command of the Yorktown district including Williamsburg, decided to put a stop to these incursions. "I am of the deliberate judgment that the only way of our immunity lies in the destruction of Williamsburg," he advised his commanding officer, General John Dix at Fort Monroe, on 26 March; "and if you will approve it I would give the inhabitants notice that upon a repetition of these attacks the place should be destroyed." Dix immediately shot back, "We must not destroy towns unless they are actually taken possession of by the enemy, and then not unless absolutely necessary for our own safety." As if to meet these requirements, three mornings later Colonel William Tabb led two regiments of Virginia cavalry to the outskirts of Williamsburg and attacked at dawn from two directions with the objective of capturing Fort Magruder. Failing in this, Tabb's force held the town only long enough to collect needed supplies and left the Federals once again eager to apply the torch. Busteed forbade that retaliation, but, with evidence that the raiders were aided by civilians, ordered all citizens to take the oath of allegiance to the U.S. government or be placed beyond Federal lines outside of Williamsburg. Again Dix countermanded Busteed's order but warned that if it "be found that any house in Williamsburg was occupied by the enemy with the consent of the owner for the purpose of firing upon our troops it will be razed to the ground."

Wise's Last Raid. Skirmish at the College. April 9th 1863.

Provost marshal David E. Cronin sketched the ruins of the college as a backdrop for the April 1863 raid by Confederate General Henry Wise. The marble statue of Lord Botetourt (see color plate 21 and pp. 90, 141, 149, & 152) providing cover for Federal defenders survived the war and is presently housed in the college library.

Courtesy, Collection of the New York Historical Society

When Tabb's raid failed to meet Dix's conditions for destroying Williamsburg, the gray soldiers tried again–or so it seemed to the blue. Actually, General Longstreet was planning an attack on Suffolk and needed a diversion on the Peninsula. This task went to a former Virginia governor and lawyer who often practiced in Williamsburg–General Henry A. Wise. Early in the morning of 11 April, Wise had his 1,700 infantry, cavalry, and artillerymen poised on the western edge of Williamsburg, totally surprising the Federal guard and driving it all the way from the college into Fort Magruder. As Wise's men took cover along the streets, Union artillery in the fort commenced shelling the town "very fast." Rudely awakened townspeople fled to safety, many taking refuge in the asylum, where the Federal surgeon in charge, Dr. Peter Wager, warmly welcomed them with coffee. Most houses on the eastern edge of Williamsburg, including Bassett Hall, the Galt house, and the present Benjamin Powell house (see p. 46), were hit. "Many other houses were struck and portions of them torn to pieces," wrote John Coupland, whose family was temporarily living in the Vest house (now called the Palmer house); "but strange to say none took fire, all that portion of town from the Episcopal church down embracing much the larger part was pretty well peppered."

Worried that his presence would cause more damage, Wise withdrew out of range to the college. He remained around Williamsburg a few days, trying more feints toward Fort Magruder and allowing civilians their first opportunity in nearly a year to move freely between Williamsburg and Richmond. Many, weary of their confinement and longing to reunite with absent loved ones, surrendered their homes and "refugeed" into Dixie during this time. Wise pulled out of Williamsburg on 16 April amid fears that the "Yankees will certainly fire the town when our men leave." Again Williamsburg was spared the torch, but General Dix was so enraged by Wise's raid he reiterated his threat to raze any house used "for the purpose of firing upon the troops stationed there." No wonder one citizen was quoted offering the politician's prayer: "Good Lord, save me from my friends! I can take care of my enemies myself."

Tempers eventually cooled, raids subsided, and Williamsburg settled down to "comply with Federal rules as gracefully as possible" through the summer and into the fall of 1863. During winter, a visiting Massachusetts soldier found a "great many of the houses present the usual appearance of a captured town, that is they look as if a 'dose of salts had been through them' and they had been cleaned out." At that point, January 1864, the town entered its next crisis. A Federal plan to raid Richmond in force, by way of the Peninsula, led to a mandate that all citizens take the oath of allegiance or be placed outside the lines. Sally Galt best expressed the alarm of many Williamsburg natives in a protest letter she addressed to the commanding officer: "We cannot, without bitterest, deepest anguish, leave the homes of our childhood, the scenes of our youth, those grassy mounds–Oh! Holy Dust, we can not give Thee up, all that is left to some bereaved hearts of what made life precious." Miss Sally knew well the fate of unoccupied dwellings, yet she could not in good conscience take an oath contrary to her beliefs. Neither could Lucy Tucker bear the thought of dishonoring her name with the oath and frantically "packed up everything that could be taken." At the last minute, she was notified that all could remain in their homes without swearing allegiance to what they considered a foreign government.

The Richmond raid failed anyway, and Williamsburg enjoyed relative tranquility during the summer of 1864 under its most benevolent provost marshal, Captain David Cronin of the First New York Mounted Rifles, which had relieved the Fifth Pennsylvania. In September, soon after Cronin's departure to rejoin the Union army besieging Petersburg, orders were issued by department commander General Benjamin Butler that all civilians must take the oath of allegiance or be sent across the lines. Sally Galt's letter-writing campaign was not effective this time. Butler adamantly refused anyone permission to stay; and, by the end of October, all loyal Southerners had been banished from their homes. Some made it to Richmond, but others, notably Lucy Tucker, Dr. Garrett, and probably Sally Galt, were waiting in Norfolk for transportation to Richmond when they received word they could return to Williamsburg without taking the oath. As they feared, they found their houses ransacked, furniture gone, and rugs stripped off floors. A short time later "the burning and pulling down of houses" occurred. Despite Dr. Wager's best efforts to save them, both homes on the palace grounds were "torn to pieces and the bricks carried away" with nothing left "save a heap of rubbish," Cynthia Coleman lamented. "The last remnant of the circumstance and pomp of Colonial days passed away with the total destruction of the Palace buildings."

The Nelson-Galt house (shown here ca. 1905-1926) situated near the eastern end of town drew Federal fire from Fort Magruder during Wise's raid, yet Sally Galt refused to abandon it even as shells burst beneath her window sill. When she was forced to vacate temporarily in November 1864, her servant, Arena Baker, probably remained to protect the old home.

Courtesy, Colonial Williamsburg Foundation

"It is really a magnificent Establishment. No House in the City, public or private, can compete with it." Such was Dr. Samuel Griffin's evaluation of this residence in September 1858, shortly before it was completed. Owned by Williamsburg's leading lawyer, Lemuel Bowden, this impressive example of Greek revival architecture was built of Baltimore brick at the exorbitant cost of $10,000 and was conspicuously located next to Bruton Church. Bowden, called a "Virginia Yankee" for his unpopular Unionist views, nearly lost his mansion early in the war for refusing to pay property taxes to what he considered an illegitimate government. He was threatened again in the spring of 1862 when some Louisiana soldiers, incensed by his disloyalty, planned "to attack the house, drive out the inmates, break up the furniture, &c & do Mr Bowden some bodily harm"; but he had already fled the city to avoid capture by his old political enemy, Confederate General Henry A. Wise. After the 5 May 1862 Battle of Williamsburg, Bowden returned home to serve as mayor with Federal protection. That August, as the Union army evacuated the Peninsula, he left again, never to return. Though his home survived the war unscathed, Bowden died in January 1864 while serving as Virginia's Unionist senator in Washington. (See p. 229.)

Courtesy, Colonial Williamsburg Foundation

All that was left of the Governor's Palace west advance building after its dismantling shows in this postwar photograph. Through trees and overgrown brush, the Saunders house peeks out to the right and the Wythe house to the left, with Bruton Church's spire in the distance. (See p. 136.)

Courtesy, Colonial Williamsburg Foundation

At the close of the war in April 1865, Williamsburg refugees—defeated, destitute, and disheartened—returned to find great gaps where four years earlier stood beloved domiciles, doctors' offices, drugstores, hotels, and barns. Indeed, "every vacant frame house in the city, with very few exceptions, were torn down by the 'Yanks,' or fell prey to the axe of citizens who had no other way of securing dry kindling wood," one resident later lamented. If not for the courage and foresight of citizens such as Sally Galt, Lucy Tucker, Harriette Henley, Edmund Parsons, Dr. Robert Garrett, James Griffin, Mary Southall, Robert Cole, and Virginia Smith, many more of Williamsburg's colonial treasures would no doubt have been lost.

One of the many pieces of sheet music published to celebrate Civil War victories. Nothing is known of the composer Coyle, but Union Brigadier General Winfield Scott won his fame at the battle of Williamsburg, after which he was known as "Hancock the Superb."

Courtesy, Virginia Historical Society, William W. Cole Sheet Music Collection

Selected Sources and Suggested Readings

Most of the sources for this essay reside in Swem Library, College of William and Mary: Galt Family Papers, including the 1861-1862 Diary of Dr. John Minson Galt II, Tucker-Coleman Papers, Dorsey-Coupland Papers, Page-Saunders Papers, Civil War Collection, Williamsburg City Papers, James L. C. Griffin's Commonplace Books in the Faculty-Alumni File, and Harriette Cary's Diary.

Charles, John S. "Recollections of Williamsburg, Virginia, As it was at the Beginning of the Civil War," transcript of an interview (1928). Colonial Williamsburg Research Library.

Cronin, David. "The Vest Mansion," unpublished. Colonial Williamsburg Research Library

Dain, Norman. *Disordered Minds: The First Century of Eastern State Hospital in Williamsburg, 1766-1866* (Williamsburg: Colonial Williamsburg Foundation, 1971).

Godson, Susan H., Ludwell H. Johnson, Richard B. Sherman, Thad W. Tate, & Helen C. Walker, *The College of William & Mary. A History*. 2 vols. (Williamsburg: King & Queen Press, 1993). Esp. Johnson, "Between the Wars, 1782-1862," I: 165-329, and Walker, "'So Decayed an Institution': Colonel Ewell's College, 1862-1888," I: 333-435.

Goodwin, M.R. "Historical Notes on the College of William and Mary," unpub. (1954).

Colonial Williamsburg Research Library and Swem Library, College of William and Mary.

Hastings, Earl C., Jr., and David. *A Pitiless Rain: The Battle of Williamsburg, 1862* (Shippensburg, Pa: Whitemare, 1997).

Hudson, Carson O., Jr. *Civil War Williamsburg* (Williamsburg: Colonial Williamsburg Foundation, 1997).

Lafayette McLaws Papers. Southern Historical Collection of the Manuscripts Department, University of North Carolina.

U.S. War Department. *The War of the Rebellion: A Compilation of the Official Records of the Union and Confederate Armies* (Washington: Government Printing Office, 1880-1901).

Yetter, George Humphrey. *Williamsburg Before and After: The Rebirth of Virginia's Colonial Capital* (Williamsburg: Colonial Williamsburg Foundation, 1988).

Three Hundred Years of Faith

by: John Turner

Since its beginning, Williamsburg has been a community with an active, vibrant religious life. With more than eighty-five houses of worship in the town and surrounding area today, there would seem to be great promise for the continuance of that tradition into the twenty-first century and beyond. What follows here is an attempt to highlight just a few of the lives and events that have enriched local religious life over the past three centuries.

The Reverend James Blair (ca. 1655-1743), portrait painted in 1705 by James Hargrave. Blair was commissary to the Bishop of London, founder of the College of William and Mary, member of the Governor's Council, and rector of Bruton Parish Church. (See p. 152 & color plate 5.)

Courtesy, Muscarelle Museum of Art, College of William and Mary, gift of Mrs. Mary M. Peachy

In 1699 Williamsburg was a new development site. The college main building was just several years old; the first brick Bruton Parish Church had been in place for only sixteen years (see color plate 4); and although Middle Plantation had been used as an interim meeting site for the House of Burgesses before 1699, a new capitol building was still only a vision in the planners' minds. Besides the more strategic and healthier location this area offered, a major reason for relocating the government from Jamestown to Williamsburg was that the college and church were already here.

The three C's of the town were to be college, church, and capitol; and Williamsburg's first eighty years were marked by the intertwining of education, religion, and government. No one person in seventeenth- or eighteenth-century Virginia is a better symbol of such interconnectedness than the Reverend James Blair. Born in Alvah, Scotland, in the mid-1650s, Blair arrived in Virginia in 1685 to accept the rectorship of Varina Parish in Henrico County. In December of 1689, Blair was named Commissary to the Bishop of London, a position that gave him supervision over all the Anglican clergy in Virginia. Soon after this, Blair began to advocate the creation of a college that would provide native-born ministers for Virginia.

Medal from 1772 showing Reverend James Blair receiving the charter of the college from William III and Mary II. In 1770 Lord Botetourt, the colonial governor and great friend to the college, endowed a medal to be awarded annually to the student who excelled in natural philosophy. The steel dies from which Thomas Pingo struck the medals in London survive at the college.

Courtesy, Colonial Williamsburg Foundation

In February 1693, Blair persuaded William III and Mary II to grant a royal charter for the college subsequently named after them, and was named its first president. Then, upon his return to Williamsburg from England in 1694, he was appointed to the Governor's Council, the most powerful political group in the colony. In 1710, he became rector of Bruton Parish Church, thus completing his triangle of leadership: college, colony, and church. For the remaining thirty-three years of his life, Blair exercised power in a government that was inextricably bound to its established religion, in an educational institution begun for the express purpose of furthering that religion, and in a church that had considerable official, legal influence over the daily lives of its parishioners.

For all Blair's power, he represented change and a gradual lessening of England's power over her colonies, ecclesiastical and otherwise. Virginia society was relatively stable by 1699, and the church in particular had been evolving as an American institution for nearly a century. There were no bishops, no ecclesiastical courts, and vestries had emerged with more extensive powers and greater autonomy than their English counterparts. The great majority of white residents of the new capital of the colony were professing members of the Church of England in Virginia, a powerful force concerned with conducting the affairs of the community largely under the control of the landed gentry. For most free citizens of Williamsburg, religion informed the pace and conduct of societal life and supported its hierarchical structure.

The dominance of the established church and its role in Virginia society had not been seriously challenged in the seventeenth century. Quakers, the only religious group actively persecuted in Virginia prior to 1700, had mostly left the colony for friendlier settings. Presbyterians, in small groups organized by Francis MaKemie, were confined mostly to the eastern shore of Virginia. Anti-Catholic sentiment, identified by recent historians as an essential part of British patriotism, effectively kept Catholic settlers away from all but the most northern portions of the colony, along the Maryland border.

At the beginning of the eighteenth century, the degree of participation of the church in the lives of slaves varied greatly from parish to parish, minister to minister, plantation to plantation, and master to master. For many slaves in 1699, assimilation into Virginia society was still a relatively recent experience. African religions–and/or exposure to Christianity, Islam, or other religions while still in Africa–would still have been fresh in the minds of some. It is likely, however, that at their masters' discretion, some slaves were already attending services at Bruton when the capital moved to Williamsburg. By the end of the colonial period, more than a thousand slaves, both adults and children, would be baptized at Bruton.

Whether they attended services at Bruton, Williamsburg area slaves were certainly attending to their spiritual life with whatever was available to them in terms of time, remembered traditions, and objects substituted for or adapted to sacred use. By 1699, many Virginia slaves would have professed Christianity, though the opportunities to express or practice their faith would have been largely limited to their work and living environments. Religion was ever one of the most important tools available to a slave for coping with the horrors of slavery.

The eighteenth century would witness tremendous growth in the understanding of the place of personal faith in the lives of Virginians both free and enslaved. Williamsburg's first face-to-face encounter with the first series of revivals generally referred to collectively as the "Great Awakening" (roughly 1720-1750) came in December of 1739. At the invitation of Commissary Blair, the Reverend George Whitefield, celebrated English evangelist, preached at Bruton on the sixteenth. The first true Anglo-American celebrity, Whitefield delivered a powerful and emotional message on the importance of every human being to God. Celebrating his twenty-fifth birthday while in Williamsburg, Whitefield was entertained by the governor and by Blair, whom he announced to be the most impressive fellow clergyman he had yet met in the colonies.

Here was a religious idea that many people—black, white, slave or free—could really get excited about. The God of all that is, is interested in me, and loves me. Scripturally, of course, it wasn't anything new; but the effect of *hearing* this message for the first time was explosive, especially on the vast majority of whites and blacks who were not part of the Anglican leadership.

Print after John Russell's 1768 painting of the Reverend George Whitefield, celebrated English evangelist, preaching in the fields outside London. Whitefield preached at Bruton Parish Church on 16 December 1739, bringing revivalism to Virginia.

Courtesy, Colonial Williamsburg Foundation

Since the Act of Toleration of 1689, dissenters –those who chose to express religious belief in formal ways other than those practiced by the Church of England–had supposedly been protected from active persecution; but they had not been freed from the obligation to support financially the established church and its activities. Whether the 1689 Act applied to Virginia was still being contested in some political circles as late as the 1770s. After 1689 dissenting ministers could obtain licenses to preach, though they were to do so only at fixed locations–a requirement that some ministers challenged and defied.

By the 1740s, Williamsburg was being visited by more dissenters, and of increasing variety. Samuel Davies, a Presbyterian minister, journeyed to the capital in 1747 to obtain a license to preach in Hanover County. Davies was successful in his quest and by many accounts conducted a significant evangelical ministry over a wide area in central Virginia, paying special attention to the needs of slaves and free blacks. He was criticized for his efforts at teaching slaves to read the Bible themselves and for encouraging them in the singing of popular hymns.

Many other dissenting ministers and itinerant preachers–most frequently Presbyterians, Baptists, and Methodists–made their mark in Williamsburg during the course of the eighteenth century. A group of local citizens successfully petitioned the York County court in 1765 to be allowed to meet publicly as Presbyterians. Following twenty-eight days of imprisonment in Spotsylvania, Lewis Craig, a Baptist itinerant, came to town seeking the release of colleagues who, like himself, had been arrested for disturbing the peace. Craig found able assistance in Williamsburg and accomplished his goal. The case itself drew the attention of a young James Madison, who later, along with Thomas Jefferson, championed the cause of religious freedom and separation of church and state. After six months imprisonment in Culpeper, James Ireland, another Baptist itinerant, came to Williamsburg to secure a license to preach in Culpeper County.

In 1772, Joseph Pilmore, Methodist itinerant, described in the *Virginia Gazette* as "that dear, divine man," made the first of several preaching visits to the colonial capital. He was followed, a decade or so later, by the Reverend Francis Asbury, one of the giants of American Methodism; and in 1785 Jeremiah Mastin was assigned to be the first itinerant minister to the Williamsburg Circuit. Also, despite persecution in the seventeenth century, there was a small community of Quakers, who worshiped at the Skimino meeting house built in 1767.

Despite these developments, religious diversity was not in strong evidence in the eighteenth century. There were probably no more than several hundred Catholics in the entire colony by the time of the American Revolution, with no known significant presence in the Williamsburg area. Richmond and Norfolk had small Jewish populations by the end of the century; but there were no Jews in Williamsburg other than the esteemed Dr. DeSequeyra, administrator of the mental hospital.

Of the three aforementioned Protestant dissenting traditions, the one that apparently had the greatest appeal to Williamsburg's African-American population was Baptist. *Virginia Gazette* advertisements chronicle runaways known to preach at suspected slave gatherings. Other slaves and free blacks are described as "styling themselves preachers." Clearly, the long-range effects of religious revival were felt strongly in the African-American community.

By oral tradition, the ancestors of the First Baptist Church of Williamsburg had gathered together by 1776, meeting in out-of-the-way locations including a site near Green Spring Plantation. More oral tradition has it that African Americans were worshiping in a building on Jesse Cole's property on Nassau Street. More certain written documents and denominational records have them participating in the Dover Baptist Association in the 1780s and 1790s. Under the leadership first of the slave Moses, then of Gowan Pamphlet, this congregation is believed to have been the earliest church in America organized and administered by African Americans: at least as early as 1818, the Baptist church was cited as a boundary for the Bryan property.

The year 1776 signaled several epochal shifts. At least one that preceded the American Revolution and the many important decisions made in Williamsburg concerning it was in the realm of faith. The town was home to several active religious groups at the beginning of the final quarter of the eighteenth century; and even though official disestablishment of the Church of England in Virginia did not occur until 1784, the formal political break in 1776 from the government of England was also a *de facto* break from its church. The political center of the soon-to-be Commonwealth of Virginia was no longer homogeneous in a religious sense. Even enslaved members of the community had their own church with considerable control over its direction and governance.

Before the capital moved to Richmond in April 1780, one of Virginia's most important legacies to the world had already been initiated. Following on the heels of the Virginia Declaration of Rights with its sixteenth article guaranteeing the "free exercise" of religion, Tho-

Xt H. 90a. 84

A BILL *for establishing* RELIGIOUS FREEDOM,
printed for the consideration of the PEOPLE.

WELL aware that the opinions and belief of men depend not on their own will, but follow involuntarily the evidence proposed to their minds, that Almighty God hath created the mind free, and manifested his Supreme will that free it shall remain, by making it altogether insusceptible of restraint: That all attempts to influence it by temporal punishments or burthens, or by civil incapacitations, tend only to beget habits of hypocrisy and meanness, and are a departure from the plan of the holy author of our religion, who being Lord both of body and mind, yet chose not to propagate it by coercions on either, as was in his Almighty power to do, but to extend it by its influence on reason alone: That the impious presumption of legislators and rulers, civil as well as ecclesiastical, who, being themselves but fallible and uninspired men, have assumed dominion over the faith of others, setting up their own opinions and modes of thinking, as the only true and infallible, and as such, endeavouring to impose them on others, hath established and maintained false religions over the greatest part of the world, and through all time: That to compel a man to furnish contributions of money for the propagation of opinions which he disbelieves and abhors, is sinful and tyrannical: That even the forcing him to support this or that teacher of his own religious persuasion, is depriving him of the comfortable liberty of giving his contributions to the particular pastor whose morals he would make his pattern, and whose powers he feels most persuasive to righteousness, and is withdrawing from the Ministry those temporal rewards which, proceeding from an approbation of their personal conduct, are an additional incitement to earnest and unremitting labour for the instruction of mankind: That our civil rights have no dependance on our religious opinions, any more than on our opinions in physicks or geometry: That therefore the proscribing any citizen as unworthy the publick confidence, by laying upon him an incapacity of being called to offices of trust and emolument, unless he profess or renounce this or that religious opinion, is depriving him injuriously of those privileges and advantages to which, in common with his fellow citizens he has a natural right: That it tends also to corrupt the principles of that very religion it is meant to encourage, by bribing with a monopoly of worldly honours and emoluments, those who will externally profess and conform to it: That though indeed these are criminal who do not withstand such temptation, yet neither are those innocent who lay the bait in their way; that the opinions of men are not the object of civil government, nor under its jurisdiction: That to suffer the civil Magistrate to intrude his powers into the field of opinion, and to restrain the profession or propagation of principles on supposition of their ill tendency, is a dangerous fallacy, which at once destroys all religious liberty, because he being of course Judge of that tendency will make his own opinions the rule of judgment, and approve or condemn the sentiments of others only as they shall square with, or differ from his own: That it is time enough for the rightful purposes of civil government for its officers to interfere when principles break out into overt acts against peace and good order: And finally, that truth is great and will prevail if left to herself; that she is the proper and sufficient antagonist to errour, and has nothing to fear from the conflict, unless by human interposition, disarmed of her natural weapons, free argument and debate; errours ceasing to be dangerous when it is permitted freely to contradict them.

WE the General Assembly of *Virginia* do enact, that no man shall be compelled to frequent or support any religious Worship place or Ministry whatsoever, nor shall be enforced, restrained, molested, or burthened in his body or goods, nor shall otherwise suffer on account of his religious opinions or belief, but that all men shall be free to profess, and by argument to maintain their opinions in matters of religion, and that the same shall in no wise diminish, enlarge, or affect their civil capacities.

AND though we well know that this Assembly, elected by the people for the ordinary purposes of legislation only, have no power to restrain the acts of succeeding Assemblies, constituted with powers equal to our own, and that therefore to declare this act irrevocable would be of no effect in law; yet we are free to declare, and do declare, that the rights hereby asserted are of the natural rights of mankind, and that if any act shall be hereafter passed to repeal the present, or to narrow its operation, such act will be an infringement of natural right.

A Bill for establishing Religious Freedom. *First proposed in Williamsburg, passed into Virginia law on 16 January 1786.*

Courtesy, Colonial Williamsburg Foundation

mas Jefferson proposed the separation of church and state. What would become Virginia law on 16 January 1786 was first submitted in initial form in Williamsburg in 1779. Jefferson later called the Virginia Statute for Religious Freedom the most important governmental achievement of his era.

Disestablishment was difficult for many congregations of the former Church of England; and some of the churches fell into disuse or disrepair, or were sold to other denominations. Lack of governmental support, a diminished congregation, and the unfamiliar need to depend on voluntary support contributed to lean times for Williamsburg's remaining Episcopal church. But survive it did, and the next two centuries would witness a Bruton Parish Church that consistently was of tremendous importance to the life of the community (see pages 28 & 42 and color plate 16).

By 1799, the future presented a different prospect than it had in 1699. The Great Awakening had a profound effect on the colonies in general, and had, as previously noted, considerable influence on developments in Williamsburg. In about 1795, another revival, sometimes referred to as the Second Great Awakening, began in the new United States and was to last about forty years. Country-wide, this revival caused significant increases in church memberships, put the focus of ministry on winning souls, and gave new importance to the role of women in benevolent causes in this country as well as in foreign mission fields.

Locally, the first few decades of the nineteenth century saw considerable church growth for the size of the town. As already noted, the first documentary reference to the black "Baptist Meeting House" on Nassau Street appears in 1818, by which time it had more than five hundred members. In response to Nat Turner's Rebellion in Southampton County in August 1831, it was closed for part of the next year; and when it reopened, it was for a time under white supervision. Twenty-five years later, on 11 May 1856, the African-American Baptist congregation (today's First Baptist Church) dedicated its new brick church on Nassau Street. At the end of the Civil War, this congregation, along with most other black Baptist groups, withdrew from the white Baptist associations and formed regional associations of their own.

In 1828, a white Baptist congregation was organized and met for some time in the powder magazine, and in 1832 this congregation of seventy-five or so was accepted into the Dover Baptist Association as Zion Baptist Church of Williamsburg. Twenty-five years later the congregation moved into a new church building on Duke of Gloucester Street, just east of the magazine.

Other denominations also grew in this period. The Methodist presence in Williamsburg that had been nurtured by Francis Asbury's frequent visits (five times between 1782 and 1801) was large enough that in 1842 the congregation built a brick church just west of the magazine. From their beginnings in the "house belonging to Mr. Davenport" (near Campbell's Tavern), Williamsburg's Presbyterians had grown enough to erect a church on the palace green (present site of the Elkanah Dean house). The largest new denomination to grow out of the Second Great Awakening was the Christian Church (Disciples of Christ). Though no Christian Church was organized in town, twenty men and women meeting at Hill Pleasant Farm (in present Norge) founded Olive Branch Christian Church in 1833; and by 1835 the congregation had built a brick church and was visited by Alexander Campbell, one of the founders of the denomination.

African Baptist Church (later First Baptist). The building on Nassau St. was dedicated in 1856.

Courtesy, Colonial Williamsburg Foundation

Methodist church built in 1842 on Duke of Gloucester St. west of the powder magazine.

Courtesy, Colonial Williamsburg Foundation

By 1850 increasing population in James City and York counties brought with it more churches and an increasing diversity of religious choices, but in town the number of houses of worship had stabilized. Bruton, of course, occupied the same spot it had since the third building was completed in 1715. Zion Baptist (today's Williamsburg Baptist) and Williamsburg Methodist were on either side of the powder magazine. The African Baptist Church remained at its Nassau Street site, and the Presbyterian Church fronted on the palace green.

Later in the century, nationwide revivals gave new life to local churches. The short-lived prayer meeting revival of 1857-1858 swept American towns as a result of a nationwide financial panic. Unfortunately, war came to Williamsburg again, drawing heavily on the reserves of the churches and their members. Virtually all of the churches in town served as hospitals for soldiers from both sides. Olive Branch became a stable for Union horses, and its pews and flooring were broken up for firewood. In spite of such hardships, the community of faith endured its country's internecine war, starting over again as the fourth quarter of the

Williamsburg Baptist Church (formerly Zion Baptist), ca. 1856, on Duke of Gloucester St., east of the powder magazine. It is generally believed that the Zion Baptist congregation was constituted in 1828. At the time of its admission to the Dover Association in 1832, the church had seventy-five members. Its first minister was Scervant Jones, a wealthy lawyer and property owner, who served without pay until his death in 1854. The congregation had increased to 431 (179 whites and 252 blacks) by the time of Jones' death and had outgrown the powder magazine, where it had met throughout Jones' tenure. The cornerstone for a new church was laid in 1853; and the Episcopal, Methodist, and First Baptist churches held suppers and fairs to raise funds for the new building. In 1866 segregation was taking its hold on every aspect of social life, and only white members remained in the church, so that membership dropped greatly.

Courtesy, Colonial Williamsburg Foundation

century began. Throughout this period, Williamsburg's women markedly worked together in an increasing number of church-related organizations.

The situation for Jews changed slowly but steadily in the nineteenth century. Jewish merchants and their families were living in Williamsburg by the middle of the century; and several families of Hofheimers, immigrants from Germany, appear in the 1860 census. Prior to that, the eldest of the Hofheimers, Isaac, was elected to several offices within Williamsburg Masonic Lodge Number 6. Catholic priests from Newport News visited Catholics in Williamsburg from 1908 to 1912 and may have done so earlier.

In the second half of the nineteenth century, Williamsburg's African-American community had to deal with tremendous change. The church provided not only most of the black leadership after emancipation and during reconstruction, but was the physical as well as spiritual center of development in the African-American community. First Baptist had been "the" church for blacks in the Williamsburg area since the fourth quarter of the eighteenth century. Soon after the war, it began parenting new congregations in the area. Among these offspring

were: Queen Street, Hampton (1865); St. John's, York County (1879); and Oak Grove, York County (1914). Additional churches with a First Baptist lineage founded in the late nineteenth or early twentieth century were: First Baptist Church Morrison, Newport News (1882); Little Zion, Grove (1889); and Lincoln Park, Hampton (1911).

Mount Ararat Baptist Church, an African-American congregation organized in 1882, became an important center for blacks in the central to eastern part of Williamsburg. From a frame church on Francis Street, the congregation moved in 1932 to the present brick building on Franklin Street. In town, First Baptist, Mount Ararat, and Union churches served in the late nineteenth and early twentieth centuries as the soul of the African-American community. As in biblical times, these churches were involved in all aspects of the lives of their people. They were civil, educational, social, and spiritual centers all rolled into one. This centrality, physically and emotionally, of religion in the life of the community continued to sustain and contribute greatly to the life of the larger community for the next hundred years.

The Williamsburg area absorbed a number of Norwegian and Danish immigrants in the nineteenth century and began the twentieth by adding the Lutheran traditions to its pantheon of denominations. The first Lutheran congregation was organized in 1898, building a church west of town on Richmond Road in 1904. What began as the Zion Scandinavian Evangelical Lutheran Church dissolved in 1908, breaking into two congregations, Zion and Bethany. They were served by one pastor in 1918 and came back together in 1932 as Our Savior's Lutheran Church.

The gradual changes of the nineteenth century mushroomed in the twentieth, especially after the restoration of Williamsburg and the emergence of the Colonial Williamsburg Foundation. Dr. W. A. R. Goodwin had been instrumental in an earlier restoration of Bruton Parish Church while its rector from 1903 to 1909; and brought back to Williamsburg in 1923 by the college president, Dr. Chandler, to direct an endowment campaign, Goodwin renewed his dream of having the entire town restored. By the end of 1926, Goodwin was again rector of Bruton, and had successfully convinced another committed churchman, John D. Rockefeller, Jr., to become involved in Williamsburg's restoration.

Methodist Church built in 1926. In order better to serve William and Mary students, the Methodists moved to this building at the corner of Duke of Gloucester and North Boundary streets in 1926. By 1964, not only had the congregation outgrown the building, but Colonial Williamsburg objected to its 20th-c. architecture just across the street from the Wren Building. Colonial Williamsburg bought the property and demolished the building in 1981.

Courtesy, Williamsburg Methodist Church.

Williamsburg's community of faith continued to thrive and meet the new challenges of this latest, different revival. The restoration caused an increase in population, and a more diversified one. It also increased tourism and created the need for an ever-growing service industry, which caused all of the churches in the historic area besides Bruton (see pages 28 and 42) to relocate. Nineteenth-century structures on Duke of Gloucester, Nassau, Francis, and Palace Streets were eventually torn down. New churches appeared on Franklin Street (Mt. Ararat), Scotland Street (First Baptist), and Richmond and Jamestown roads (Presbyterian, Baptist, and Methodist).

By 1908 there were several Catholic families living in or near Williamsburg. At first, they met in their homes, but later that year a priest from Newport News began saying Mass at

The Forster gift shop passing by Bruton Parish Church as it is moved down Duke of Gloucester St. on 29 March 1968, en route to its new location and use as a synagogue on Jamestown Rd. Dr. Paul Sternberg, an optometrist, had acquired the site, and arranged the purchase of the shop building for a modest sum from Colonial Williamsburg.

Courtesy, *Daily Press*

Cameron Hall for hospital patients and a few townspeople. However, these services were discontinued in 1912. These early years saw a growth in the number of Catholic college students, and they outnumbered the resident Catholics. In the 1920s the students formed the Gibbons Club and met for worship in the William and Mary Chemistry Laboratory. It was largely through the desires and efforts of the students that St. Bede's Chapel came to be built on Richmond Road, opening in 1932. Benedictine priests from Richmond served the church until 1939 when Rev. Thomas J. Walsh was appointed the first resident pastor.

Four years later, Elder Lightfoot Solomon Michaux and his organization purchased some nine hundred acres near Jamestown for the development of an African-American religious, recreational, and cultural center–the National Memorial to the Progress of the Negro Race in America. Michaux, pastor of the radio Church of God, established a dairy farm on the property to begin to realize his vision of economic improvement for underprivileged African Americans. Though many of his particular dreams were not realized, his ministry had far-reaching effects on the Williamsburg area and the country.

World War II brought yet another challenge for the community of faith, as well as many opportunities, when servicemen were brought through Colonial Williamsburg for training. Leaders of America's war effort thought it worthwhile to expose servicemen to the ideals of freedom and patriotism that had been given birth in Williamsburg in the eighteenth century—ideals that often had a religious base and had been greatly influenced by Virginia's religious history. This effort was substantially financed by Mr. and Mrs. Rockefeller. In a variety of ways, area churches and residents interacted with thousands of members of America's armed forces; and like most communities in the country, Williamsburg sent many of its sons and daughters to join their ranks.

After World War II, revivals again swept the United States. Williamsburg area churches increased in size and number as Billy Graham and other popular evangelists captured the attention of large audiences around the world. Also, Temple Beth El was founded in 1959.

The Reverend John M. Dawson (1835-1915). Born a free man, Dawson attended Oberlin College before the Civil War. Elected pastor of First Baptist Church of Williamsburg in 1866, he served for forty-six years. In 1872 he began purchasing real estate and twenty years later owned fifteen houses and lots. From 1865-1895 he was treasurer of James City County, in 1874 was elected to the General Assembly, and in 1882 ran unsuccessfully for Congress as a Republican.

Courtesy, Marie Sheppard and First Baptist Church

Services were held at the Wren Chapel and the Williamsburg Community Center for many years before a permanent place of worship was constructed on Jamestown Road in 1968. Furthermore, in the turbulent 1950s and 1960s, Williamsburg's church leaders, black and white, were in the forefront locally (and some nationally) of the civil rights movement.

Faith is a journey, and the journey continues. Along the way for the three hundred years of Williamsburg's history there have been many spiritual luminaries. In addition to those of the eighteenth century already mentioned, among those of the nineteenth century were the reverends Scervant Jones (Williamsburg Baptist), William H. Wilmer (Bruton Parish), John M. Dawson (First Baptist), L. W. Wales, Sr. (Mt. Ararat Baptist), and J. G. Anderson (Williamsburg and York Presbyterian).

The twentieth-century luminaries are too numerous to mention here, but their work has supported a rich environment for faith that is evidenced by a large and diverse population of religious organizations. At the close of the twentieth century, those main-stream churches already mentioned continue to operate with increased memberships, large budgets, and greater responses to community needs. Population growth has resulted in more than twenty Baptist churches in the Williamsburg area, two Presbyterian churches, three Lutheran churches, three Episcopal churches, and two Methodist churches. Even though the physical building of St. Bede's Catholic Church has grown during the years, it is now too small for its membership, so that services are also being held at St. Olaf's in Norge; and a new church building is on the drawing board. During recent decades, many diverse denominational and non-denominational churches have started new congregations. They cannot all be named, but among them are the following: Ascension of Our Lord Byzantine Catholic Church, First Church of Christ Scientist, Church of Christ, Greenspring Chapel, Seventh Day Adventist Church, Mennonite Church, Community Chapel, and Unitarian Universalist. The renovated Temple Beth El remains the religious home of Jewish students and townspeople, now ably served by its first rabbi, Sylvia Scholnick. The growing number of Asians in the community must still, however, go to the larger cities of Richmond and Newport News for their religious services.

Guided by people of vision, Williamsburg's journey of faith goes on.

Selected Sources and Suggested Readings

Dorsey, Susie. *A History of the Williamsburg Baptist Church* (Williamsburg: Williamsburg Press, 1978).

Fithian, Philip Vickers. *Journal and Letters of...*, ed. Hunter Dickinson Farish (Williamsburg: Colonial Williamsburg Foundation, 1957).

Gaustad, Edwin S. *Revival, Revolution, and Religion in Early Virginia* (Williamsburg: Colonial Williamsburg Foundation, 1994).

Goodwin, W. A. R. *Historical Sketch of Bruton Parish Church* (1903; rep. Baltimore: Genealogical Publishing, 1997).

Holmes, David. L. *A Brief History of the Episcopal Church* (Valley Forge:Trinity Press International, 1993).

Isaac, Rhys. *The Transformation of Virginia, 1740-1790* (Chapel Hill: Univ. of North Carolina, 1982).

McCartney, Martha W. *James City County: Keystone of the Commonwealth* (Virginia Beach: Donning, 1997).

Raboteau, Albert J. *Slave Religion: "The Invisible Institution" in the Antebellum South* (N.Y.: Oxford Univ., 1978).

Rouse, Parke, Jr. *James Blair of Virginia* (Chapel Hill: Univ. of North Carolina, 1971).

Upton, Dell. *Holy Things and Profane: Anglican Parish Churches in Colonial Virginia* (Cambridge: MIT, 1986).

Yetter, George H. *Williamsburg Before and After: The Rebirth of Virginia's Colonial Capital* (Williamsburg: Colonial Williamsburg Foundation, 1988).

African Americans in Williamsburg, 1865-1945

by: Linda Rowe

Despite the initial promise of post–Civil War times, African Americans in Williamsburg and the rest of Virginia found life in the last twenty-five years of the nineteenth century and the first half of the twentieth century increasingly difficult. By 1885, white politicians friendly to the old southern guard had reasserted themselves. In 1902 they succeeded in disenfranchising most black voters, drawing an unmistakable race line in the sand. In good times and bad, however, blacks in the Williamsburg area relied on family and a sense of community, their churches and, eventually, schools to sustain and protect their rich and vibrant culture.

In 1865, Williamsburg had the near-moribund look of hundreds of other southern towns in the wake of the war. A young man, on first setting foot in the former colonial capital in 1870, told his folks that it "betokened poverty and paralysis." Nonetheless, by 1877 blacks in Williamsburg were poised to make the most of a Virginia society "reconstructed" according to federally legislated requirements. Former slaves now worked for pay or a share of the crop, and black men got the vote. During reconstruction, more than sixty percent of registered voters in Williamsburg and James City and York counties were African American, and Republicans kept a grip on Virginia politics for nearly two decades with the help of black voters.

One Williamsburg black, Daniel M. Norton, was a delegate to the Virginia constitutional convention of 1868. The constitution that came out of that convention enfranchised black men in the state and called for "a uniform system of public free schools and for its gradual, equal, and full introduction into all the counties of the state by the year 1876." Norton later served for several years as a state delegate and state senator. Likewise, the Reverend John M. Dawson, pastor of First Baptist Church, was elected to the state senate, where from 1874 to 1877 he represented the district comprised of Charles City, James City, York, Warwick, and Elizabeth City counties. He was still active in local government as treasurer into the 1890s. Another elected official was barber John Cary, who served on the city council and was a delegate to the Republican National Convention.

Samuel Harris, a black entrepreneur and real-estate investor (see p. 157), began a six-year term on the Williamsburg School Board on 27 August 1883 and also supplied anthracite coal and wood to the schools. In 1860 blacks outnumbered whites in Williamsburg (864 to 742), about as they had in 1775. Among the 864 were 121 free blacks who made a living in a variety of ways—on the water as pilots, water men, fishermen, oyster men, and a steamboat fireman, or in the trades as skilled carpenters, wheelwrights, shoemakers, blacksmiths, barbers, and gardeners. Other free blacks found work as farm hands and ditch diggers; women sewed or took in washing; and both sexes found employment as domestic servants.

After the war, although some freedmen left Williamsburg, others remained, sometimes in the employ of their former owners. For instance, Malachi could be seen driving his former master, Benjamin Ewell, into town to ring the bell during the years William and Mary was closed (1881–1888). Many whites resolutely regarded their black household servants as family members, and blacks often felt strong ties to whites. But resentment simmered beneath the surface. An African-American woman recently acknowledged that relations between the races were cordial, even friendly—as long as blacks knew their place. One Eli Brown could no longer keep his "place." In February 1895, white boys, walking along the path children of both races made use of to get to and from their separate schools, pushed Brown aside. A scuffle ensued, and Brown was suspended from the black school for "unbecoming conduct in the street." Questioned by the superintendent of schools, Brown declared "he would die before he would give the path to those boys."

Black churches took an important role in providing education for black youths before Virginia's public school system came into being. In 1873, the State Sabbath School Union recognized Rachel Dawson, eight-year-old daughter of the reverend and member of the Williamsburg Sabbath School, for memorizing eighty-four Bible verses. The Union reported there were seventy-five students under the superintendence of Dawson and eight teachers at the church. And, First Baptist had a library of 250 volumes, which is further evidence of the important role it played in educating its members.

Negro History Week, promoted by Carter G. Woodson, was first observed in Williamsburg in February 1926. James City County Training School offered the venue for orations, musical concerts, and plays in which black students portrayed scenes and personalities from African-American life and history.

In many localities including Williamsburg, blacks more enthusiastically embraced public education than did whites. Booker T. Washington wrote movingly that freed persons' desire for education "was a whole race trying to go to school. Few were too young, and none too old, to make the attempt to learn." These same sentiments echoed in the words of a James City County man in 1871 when he said, "great excitement prevails among the colored race. Young and old, little and big, seem eager to obtain knowledge." In a related development, a number of white northern industrialists established foundations that made grants to southern school systems (including Williamsburg's) to help them build or improve schools for blacks.

On 27 January 1871, the Williamsburg school board appointed its first teacher. James W. Edloe was to teach at the "colored school of this City, no other person having regularly applied." In December 1874, the school board hired Miss M. A. Bright to be the assistant teacher for the black school. She taught the girls and Edloe taught the boys. At first, salaries of not more than twenty-five dollars a month were distributed equally among Edloe and two teachers appointed for the white school; but within a year, white teachers took home double what the black teachers did.

For a number of years after public education got going in Williamsburg, the school board rented spaces in private homes or other buildings for students of both races. These rooms were often crowded, inadequately lit, poorly ventilated, and furnished with makeshift desks. On the first day of public school in Williamsburg–1 February 1871–it is believed Edloe gathered the first class of black students together in just such a room or building. To improve accommodations for black pupils, in 1883 the school board asked Samuel Harris, its only black member, to oversee the transfer of the furniture from the black school to Mt. Ararat Baptist Church on Francis Street. Meanwhile, in 1873 the school board had leased the old Mattey School on the site of the colonial governor's palace for the white school. The next year, the city earmarked $950 for the first new school building in Williamsburg.

As this new building was for black students, the board appointed Samuel Harris to keep tabs on its construction on the north side of Francis Street. The building had a shingled roof painted red, a brick foundation, and two schoolrooms. "School No. 2," as it was designated by the school board, was ready for occupancy in early 1885; and in 1920 the school board

Public School No. 2 for black students. Beginning in 1871, the school board rented various residential spaces for the black school and the white school. School No. 2, completed in 1885, was the first school built from the ground up for either race by the school board. Originally located on Francis St., School No. 2 was moved to Nicholson St. in 1907.

Courtesy, James City County Training School Alumni Association

rented the "Colored Odd Fellows Hall" at Nicholson and Botetourt streets, probably for temporary additional space for the expanding black student population.

The Supreme Court ruled in 1896 that "separate but equal" facilities, including schools, for blacks and whites were constitutional. Southern school districts were chronically short of money, and black schools usually felt the pinch first. Disparities that had existed all along persisted in the 1920s and 1930s. For instance, in 1931, the operating expenses for the James City County Training School and the new, white Matthew Whaley School stood at about $1,500 and $5,470 respectively.

Before the turn of the century, the black community had formed the Williamsburg School Improvement League to make up some of the difference. In 1906, the school board withdrew housekeeping services from the black school, so teachers and students took on the tasks. Black parents provided more than half the cost of a sewing machine for the school, half of the funds for a school library, and half the rental price when additional space was needed in 1914. That same year, school board members agreed to have the school interior painted, but only if the school bought the paint. At another time, black parents bought a vehicle and paid $1.35 per month to transport their children from the Grove area to school in Williamsburg.

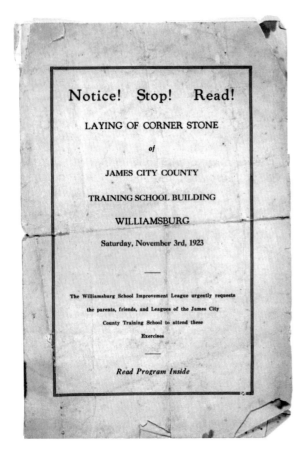

Events such as laying the cornerstone for the James City County Training School on 3 November 1923 were important community milestones for black residents. Grants from the Rosenwald, Sclater, and Jeanes Funds as well as the General Education Board helped fund the new school and its operations.

Courtesy, John D. Rockefeller, Jr., Library, Colonial Williamsburg Foundation

In early 1919, the League kept up the pressure for better facilities by asking the school board to authorize a new building for the black students. In a letter to the superintendent of schools, the League stated that the black community was "ready to ra[i]se their portion of the money needed." In 1922 Andrew Jones and W. H. Hayes (principal of School No. 2) of the "colored school League" came before the school board to pledge $2,500 in addition to the $1,200 already in hand and to put forward their own plans for a new school.

Finally, in 1924, the new school, named the James City County Training School, opened its doors. Standing on the northeast corner at the intersection of Nicholson and Botetourt streets, the James City County Training School was Williamsburg's first African-American high school, and it also housed the lower grades. In the training school tradition, the curriculum included agricultural courses particularly helpful to students from rural areas and professional training for high schoolers who wanted to meet state qualifications in order to become teachers themselves. An early beneficiary of the Rockefeller, Rosenwald, Slater, and Jeanes foundations, the James City County Training School served the African-American school population in the Williamsburg area for about sixteen years.

A small but strong group of black professionals—particularly ministers and teachers—was in evidence in Williamsburg soon after the Civil War. In the 1870s, there had been relatively few educated African Americans in Virginia to fill teaching positions in local schools, but by 1890 there were nearly as many black teachers as white in Williamsburg and James City County. Black-owned businesses gained a foothold in late nineteenth-century Williamsburg as well: a blacksmith shop and a butcher shop patronized by both races, Samuel Harris' "Cheap Store," Theodore Harris' vaudeville

The James City County Training School (1924-1940) accepted students from Williamsburg and nearby districts of James City and York Counties. The school included all the elementary grades as well as Williamsburg's first high-school classes for African-American students. Today a historical marker near the corner at Nicholson and Botetourt streets commemorates this important school.

Courtesy, John D. Rockefeller, Jr., Library, Colonial Williamsburg Foundation

*Training School
graduating class of 1937.*

Courtesy, John D. Rockefeller, Jr.,
Library, Colonial Williamsburg
Foundation

theater, the Crump Restaurant, John Cary's barbershop, Crutchfield barber shop and teahouse, Hitchens Store, and Skinner's Tavern were among the most notable. Julia Oxrieder has concluded that an 1897 observer was probably right when he reported that "Mr. Samuel Harris, the well-known merchant of Williamsburg, Virginia, does probably the largest business of its kind of any colored man in the United States." In 1901, when the business license was based on total sales, fifty of the fifty-seven licenses issued in Williamsburg that year cost five dollars or less. Harris paid more than anyone - $203!

While black professionals in Williamsburg during the first quarter of the twentieth century continued to be dominated by ministers and public school teachers, there were a number of nurses added to their ranks. African-American shopkeepers continued to do business on Duke of Gloucester Street: at the time Rockefeller and Goodwin were imagining a restored colonial town in the late 1920s, Robert Smith had a meat market on Duke of Gloucester

Samuel Harris' Cheap Store on Duke of Gloucester St. (where the restored 18th-century Davidson Shop is today) catered to black and white residents. Harris carried a wide variety of merchandise at the store, supplied coal to local residents and schools, and invested in local real estate.

Courtesy, Colonial Williamsburg Foundation

Street, and a "colored restaurant" was operating there. George Tabb opened the first black funeral parlor in Williamsburg, located on York Street, and the Tabb family's disposal company remained an important commercial service for decades.

More commonly, however, black men found work as drivers or porters for white shopkeepers, as day laborers (some on nearby farms), or as cooks, janitors, waiters, porters, and butlers in private homes and local hotels. Both the black and white public schools hired black men to keep the buildings clean, while black women worked in private homes. Work outside white private homes was found primarily at the College of William and Mary and at Eastern State Hospital where blacks cooked, served food, hauled goods, ran errands, tended the grounds, washed clothes, or cleaned up. Henry Billups was bell ringer and janitor at the college for more than thirty years. African-American tenant farmers brought produce into town for sale. Black laborers and hammer men found jobs laying track in the Williamsburg area for the C & O Railroad in 1881, and they took jobs as porters and laborers once it was completed. The steady demand for drivers and haulers created regular economic opportunity as well.

In the Jim Crow era, African Americans in Williamsburg formed community groups to socialize, perform community service, and provide financial aid. They met in private homes, black churches, or in the Colored Odd Fellows Hall at Nicholson and Botetourt streets, in an area of town where a number of African Americans lived. Black women especially belonged to organizations formed to aid their churches or communities. Two such groups were the Willing Workers Club at First Baptist Church and a King's Daughters circle founded in 1924 with Clara Baker as president. As much for necessity as social reasons, black men belonged to the Odd Fellows or Good Samaritan benevolent societies. As Virginia further restricted African-American rights–before the 1902 Constitution 192 black men were registered, but only

Odd Fellows Hall. The Commonwealth's commitment to the civil rights won by black Virginians after the Civil War began to wane as the 19th-c. wore on. Self-governing African-American benevolent organizations, such as the Odd Fellows and the Good Samaritans in Williamsburg, stepped in to support black businessmen and to offer members an early form of insurance against illness and death. About 1920, the school board rented the Samaritan Odd Fellows Hall to augment the classroom space at the Training School.

Courtesy, Colonial Williamsburg Foundation

thirty-six after–these societies provided services such as business and personal support, as well as financial and insurance needs not available elsewhere.

Churches in Williamsburg provided perhaps the most important centers of community support for blacks in Williamsburg. First Baptist, Union Baptist, and Mt. Ararat Baptist and other churches nourished strong family life, sometimes suspending members who breached marriage vows or had children out of wedlock. In these churches, several generations attended services together, which further strengthened black families and the community. At First Baptist, members honed other skills as well when dues paying members of the congregation voted on church affairs and represented their church at state and national church conventions.

Meanwhile, the local development that had already brought major changes to the Williamsburg community at large was to have profound consequences for public education, particularly black education. John D. Rockefeller, Jr.'s 1926 decision to carry out the vision of the Rev. W. A. R. Goodwin to restore Williamsburg to its eighteenth-century appearance was well on the way to becoming a reality by the end of the decade.

At that time, a number of African-American and white households in

At the West End Market owned by the Hitchens family, black and white clerks and butchers worked side by side in the 1930s. The shop was on the corner of Boundary and Prince George streets. Rear: Clifton Gardner, James Randall, & Wilbur Wells. Front: [unknown] & Jefferson D. Bull.

Courtesy, Gardner Family

Williamsburg were in close proximity along Duke of Gloucester, York, and Nassau streets, and in an area known as Buttermilk Hill near the old palace grounds. There were eleven black households living side-by-side with eighty-six white households on the main street, Market Square, Palace Green, and the capitol grounds. Five black families and thirty-three white households were neighbors on Francis Street. Both African-American and white families lived on Prince George, Henry, Nassau, and York streets.

Black and white Williamsburgers may have been neighbors, but African-American voices were not among those heard at the Williamsburg town meeting in 1928, when white citizens voted in favor of Goodwin's project. The *Journal and Guide*, an African American newspaper published in Norfolk, did not make reference to the restoration until two years later. People who owned lots and houses in the area of Williamsburg targeted for historical development stood to make money on the sale of their holdings to the restoration, but black property owners dealt warily with agents who sought to purchase their properties. The last black business on Duke of Gloucester Street, the Banks Café owned by a Newport News woman, was removed in 1930.

Relocating displaced residents, black and white, established racially segregated residential areas along lines unknown in pre-restoration days—as the map on the inside of the dust jacket of this volume demonstrates. Blacks were funneled into specific areas northeast of town on Scotland Street and south of Francis Street on Henry Street. Others moved to the vicinity of Nicholson and Botetourt streets. A group of white-painted houses, built in that part of town

African-Americans were quick to recognize advantages the Restoration had to offer them. Many found steady work, albeit in traditional roles reserved to blacks in the south, such as housekeepers, bell hops, laborers, waiters, and groundskeepers. With the support of the Restoration, blacks also pressed for better educational facilities. Here, John D. Rockefeller, Jr. and the Rev. W. A. R. Goodwin confer with Alec Pleasant, who interpreted the powder magazine in the early 20th c. after the APVA purchased the structure. He was also sexton at Bruton Parish Church for a time.

Courtesy, Colonial Williamsburg Foundation.

for some of the blacks who sold their properties to Colonial Williamsburg, came to be known as "white city."

Churches, too, came under some pressure to make way for the Restoration. Mt. Ararat on Francis Street (wood-framed, clapboard) was declared a firetrap in late 1933 (see p. 115). The congregation moved to Franklin Street, where it still meets today. Union Baptist held services in a building on Duke of Gloucester Street until it, too, moved to the Franklin Street area. First Baptist Church continued to meet in the brick church on Nassau Street (see p. 113) just outside the historic area until 1955. Under an agreement with Colonial Williamsburg, the congregation transferred operations to a new brick church on Scotland Street; and Colonial Williamsburg razed the historically important nineteenth-century church shortly thereafter.

Ironically, the process of removing inappropriate buildings and the excavation of historical sites, many of them once black-owned, provided jobs for local blacks. Many worked as day laborers, but others held

Mother and daughter Nannie Ashby Frasier and Lydia Frasier on Nicholson St. up the hill from the old Public Gaol (1920s).

Courtesy, Gardner Family

a variety of jobs. For example, Levi Wallace helped excavate the Governor's Palace site, and William Baker, local handyman and sexton at Bruton Parish Church, also served as a guide at the church for many years. Between 1927 and 1931, although Lydia Frasier Gardner was a guide at the George Wythe house, she eventually lost her job to a white woman, after which she became a maid for the foundation. From 1939 to 1941, James Payne and his family lived in the upper floor of the kitchen building of the Wythe house; and at the behest of Colonial Williamsburg, the family wore colonial costumes when at home and tended a cow, a few chickens, and a garden on the grounds to give the house a more colonial look.

Music in the African-American community of Williamsburg was a source of entertainment and expression in the 1930s, '40s, '50s and beyond. It was also a valuable asset. In 1938 William King of James City County Training School wrote to Colonial Williamsburg offering the services of the Colonial Glee Club. By the 1940s, Levi Stephens, Lisbon Gerst, Clifton Gardner, and Fred Epps made up the Williamsburg Quartet, a black vocal group that sang at the Williamsburg Inn every Sunday evening. They were popular entertainment for local bigwigs and visitors to Williamsburg, including heads of state and other notables. The Williamsburg Quintet (Stephens, Gerst, and Fred Epps from the Quartet with Archie Rucker, and Alfred Epps) (see p. 242) sang in the lounge at the Williamsburg Lodge until 1944 and made a commemorative record album for Colonial Williamsburg in 1950.

In the 1930s, blacks in Williamsburg began taking a more public stand against the injustices of the times. William H. Hayes, principal of the Training School, wrote to the NAACP about starting a local chapter but did not pursue the issue. The *Journal and Guide* reported that blacks were barred from Jamestown Island. In Williamsburg, Rockefeller did not exclude African-American visitors, but Foundation policy rarely tested the racial mores of the town: African Americans were not encouraged to visit the historic site or stay in the Williamsburg Inn. Over time, however, black school administrators in town arranged for groups of their students to tour Colonial Williamsburg.

The Training School was not only bursting at the seams by the late 1930s but badly in need of repair. A movement toward an improved educational plan for their children was once again afoot in the black community, and the usefulness of the Restoration in attaining that goal was not lost on the twenty-three percent of Williamsburg's population that was African-American. Addressing themselves to the Williamsburg Holding Corporation in 1937, the James City County Training School League not only pushed for improved educational and community facilities, but pointedly justified their demands with a history lesson: "We believe you appreciate the contributions colored people have made to Virginia's historical progress and prestige." The league's vision was clear:

> (1) colored people were among the earliest settlers in this area, (2) we have helped to build up and to preserve the Nation and stand willing to sacrifice again and again to uphold law, order, and peace, and (3) we desire our sections of these communities, wherever they might be, to harmonize with the Restoration Movement.

The league had in mind a central school facility that would house students from the first grade through high school; they also envisioned the school as a community center. Although the league's letter was not acknowledged by either the Restoration or the school board, school officials soon developed a plan for a new school that incorporated several of the league's ideas. Prominent educator Jackson Davis observed that it was "the best plan of Negro education which has ever been developed in this country up to the present time; and, if the program should be put into effect, it would be the only place in the country to have such a program." More than $245,000 from the Public Works Administration, the Virginia State Literary Fund, the sale of the Training School property, a city bond issue, and the Rockefeller family made the state-of-the-art Bruton Heights School a reality. Local newspapers carried the story on 16 December 1938, reporting that Abby Aldrich Rockefeller had personally contributed $50,000 toward the proposed black school. True to form, the African-American community promised to raise about a thousand dollars towards the cost of landscaping.

Land belonging to John D. Rockefeller, Jr., on York Street between the city limits and Quarterpath Road looked like a good location for the new school until white residents of the area objected. A parcel of land in an area called Bruton Heights north of the railroad tracks provided a suitable alternative. Williamsburg Restoration, Inc., bought the old Training School for $10,000 and deeded the thirty-acre Bruton Heights site to the school board. Having calmed the objections of white residents along Capitol Landing Road whose property would back up to school grounds, local officials broke ground for the school on 15 December 1938.

While the new school was under construction, board members set about assembling a faculty. On the recommendation of the Virginia Department of Education, in June 1939 the school board approved H. D. Carpenter as principal. Some members of the black community wanted R. L. Rice, principal of the Training School, to move over to Bruton. His supporters described Rice as a Christian leader "who is greatly qualified to guide our youth's interests" and praised his years of hard work to "build a fortress of interest that can not easily be torn down." Rice, however, resigned in August 1940 to become principal of the Gloucester County Training School.

In addition to the Training School, there were several black elementary schools in James City County: Chickahominy, Oak Grove, Centerville, Mount Pleasant, and Croaker were in operation when Bruton Heights opened. Some of these traced their beginnings to black church schools where children had been taught to read the Bible. As planned, elementary students from these schools transferred to Bruton Heights. Classes began in September 1940.

Bruton Heights offered instruction in both academic subjects and vocational training. Many parents insisted that their children receive academic training comparable to what white students got at Matthew Whaley; others recognized the practicalities of vocational and agricultural training. By the early 1950s, stricter academic standards and a greater emphasis on college preparatory courses was the norm at Bruton Heights. In spite of limited expectations from

On 25 May 1941, three hundred people, black and white, attended the dedication ceremony for the $245,000 Bruton Heights School. This 1960s photograph shows additions to the north and south sides of the main building.

Courtesy, Colonial Williamsburg Foundation

One of three buildings in the original Bruton Heights complex, the Home Economics cottage contained a living room, dining room, kitchen, and bedroom on the ground floor and classrooms and demonstration kitchen and laundry on a lower level. The restored cottage, now part of the Colonial Williamsburg Bruton Heights School Education Center, is a residence for visiting scholars.

Courtesy, John D. Rockefeller, Jr., Library, Colonial Williamsburg Foundation

Bruton Heights School faculty, ca. 1949. As well as being educators, teachers were role models for their students.

Courtesy, Colonial Williamsburg Foundation

the white community, a number of Bruton Heights graduates went on to become educators, accountants, neurosurgeons, and lawyers. Even for those who did not go on to college themselves, Bruton Heights instilled self-reliance and a determination to see their own children educated.

The comprehensive design of the program at Bruton Heights included plans for the complex to be an African-American community center. Night classes for adults soon got under way. In September 1940 the movie, *The Howards of Virginia*, partly filmed in Williamsburg, was screened in the school auditorium in conjunction with the film's regular run at the segregated Williamsburg Theatre. By early 1941 the building was open one night a week for group meetings; and the library, shops, clinic and gymnasium were widely used.

The full recreational potential of Bruton Heights was yet to be realized, however. For one thing, the black community had anticipated a full-fledged, up-to-date movie theater in Bruton Heights. Even the Rockefellers, during their December 1940 visit to the school, had "expressed their hope that permanent moving picture equipment would be installed very soon." What they got fell far short of expectations. The lightweight movie projector and small speakers used to show *The Howards of Virginia* and other films through

Students prepared and served meals in the domestic setting of the Home Economics cottage. Parents (as in this picture) and school board members were invited guests.

Courtesy, John D. Rockefeller, Jr., Library, Colonial Williamsburg Foundation

the Spring of 1941 made for poor picture and sound quality in the large school auditorium setting. Neither did movie patrons want to see films that were months or years old when they knew that recently released movies were being shown in black theaters in Newport News and Richmond.

Under pressure from the black community and the Rockefellers, the school board finally installed theater-grade

The first graduating class of Bruton Heights (1941).

Courtesy, John D. Rockefeller, Jr., Library, Colonial Williamsburg Foundation

Designed to be not only a school but also a community center, Bruton Heights provided space for groups and club meetings and included a movie theater. The black community also used the library, attended night classes for adults, and could get treatment in the medical and dental clinic.

Courtesy, John D. Rockefeller, Jr., Library, Colonial Williamsburg Foundation

35mm equipment and large speakers, the projection booth rigged for fire emergencies, and the auditorium better lit for the safety of moviegoers. The first public showing was on 19 September 1941. After that, the regular schedule called for movies on Friday and Saturday evenings. Admission was twenty cents for adults and ten cents for children.

In the first two months, bookings included *The Sea Wolf, The Road to Zanzibar, Meet John Doe, I Wanted Wings, Ziegfeld Girl, Billy the Kid, A Woman's Face,* and *Caught in the Draft.* By popular demand, movies with African-American casts, such as Paul Robeson's *The Tunnel* and *I Am Guilty,* played at the school. By November, there were three showings per week, playing to several hundred patrons each.

After the United States entered World War II, the selective service periodically reduced the teacher corps at both Bruton Heights and Matthew Whaley, but shop teachers who could "carry on defense classes for adults in a mechanical field" sometimes got deferrals. With defense programs going into high gear, skilled workers were in demand, but defense contractors resisted hiring African Americans, prompting protests from numerous black organizations. In March 1941, the State Defense Council of Virginia, chaired by Dr. Douglas S. Freeman, called upon defense contractors, trade unions, and employers not to make a mockery of democracy by refusing to hire African-American workers. At about the same time, Hampton Institute announced that the American Federation of Labor had agreed to charter the "first Negro local in Virginia of the Carpenters and Joiners' Union." With more jobs opening up to African Americans, enrollment at Bruton Heights School began to fall off as students in the upper grades left school to find work in the defense industry.

On 6 October 1941 superintendent of schools Rawls Byrd reported to the school board that "there is one battalion of Negroes at Fort Eustis and the question of making available some of the facilities at Bruton Heights to this group of men had been brought to him." Soon, large numbers of black soldiers joined local movie patrons at Bruton Heights, which continued throughout the war years. It was not until March 1943 that the question of using the Bruton Heights gymnasium for a "Negro USO" came up at a school board meeting. Later that month, a special committee of local black citizens proposed that a recreational plan be developed for black sailors at Camp Peary and black soldiers at Fort

Black military personnel stationed near Williamsburg flocked to USO facilities housed at Bruton Heights. In 1943, one hundred sailors attended the first dance. Local residents such as Fred and Fannie Epps also attended USO dances. By 1944 the expanding USO program had its own director and served several thousand people a week.

Courtesy, Colonial Williamsburg Foundation

Eustis, and a dance attended by a hundred sailors from the Naval Mine Depot and Camp Peary was held at the school on Wednesday, March 24.

By April the school was opened to blacks in the military on Tuesdays and Wednesdays between seven and ten in the evenings and Saturday and Sunday afternoons from three o'clock until six. Soldiers and sailors came to dances and informal parties or joined in games, singing, and dramatics. Music for USO dances was usually recorded, but musicians among the servicemen often performed during intermissions. One of the classrooms at the school was outfitted with "comfortable furniture, lounging chairs, and reading tables." By late 1943, black USO activities at Bruton Heights had developed to such an extent that the regional office of the USO had employed Marie Sheppard, a local African-American, as social director. She oversaw the program at the school in conjunction with the local committee of black citizens. Several thousand people attended USO activities at the school every month.

Despite the enormous betterment of African-American life after emancipation, the racial divide in communities like Williamsburg was unmistakable from the late nineteenth century onwards. African Americans had few economic opportunities in Williamsburg and still worked at jobs that required strong backs, long hours, and a willingness to take orders. As elsewhere in the south, black students in Williamsburg did not share equally the resources available for public education as inequities in the segregated schools of Williamsburg were prolonged until the late 1960s. African Americans met these challenges and bore the inequities with dignity; and armed with a rich cultural heritage and growing sense of purpose, they prepared to enter a new era of achievement after World War II.

Selected Sources and Suggested Readings

Byrd, Rawls. *History of Public Schools in Williamsburg* (Williamsburg: 1968).

Ellis, Rex Marshall. "Presenting the Past: Education, Interpretation and the Teaching of Black History at Colonial Williamsburg," Ed. D. dissertation. College of William and Mary, 1989.

Hudson, Carson O., Jr. *Civil War Williamsburg.* (Williamsburg: Colonial Williamsburg Foundation, 1997).

Foster, Andrea Kim. "'They're Turning the Town All Upside Down': The Community Identity of Williamsburg, Virginia Before and After the Reconstruction," Ph.D. dissertation. George Washington Univ., 1993.

McCartney, Martha W. *James City County: Keystone of the Commonwealth*. (Virginia Beach: Donning Co., 1997).

Morgan, Philip D. *Black Education in Williamsburg-James City County, 1619-1984.* (Williamsburg: Williamsburg-James City Co. Public Schools and the Virginia Foundation for the Humanities, 1985).

Morton, Richard L. *The Negro in Virginia Politics, 1865-1902.* (Charlottesville: Univ. of Virginia, 1919).

Oxreider, Julia Woodbridge. *Rich, Black, and Southern: The Harris Family of Williamsburg (and Boston).* (New Church: Miona, 1998).

Pearson, Charles Chilton. *The Readjuster Movement in Virginia.* (New Haven: Yale Univ., 1917).

Rouse, Parke, Jr. *Cows on the Campus: Williamsburg in Bygone Days* (Richmond: Dietz, 1973).

School Board Minutes, City of Williamsburg, 1907-1952, Williamsburg-James City Co. School Board Office.

Trustees of the Free Schools of the City of Williamsburg Minutes, 1870-1907. H. D. Cole Papers, Swem Library Special Collections, College of William and Mary.

Wynes, Charles E. *Race Relations in Virginia, 1870-1902.* (Charlottesville: Univ. of Virginia, 1961).

136

Late 19th-c. snapshots from Drewery Jones' album (see p. 169), which became part of Tom Williams' collection (see p. 229): (top l and bottom middle) the ruins of the two advance buildings of the Governor's Palace (see pp. 95 & 104); (top middle) the powder magazine (see pp. 35 & 41), which in the 19th c. had many uses, including a meeting place for a white Baptist congregation, a warehouse, and a stable; (top rt) Duke of Gloucester St. viewed from the Wren Building; (bottom l) Duke of Gloucester St. viewed from the Wren Building; (bottom l) the Nicholas-Tyler house (no longer standing), where Vice President John Tyler lived; (rt) a butcher slicing ham in winter on Duke of Gloucester St.

Courtesy, Thomas L. Williams archive

Town and Gown Through Three Centuries: William & Mary in the Life of Williamsburg

by: Thaddeus W. Tate, Jr.

"Town and gown" is a familiar phrase that instantly suggests the close relationship that customarily exists between a college or university and its host community. In its derivation, it most likely denoted rivalry or hostility between the people of a town and a faculty and its students, but its usage widened to embrace harmonious relationships as well. The three-century connection between the city of Williamsburg and the College of William and Mary has produced both discord and harmony, although the latter, fortunately, has been the rule. Advantageous as this relationship has been for both, it has been complex and changing.

The decision of the Virginia Assembly in September 1693 to locate the new College of William and Mary "as neer the church now standing in Middle Plantation old fields as convenience will permitt" and its vote a few years later to relocate the capital of the colony from Jamestown to the same area, renamed Williamsburg, were the consequences of well-orchestrated moves that closely linked the city and the college from their very inception. The prime movers were undoubtedly Francis Nicholson, the royal governor, and the Reverend James Blair (see pp. 107 & 152 and color plate 5), the commissary of the bishop of London, which made him the leader of the Anglican clergy of Virginia.

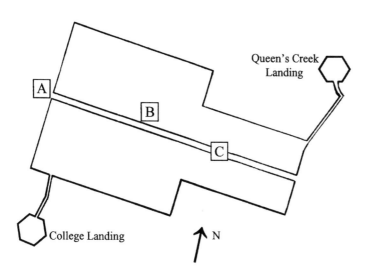

Modern redrawing of the central detail in Theodorick Bland's 1699 survey for the original town site of Williamsburg. Bland's survey included three buildings: the recently built college main building (A); Bruton Parish Church (B); and the proposed capitol (C). It visually represents the manner in which the college and the town were linked from the founding of both. (See color plate 23.)

Courtesy, David F. Morrill

When Blair returned from England bearing the royal charter of 1693 (see p. 108) that created the college, the dual effort gained force. Before the end of the year, Blair moved promptly to purchase from Thomas Ballard land on which William and Mary still stands and by 1695 began to construct the first college building (see p. 29). Moving the capital took a bit longer, but a fire that destroyed the last state house at Jamestown in 1698 made it possible to raise the question at a session of the assembly that convened on 27 April 1699. Within days, on 1 May the governor brought legislators to the college for carefully contrived "Scholastick Exercises," in which five students delivered Latin orations promoting the advantages of education and of bringing the functions of education and government together at Middle Plantation. In proclaiming that "the Colledge will be a great help towards the making of a Town and the Town towards the improving of the Colledge," one young orator set the stage for a successful vote on 7 June. Nicholson's town plan for the new capital added a further symbolic dimension to the relationship by placing the new college building, now nearing completion, and the proposed "Capitoll" in dominant positions at opposite ends of the broad main street that would be named Duke of Gloucester (see pp. 25 & 40 and color plate 9). A union of town and gown in the new city of Williamsburg was now forged.

For its first thirty-five years, from 1694 until 1729, the college struggled to maintain itself, experiencing the destruction of the interior of its original building by fire in 1705, attracting only a small number of students, and falling far short of filling out its full complement of six professors. The college operated only its Grammar School, providing what we would think of today as secondary schooling in the classics. Yet, for a number of reasons William and Mary in these years cemented its relationship with leading citizens of a capital town that also remained small and did not experience its full development until mid-century. For many who lived in or near Williamsburg, the Grammar School emerged as the best choice for educating their sons.

James Blair, who served as president for fifty years, played a central role in bringing town, colony, and college together. Within two years of his arrival in Virginia, the Scottish-born cleric married into the powerful Harrison family, thereby gaining appointment to the Governor's Council and identifying himself ever more closely with the political elite of the colony. The same group of leaders, a number of them Williamsburg residents and others frequent visitors to the capital, also dominated the self-perpetuating Board of Visitors, the governing body of the college. Blair developed additional ties to the local community, especially after becoming rector of prestigious Bruton Parish in 1710. For more than three decades, he remained a prominent figure in the religious, educational, social, and political life of the colony and its capital.

In 1729 President Blair finally achieved a long-sought objective for the college—the completion of its full complement of six professors. This made it possible to offer advanced instruction in moral and natural philosophy, the two main components of the liberal arts in the eighteenth-century, and in divinity. Enrollment also doubled, although seldom exceeding sixty or so for much of the remainder of the colonial period. Most students were still scholars in the Grammar School, but a number began to study with the philosophy professors. None, however, sought the baccalaureate degree, and William and Mary continued to function as a "finishing school" for training a few sons of the élite for future leadership in the affairs of the colony. If a larger number of the students came now from relatively more distant parts of

Virginia, they, too, became an integral part of the local community, some boarding with Williamsburg families and many, despite their youth, regularly patronizing the local taverns.

As long as Blair lived, these changes in the character of the college seemed to enhance the harmony between town and gown. Blair carried through the completion of the colonial campus (the Brafferton, the President's House, and the chapel wing of the original building); the enlarged faculty remained relatively stable; and Sir William Gooch, the resident lieutenant-governor from 1727 until 1749, proved a loyal supporter of an institution that he called "that Seminary of Learning and Ornament to Virginia."

Soon after Blair's death, however, the college entered a troubled period in its history. The faculty, although still few, became more cohesive: mostly British-born and -educated Anglican clerics, they sought to control the affairs of the college and to inculcate in its students the culture of the mother country. The Virginia laymen who dominated the Board of Visitors were equally determined, however, to shape the college in other ways that they thought best for training a small cadre of Virginia leaders. Blair's successors as president, lacking his personal and political authority, were powerless to prevent a seemingly endless struggle that damaged town-and-gown relations but nonetheless testified to the importance that both sides still attached to Williamsburg's college.

Indeed, the struggle in many respects was a microcosm of the larger contest between the colonies and Great Britain that was beginning to unfold in the same years. The college battles spilled into the politics of the colony, as some faculty took the imperial side against that taken by Virginians in disputes such as the Parsons' Cause (a fight over the salaries paid Anglican clergy). The central issues, however, concerned the college itself. The visitors sought to establish their complete authority to hire and fire faculty, enforce rules of discipline for students, and alter the course of study to lessen the emphasis on the classics and institute more practical courses— surveying, for example, in place of pure mathematics. The faculty held out for autonomy and the traditional curriculum they had studied in Britain and appealed to imperial and church authorities for support.

The fight was, moreover, thoroughly public. Both sides published heated essays in the *Virginia Gazette* and in pamphlets issued by Williamsburg printers. In many of them, faculty members bore the brunt of biting satire. During a protracted dispute in 1756 and 1757, the visitors fired four of the five members of the faculty, sparing only the inconsequential Indian master. In 1760 Jacob Rowe, one of the masters who had been appointed as a replacement and who had already been censured for public drunkenness and "other flagrant improprieties," led the college students in a fight with town apprentices. When two Williamsburg citizens sought to intervene, Rowe held a pistol to the breast of one of them, who turned out to be none other than Peyton Randolph, the attorney general of the colony, a member and former rector of the Board of Visitors, and longtime college representative in the House of Burgesses. Rowe's discharge was not long in coming.

Although there is some indication that such battles between town boys and students were not uncommon, the more normal contest between their elders was verbal. Yet, it took its toll on the reputation of the college and at times damaged the town-gown relationship. At the same time, one has to remember that in the very year of Jacob Rowe's escapade Thomas Jefferson entered William and Mary for two years of study under the tutelage of William Small who, Jefferson recalled, "fixed the destinies" of his life. Also, Small's introduction of his young protégé into the small circle of friends whom Governor Francis Fauquier frequently invited to the Governor's Palace for music and intellectual conversation was surely an indication of how accessible even the best of the social and cultural life of the capital might be for an exceptional student.

In the last years before the outbreak of the War for Independence, the struggle between the British faculty and its Virginian governing board eased. The popular next-to-last royal governor, Lord Botetourt, proved so staunch a patron of the institution that at his death in 1770 he was buried with great ceremony in the crypt of the Wren Chapel. John Camm, once the most contentious of the professors, assumed the presidency in 1772, stayed out of public controversies, kept the college solvent, and oversaw the granting of its first baccalaureate degrees.

The college could not, however, escape the Revolution. Two principal faculty members who were loyalists returned to England, while an equally pro-imperial Camm was removed from office in 1777 but permitted to remain in Virginia. The new president was the Reverend James Madison, a cousin of the future U. S. President of the same name. Although an Anglican cleric, he was a Virginian, a graduate of the college, and a strong advocate of independence. Nonetheless, the college suffered from the uncompromising loyalism of its key faculty, the loss of students to military service, and the generally dislocating effects of the war. The popular Madison set out, nonetheless, to rebuild a depleted faculty and "to new-model our College." That effort culminated, in October 1779, in a reorganization implementing some parts of a more sweeping plan that Jefferson had formulated. The statute adopted by the visitors eliminated the Grammar School and instruction in divinity, redirecting the vacated chairs to medicine, law, and modern languages. The most positive outcome was the appointment of George Wythe, Williamsburg's most prominent lawyer and Jefferson's teacher, to the law professorship; but as the war moved ever closer to Williamsburg during 1781, Madison reported that "the College is entirely broke up." He had to close it, leaving the buildings to be used by French forces as a hospital during the Yorktown campaign.

When Madison bravely reopened the college in the fall of 1782, he faced a very different world. A successful war for independence, which had given Williamsburg its greatest moment in history, ironically proved disastrous for both the town, which lost its position as the seat of the government of the new state, and the college, which saw the support it had long received from both private and public sources in Britain and much of what had come from the colonial legislature evaporate.

Both town and college survived, however precariously. Indeed, in their straitened circumstances they needed each other more than ever. From the end of the Revolution to the Civil War, the population of Williamsburg remained small and static, never exceeding fifteen hundred. Despite the critical observations of travelers who often described a town virtually in ruins, a few leading families remained "who were in sufficiently easy circumstances to live well, but not to throw away money in ostentatious expense." Students from these years often remembered the town fondly, finding "not only beauty, but sociability in the ladies." The college likewise remained small, enrolling 140 students in its very best year, but sometimes two dozen or fewer, taught by a faculty of never more than a half dozen. Yet, despite some close calls, it never collapsed. (For more on the ante-bellum period, see pp. 75-78.)

This setting inevitably made for an intimate relationship between town and gown. The faculty, some beloved and popular, some roundly disliked, some having come from far away and some being either alumni or Williamsburg natives, were almost by default central figures in the small community. Students, too, were an integral part of town life, boarding at times with local families, fully participating in the social life of Williamsburg, and sometimes drawing condemnation for their rowdy behavior.

In such a setting, social and political alignments in the town inevitably affected the circumstances of the college; and townspeople, who were well represented on the Board of Visitors, were no less involved in college affairs. At its best, then, the relationship between town and college was both close and congenial, a circumstance best illustrated by the decade from 1836 to 1846 when Thomas Roderick Dew

Lithograph of the college campus, ca. 1840, by Thomas Millington, son of Professor John Millington. The image captures the intimate, rural setting of the campus in the early 19th c.

Courtesy, Swem Library, College of William and Mary

(see p. 77) held the presidency. Dew, from a Tidewater family, became well known for his writings in political economy and in defense of slavery. He and the members of his faculty, which included some of the ablest professors of this era, developed a strong affinity for Williamsburg and were remarkably integrated into its life. Nathaniel Beverley Tucker, professor of law (see p. 75), had returned from Missouri to his hometown and to the college where his father St. George had also taught. The English-born John Millington was an able scientist who built or bought with his own money scientific equipment for the college and who became much beloved by both the adults and children of the town. Recently arrived from Germany, Charles Frederick Ernest Minnegerode served as professor of modern languages and he became virtually a member of the Tucker family, married a Virginia woman, and is sometimes remembered for having introduced the first Christmas tree to Williamsburg. Rob-

Daguerreotype, ca. 1858, of the second college main building. Except for the large columns supporting a balcony over the main entrance, the historic main building of 1709-1716 remained largely unaltered after a century and a half; but a fire on 18 February 1859 left only its outer walls standing.

Courtesy, Swem Library, College of William and Mary

ert Saunders, the professor of mathematics, was from an elite Williamsburg family long active in college affairs.

Such halcyon days were not always the rule. Occasionally, the college faced serious crises, often compounded by differences between the president or faculty and town leaders, or by local disputes that affected college affairs. As soon as the college had reopened in 1782, a division developed between those who wanted to carry forward the 1779 Jeffersonian reforms and those, many of them citizens of Williamsburg, who wished to return to the old

The first college or university humor magazine published in America, The Owl *has most of the perennial qualities of such publications, including jokes at the expense of its surroundings and the faculty. Most of the references are so obscure as to be unrecognizable, but the smugness of the tone is fairly evident. Especially condescending is the attitude toward both blacks and the north. For example, on a page not shown here, a cartoon depicts a starving white northern woman warming her hands before a solitary candle in a drafty shack with icycles hanging from the ceiling, while beside it another cartoon depicts southern blacks dancing and singing merrily. Such attitudes reveal the depth of the sectionalism that by 1854 had divided the country beyond repair. On a positive note, the only dirty joke requires knowledge of Latin to be comprehended.*

Courtesy, Rare Books and Manuscripts, Swem Library, College of William & Mary.

days by reopening the Grammar School and reinstituting instruction in divinity to train Episcopalian clerics. When the reform effort began to weaken and a disenchanted Thomas Jefferson proposed to found his new university in Charlottesville, one wing of defenders of the old college proposed relocating in Richmond, thinking that locating in the capital would revitalize William and Mary and head off its new rival. Others, loyal to Williamsburg, fought removal. The bitter contest reached a climax in the legislative session of late 1824 and early 1825, where

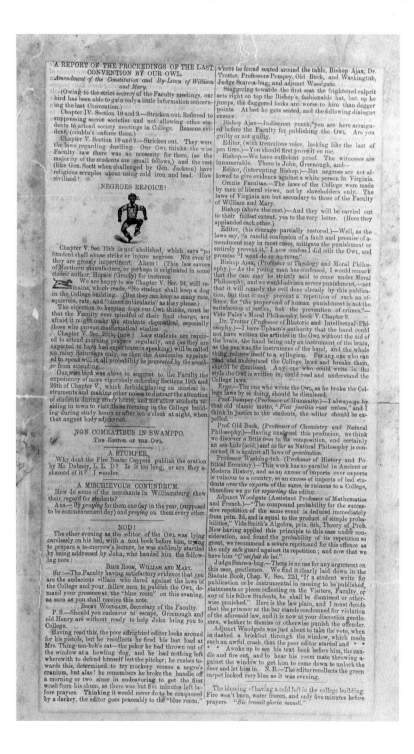

Jefferson's supporters beat down removal to Richmond, saving the day for the new University of Virginia and leaving William and Mary to live or die in Williamsburg.

    The college remained in a precarious condition until the early 1830s, when it recovered and achieved new heights during Dew's presidency only to enter another period of crisis after his death in 1846. For all practical purposes the college simply disintegrated as a result of an increasingly bitter fight between a dominant group of the visitors and the faculty and students.

Drawing by L. J. Cranstone of the President's House and the third main college building of 1859-1862. After the 1859 fire, the main building was rebuilt much altered with Italianate towers. This view from Richmond Road shows the President's House and dependencies in the foreground.

Courtesy, John D. Rockefeller, Jr., Library, Colonial Williamsburg Foundation

    The board determined to establish its control by forcing the appointment to the faculty of a Williamsburg native, Archibald Peachy. Questioning Peachy's qualifications, all but one of the professors and nearly all their students rallied in opposition behind Robert Saunders, a long-time faculty member who had recently been narrowly elected president. The Peachy faction won out, but its victory was Pyrrhic. They had driven away or dismissed all but one of the professors; alienated a majority of the students (who had protested in noisy demonstrations and by wrapping the statue of Lord Botetourt in black); and, by branding some of the departing faculty as "damned foreigners," given the appearance of a takeover of William and Mary by the more provincial of Williamsburg's citizens.

Italianate fourth main college building, flanked by the Brafferton on the left and the President's House on the right. This drawing by David Henderson, a Confederate soldier, was done in 1862 before Union troops burned down the main building in September.

Courtesy, Virginia Historical Society

Somehow, William and Mary, as had happened so often in the past, struggled back for a few years only to face a new threat in 1859, when on 8 February the Main Building—today's Wren Building—was gutted by fire. The disaster confirmed, however, an enduring bond between college and town. New suggestions of moving elsewhere were resisted and townspeople and other friends rallied to keep the college open and to rebuild its central structure rapidly, albeit in an Italianate style that bore no resemblance to its colonial predecessor.

The fire was a prelude to an even more wrenching dislocation by the outbreak of the Civil War two years later: the college closed as most of its students left to join the Confederate forces, and then a long occupation of Williamsburg by Union forces began (see color plate 18). A briefly successful Confederate attack on the town in September 1862 so enraged and humiliated one of the Union regiments that soldiers burned the main building, once again leaving it in ruins (see p. 102).

By 1869 a fourth version of the Wren Building was in place, but its completion hardly signalled a successful renewal of the college. Finances were shakier than ever and recruitment of students able to pay their way, difficult. President Benjamin S. Ewell, one of the heroic figures in the history of William and Mary, kept it open from 1865 to 1881, but with depleted enrollment and few resources. Without formally suspending operations, he nevertheless presided from then until 1888 over an institution without students while he struggled to find private, state, and federal funds.

As had so often been the case, these difficulties only strengthened the determination by all to keep William and May in its historical location as an integral part of Williamsburg. Numerous new proposals for relocation within Virginia met resistance, as did one effort to merge it with the Episcopalian University of the South in Sewanee, Tennessee. The commitment to Williamsburg was further confirmed when, in the search for funds, college officials discovered that Mary Whaley's bequest in 1741 for support of education in Bruton Parish in memory of her young son, Mattey, had lain untouched in England for more than a century. The college was able to draw on the proceeds for something over $8,000 in return for accepting some of the poorest boys of the town into the Grammar School and constructing a school building.

Precarious as conditions were after the Civil War, the small group of students who studied there in the late 1860s and the 1870s have left an unusually rich record of their happy memories of the experience of boarding at the Tucker and Wythe houses, enjoying a rich social life that did not always exclude drinking and card playing, and engaging in a round of student pranks that included moving outhouses decorated with the names of local doctors and lawyers to the middle of the street. One student later recalled that "there was no town-gown hostility; for town and gown were one and not separate bodies."

Students in the college library, late 19th c. When the college reopened after the Civil War, the library was housed at the rear of the chapel wing of the fourth main building.

Courtesy, Swem Library, College of William and Mary

In 1888 Ewell secured a grant from the state legislature, which enabled the college to reopen. In return, it agreed to undertake the training of white male teachers for Virginia schools. Relocation was no longer a threat. Yet, in undertaking to perform a statewide educational service and in agreeing that the governor would appoint half of the Board of Visitors, the college was moving a few steps away from the close linkage with the town that had so shaped its nineteenth-century history.

That trend continued after Ewell retired and Lyon G. Tyler, son of U. S. president John Tyler, succeeded him. Tyler carried through the considerable remaking of William and Mary that had been foreshadowed in the state grant. Enrollment climbed to an average of around two hundred before the outbreak of World War I. If the total seems tiny by today's standards, it was a remarkable increase, and enough to make students a far more visible presence in the small town, especially since many came from across the state and even a few from other states. The college also sought to reinvigorate its traditional collegiate program at the same time that it instituted teacher training. In 1906 William and Mary became a full-fledged state institution with a Board of Visitors appointed by the governor. The opening of the college to women students followed in 1919, further increasing the geographical diversity of the enrollment as women students from across Virginia were attracted to the only state-supported coeducational institution.

William and Mary had not altogether outgrown its Williamsburg setting, however. The eight new buildings constructed in the Tyler administration were clustered near the three original buildings or else just across Jamestown Road, squarely in the center of town. The setting was sufficiently bucolic that the visitors asked Tyler to cease allowing his horse and cow to graze freely across the campus. Moreover, the first faculty that Tyler assembled, known in college tradition as "the Seven Wise Men," were all Virginians, and all but one settled into the local community and spent the remainder of their careers at William and Mary.

This 1910 photograph, with unpaved town streets in the foreground, indicates that although William & Mary had begun its 20th-c. revival, it was still a small college in a small town.

Courtesy, John D. Rockefeller, Jr., Library, Colonial Williamsburg Foundation

The "Seven Wise Men." In the first years after the college reopened in 1888, President Tyler, who also taught, brought six faculty members to the campus. The group's long tenure and long residence in Williamsburg created perhaps the closest union of town and gown in the long history of the college.

From left to right: standing–Hugh S. Bird, professor of pedagogy; Thomas Jefferson Stubbs, professor of mathematics; and Charles Edward Bishop, professor of Greek, French, and German. Seated–the Reverend Lyman B. Wharton, professor of Latin; Lyon Gardiner Tyler, college president; Van Franklin Garrett, professor of natural science; and John Lesslie Hall, professor of English and history.

Courtesy, Swem Library, College of William and Mary

Only one major town-gown dispute in these years is recorded. It arose in 1894. After the town had created a public school, it wished to take over the old Mattey school, whereas the college, having upgraded it as the Matthew Whaley Model and Practice School (see p. 160), sought to keep it for training its growing number of student teachers. It took twenty-five years and the threat of litigation for the college and the school board finally to agree, in 1919, that the city would operate the entire school system and receive qualified William and Mary students as teacher trainees. The college, even as it underwent a significant transformation, retained a central place in the life of Williamsburg.

The retirement of Tyler and the accession of Julian A. C. Chandler to the presidency on 1 July 1919 was, as a recent history of William and Mary has aptly noted, "probably as meaningful a date as any to mark the beginning of the emergence of the modern College." At the end of Chandler's fifteen-year administration, the college had experienced increases in student enrollment from 333 in his first year to a peak of 1,682 in 1931-1932 in faculty from twelve to seventy-eight, and in physical plant by the addition of some ten major new buildings and the enlargement of several others.

The restoration of the Wren Building, 1928-1931. The restoration of 18th-c. Williamsburg, including the original college buildings, signaled a key transformation in both the town and the college. Here the main building, now officially named the "Sir Christopher Wren Building," is undergoing restoration to the 1709-1716 structure that would make it a centerpiece of that transformation.

Courtesy, John D. Rockefeller, Jr., Library, Colonial Williamsburg Foundation

Although by today's standards William and Mary remained relatively small, it was scarcely an intimate college whose two or three hundred students and dozen or so faculty fitted with complete comfort into the small community. Growth had changed the college in other ways as well. By 1931 the student body was almost half female and approaching forty percent out-of-state—both categories passed fifty percent mark before the end of the decade. Chandler had also instituted an ambitious expansion of curriculum and educational mission that emphasized vocational and technical training and off-campus extension programs both in Richmond and throughout the Tidewater region. While promising to maintain strength in the traditional liberal arts, he also envisioned a range of service functions that would establish a strong position for the college across the state.

The Williamsburg campus remained, however, essentially residential. Strict regulation of student life limited the impact of a larger and more diverse group of undergraduates on the placid ways of the town. No student could keep an automobile; and parietal rules for women limited social hours and absence from their dormitories, forbade their leaving the campus alone after dinner, and required permission for a whole range of activities. Sororities now took their place alongside men's fraternities, and much of the social life of students took place on campus: although "shimmying, cheek-dancing and all objectionable dancing" were prohibited, chaperoned balls and cotillions became especially popular. Students being students, there was occasional unrest, the most spectacular episode taking place in April 1932, when a group of freshmen, thwarted by a student informer in their plan to rush into the Williamsburg Theater, rioted in an effort to catch their betrayer. In the process they knocked down the dean of men, William T. Hodges, breaking his glasses. They then staged a strike in protest against the punishment of four of their number, who had been suspended and ordered to leave town.

The Chandler presidency saw, too, a development that perhaps transformed both Williamsburg and the college more profoundly than anything that had happened since the Revolution—the restoration of the eighteenth-century town with the backing of John D.

Rockefeller, Jr. The events that led to Rockefeller's decision scarcely require retelling, but it was the Reverend W. A. R. Goodwin, acting in his capacity as director of a college endowment campaign, who opened up the initial contacts with the philanthropist and who succeeded in winning his backing for the Williamsburg restoration. In a recent essay, former President Davis Y. Paschall has presented an important body of evidence that demonstrates the vital role that Goodwin, J. A. C. Chandler, and others at the college played in bringing about the restoration. Once the plans for the restoration became public in 1928, work on the three colonial buildings of the college became one of the first priorities, and the Board of Visitors formally accepted the restored buildings and adjacent grounds on 28 December 1932.

At the height of the Great Depression with limited state funding even further reduced, the college had hardly escaped its traditionally dire financial straits. Yet the attractiveness of the historic campus and its strategic position as one focus of the burgeoning efforts to restore the eighteenth-century town gave William and Mary a wider visibility. It opened the way as well for a vigorous reassertion of its colonial traditions; and while the restoration did not and could not of itself provide a national reputation for William and Mary, if a young student orator could predict in 1699 that the College would make the town, one might conceivably have turned that equation on its head in 1932.

20 October 1934 was a double event: the opening of the restored Duke of Gloucester Street and the inauguration of John S. Bryan as the president of William & Mary. At the inauguration, Roosevelt was honored with a doctorate in law.

Courtesy, John D. Rockefeller, Jr., Library, Colonial Williamsburg Foundation

The president who took office in 1934, John Stewart Bryan, was unusually well qualified to reemphasize the mission of William and Mary as a liberal arts college and temper its recent emphasis on vocational and technical education. A Virginian, Richmond newspaper executive, and man of urbanity, Bryan was the candidate of those who had that goal. He moved promptly to seek further improvement of the faculty, curriculum reform, and higher academic standards. He brought as well a new sense of style to more ceremonial and social occasions. To begin with, as Franklin D. Roosevelt had been invited to open the restored Duke of Gloucester Street, the college installed Bryan at the same time and awarded Roosevelt an honor-

This Christmas celebration with President John S. Bryan escorting Abby Aldrich Rockefeller in colonial costume demonstrated his interest in reviving the traditions of the colonial college during the 1930s. One that he revived and that still continues is the Yule Log ceremony.

Courtesy, Swem Library, College of William and Mary

ary degree. Also, Bryan instituted the formal observance of Charter Day and the Yule Log ceremony at the Wren Building, which participants attended in colonial costume–to mention but one of the social occasions that he encouraged. Bryan likewise sought to strengthen academic programs in the fine arts and increase the number of such campus events as concerts, plays, and lectures.

The activities that Bryan encouraged almost certainly offered citizens a richer cultural life than had been available; and men's intercollegiate athletics, which had begun to build under Chandler, now advanced to a higher level with the completion of Cary Field in 1935 and admission in the following year to the Southern Conference, which then included most of the present members of the Atlantic Coast Conference. By the end of the decade the football team won two state titles, and the college had attracted a following among still another group of townspeople. The beginnings of a tourist industry also brought a significant number of students into the local work force. Finally, many of the faculty whom Bryan recruited, not excluding those who came from out of state, remained at the college throughout their careers and often became active participants in the life of the town.

As it headed into the 1940s, both town and college remained small, however much a foundation had been laid for a major transformation of both. For the college, the advent of World War II put such changes in a holding pattern. Male enrollment rapidly declined to the point that by 1944-1945 women constituted almost three-quarters of a reduced civilian student body. From the spring of 1943 to November 1945, however, the college hosted the Navy Training School for chaplains, which enrolled successive eight-week classes of 250, as well as in 1943-1944 a short-lived unit of the Army Specialized Training Program.

Bryan having resigned in April 1942, leadership during the difficult war years fell to a new president, John E. Pomfret, a historian who had been serving as dean at Vanderbilt University. His election marked a second consecutive victory for those who sought to continue an emphasis on building a strong liberal arts institution. After the war ended, Pomfret had some limited success in advancing that effort, but he faced almost insurmountable difficulties. Among them were rapidly growing enrollment as veterans returned to college, inability to rebuild the faculty fully in the face of low salaries and heavy teaching loads, continuing financial problems, and, above all, a major athletic scandal that involved alteration of the grades and credits on the high school and college records of football players. Although Pomfret was not personally involved, this last crisis prompted his resignation in September 1951.

The election of a successor was, in effect, the result of a quickly executed coup by those state politicians, alumni, and board members who were determined to return the college to the course that had been set in the J. A. C. Chandler era. Their choice to carry out the mission was, in fact, the elder Chandler's son, Alvin Duke Chandler, an alumnus, Naval Academy graduate, and retired rear admiral. He determined from the outset to pursue a taut-ship style of management that produced a running and open battle with faculty and students. By stages, he and those who supported him moved toward creation of a vast service institution extend-

The landmark statue of Lord Botetourt, the popular penultimate colonial governor, who is buried under the college chapel, had so deteriorated by 1958 that it was removed from the yard in front of the Wren Building to safe storage. Here, in 1965, the statue is being welcomed back to campus for installation in the new Swem Library (see color plate 21 and pp. 90, 102, 141, & 152).

Courtesy, Archive of Thomas L. Williams

ing from Richmond through Hampton Roads, which by early 1960 culminated in the establishment by law of the Colleges of William and Mary, embracing the Williamsburg campus, the existing divisions in Norfolk and Richmond, and new two-year colleges, Christopher Newport in Newport News and Richard Bland in Petersburg. Surprisingly, the apparent triumph of this expansionist vision proved transitory. In February 1962, by votes of eighty-six to two in the House and thirty-three to three in the Senate, the General Assembly abolished the combined system and created independent state universities in Richmond and Norfolk, leaving to William and Mary its original Williamsburg campus and oversight of the two new two-year branches, one of which, Christopher Newport, later became an independent four-year university. The move also terminated the position Chandler had assumed as head of the colleges, although he remained as the largely honorary chancellor of the original William and Mary. Davis Y. Paschall continued as president of William and Mary, an office he had assumed in August 1960.

In the absence of substantial documentary evidence, it is not easy to explain such a sudden and definitive change; but clearly there was strong pressure from both Richmond and Norfolk to have their own autonomous institutions, which became Virginia Commonwealth and Old Dominion universities. Many, too, especially in Williamsburg and among those associated closely with the college, quickly had come to fear that the 1960 plan would adversely affect the traditional character of William and Mary. Russell Carneal, the member of the House of Delegates who represented Williamsburg, introduced the legislation that dissolved the combined colleges. The close association of town and gown remained intact.

When Chandler's ambitious plans collapsed, William and Mary had not yet fully experienced the more general growth in American higher education that had begun after World War II. Its enrollment, although double its pre-war maximum, still stood at just under 2,500; and although Chandler had projected a major physical expansion of the campus, two new dormitories, the present Phi Beta Kappa Hall, and a new Campus Center were as yet the only major additions. Nor had the establishment of new schools of law and marine science made professional and graduate education as visible a part of the institution as it would soon become. Clearly, many faculty, students, and alumni as well as Williamsburg residents hoped the college might now resume the mission that it had pursued in the 1930s and 1940s as a relatively small undergraduate liberal arts institution. In the decades that followed, however, the college moved in a different direction, experiencing an unprecedented degree of growth and change; and those who spoke for it officially often described it as a university, albeit a "small university." As early as January 1968 such a definition received formal recognition from the Board of Visitors and the State Council of Higher Education.

To trace in full the manner in which the college evolved would require a lengthy discussion. A brief account can at best outline a few key trends and suggest some of their implications for the ongoing relationship of town and gown. Four presidents have held office in the past four decades: Davis Y. Paschall, from 1960 until his retirement in 1971; Thomas A. Graves, Jr., from 1971 to 1985; Paul R. Verkuil, from 1985 to 1991; and the incumbent, Timothy J. Sullivan, since 1992. Three were alumni, but all differed in their backgrounds, styles of leadership, and even priorities for the college. Yet, over these years the course of development of the college displayed a remarkable consistency.

The most apparent change was, of course, in size. Enrollment in 1997-1998 stood at 5,193 undergraduates and 1,343 students in graduate and professional programs—more than double that in 1960, with a comparable increase in faculty. Although the completion of new buildings and extension of the campus west of the Sunken Garden in the Paschall administration was particularly noteworthy, further additions and renovation of older buildings have occurred under each of his successors. Expansion of the four professional schools in law, business, education, and marine science and the development of several graduate programs in arts and sciences account for some of the growth. Yet, undergraduates still number three-quarters of total enrollment, and those outside the college are still likely to perceive it as primarily an undergraduate institution. The frequent description of William and Mary as a small university is, however, undeniably appropriate.

Far from diluting the quality of students, such growth has been accompanied by the emergence of William and Mary with a more prestigious national reputation than it had ever before achieved. Some of the circumstances that made this possible were external to the college itself: a national trend toward a rising number of college applicants that helped to raise admission standards; a similar increase in the output of trained academics that made recruitment of a strong faculty possible despite continued heavy teaching loads and relatively low salaries; and, for much of the 1980s, a marked increase in state funding for public colleges and universities. But the college had to exert itself to capitalize on such opportunities and also had to seek additional private support, including a successful campaign to raise $1,500,000 during the observance of its three hundredth anniversary in 1993. Although its financial situation worsened in the early 1990s because of declining support of higher education by the state, William and Mary has continued to receive high rankings in several national evaluations of colleges and universities. Its highly selective admissions standards and the high percentage of graduates who have been accepted at major professional and graduate schools may, however, be the best measure of its standing.

Because of size, breadth of educational mission, and accountability to the state government, William and Mary could hardly remain the same intimate, "small-town" institution that it had been for all of the nineteenth and half of the twentieth century. Its relationship to the town had inevitably changed as a consequence. But the Williamsburg area itself experienced, what was probably an even more profound and far-reaching transformation. From the first years after World War II, it had rapidly developed as a major national tourist attraction that included the Colonial Williamsburg restoration and nearby historical sites at Yorktown and Jamestown, and now includes Busch Gardens, an amusement theme park.

An increase in population extended, moreover, well beyond the sizeable number of persons needed to staff the facilities that served the vast number of visitors. Despite a new degree of sprawl that tourist-oriented services necessarily produced, many retirees and others not directly connected with the Williamsburg economy also found the Williamsburg area attractive. Since the city extended its boundaries only slightly and did not itself record much population growth, James City and York counties absorbed most of the quadrupling residential population of "Greater Williamsburg." The community, like the college, had become increasingly more diverse and perhaps less local in its outlook. For that reason it is scarcely possible any longer to discern a single set of community expectations for the college. There

*William & Mary's 300th birthday in 1993 was an endless series of special
events and creations. Three historical statues that will enhance the campus for
future generations were set in place during the year. A life-size bronze of
William & Mary's pre-eminent alumnus Thomas Jefferson, a gift from the
University of Virginia, which was founded by Jefferson, was set in place west
of Washington Hall. Sculptor Lloyd Lillie's engaging, informal Jefferson
quickly socialized with students (top rt).*

*Bronze sculptures of the college's first president, Rev. James Blair (rt) and of
notable 18th-c. benefactor Lord Botetourt (top l) were dedicated during
Homecoming in October. Alumni bowed to tradition in doffing their caps to
Botetourt, recreated in bronze by alumnus Gordon Kray ('73), who worked
closely from the original 1772 marble statue preserved in Swem Library
Presented to the college as an alumni gift, the bronze was installed in front of
the Wren Building where the original had stood for more than 180 years. (See
color plate 21 and pp. 90, 102, 141, & 149.)*

*The larger-than-life monument to Rev. James Blair was commissioned by the
college from faculty sculptor Lewis Cohen, whose powerful
image of the college's founding president was installed on a
plaza between Blair and Tyler halls. Blair, dressed in formal
clerical robes, grasps the royal charter he worked so hard to
obtain in 1693. At the conclusion of the tercentenary, Cohen
(l) prepared a model of the statue for presentation by Rector
Jim Brinkley (rt) on behalf of the Board of Visitors to
Martha Hamilton-Phillips, the executive director of the
tercentenary.*

Photo credits:
Botetourt, Blair, & Cohen: Courtesy,
College of William & Mary
Jefferson: Courtesy, William K. Geiger

Thousands of alumni returned to campus for Homecoming 300th, whose 167 events filled five days and included the first Academic Festival, statue dedications, a tercentenary ball, and a historical parade. During a victorious Tribe game marking 100 years of William & Mary football, a commemorative banner in the shape of a star was unveiled (top l). That night, Busch Gardens hosted a party for 15,000, with spectacular fireworks and a ceremonial cake-cutting by Society of the Alumni President, Joseph W. Montgomery (below rt).

The college published a 1,000-page authoritative History of itself, edited by Thaddeus W. Tate, Jr., who presented it (above l) to President Timothy Sullivan. The highlight of the year was Charter Day, when H.R.H. The Prince of Wales, an Honorary Fellow of the college, gave the address. Prince Charles, shown (below rt) with British Ambassador Sir Robin Renwick, received a standing ovation. President Sullivan announced in 1993 that former British Prime Minister Lady Margaret Thatcher would be the new chancellor of the college—the first British citizen since the Revolution to hold the office. Lady Thatcher began her term at Charter Day 1994, where she is shown (below l) with Gov. George Allen, Sullivan, Rector Jim Brinkley, and her predecessor as chancellor, Chief Justice Warren Burger.

are instead a whole series of town-gown relationships—and perhaps some loss of the intimacy that once prevailed between the two.

Such changed circumstances have undoubtedly produced problems and tensions, which are nonetheless probably milder than those of many university towns. One could point to such an obvious example as the additional burden that larger numbers of students—as addicted to the automobile as are most Americans—contribute to already strained parking and traffic in the central parts of the city. A more mobile faculty, who may teach at several institutions in the course of their careers and who face increasing demands on their time for more research and publication, are less likely to become long-term residents who involve themselves closely in the life of the town. Heavier demands by the college community itself on campus facilities likewise reduce their availability to community groups.

On the other hand, one has to remember that, when the relationship of a small college and equally small town was more intense, there were periods of open rancor that have almost no counterpart today. The present relationship between the two is possibly more formalized and institutionalized, but is still vital to both. The location of the college as a fundamental part of the historical setting of Williamsburg continues to help in building its reputation and attracting students. At the same time the existence of the college enhances the appeal of Williamsburg as a residential community. If the city has admirably expanded its own cultural facilities and agencies, college-sponsored programs in art, music, theater, and lectures and its library resources remain an indispensable part of the cultural life of Williamsburg. College expenditures and those of its faculty, students, and staff still make a sizeable contribution to the local economy. The college's Bureau of Business Research, founded in 1958 and ultimately absorbing an older Williamsburg Business Index, provided useful information and services to businesses and governmental agencies locally and statewide. Today, the Crossroads Project begun by President Sullivan in December 1997 brings together local public and private leaders as well as nationally known consultants to create a shared vision of future planning throughout Williamsburg's newest entry corridor, the Rt. 199/Monticello Avenue/Ironbound Road area. Students, too, continue to furnish a significant and capable addition to the local work force, while receiving help in meeting the growing costs of their education.

As Director of Publications for thirty-two years, S. Dean Olson (1938-1999) captured the spirit of the college and its community in numerous award-winning books, magazines, and catalogs. He oversaw many special publications for both William & Mary's Tercentenary in 1993, and the city's in 1999. The college honored him in 1999 with the Algernon Sydney Sullivan Award given to a person who possesses "characteristics of heart, mind, and conduct as evince a spirit of love for and helpfulness to others." Like previous recipients such as Baxter Bell (see pp. 170-171), Dudley Woodbridge (pp. 170-171), and Lois Hornsby (pp. 214 & 243), Dean was recognized for his commitment to public service and his active volunteer work in the community.

Courtesy, College of William & Mary

If we think only in terms of a relationship between the college and the city as one between two institutional entities, however, we risk losing sight of how much individuals remain the ultimate base on which the intersection of town and gown rests. The examples are many. Some go largely unheralded, as, for example, the extent to which William and Mary students perform many hours of volunteer work in a variety of local social service organizations. A recent survey concluded that seventy per cent of undergraduates participated in some kind of volunteer community activity, contributing more than 150,000 hours of service in the 1997-1998 academic year. Other instances of cooperation between the college and local citizens are more visible, as in the case of two flourishing groups that involve local citizens, especially retirees. One, the members of the Christopher Wren Association, receive support and space for a series of voluntary classes from the college and in return contribute many kinds of forms of voluntary assistance to the college. The other, organized at the initiative of college faculty members, sponsors a well-attended weekly town and gown luncheon that provides a useful interchange between the college and the community.

Sometimes the bond between Williamsburg and the college finds expression, too, in unpredictable and utterly spontaneous ways. One striking instance took place on the wintry night of 20 January 1983 when a college dormitory, Jefferson Hall, was largely destroyed by fire. The 185 student residents escaped safely but with the loss of virtually all their possessions. Almost immediately, local residents and merchants, in an effort that the local American Red Cross chapter coordinated, rallied with support that ranged from donations of clothing and provision of temporary housing to substantial gifts of money. Local regulations were also amended to permit the displaced students to occupy a motel that was closed for the season. An editorial in the *Daily Press* commented on the generous support for the displaced students that had come from both "the town and the gown." Its author concluded, "Out of the wreckage of Jefferson Hall has come a new reminder of what this venerable institution is about. It has helped to reawaken the spirit which has permeated Williamsburg and its college since colonial times."

In many ways, then, an institution of higher learning and a community, both of which have been transformed in the past forty years more than at any other time in their history, still benefit from the support that they give one another and from the mutual advantages they derive from their relationship.

On 14 May 1694 the College of Arms in London granted a coat of arms to William & Mary. Since the college had not yet been built, the architecture is reminiscent of ancient universities such as Padua and Oxford. William & Mary was the first American colonial college to receive a coat of arms, and continues to use this as its proud emblem today.

Courtesy, Special Collections, Swem Library,
College of William & Mary

Selected Sources and Suggested Readings

Godson, Susan H., Ludwell H. Johnson, Richard Sherman, Thad W. Tate, and Helen C. Walker. *The College of William and Mary: A History*. 2 vols. (Williamsburg: King and Queen, 1993).

Kale, Wilford. *Hark upon the Gale: An Illustrated History of the College of William and Mary* (Norfolk: Donning, 1985).

Vital Facts: A Chronology of the College of William and Mary (Williamsburg: College of William and Mary, n.d.)

Williamsburg Claims the Amenities of Life, 1880-1920

by: Julia Woodbridge Oxrieder

In April 1913, the Williamsburg City Council failed to appropriate the usual fifty dollars to pay a man to wind the town clock in the tower of Bruton Parish Church. A month later, part of an editorial in the Richmond *Times Dispatch* read,

> No one really believes that this town of twilight and dreams cares for the clock. It has too much sense. It doesn't really care when it gets up, if ever, or when it goes to bed, if never. Everything can be put off until tomorrow, and tomorrow will never come. Belles for whom the relentless passing of time made life miserable can forget their birthdays. Notes can be extended until judgment day.

Such writing caused post-Civil-War Williamsburg to be labeled lazy and sleepy. Nothing could be further from the truth.

To begin with, the continued presence of Eastern State Hospital and the College of William and Mary (except from 1881 to 1888, when financial woes forced it to close) ensured that Williamsburg would remain a place of more than usual activity; and late nineteenth-century Williamsburg also provided a central location for businesses, churches, schools, and society. The needs of the 1,500 inhabitants were met by five blacksmiths, two corn and flour mills, a saw mill, and twenty two general merchants. Four of the merchants were African Americans, including the most prominent merchant of all, Samuel Harris (see page 125); and one notable merchant was a woman–Mrs. W. H. Braithwaite, who operated an undertaking business and a general store after her husband's death.

In the 1890s, the town became even busier when it began to meet the needs of the midwestern farmers who were settling in the area of present-day Norge. These families of Scandinavian descent were lured by land and railroad agents who exaggerated crop production, climate, and healthy environment. They were also attracted by the rural character of Williamsburg, where there were thirty-six principal farmers, not to mention the lesser ones. So important was farming that farm animals wandered about the streets and gardens as freely as the townspeople, a mingling that was changed only by ordinance in the early 1900s.

Samuel Harris owned several businesses, the most prominent of which was his "Cheap Store." He came to Williamsburg in 1872 and was a leading citizen until his death in 1904.

Courtesy, John D. Rockefeller, Jr., Library, Colonial Williamsburg Foundation

One sign that Williamsburg was recovering from the hard times following the Civil War was the coming of the C. & O. Railway to the Peninsula in time for the Yorktown Centennial celebration in October 1881. Although in the last-minute rush to beat the deadline a "shoofly" track had to be laid down Duke of Gloucester Street, it was moved two months later; and a regular schedule was finally established on 1 May 1882.

In addition to being a merchant and an undertaker, Mrs. W. H. Braithwaite (1847–1918) rented horses and buggies to drummers (traveling salesmen).

Courtesy, Adelia Peebles Moore

Another sign of recovery was the reopening of William and Mary in 1888. By 1891 President Lyon Gardiner Tyler had assembled a high-caliber staff of six professors. These "Seven Wise Men" (see p. 146) labored to reestablish William and Mary's prestige. Also, even before women were admitted as students, three women held staff or faculty positions. Blanche Moncure became the college librarian in 1899, and Emily Christian followed in 1902. Nannie Davis, assistant professor of education from 1905 until 1908, also served as principal of the Model School.

During most of the nineteenth century, the *Virginia Gazette* had suffered difficult times and had been published only about a third of the time; but in May 1893, a new editor, W. C. Johnston (1870-1948), revived it. A native of Ohio and an alumnus of William and Mary, Johnston served the city in many capacities: as clerk of the City Council, as a member of the Board of Registrars and the Williamsburg Business Association, and later as postmaster. Johnston wanted to see Williamsburg grow and prosper and, as editor, constantly pleaded for industries to open here. Two such were the planing mill and corn and cob crusher that James Banks began to operate in 1895 behind the C. & O. Depot. The *Gazette* described this new industry as "the morning star of the future that heralds a glorious dawn of prosperity upon this little city." In 1898, Arthur Denmead's ice factory opened; and, becoming successful, four years later he was making daily ice deliveries. Almost, simultaneously, Peninsula Bank, Williamsburg's first, opened in 1897. Judge R. L. Henley served as president without compensation, although cashier Harry N. Phillips received $1,000 a year.

The population nearly doubled to 2,714 in the thirty years after 1880; and in 1898 rapid growth took place specifically in the suburb known as West Williamsburg. In 1902, the city used this continuing growth to justify the extension of the corporate limits to take in the College of William and Mary. On 1 April 1905, Johnston wrote, "Who says Williamsburg is not growing? The West End lots are practically all sold. Soon another section will be opened out that way." The trend continued, and in 1916 a plat was drawn showing lots along West Duke of Gloucester Street (present day Jamestown Road), Texas Avenue (Griffin Avenue), and Oklahoma Avenue (Cary Street). (For development in that area, see pp. 173-78.)

A steam laundry opened in August 1900, but even more notable was the opening of the Williamsburg Knitting Mill in December of that year. The mill provided jobs for men and women, the latter earning thirty-five cents a day. Shortly after opening, the mill turned out fifty to sixty dozen suits of underwear a day; but, unfortunately, financial problems arose before the end of the decade, and the mill closed for good in 1916.

The King's Daughters, the first interdenominational charitable group, was organized in 1888 under the leadership of Miss Catherine (Kate) Wharton Curtis. Its members ministered to the needs of both blacks and whites. Initially, dues of one penny a meeting were collected to fund their projects; and five years later, dues doubled. Silver teas were a favorite fund-raising occasion of the King's Daughters. Also, men of the town became active in fraternal organizations and supported a variety of church and school fund raisers organized by the women–for example, box suppers and oyster suppers that raised money for various causes.

Other women of the community, recognizing the rich history of the area, sought to preserve local historical shrines. The Association for the Preservation of Virginia Antiquities (APVA), co-founded in 1889 by Mrs. Cynthia Beverley Tucker Coleman (see color plate17) and Miss Mary Jeffrey Galt, began to purchase historic properties, such as the powder magazine and the capitol grounds (see p. 180).

Although Bruton Parish Church had been active since colonial times, that historic building had fallen into disrepair. In February 1903, newly arrived Rector W. A. R. Goodwin was dismayed at the condition of the church. He resolved not only to renovate it, but to restore it to its colonial appearance. It took time to assess the damage, raise the required funds, and do the repairs; therefore, it was not until 12 May 1907 that the restored church was consecrated. Appreciating the historic sensitivity of the APVA, after the restoration of Colonial Williamsburg began Goodwin acknowledged the APVA's steadfast efforts, noting that "These devoted ladies of Virginia bent like priestesses over the dying embers of ancient flames and breathed upon them and made them glow again."

The Underwood Constitution of 1869 had provided for free public education of all children; and in accordance with the new state law, the Trustees of the Free Schools of Williamsburg met on 2 December 1870 and ordered the clerk "to proceed forthwith to take the census of persons between the ages of five and twenty-one in this district." This meeting, presided over by R. H. Armistead, marked the beginning of public schools in Williamsburg. At the second meeting, on 27 January 1871, resolutions were passed to hire Mrs. V. T. F. Southall, Miss Lucy H. Hansford, and Mr. James W. Edloe to teach, respectively, white females, white males, and all black children. The school term was set to run only from 1 February through 1 July, using rented classrooms.

During most of the nineteenth century, the Grammar School at William and Mary had provided basic education for young white males. In 1866, the college had finally received money from the 1741 bequest of Mary Whaley, who had wished to "eternalize forever" her dead son Mattey. In 1870 a brick building was erected by the college's Board of Visitors on the site of the colonial Governor's Palace, and it was named Mattey School. The city leased the school from 1873 to 1884 for the free public education of white males; but when the lease was renewed, girls were admitted. In 1894 the college dissolved its ties to the city and began to operate the Model and Practice School in conjunction with its teacher education program; but in 1912, the school was again jointly operated by the college and the city.

Miss Mary Jeffrey Galt (1845–1922), a native of Norfolk, was a co-founder of the Association for the Preservation of Virginia Antiquities. She is credited with naming the organization.

Courtesy, Galt Family Papers, Swem Library, College of William and Mary

White pupils met in rented rooms until the first city-owned school, the Nicholson School, opened in 1897. It was located on Nicholson Street, almost due north of today's

Mattey's Observation and Training School built on the site of the colonial Governor's Palace in 1870 was also known as the Model and Practice School. The two women shown in the photograph are Nannie C. Davis, principal, and Elizabeth A. (Pinky) Morecock.

Courtesy, Swem Library, College of William and Mary

The Association for the Preservation of Virginia Antiquities and most of the William and Mary faculty opposed the palace green site for the Williamsburg High School. Nevertheless, the school was built there. It served the community from 1921 to 1930.

Courtesy, John D. Rockefeller, Jr., Library, Colonial Williamsburg Foundation

Chowning's Tavern. Williamsburg High School, located in front of the Mattey School, was completed in 1921. Black children met first in homes and, later, at Mt. Ararat Baptist Church (see p. 115); but in 1885 the city opened a school for them on Francis Street near the powder magazine. That school building was moved, in 1907, to the corner of Nicholson and Botetourt streets (see p. 123), being replaced in 1924 on the same site by the James City County Training School (see pp. 124 & 125).

For a number of years, free public schools in the state did not extend beyond grade school; and when high school was introduced, it stopped at the ninth or tenth grade. So, to pursue a better education, many of the local girls went away to normal schools, institutes, colleges, and music conservatories. Most of them became teachers.

One unusual young woman, Minnie C. Brathwaite (1874-1954), applied to the college faculty in 1896 for permission to take chemistry classes and was refused. She began teaching when she was but seventeen, her first years being spent in James City and York counties. In 1901 she passed the examination required by the Office of Indian Affairs and taught first at Blue Canyon, Arizona, and then at Fort Mojave, Arizona, later recording her experiences in her book, *Girl from Williamsburg*. She married in 1906 and lived the rest of her life in Sutter County, California.

Minnie was not the first Williamsburg woman to go west and work with the Indians, however. Susan Garrett, sister of one of the "Seven Wise Men" at William and Mary, worked as a missionary in Arizona, Utah, and Idaho from 1893 to 1910. In Idaho, she met and married Peyton Randolph Nelson, great-grandson of Thomas Nelson, Jr. (a signer of the Declaration of Independence), a former Klondike gold miner and, then, a cowboy. On their return to Williamsburg, they lived in Tazewell Hall (see p. 98). Colonial Williamsburg bought the house and gave the Nelsons life-rights. Susan didn't live long afterwards, alas, so local memories are mostly of the colorful Peyton—a remarkable sight with his long hair and beard grazing his cows on the palace green. He was to take care of the small repairs to the house, and Colonial Williamsburg, the large ones; however, he saved himself a great deal of time, trouble, and money by ignoring all problems until the minor repairs became big ones. The Williamsburg Lodge now stands where Tazewell Hall once did.

Minnie C. Braithwaite (1874-1954), having been refused permission to enroll in chemistry courses at the college, turned to teaching. In 1901 she passed the examination required by the Office of Indian Affairs and accepted a post teaching in Arizona. She remained in the west and recorded her experiences in her book Girl from Williamsburg.

Courtesy, Dorothy Ross

Informal snapshot of Peyton Randolph Nelson, who was a familiar sight as he took his cows to graze on the palace green. The youth of the town affectionately called him "Pony Nelson" and "Old Man Nelson."

Courtesy, John D. Rockefeller, Jr., Library, Colonial Williamsburg Foundation

Finally, local girls had the opportunity to attend a private high school in town. The Williamsburg Female Institute, financed by the Norfolk Presbytery and donations from local residents, opened in 1908 and ran until 1916. The school offered girls, at an affordable price, "the elements of culture which make the life of the well-educated Christian woman." The strongest department was music, and student recitals enriched the cultural life of Williamsburg. After the school closed in March 1916, the building served many purposes before being torn down to make room for Matthew Whaley School, which opened in the fall of 1930.

Whereas the Episcopalian rector had but one congregation, the Baptist, Methodist, and Presbyterian ministers served churches in both the outlying counties and the city; and the Scandinavian newcomers in the Norge area were mostly Lutherans. The black community was largely Baptist and worshiped in its own churches. Catholics were few; and the first mention of Catholic services appears in 1908, when two priests began coming occasionally from Newport News to conduct Mass in Cameron Hall at Eastern State Hospital for patients and townspeople. Sparse numbers, however, caused the services to end in 1912.

The Jewish presence in Williamsburg during the nineteenth century was never large enough to establish a synagogue. However, the Hechts and Hofheimers were successful merchant families in the 1850s and 1860s, and four of the men were active members of Masonic Lodge No. 6 in Williamsburg. Zach Hofheimer was the only Jewish student attending William and Mary during the years 1869-1871. In 1891 another Jew, David Lichtenstein, briefly lived in the William Byrd III house. After that date, however, there are no records of Jewish families in Williamsburg until the late 1920s or early 1930s.

In 1903 the first car appeared on the streets of Williamsburg. Shortly thereafter C. J. Person became the first resident to buy a car, and in 1908 he started selling them. In 1911 he was called to the scene of the first accident involving Williamsburg residents. Passengers in the wrecked Ford driven by W. A. Bozarth included his daughter, Grace, and two O'Keeffe sisters, Claudia and Georgia, the famous artist.

In the early part of the twentieth century, the health of the residents was improved. Dr. David J. King, a Canadian, exerted a great deal of influence both in private practice and as the college physician from 1916 until his death in 1935. William and Mary recognized his contri-

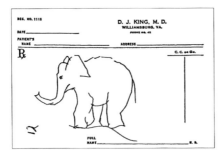 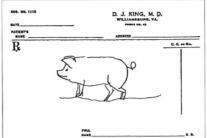

On a house call to John Clemmitt (ca. 1928), Dr. David J. King drew these pictures on pages of his prescription pad. Dr. King made a practice of entertaining his young patients in this way.

Courtesy, Swem Library, College of William and Mary.

bution by renaming the infirmary in his honor. King advocated strict sanitation rules and was credited with clearing the town of typhoid fever and diphtheria. *Virginia Gazette* writers declared that all lives seemed equally precious to him, that he answered calls at any hour, that he often paid for the medicine for some of his poorer patients, and that he was never known to send a bill to either rich or poor. Dr. King's practice overlapped with that of Dr. Baxter Israel Bell, a man cut of much the same cloth.

The Civic League came into being in early 1907, as Williamsburg women began to endeavor to beautify the "village" in time for the celebration of Jamestown's three hundredth anniversary. To accommodate the anticipated crowds and dignitaries, the Jamestown Exposition (26 April-30 November) was actually held in Norfolk. The opening date commemorated the anniversary of the settlers' landing at Cape Henry. Organizers expected many visitors would visit Jamestown and Williamsburg and used convict labor to build an improved road connecting the two places.

In the midst of this planning and activity, the women of Williamsburg became concerned about the inadequacies of their community, which would soon see the spotlight. The twenty-eight women who gathered at the Model School on 25 January 1907 founded the Village Improvement Society (later, the Civic League), with Miss Elizabeth Scott as president. Members committed themselves to beautification and sanitation, to extending hospitality to strangers, and to paying twenty-five cents a year in dues. Working alongside their servants, the women wielded rakes and shovels, and loaded carts and horses.

In subsequent years, the women supported Dr. King, battling typhoid fever by promoting safe drinking water and the eradication of flies. The league is also credited with sponsoring TB clinics, organizing Boy Scouts and Campfire Girls, starting a public library, sponsoring the Swarthmore Chautauqua, and presenting the town with its first community Christmas tree.

The Woman's Christian Temperance Union was also active in Williamsburg and James City County from 1903 to at least 1922, and the local Anti-Saloon League was founded in 1901. Kate Waller Barrett, the second woman to serve on the Board of Visitors of William and Mary, participated at the state level of the WCTU and sometimes lectured in Williamsburg.

Compared to the state institutions in town, the rest of Williamsburg was slow in getting the modern conveniences of electricity, water, and sewage. The public hospital (which changed its name, in 1894, to Eastern State Hospital) had hot running water in 1883 and in 1884 had electricity during the night. Following the installation of a power plant in 1911, William and Mary was thought to have a thoroughly modern system of utilities. The artesian well dug at the Williamsburg Knitting Mill in 1900 became the fourth such well in the town, but not until 1916 did the town have pipes for a water system and a sewage plant. The following year, in the interest of public health, an ordinance compelled all citizens to connect with the water and sewage systems.

Despite considerable protest from the City Council, the Chesapeake Telephone and Telegraph Company erected poles down Duke of Gloucester Street in 1901. That the most important street should be so disfigured became an issue whenever the Civic League worked on beautification projects. Finally, in 1932, the poles came down and the lines were put underground.

Before the introduction of electricity, kerosene was the accepted fuel for lighting and to a lesser degree for cooking and heating. In 1905, when there was a shortage of kerosene, the *Gazette* wrote, "Williamsburg is suffering from a kerosene oil famine. Perhaps Rockefeller's scheming to raise the price of oil here to enable him to donate to a local institution here. That's the Standard Oil Magnate's way."

Two private businesses had electricity in 1915, but the town as a whole did not offer such a convenience until the Williamsburg Power Company began operating its generating station on 3 September 1917. Citizens were invited to come out on Saturday night, the fifteenth, to see the electric lights on Duke of Gloucester Street.

The Chesapeake Telephone and Telegraph Company erected telephone poles down Duke of Gloucester Street in 1901. The lines were put underground in 1932 during the restoration.

Courtesy, John D. Rockefeller, Jr., Library, Colonial Williamsburg Foundation

Williamsburg residents met and entertained each other at home, church, and school, and in the great outdoors. The white community also attended special events at Cameron Hall, the amusement hall at Eastern State Hospital. This building, completed in 1885 on the grounds near the intersection of Francis and Nassau Streets, met the recreational needs of the patients but was also the focal point for many of Williamsburg's social affairs. Fraternal and civic groups used the building; and townspeople in general went there to enjoy comedy acts, lectures, moving pictures, minstrel shows, musical programs, plays, and stereoptican exhibitions. The admission charges for these events usually went to a worthy charitable or educational cause.

The children of the community shared many happy occasions, such as birthday parties, Easter egg hunts, Sunday School Christmas parties, and May Day and Fourth of July celebrations. Often groups took picnic baskets and went looking for chestnuts. An opossum hunt at Oak Tree in York County was evidently a highlight of the 1900 season. Youth at house parties participated in many activities, including driving, candy making, riding, dancing, singing, card games, picnics, and masquerade balls. William and Mary, a male college until 1918, hosted dancing parties to entertain the young ladies of the town.

The C. & O. train station is shown here on the left. To its right is the Virginia Electric and Power Company building, formerly the Williamsburg Knitting Mill. The area was behind the site of the Governor's Palace.

Courtesy, John D. Rockefeller, Jr., Library, Colonial Williamsburg Foundation

"Pounding" the minister with gifts of food was a special social activity. Although ministers were poorly paid, they benefited from this custom: each person would bring a pound of sugar, or flour, or bacon, etc. The 8 January 1920 *Gazette* reported the bounty the Baptist minister, Reverend Peyton Little, received:

> His members came from every direction and proceeded to "pound" him and his family severely. The minister's wife was "hit" in the head, he got "struck" in the throat, and his feet were "pounded" until they presented a gray appearance. And the stomachs of the whole family were "loaded" with the best that the markets afford.

Those going about their business in town could take advantage of various places to rest and socialize. In 1913, the Hotel McGinnis advertised a rest room for women. The newly opened Peninsula Co-Operative Association placed the following notice in the 15 April 1915 issue of the *Gazette*: "We also want you to know that two rooms are set aside and fitted up for our customers and others for rest rooms—one for the ladies and one for gentlemen—where people can meet, rest, and get socially acquainted." In 1918, the Civic League sponsored a rest room in the Blair House. Notice that no mention was made of plumbing: the rooms were, as advertized, for rest and socialization.

The building on the far left in this 1916 souvenir photo-graph was put to various uses. At one stage it was the Williamsburg Hotel, and from 1925 to 1930 it was Dr. B. I. Bell's hospital. During the two months in 1881 that the railroad ran down Duke of Gloucester St., it was the C. & O. Station.

Courtesy, John D. Rockefeller, Jr., Library, Colonial Williamsburg Foundation

Williamsburg's first movie theater, operated by Charles M. Carey, is noted in several 1910 issues of the *Gazette*. Hospital records show that patients were encouraged to attend the movies there. The theater does not appear to have lasted long; and, in 1913, Councilman B. F. Wolfe opened "The Palace" theater opposite the palace green. A talkaphone was added the following October. Wolfe's successful theater was sold for $12,000 early in 1920 to a joint stock company.

In July 1915, the Odd Fellows' Hall at Nicholson and Botetourt streets (see p. 126) began showing movies for blacks on Monday and Friday nights—for an admission fee of five and ten cents respectively. After the James City County Training School opened in 1924, talking pictures were shown there on Saturday evenings.

When author Mary Johnston came to Williamsburg as a guest of President and Mrs. Tyler to lecture on woman suffrage in the Wren Chapel in March 1911, it was

Mrs. Merrill Proctor Ball, wife of land agent F. H. Ball, was the first woman to register to vote in Williamsburg.

Courtesy,
Gertrude Ball
Daversa

only natural that the women already heavily involved in other causes should be in the audience. Twenty-one highly enthusiastic ladies met with Miss Johnston the next day and organized a Williamsburg League. The officers came from the ranks of women prominent in the community, and included Mrs. Lyon G. Tyler as president. Vice President Nannie Davis was well known for her long service as principal of the Model School and as the originator of the Civic League; Mrs. L. S. Foster, Williamsburg League treasurer, was the wife of the former superintendent of Eastern State Hospital; and Mrs. Margaret Hansford, one of the charter members of the King's Daughters, served as secretary. The first president of the Civic League, Mrs. R. M. Crawford, née Elizabeth Scott, succeeded Mrs. Tyler as president.

The Williamsburg League had an uphill fight all the way. The ladies in town who found the idea of suffrage repugnant vowed to save the women of Williamsburg from the new movement, and W. C. Johnston used the power of the press to oppose women's suffrage. Less than a month after the ratification of the Nineteenth Amendment, Mrs. Merrill Proctor Ball, a music instructor at the college, paid her poll tax and registered to vote. Registrar Cole asked the other ladies to see him as soon as possible and "get the agony over." Thirteen members of the Civic League, ages twenty-four to seventy-four, answered his appeal and registered to vote that year.

In 1915, the city fathers determined that Marie Marshall, an Eastern State Hospital patient living in the William Byrd III house (today leased by Colonial Williamsburg to Legg, Mason, Wood, & Walker), owed a whopping half million dollars in back taxes on her intangible property. A 16 September 1915 article in the Newport News *Daily Press*, poked fun at the neighbor up the road:

> If the plans and specifications of the examiner of tax accounts do not miscarry, Williamsburg will be the richest city to its inches in the State. Fancy the old 'burg with over a half a million dollars in her inside pocket!
>
> But what will Williamsburg do with half a million dollars? The city could take out enough to erect waterworks, establish a county fair, employ a man to wind the town clock, and then have a sufficient endowment to relieve the town forever from local taxation. It would be a windfall, and we fear our friends would be [so] stuckup and purse-proud that they would not notice a little old poor town like Newport News. However, we heartily congratulate the ancient city upon its brilliant prospects.

The case was decided in the Virginia Supreme Court in 1921 in Miss Marshall's favor. It was argued that when Miss Marshall, originally a resident of New York, had entered the mental hospital in 1872 she had no intention of permanently changing her domicile and did not have the mental capacity to change her domicile after that time, and that no one else had the authority to do so. Since she was not domiciled here, the court decreed that the city could not collect these particular taxes from her. The law governing domicile has since been changed.

When the United States entered World War I, women and children did what they could on the home front. In 1916 a wartime industry, the Du Pont Powder Company, was built at Penniman (now Cheatham Annex). By 1 June, a railroad had been laid from Williamsburg to Penniman, and six hundred carloads of material had been shipped there. Later that month, the semi-monthly payroll amounted to $24,000; and it was forecast that the company would have ten thousand employees by October.

The 20 July 1916 *Gazette* called Williamsburg the new Du Pont Wonder City, and the town prospered as never before. When landlords doubled rents, Johnston wrote an editorial cautioning that extortion was bad business and would drive newcomers out of town into such subdivisions as Delta Park, Forest Heights, York View, and Kenton Park. Although highly advertised, most of these subdivisions were hardly developed, if at all.

In 1918, the War Department added plants for manufacturing and loading of shells. The increase in employment at Penniman required six trains daily to run each way between the munitions plants and Williamsburg. Penniman disappeared at the end of World War I, however; and the site was not developed into Cheatham Annex until another wartime economy required it in 1943.

Williamsburg of the 1880-1920 period has been commonly described as the town that couldn't afford to pay a man to wind the town clock, the town that forgot to hold an election, the sleepy town where "the lazy lived off the crazy." But Williamsburg was much more than that. It pulled itself out of the despondency and poverty that followed the Civil War; and as it entered the third decade of the twentieth century, offering its residents new amenities such as electricity, a rudimentary sanitation system, movie theaters, and a functioning public-school system, it was ready for the exciting days of the Restoration that would soon follow. The 1905 prediction that Rockefeller (albeit his son) would donate something to a local institution was about to be fulfilled.

Selected Sources and Suggested Readings

Bureau of Information of the Business Men's Association of the City of Williamsburg, Va. *Facts About Williamsburg and Vicinity* (Richmond: Whittet and Shepperson, 1900).

Byrd, Rawls. *History of Public Schools in Williamsburg* (Williamsburg, 1968).

Charles, John S. *Recollections of Williamsburg: as It Appeared at the Beginning of the Civil War and Just Previously Thereto, With Some Incidents in the Life of Its Citizens* (Williamsburg: Colonial Williamsburg Foundation, 1928).

Directory and Handbook of the City of Williamsburg and the County of James City, Virginia (Williamsburg: Virginia Gazette, 1898).

Goodwin, Rutherfoord. *A Brief & True Report Concerning Williamsburg in Virginia.* 3rd edn. (Richmond: Dietz, 1959).

Jamestown Ter-Centennial Exposition, Norfolk, Virginia, April 26 to November 30, 1907 ([Norfolk]: Jamestown Exposition Co., 1906).

Mueller, Walter J. *History, Colonial Capital Branch Association for the Preservation of Virginia Antiquities, 1889-1988* (Williamsburg: Colonial Capital Branch of the Assoc. for the Preservation of Virginia Antiquities, 1988).

Schneider, Megan Elaine. "The Distaff Side: The Williamsburg Civic League, 1907-1937," M.A. thesis (College of William and Mary, 1991).

Stevens, John Austin. *Yorktown Centennial Handbook: Historical and Topographical Guide to the Yorktown Peninsula, Richmond, James River, and Norfolk* (N.Y.: C. A. Coffin & Rogers, 1881).

Virginia Gazette, 20 May 1893–8 December 1921.

Vivian, William R. "The C. & O. Peninsula Extension, 1881 to 1981," *Chesapeake and Ohio Historical Newsletter* 56, no. 10 (1981): 4-8.

Williamsburg Garden Club. *A Williamsburg Scrap Book*, 3rd edn. (Richmond: Dietz, 1937).

Wiseman, Howard W. *The Seven Wise Men* (N.Y.: Jacques & Co., 1948)

Street Scenes, ca. 1890-1910

Photo of Duke of Gloucester St. ca. 1901 (top rt).

Courtesy, John D. Rockefeller, Jr., Library,
Colonial Williamsburg Foundation

Snapshots from Drewery Jones' album (see p. 136),
which became part of Tom Williams' collection (see
p. 229).

Courtesy, Thomas L. Williams archive

Neighbors and Humanitarians

In mid-twentieth century Williamsburg, two especially beloved and respected men were physician Baxter Israel Bell (1889-1963) and law professor and dean Dudley Warner Woodbridge (1896-1969). Woodbridge spent all, and Bell spent almost all, of his professional years in Williamsburg in unselfish service to the community.

Dr. Bell was born in Swanquarter, North Carolina, and did two years of pre-medical study at the University of North Carolina before taking his M.D. at the Medical College of Virginia. After interning in Abingdon, Virginia, and practicing briefly in Eastern Kentucky, he became a staff physician at Eastern State Hospital in 1918. There he met Imogene Black, an occupational therapist, whom he married in 1925.

In 1926 he opened an office in the old Williams-burg Hotel next to the powder magazine on Duke of Gloucester Street and set up a small "hospital" of two or three rooms where patients could stay overnight

*Baxter Israel Bell
(1889-1963)*

*Dudley Warner Woodbridge
(1896-1969)*

(see p. 165). In 1927 he and his associate sold the building–the buyer later being revealed as John D. Rockefeller, Jr. Three years later, Dr. Bell built the Bell Hospital at the corner of Oklahoma (now Cary) Street and Wythe Lane and erected his home beside it. The staff of the ten-bed hospital, which was the only one in the Williamsburg area, included Mrs. Bell, who became the dietician; Anna Debridge, the cook; Spencer Tyler, the orderly; and the nurses.

Dr. Bell was also staff physician at the College of William and Mary for thirteen years and acted as physician to Colonial Williamsburg. He spent all his waking hours serving residents and college students and was on call for births, illnesses, and accidents during the night.

His untiring devotion to his profession was recognized and rewarded. In 1955 William and Mary gave him the Algernon Sydney Sullivan Award, which is given annually to a person having a "close relationship to the college" and who possesses such "characteristics of heart, mind, and conduct as evince a spirit of love for and helpfulness to other men and women." Two years later, the Medical Society of Virginia selected him as the "Practicing Physician of the Year."

Dr. Woodbridge was born in Bellaire, Ohio. His family moved to Seattle while he was just a young boy; but he received his B.A. and J.D. degrees from the University of Illinois and came further east in 1927 to Williamsburg, where he began teaching at William and Mary. Credited with building the law school into a nationally-recognized institution, Dr. Woodbridge was honored by being awarded one of the first two Chancellor professorships; and in 1963 he was the first recipient of the college's Thomas Jefferson Award, the recipient of which "exemplifies, through his life, his character, and his influence, the principles and ideals of Thomas Jefferson." In October 1950, *Life* magazine named him one of the eight most outstanding professors in the country;

After several days of freezing weather, Dr. Woodbridge would take the neighborhood children to Ice House Cove on Lake Matoaka. He had dozens of ice skates in all sizes and handed them out to children and taught them how to skate.

Courtesy, Julia Woodbridge Oxrieder

Bell Hospital at 109 Cary Street, built in 1930. Until Williamsburg Community Hospital was built, Bell Hospital was the only hospital in the Williamsburg area. It had a capacity of ten beds until 1939, when it was expanded to accommodate twenty-two patients. It was closed in 1966 and was used as an office building until 1999, when the building was purchased by William & Mary.

Courtesy, *Daily Press*

Community Testimonial Night honoring Dr. Bell at Matthew Whaley School, 27 May 1957.

Courtesy, Thomas L. Williams archive

and in 1962, seven years after Bell, Woodbridge also received the Sullivan award.

Although he told his students that the law was a "jealous mistress," Woodbridge found time to enrich the lives of children and was never happier than when he was teaching them to play tennis, ride bicycles, or ice skate. When children were sick and homebound, he visited them and helped them keep up with their class assignments; and he tutored older children in algebra and Latin. It is small wonder that the children claimed him as their own.

Woodbridge was also a man well ahead of his times in racial attitudes and civil rights. It may seem trivial now, but his making his bicycles available to black children well over half a century ago was a strong public statement of fairness. He also privately taught black law students, who were forbidden by state law to attend his summer classes that coached students prepping for the bar exam. He was well suited for his seat on the inter-racial council in Williamsburg.

Dr. Woodbridge was affectionately called "the good dean" and, upon his death in 1969, "the eighth wise man" (see p. 146). He was buried just a few feet from Dr. Bell in Cedar Grove Cemetery. As they were before, the two men are still neighbors.

Woodbridge's amusing remarks at Bell's Testimonial Night in 1957 reveal some of the endearing qualities of both men:

> Back in the time of World War II when Dr. Bell was worked to death, when cars were almost impossible to get, and when there was a sailor every two feet, Dr. Bell left the keys to his car in the ignition while he went into the hospital to get some articles he needed. A sailor saw his chance, jumped in the car, and sped south on Cary Street. When he discovered it was a dead end road, he slowed down as much as he could, opened the door, and jumped out. The car smashed into the porch of the last house on the street. I said to Dr. Bell, "I'll bet they'll court martial that thieving sailor and throw the book at him." He replied, "Not on my complaint. The poor fellow is probably just back from combat duty." Dr. Bell's deeds speak far more eloquently than anything I can say, so I'll close with these few lines:

> > We all love you, Dr. Bell;
> > The reasons why aren't hard to tell....
> > Your kindest heart of purest gold
> > Beats for us all, both young and old.
> > You've let us make a travesty
> > Of your sacred right to privacy.
> > You've kept our wheezes and our sneezes
> > From turning into dread diseases.
> > You've prevented wicked germs from killin'
> > With many shots of penicillin....
> > If all men, Dr. Bell, were as good as you
> > What in the world would we lawyers do?

by: Julia Woodbridge Oxrieder

Greening the Grid:
Chandler Court, Pollard Park, and the
Early Suburbanization of Williamsburg

by: Edward Chappell

In 1920, William and Mary President J. A. C. Chandler hired Charles M. Robinson's Richmond architectural office to plan a grand campus expansion. Robinson and his staff designed the new college buildings in an idiom that respected the mass and character of the three still unrestored colonial collegiate buildings without literally lifting their details. They organized the new campus around the Sunken Garden and aligned dormitories along the adjoining streets, drawing inspiration from Christopher Wren's Chelsea Hospital and Francis Nicholson's Williamsburg town plan. Earlier, McMillan Commission members planning the expansion of Pierre L'Enfant's design for Washington, D.C., had visited Williamsburg in search of ideas, attracted by the town's vistas, greens, and diagonal streets.

But the concept of cultivating a distinctive identity by drawing on the community's past and preserving open space was lost on private land developers. By the 1920s, half a dozen subdivisions had been platted with conventional grid patterns of parallel streets north, south, east, and west of the old town. Developer C. J. Callahan planned six blocks of narrow, rectangular building lots filling over thirty acres south of the college across Jamestown Road (then called West Duke of Gloucester Ave.). There was no hint that personal taste or uneven topography might affect the shape or placement of lots. Nor did the plan take into account the ravine that cuts deeply into the area, which caused some lots to be so irregular that any rash homebuilder would have needed climbing gear to enter or exit the house.

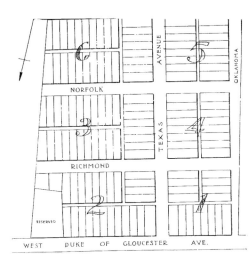

Developer C. J. Callahan's uninspired grid plan for thirty acres of housing off Jamestown Rd. (then called West Duke of Gloucester St.).

Redrawn courtesy, David F. Morrill

John Garland Pollard (see p. 259) was cut from a different cloth than were developers like Callahan. Pollard moved to Williamsburg in 1922 to become professor of constitutional law and history at William and Mary. The next year Chandler appointed him head of the Marshall-Wythe School of Government and Citizenship (now the Marshall-Wythe School of Law), a position he held until elected Governor of Virginia following Harry Byrd in 1929.

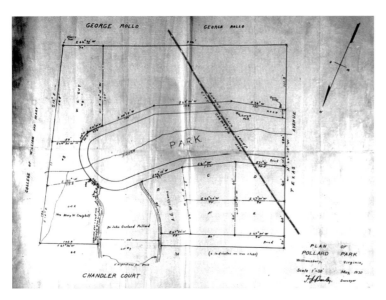

Pollard played a progressive role in Williamsburg in the years of his residency, which coincided with W. A. R. Goodwin's wooing of John D. Rockefeller, Jr., and the opening stage of restoration. He was elected mayor in 1926, led an effort to create the city's first planning commission, and personally planned and partially financed the Chandler Court and Pollard Park neighborhoods.

Both Rockefeller and Williamsburg's countless subsequent admirers saw the town's restoration as Janus-faced, looking back toward a more refined and beautiful time and forward by providing a model of thoughtful community design worthy of emulation by future American planners. While some of the local leadership resisted newly-imported authorities

Plan of Pollard Park, 1930.

Courtesy, Rare Books and Manuscripts, Swem Library, College of William & Mary

and opportunities, Pollard, like Chandler, embraced the new model town perspective, seeing the place's historic pedigree as a lever that, properly manipulated, could create a more progressive Williamsburg. Both Pollard and Chandler had already taken their own steps toward civic improvement before Rockefeller arrived on the scene.

Pollard thought Callahan's development a mindless disaster and quickly remade the subdivision according to his own aesthetics and perception of how twentieth-century Williamsburg should evolve. He began buying the properties in 1922, and two years later he successfully petitioned City Council to vacate the established street plan and permit him to create a small suburban neighborhood called Chandler Court in honor of his boss. About a dozen lots were arranged to face the lanes and a public green and to provide room for consistent setbacks, varied plantings, and privacy without surrounding the houses with large lawns.

In 1930, Pollard charted the second phase of his development, ten lots strung around a hairpin-shaped lane circling the streambed. The topography was irregular, and the houses looked down on the wooded ravine from lots of varied sizes and orientations. Two public walkways were to link Chandler Court with the new section, called Pollard Park. Pollard built a small gambrel-roofed house beside the east path with a charming and downright un-American absence of auto access. A second small lane, now called Ballard, was snaked up between the two enclaves, providing snug sites for only two other houses. What Pollard's designs share is an emphasis on individuality or imagination, on a sense of character that distinguishes them from the predictable subdivisions Callahan and others imposed on the town.

Neighborhood tradition identifies Chander Court's communal lawn as inspired by English and New England village greens. Such greens were an enduring image among garden suburbs on both sides of the Atlantic. But a more prosaic model, closer in scale to Chandler Court's nucleus were the bungalow courts built across much of the United States in the second and third decades of the twentieth century. Ten to twenty bungalows grouped around a central green shared a design style and yet had an individual personality. Pollard's choice of name, Chandler "Court," suggests that such developments were part of his conception. Robert Braxton used the same terminology when naming Braxton Court, which he developed off Scotland Street in the same period. Like the black citizens who bought lots in Braxton Court, Pollard's white clients built houses that partook more of the colonial than the bungalow style.

Pollard was an amateur designer, and in the 1970s Colonial Williamsburg architect Edwin Kendrew criticized his neighborhoods for their small lots and impractical, narrow lanes. Kendrew favored Indian Springs Road, laid out more generously by a Norfolk architect. But Chandler Court and Pollard Park are among the community's best-loved neighborhoods, largely because of their intimate scale, gentle treatment of the landscape, and accommodation

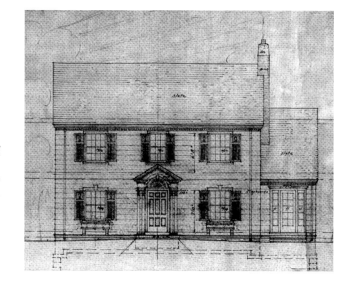

Charles M. Robinson's design for the Geiger house on Chandler Court and the house as constructed in 1928 illustrate the degree to which various architectural styles intersected in pre-Colonial Williamsburg neighborhood houses. Hired by Philosophy professor J. K. Geiger to draw plans copying a Georgian-style house recently built on Richmond Road, Robinson's firm designed a two-story frame house, rendered with a neoclassical American flavor. Finding the proposal too expensive, however, the Geigers worked with their contractor to reduce its size and complexity. They kept elements of Robinson's floor plans but reduced the number of rooms and enclosed them in a very different story-and-a-half brick house with an extremely steep roof, broken by a long dormer.

Drawing courtesy, M. L. Geiger; Photo courtesy, Edward Chappell

for people of varied means. Townspeople have rallied more than once in recent years to protect them against buildings that would alter the scale and confuse the scene.

As development of Chandler Court began, little attention was given to creating a distinctly local or regional flavor in the houses. The most common idiom, ironically, was what in the 1920s was considered Dutch colonial. Professor P. A. Warren and Pollard built houses for

Elmer Cappelman's presentation drawing of the Guy house in Pollard Park, 1930. Gladys Guy and her husband, William, longtime chair of the Chemistry Department at the college, hired Richmond architect Cappelman to design a medieval cottage, which he was shocked to find the Guys accepting without any changes. The Guys' house, dramatically situated on a hillside overlooking Pollard Park, is the most sophisticated building in the neighborhoods Pollard planned, and is more stylized and eclectic than the colonial-style houses that predominate in Pollard Park.

Courtesy, Joan Eastman Bennett

themselves with long dormers breaking through exaggerated gable or gambrel roofs. These roof treatments and small door hoods quaintly rolled out from the eaves were the product of 1920s domestic images rather than features one might find in eighteenth-century rural New York. Librarian Earl Gregg Swem's large, two-story, weatherboard house with classical porches and deep, exaggerated cornices is a familiar early-twentieth-century rendering of a Georgian house without being recognizably drawn from any particular historical model or region. The respected Virginia historian Richard L. Morton built a picturesque cottage that combines steep roofs and brown shingle siding with jumbo cylindrical porch columns in an eccentric manner that suggests he, as an architectural aficionado, designed his own house with the aid of published arts and crafts plans.

By 1930, such freely interpretive historicist designs had become old-fashioned, replaced by the more literal colonial style houses that began to be built on Pollard Park. Colonial Williamsburg's impact was immediate and was both direct and indirect. While Virginia's surviving eighteenth-century buildings had long affected perceptions of the region, Goodwin and Rockefeller's project raised them to a new status. For many people, they came to represent models of how to live a wholesome life. Pollard, college faculty, and other successful townspeople naturally gravitated to the newly brushed-up local style. Unlike their counterparts elsewhere in the state, Williamsburg's literati had direct access to the new designers. Thomas Tileson Waterman, a prolific draftsman working on the restoration from 1928 to 1932, moonlighted extensively, designing four houses in and near Pollard's development. In 1931 he designed a cozy six-room brick house that Richard Morton built as a rental property on the north side of Pollard Park. Morton's tenement has exaggeratedly tall roofs, whimsically small

Designed by Thomas L. Waterman, History professor Richard L. Morton's rental house in Pollard Park illustrates the literal colonial style that gained popularity after the restoration of Williamsburg began.

Courtesy, Edward Chappell

end windows, and a diminutive wing, all raising the volume of cuteness. Yet virtually every detail is drawn from the vocabulary of what Waterman perceived as early eighteenth-century tidewater architecture. Clarence Wright Huff, Jr., was one of numerous Richmond architects who specialized in Virginia revival houses in the decade before World War II. He designed a pair of gambrel-roofed residences for the sooth side of Pollard Park, both consciously more reserved renderings of the local eighteenth-century style, in 1939 and 1940.

Pollard Park represents a shift from intimate, actively shared spaces on essentially flat ground to emphasis on a natural feature serving as a substantial buffer or visual screen between the properties. Some American architects and domestic reformers had argued since the mid-nineteenth century for the picturesque arrangement of personalized houses, but it was in the early twentieth century that planners within striking distance of Williamsburg focused the attention of new neighborhoods or streets—like Riverside Drive in Richmond—on relatively untamed scenery. That Pollard had a prescient perspective by the time his attention turned to Pollard Park is illustrated by the fact that his small loop predates such romantically conceived scenic roads as the Colonial Parkway and its grander Blue Ridge counterpart.

Suburban growth is a potent force that continues to change the face of Williamsburg, as it does most active towns and cities in the western world. Residential and commercial developments now stretch out along all the full-access roads leading from Williamsburg, profoundly affecting the character of the place. Much of the roadside developments of the 1950s and '60s are now being recast as larger hotels and stores, surrounded with seas of undivided parking. Residential complexes built since the 1970s are increasingly cast as separate communities, with aggressive entrances announcing arrival like some earth-bound pearly gates. Graceland's gateway has become modest by comparison.

The lesson of Chandler Court and Pollard Park is that individuals with a little imagination and concern can make development a contribution rather than detriment to the visual health of the community. As ever-bolder suburbs rapidly make Williamsburg more socially segregated and less green, Pollard's personal effort is worth a second look.

Selected Sources and Suggested Readings

Architectural drawings for the Guy, Gieger, Julian, and Morton House in private collections.

Chappell, Edward, William Geary, Victory Smith, and the City of Williamsburg. National Register of Historic Places Nomination, 1995. Dept. of Historic Resources, Richmond.

John Garland Pollard Collection, Rare Books and Manuscripts, Swem Library, College of William & Mary.

Property Deeds, Clerk's Office. Williamsburg/James City Co.

Waterman Family Collection, Prints and Photographs Division, Library of Congress.

The Restoration of Williamsburg

by: Thomas H. Taylor, Jr.

In the 1920s the character of the former colonial capital was still apparent in its nearly one hundred eighteenth- and early nineteenth-century structures; and, local efforts to preserve the physical remains of the eighteenth century were periodically rejuvenated by regional, state, and national expositions at Jamestown, Williamsburg, and Yorktown that brought thousands of people to the area. As early as 1900 a guidebook to Williamsburg was published, and a hotel constructed on its main street (see p. 165). Many citizens recognized the importance of the old buildings and attempted to preserve individual examples; but with a poor economy, little could be done to protect the majority of this fabric from further neglect.

Spearheaded by the Catherine Memorial Society and later the Association for the Preservation of Virginia Antiquities (see p. 159), efforts to save Williamsburg's historic structures had been underway since the late nineteenth century. The magazine (see pp. 41 & 136) was the first building to receive attention: the APVA purchased, repaired, and opened it as a museum in 1896.

Also, the Catherine Memorial Society raised funds for the preservation of Bruton Parish churchyard; and during his first rectorship (1902-1907), Dr. W. A. R. Goodwin directed the removal of nineteenth-century alterations and restored the church itself to reflect his vision of a colonial church. The changes were completed in 1907 in time for the Jamestown Exposition. Goodwin documented the work and published one of the earliest accounts of a restoration in North America.

The George Wythe house, erected between 1752 and 1754, sat vacant for many years before Goodwin convinced the Bruton vestry to permit him to raise funds to purchase it for use as the new Parish house. Goodwin directed the restoration and opened the house to the public in 1927. In the mid 1920s Goodwin and several friends also purchased land around the magazine to protect it from encroachment.

Then, in 1928, the APVA, which in 1897 had been given the cornfield on which the foundations of the capitol were discovered in 1903, gave the land to Colonial Williamsburg on the conditions that the capitol be reconstructed within five years and the designs be approved by a committee chaired by Earl Gregg Swem, the scholar librarian of William and Mary. Next, although the city had repaired the old public gaol and opened it to the public in 1927, it needed restoration and in 1935-1936 was restored to its 1722 appearance.

Goodwin had been dreaming of restoring many other physical remains in order to invoke an appreciation for the town's social, cultural, and political history and began to use

Dr. W. A. R. Goodwin.

Courtesy, John D. Rockefeller, Jr., Library, Colonial Williamsburg Foundation

Bruton Parish churchyard, photograph taken for use in a postcard prior to the 1906 restoration of the church. The Catherine Memorial Society had restored the table tombs and put the stone slabs on supports.

Courtesy, John D. Rockefeller, Jr., Library, Colonial Williamsburg Foundation

George Wythe house after the 1926 restoration, but prior to the 1938 restoration

Courtesy, John D. Rockefeller, Jr., Library, Colonial Williamsburg Foundation

Site of House of Burgesses Looking West, Williamsburg, Va.
PUB. BY J. H. STONE

Capitol site, postcard showing the foundations of the capitol, which had been uncovered and capped by the A.P.V.A. in 1904.

Courtesy, John D. Rockefeller, Jr., Library, Colonial Williamsburg Foundation

his position as a fundraiser for William and Mary to seek philanthropic support. He first wrote to Henry Ford, asking for his help in saving the town from destruction, which, Goodwin argued, was caused by the automobile. The appeal was direct but unsuccessful. A less blunt appeal to John D. Rockefeller, Jr., did succeed; and after Rockefeller authorized the preparation of preliminary sketches, Goodwin began to look for an architect.

Goodwin wrote to the Boston architectural firm of Perry, Shaw & Hepburn, whose three principals all had impeccable credentials: Thomas M. Shaw (1878-1965), Andrew H. Hepburn (1880-1967), and William G. Perry (1883-1975) had graduated from either Harvard or M.I.T., or both, and two from the Ecole des Beaux Arts as well. The letter reveals Goodwin's vision: "it would be the most spectacular and interesting, and from the teaching point of view, the most valuable restoration ever attempted in America." Within a few hours, Perry had committed the firm to the project; and by May 1927 the preliminary plans were completed, with little optimism, however, that anything would develop from them.

After examining the plans, however, Rockefeller outlined an elaborate program. He authorized Goodwin to negotiate with the APVA to obtain the land upon which the capitol had stood; acquire property across the street from the site of the capitol in order to prevent a garage from being constructed on the site; inform the public that the Ludwell-Paradise house (see p. 45) had been acquired with the intention of its being given to the college to be

Public Gaol, pre-restoration view showing the original cell block. The gable roof, dormers, exterior stair, and chimneys were later additions. The restored structure was opened as an exhibition building on 1 April 1936.

Courtesy, John D. Rockefeller, Jr., Library,
Colonial Williamsburg Foundation

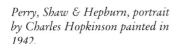

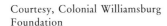

Perry, Shaw & Hepburn, portrait by Charles Hopkinson painted in 1942.

Courtesy, Colonial Williamsburg
Foundation

used as a professor's residence; acquire property at the end of the palace green for the purpose of erecting an inn; negotiate with the present owner of the Colonial Hotel for its purchase and possibly to obtain his services in the operation of the new inn; direct Perry, Shaw & Hepburn to prepare plans for the restoration of the Wren Building so that "they can be satisfactorily studied and criticized by leading colonial architects and art critics, whose judgement as to the final form which the rebuilt structure should take may be deemed the best obtainable in this country"; acquire property around the palace green and capitol and along Duke of Gloucester Street between the capitol and the palace green; acquire property between the college and the palace green only after obtaining Rockefeller's personal approval; and acquire property along Francis Street.

The Ludwell-Paradise house was the first property purchased. It was acquired on 4 December 1926 after Rockefeller authorized the acquisition in a telegram signed "David's Father." Rockefeller concealed his identity to prevent inflation of property values and to prevent speculators from competing with Goodwin in acquiring property. Goodwin acquired not only property for restoration, but also the blocks between the college and the palace green in order to create a commercial zone. By the end of the year, Goodwin had acquired sixty-five parcels, some of which contained only false-front stores and modern filling stations and garages; and as Rockefeller had requested, Goodwin sought Perry's help in obtaining the counsel of eminent authorities on colonial architecture. Those contacted included many of the people Goodwin had originally offered the job of preparing the preliminary sketches.

Architects, contractors, & corporate officers in front of the Robert Carter house, which briefly served as the corporate offices in 1930. Rear (l-rt): William G. Perry, Charles Dimmitt, J. O. Brown, Arthur A. Shurcliff, Walter M. Macomber, Webster Todd, & Kenneth Chorley; middle: Vernon M. Geddy, R. E. Parker, Robert Trimble, & Joseph W. Geddes; front: Thomas Debevoise, Dr. W. A. R. Goodwin, George Coleman, Col. Arthur Woods, Charles O. Heydt. Andrew H. Hepburn, & Rudy Bertheau.

Courtesy, John D. Rockefeller, Jr., Library, Colonial Williamsburg Foundation

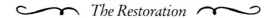
The decision to undertake the restorations occurred at a meeting in New York at the Vanderbilt Hotel in November 1927. With most of the architectural endorsements in hand, and color-coded maps and drawings hanging from the walls of his hotel room, Goodwin presented the plans to Rockefeller and his advisors. Toward the end of the first day, Rockefeller announced his intention to proceed with the entire project. At this point, three of Rockefeller's closest advisors–Charles O. Heydt, Thomas M. Debevoise, and Colonel Arthur Woods– were brought into the meeting and commented on various aspects of the project. Rockefeller authorized Goodwin to retain Perry, Shaw & Hepburn as the project architects; and Woods, Rockefeller's chief of staff, was to oversee the project. Goodwin was careful to present Perry with a clear outline of the scope of the project:

1. Christopher Wren Building: complete, with fireproof roof, estimated to cost, with architects' fees and all expenses included...$409,000.

2. House of Burgesses Building: without basement, except such basement as may be needed for furnace and coal room, fireproof construction and fireproof roof, estimated to cost, with architects' fees and all expenses included...$188,000.

3. The Golden Horseshoe Inn: fireproof construction, estimated to cost approximately...$100,000.

4. Governors' Palace: you are also authorized to prepare full plans, specifications, etc., for the fireproof restoration of the Colonial Governors' Palace, including the wings, cost approximately, including architects' fees, expenses, etc....$200,000. The question as to whether this building shall have concrete roof, or not, is left open for further consideration.

5. Town Plans: am further authorized to retain you and your firm, as architects in the Williamsburg Restoration scheme, with the understanding that you are to be paid on the basis of time and expenses for this work in accordance with our agreement.

In February 1928, articles of incorporation were drawn up creating two corporations: the Williamsburg Holding Corporation for the business activities and Colonial Williamsburg, Inc. for the non-profit educational activities. "Colonial Williamsburg" has since been adopted as the institutional name to define the entire operation. Although Rockefeller asked Woods to manage the project during the first few years, the day-to-day operations were directed by Goodwin. The organization soon, however, had grown into several corporations, innumerable departments, and an organized corps of advisors. Although Rockefeller did not hesitate to use all the resources at his disposal, including a team of advisors, most of whom remained in New York, Goodwin had primary responsibility to purchase property and orchestrate the complex political, legal, and bureaucratic processes necessary to obtain approvals for the restoration of the Wren Building and acquisition of the sites of the capitol and the Governor's Palace.

In the architect's office, "a small staff chosen for youth and enthusiasm was set upon the draughting of a city plan." In April 1928 some of them were sent to Williamsburg. They were followed in May by Walter M. Macomber, who had been appointed Resident Architect and head of the architectural team in Williamsburg. Macomber spoke of this as a tense period: "Starting with 3 junior draftsmen I found we were caught between the demands by the contractors for working drawings and our own demands for accuracy, and...more time for research and study." The architects studied the minutiae of colonial architecture, including authentic, regional details that necessitated a period of self-education. Since there were no textbooks on the subject, the architects studied surviving colonial structures in the Tidewater area.

Goodwin felt that a distinguished outside committee would inspire confidence in the architects, caution critics of the restoration, and provide valuable suggestions, which would enrich the quality of the work. Perry, Shaw & Hepburn also saw the wisdom in this approach and agreed to extend invitations and moderate the meetings. The Architects Advisory Committee met for the first time on 25 November 1928, at the Wythe house and the Chamberlain-Vanderbilt Hotel at Old Point Comfort. The following people were invited: Robert P. Bellows, president of the Boston Society of Architects and a member of the Committee on Historic Monuments of the American Institute of Architects; Edmund S. Campbell, professor of architecture at the University of Virginia and member of the State Art Commission; Finlay F. Ferguson, Sr., president of the Virginia Chapter of the A.I.A.; Fiske Kimball, director of the Philadelphia Museum of Art; Lawrence Kocher, chairman of the Committee on Historic Monuments, A.I.A.; Milton B. Medary, past president of the A.I.A.; Thomas E. Tallmadge, member of the Committee on Historic Monuments, A.I.A.; and Robert E. Lee Taylor, a Norfolk architect.

Perry saw the committee's role as one that "laid down ground rules in the early days of 1928 before the architects could go far astray." After being introduced to the project, the committee drew up and approved twenty resolutions, which were to be used by the architects as general principles. This list was later condensed to ten by Perry and became known as the "Decalogue." These principles stressed the retention of the colonial or classical traditions and the demolition or removal of everything else. They discouraged the moving in of buildings from outside the city and emphasized preservation and restoration of buildings on their original sites. Antique materials could be taken from demolished buildings, but should not be obtained by despoiling other Virginia buildings. When new materials were used they should be of a character approximating the old, but no attempt should be made to "antique" them by "theatrical means."

Advisory Committee of Architects on the front steps of the George Wythe house on 25 November 1928 during the first meeting of the committee. Rear (l-rt): Edmund S. Campbell, William G. Perry, Finlay Ferguson, Arthur A. Shurcliff, Fiske Kimball, & Walter M. Macomber; front: Milton B. Medary, Lawrence Kocher, Dr. W. A. R. Goodwin, Robert Bellows, Robert E. Lee Taylor, Andrew H. Hepburn, & Thomas M. Shaw.

The committee reviewed projects and usually gave a strong professional endorsement to the efforts of the project architects. The dominant figure at their meetings was Fiske Kimball, who introduced a third of all resolutions adopted by the committee during the twenty years that it met. From a public relations perspective it was important to bring outside specialists into the project, as they became ambassadors communicating to others in the profession as well as the general public.

Also, by now Rockefeller's backing had been revealed; and that created tremendous publicity. Although there was much speculation, Goodwin had been able to keep the secret until June 1928, when a public announcement was made at a town meeting held to determine whether the city should sell public land to the restoration project.

By 1929 it had become apparent that the historical research was too great a task for Goodwin and his part-time assistants, so the next year a department of research and record was established with Harold R. Shurtleff as recorder and historian. The new department was to supply information that would enable the architects to achieve authentic physical restoration. Shurtleff joined T. Rutherfoord Goodwin and Mary F. Goodwin, Goodwin's son and cousin, respectively, who had already done research for the architects on the Wren Building and the capitol.

Meanwhile, other specialists were needed. The architects hired Susan Higginson Nash, an interior designer, to carry out and oversee the selection of authentic furnishings for the exhibition buildings and all aspects of paint-color research; and the landscape architect Arthur A. Shurcliff (1870-1957) was hired as a consultant in 1928. At Harvard he had trained under the noted landscape architect, Charles W. Eliot, and took his first job with Frederick Law Olmsted, Sr., the father of landscape architecture in America.

In 1929 the Executive Committee of the American Society of Landscape Architects established a committee to assist Shurcliff. Shurcliff undoubtedly had a major role in selecting the blue-ribbon committee of some of the most highly respected landscape architects in the country: Rose Greely, Warren H. Manning, Fletcher Steele, Markly Stevenson, and Richard Schermerhorn, Jr. (chair). One of the committee's initial actions was to prepare general guidelines for landscape restoration, similar to the Decalogue, called the "Principles Underlying the Garden Restoration." Shurcliff was a dominant figure during this meeting, and these principles were primarily an expression of his own views.

In 1932 the Public Relations Department prepared the following statement to explain how the various components of the entire restoration project worked together:

The restoration of an existing home or building is begun with a thorough study of its history as to architecture, ownership and occupancy. Many colonial buildings have been changed and renovated in recent years. Former owners and occupants are able to recall the changes made. Valuable information is often found in the papers of persons no longer living, in old insurance policies, and on old property maps of the city which have been preserved. Court records, when available, contain interesting evidences. Archaeological investigation reveals foundations of portions and dependencies which may have been destroyed. With this information in hand, the building is dismantled, often to its frame. This permits the study of its construction and reveals any unsuspected alterations which have been made in the past. It also permits the replacement of decayed materials, although every piece of old material which is sound is retained. In some cases it is necessary to raise the building with jacks and replace decayed foundation walls and sills. With this work accomplished, the building is reassembled, the old materials which are sound and accurate being used. The building then is replastered by methods employed by colonial plasterers. It is redecorated according to the available evidences of its original decorations. Where evidence is lacking, precedent established by similar houses of similar date is resorted to.

The physical work of restoring or reconstructing the buildings was usually preceded by an unearthing of the original foundations using existing structures and the Frenchman's Map (see p. 40) as a guide. The first excavations were undertaken at the capitol site in August 1928, and in November excavations began at the Raleigh Tavern site. The architects directed the excavations without, however, the help of an archaeologist. Most of the excavations were carried out by a work force of four to six laborers and a foreman. Because the primary objective at both sites was to measure and draw the foundations, only a few artifacts were collected; but when a wall collapsed into the excavations at the Raleigh Tavern site, the architects realized they needed the help of a professional archaeologist, so that Prentice Duell was hired early in 1929. After completing the Raleigh Tavern excavation, he began work at the Wren Building, then the next year directed numerous excavations including those at the Governor's Palace.

Governor's Palace in 1935 from the palace green.

Courtesy, John D. Rockefeller, Jr., Library, Colonial Williamsburg Foundation

The person having the greatest influence in excavating sites was James M. Knight, who joined the staff in 1931. The primary purpose of excavating was to locate the positions of eighteenth-century structures and identify their original uses. Prominent landscape features were also sought to assist in the restoration of the gardens. Although artifacts were collected and labeled, most of the sites were still being dug by unskilled laborers using shovels. In addition, the enormous pressure to complete architectural plans for the Wren Building, the capitol, and the Governor's Palace and to begin work on the buildings prevented a close examination of the ground or a careful recording of the exact location and position of the artifacts uncovered; and space for storing and time for cleaning and treating the burgeoning number of artifacts became a serious problem. In order to reduce the number of artifacts that could be collected, Kenneth Chorley, chief administrative officer of the restoration in Williamsburg, at one point directed that screening of the removed earth should be stopped at most of the sites. Concerned over the lack of interest in artifacts, Rutherfoord Goodwin established an archaeological laboratory. He placed Minor Wine Thomas, a William and Mary graduate in chemistry, in charge of the lab, with responsibility for cleaning, treatment, and storage of the artifacts. Thomas also set up the first archaeological exhibit, in the old courthouse.

In 1930, with the anticipated completion of the project after the Governor's Palace and the capitol were reconstructed (see color plates 7 and 8), rumors circulated that Rockefeller might turn the whole thing over to the National Park Service. This possibility first arose during discussions surrounding the establishment of the Colonial National Monument. Most citizens did not want the town to become a national monument under government ownership and opposed the idea; and considering the protest from the citizens of Williamsburg, Congress backed down. When the Colonial National Monument was established on 30 December 1930, the only land acquired from the town was that necessary for the parkway. Rockefeller removed any lingering thoughts the staff or townspeople may have had concerning his long-term plans for the restoration when he acquired, rehabilitated, and enlarged Bassett Hall, which became known as "Rockefeller's Williamsburg white house."

In October 1930, the Ladies Advisory Committee formed itself. It was comprised of two groups, a local advisory committee and a plantation committee. The plantation committee consisted of eleven women who owned important eighteenth-century houses in Virginia–the ones the architects visited in their search for information on colonial architecture. Both committees met frequently, visited construction sites, reviewed plans for furnishing the exhibition buildings, and were extremely helpful to the architects and the research staff. When precedents were sought for such elements as moldings, paint colors, or hardware, researchers contacted committee members who lived in or knew families who lived in eighteenth-century houses and who might be able to supply the information required. In this way some of the most influential families in Virginia became involved in the restoration.

The last committee to be established was the Advisory Committee of Historians. Realizing that the original mission was nearing completion and that the research department would cease to exist if it didn't broaden its activities into education and interpretation, Shurtleff suggested that a conference of historians should be convened in Williamsburg to consider whether the Colonial Williamsburg Foundation should maintain a research department, and if so, what its functions should be, what methods its staff should use to collect and arrange information, and how it should address the needs of those involved in the restoration as well those of educators, students, and the general public, including children. Nine prominent historians were invited to the conference in October 1932: Charles M. Andrews, H. I. Brock, Samuel Eliot Morison, Thomas J. Wertenbaker, Lyon G. Tyler, Earl G. Swem, N. J. Eckenrode, Lester J. Cappon, and Alexander W. Weddell. As the participants could not complete discussions on all the issues and prepare a written report, a subcommittee met in January at the Harvard Club in New York to do so. The report recommended that research continue within the organizational framework of the Colonial Williamsburg Foundation, but that a new emphasis on public education should supplement and fulfill the program already carried out by the architectural and archaeological staffs. The report also recommended that the Foundation "promote educational publicity of a high order; and...promote a series of scholarly publications relating to the history of Williamsburg and the territory that it served, as long as it remained the capital of Virginia."

Fortunately, Rockefeller's resources allowed the restoration to continue throughout the Depression and ensured that many of the residents remained employed. In September 1932 the Raleigh Tavern became the first building open to the public (see pp. 79-80). Rockefeller decided not to attend the opening, however, as he did not want to draw too much national attention to a project that was still several years from completion. Throughout 1933, most of the activity was concentrated at the capitol, palace, and buildings along Duke of Gloucester Street. Beginning that December, all utility lines within the historic area were put underground. The next February, the capitol was officially opened during a commemorative joint session of the General Assembly held in the reconstructed building, and this time Rockefeller authorized full national coverage and addressed the legislative body assembled in the chamber of the House of Burgesses. Then, during Garden Week, the Governor's Palace opened; and in October, President Roosevelt lead a motorcade from the capitol to the Wren Building and rededicated Duke of Gloucester Street, calling it "the most historic avenue in all America" (see p. 148). Roosevelt's visit announced that Colonial Williamsburg was ready to receive the public.

The last structure to be completed under the original project outlined by Rockefeller was the Ludwell-Paradise house, which housed the Abby Aldrich Rockefeller Folk Art Collection. By the end of 1934, the pace of restoration slackened because the original project was substantially completed: fifty-nine structures had been restored, ninety-one others reconstructed, twenty-nine new shops in two business blocks at the west end of Duke of Gloucester Street constructed, and four hundred fifty-eight structures removed. In September 1934, Woods changed the contract with the architects and the contractors; and by October the only two architects who remained were A. Edwin Kendrew and Singleton P. Moorehead. The chief draftsman was Kendrew, who moved to Williamsburg permanently in 1929. At this point, Woods established the departments of Architecture and Construction & Maintenance with Kendrew and Elton Holland, a Williamsburg resident, as directors. Meanwhile, other departments increased in size, especially those involved with interpretation and education; and a Department of Education was formed in November 1933. It later merged with the Department of Research, with Harold Shurtleff as its director.

Persuaded by Perry, Kendrew, and Goodwin that the original project had not created enough sense of colonial Williamsburg's being an urban site, Rockefeller agreed to more reconstruction. The pace of reconstructing missing architectural features and providing visitor facilities steadily increased between 1938 and 1942. The Wythe house, the first exhibition building whose restoration was planned and executed exclusively by members of the foundation, opened in March 1940; and during the summer of 1941, Chowning's Tavern, the first operating tavern in the historic area, was opened for business. In May 1942, however, the organization applied wartime restraints to itself. The National Park Service, however, was able to complete the tunnel that carried the Colonial Parkway under the historic area. (The NPS had to be convinced by Goodwin and others that it ought not do as it had planned and put the parkway right through the town!)

The structure of the foundation's leadership underwent several changes between 1928 and 1942. In 1928 the trustees of Colonial Williamsburg, Inc. were identical to the directors

John D. Rockefeller, Jr., remodeled Bassett Hall as his Williamsburg residence, which signaled his continued commitment to the restoration. The Rockefellers lived here two months each year, and Mr. Rockefeller would often walk around town, retaining as much anonymity as possible.

Courtesy, John D. Rockefeller, Jr., Library, Colonial Williamsburg Foundation

of the Williamsburg Holding Corporation and consisted of Vernon M. Geddy, president; Fred R. Savage, vice president; and Goodwin, secretary. At that time, Goodwin was actually directing all the activities from his office in the Wythe house, but in the next few years he transferred control to the corporate offices run by Chorley. Once the restoration was established and operating, he was content to let others take over the detailed process of making his dream a reality. By 1935 the staff had grown to 247 employees. The principal offices had moved to occupy space above the old post office and on most of the second floor of the adjoining building in Merchant's Square. Goodwin continued to advise the administrative staff on matters relating to policy and planning until a heart attack in 1938 confined him to a bed for the remainder of his life.

Despite the scale of the project and Rockefeller's personal interest in it, Woods did not take up residency in Williamsburg; and although Chorley temporarily resided here between 1930 and 1932, he moved back to New York. Despite Goodwin's persistent urging, none of the principal architects would agree to relocate even temporarily to Williamsburg, preferring to commute. Early references by residents to a "Yankee invasion" are understandable considering that most of the key people commuted from New York or Boston.

Rockefeller's interest in Williamsburg never diminished, however; and he remodeled Bassett Hall as his Williamsburg residence, usually spending two months of the year here, one in the spring and one in the fall. According to his biographer, he was more deeply interested and more personally involved in the restoration of Williamsburg than in any other undertaking. He involved himself personally in every building that was restored or reconstructed and consistently aimed to achieve the utmost authenticity, whatever the cost in time, money, or effort. The restoration became his pet project and main challenge because it combined his love of nature, landscaping, planning, and building; and his decision to establish a Williamsburg home had an enormous effect on the organization because it demonstrated his commitment to continue the restoration. When in town, he would walk through the exhibition buildings and construction sites, often alone; and those who recognized him were asked to keep his identity a secret in order not to draw unnecessary attention to him.

John D. Rockefeller, Jr.

Courtesy, Rockefeller Archive Center; photo from Colonial Williamsburg Foundation

Although Goodwin had not been the first person to see the architectural and historical significance of the town and the need to preserve it, he was able to persuade other individuals and organizations to share his dream. At first he started with the restoration of Bruton Parish Church and the George Wythe house. Then he purchased and encouraged others to purchase property adjacent to surviving structures in order to protect them from encroachment by modern buildings. As director of fundraising for William and Mary, in 1924 Goodwin went to New York to explain the fundraising campaign for the construction of a Phi Beta Kapp Society Hall for the sesquicentennial of Phi Beta Kappa, which was founded at the college. When Rockefeller agreed to serve as the national chairman of the campaign, Goodwin took the opportunity to present to him his vision of a small Tidewater town, stripped of its modern excrescencies and restored to the historical condition of the mid-eighteenth century. The outcome is a remarkable history of remaking history.

Selected Sources & Suggested Readings

Albright, Horace M., and Robert Cahn. *The Birth of the National Park Service: The Founding Years, 1913-33* (Salt Lake City: Howe Brothers, 1985), pp. 247-51.

Business Men's Association of the City of Williamsburg, *Facts About Williamsburg And Vicinity* (Richmond: Whittet & Shepperson, 1900).

Chorley, Kenneth. *Colonial Williamsburg: The First Twenty-five Years, a Report by the President* (Williamsburg: Colonial Williamsburg Foundation, 1952), p. 5.

Fosdick, Raymond B. *John D. Rockefeller, Jr.: A Portrait* (N.Y.: Harper & Brothers, 1956), p. 272.

Goodwin, W. A. R. *Historical Sketch Of Bruton Parish Church* (Petersburg: Franklin, 1903).

Goodwin, W. A. R. *The Record Of Bruton Church*, ed. and rev. by Mary Frances Goodwin (Richmond: Dietz, 1941).

Hosmer, Charles B. Jr. "The Early Restorationists of Colonial Williamsburg," in *Preservation and Conservation Principles and Practices*, ed. by Sharon Timmons (Washington, D.C.: Preservation Press, 1976), p. 511.

Macomber, Walter M. "The Interpretation of Evidence," *in Old Cities of The New World: Proceedings of the Pan American Symposium on the Preservation & Restoration of Historic Monuments, St. Augustine, Florida, June 20-25, 1965* (St. Augustine: St. Augustine Historical Restoration & Preservation Commission, 1967), p.1.

Moscow, Alvin. *The Rockefeller Inheritance* (N.Y.: Doubleday, 1977).

Perry, William G. "Notes on the Architecture," *Architectural Record* (Dec. 1935): 363.

Shurcliff, Arthur. "City Plan and Landscaping Problems," *Architectural Record* (Dec. 1935): 382.

Simpson, Alan. *The Mysteries Of The "Frenchman's Map" Of Williamsburg, Virginia* (Williamsburg: Colonial Williamsburg Foundation, 1984).

Swem, Earl G. "Some Notes on the Four Forms of the Oldest Building of William and Mary College," *William and Mary College Quarterly Historical Magazine* 8, no. 4 (Oct. 1928): 217-307.

Tyler, Lyon Gardiner. *Williamsburg, the Old Colonial Capital* (Richmond: Whittet and Shepperson, 1907).

A Busy and Purposeful Place:
Williamsburg During World War II

by: Will Molineux

Although the news had been expected at any moment, when the announcement came over the radio it was as if "a volcano erupted" on Duke of Gloucester Street. Soldiers and sailors, who packed the USO Club to await the broadcast, raced onto Merchants Square hollering and whooping uncontrollably. In the Williamsburg Restaurant, proprietor Steve Sacalis heard the commotion and knew immediately what it meant. He told patrons their meals were free, but they had to hurry and finish eating because he was closing up. Someone burst into the Williamsburg Theatre and shouted out the news; and, almost before the lights could come on, the movie house was empty—and the size of the street celebration doubled. George Rogers, a volunteer fireman, cranked up an old pumper and, with siren sounding, lights flashing, and bell clanging, drove through the streets as celebrants climbed aboard. Servicemen and townspeople snake-danced throughout downtown. At a softball field in town, the visiting team from West Point understandably failed to show up for a championship game, and so Pittman Roane and his Williamsburg players joined the V-J festivities. Church bells rang out. Cars, loaded with cheering, boisterous revelers, moved up and down the streets, enlarging and expanding the celebration.

The pent-up jubilation burst forth at 7 P.M., Eastern Daylight Savings Time, on Tuesday, 14 August 1945, when the official announcement was made: "Japan has surrendered. Peace at last." In Williamsburg, one unidentified "old-timer" with an intuitive sense of local history told a reporter that it was "the biggest thing since the Revolutionary War."

It was certainly a history-making day at the Chesapeake and Potomac Telephone Company switchboard. Off-duty operators showed up—one walking in two miles from the countryside—to put through 12,000 local and 1,400 long-distance calls that evening. Clerks at the Western Union office typed out far more telegrams than usual.

Williamsburg had been a busy and purposeful place for four years—ever since 7 December 1941, and especially after the first test of the community air raid sirens on the evening of 17 March 1942. The steam whistles at Eastern State Hospital and at the College of William and Mary power plant could be heard within a radius of five miles. A test of blackout conditions came three months later. On 19 June there was to be, the city wardens proclaimed, "no light except from stars and lightning bugs."

On 26 March 1943, Y. O. Kent, manager of the college bookstore and chief of auxiliary police, ordered the arrest of a physician, a volunteer fireman, and the local manager of the Virginia Electric and Power Company for violating the blackout. The physician and the fireman testified they needed their auto lights to respond to emergencies; the VEPCO manager said a switch failed. The judge dismissed all charges.

In the steeple of the Williamsburg Methodist Church on College Corner, high above the city's rooftops, an airplane lookout post was established, manned around the clock by residents augmented by William and Mary students, senior Boy Scouts, and Girl Scouts. Every plane spotted was immediately reported by an open phone line to military officials. On Jamestown Island, a detail from the 85th Coast Artillery was posted on the government dock as airplane spotters from mid-summer 1942 to the summer of 1944. The only excitement the aerial sentries had to report was the crash of a single-engine Army plane that went down 4 June 1943, in James City County in the woods near Lake Powell. The pilot parachuted safely.

Everyone in Williamsburg, it seemed, participated in the war effort under the overall coordination of Vernon M. Geddy, Sr., an attorney who was vice president of Colonial Williamsburg. Martha Barksdale, the women's physical education instructor at William and Mary, taught courses in first aid; medical stations, stocked with $600 worth of supplies, were set up around town. The Colonial Parkway tunnel under the Historic Area, which by 1942 had been dug out but not paved, was designated the air raid shelter for the entire community.

Housewives gathered and cleaned 2,400 garments and sent them to families in Great Britain. (In Bristol, England, where 750,000 books were donated as scrap paper to be converted into pulp, a copy of Paolo Sarpi's *History of the Council of Trent* [1676], missing for two centuries from the William and Mary Library, was miraculously discovered and rescued. It was returned to the college after the war.)

The Reverend Francis H. Craighill, rector of Bruton Parish Church, receives a group of sponsors of convalescent servicemen prior to a dinner served in the Parish House auditorium: (l-rt) Betty Marie Ellet and Nancy Carnegie, William and Mary Red Cross volunteers; Rev. Craighill; two soldiers; Christine Cunningham, assistant field director, Langley Field; Mrs. Charles Duke; Mrs. John E. Pomfret, wife of the president of the College of William and Mary; Vonceille Tate, executive secretary, James City County Chapter of the Red Cross.

Courtesy, James City County Chapter, American Red Cross

Magazines and books were collected for patients in military hospitals throughout the Tidewater. Thousands of surgical dressings were made. Mrs. Richard L. Morton, wife of a history professor, led a contingent of Red Cross knitters who turned out socks and scarves for servicemen overseas. Coeds from William and Mary, members of the college unit of the Red Cross, spent Sunday afternoons entertaining patients in hospital wards at Langley Field in Hampton. On Tuesdays, convalescent GIs were brought to Williamsburg for dinner in various church social halls.

Residents of Williamsburg also contributed financially to the war effort. A fund-raising drive for the USO collected $1,700 and was oversubscribed. When the U.S. Treasury Department called on Americans to buy bonds for the construction of the aircraft carrier *Shangri-La,* which was to be used expressly to launch bombers for raids on Tokyo, it assigned Virginia the goal of $13 million and Williamsburg was given the quota of $3,942—which was met. Air raid wardens went from house to house selling war bonds and stamps.

Gasoline, coffee, sugar, and meat were rationed. Although leather shoes were in short supply, canvas shoes could be bought on the black market, such as the one that was operated in a rural hay barn. Dresses for schoolgirls were made from the cloth of grain bags. Victory gardens were tended in large and small plots all over town. Scrap paper was bundled up and collected every Wednesday afternoon, and the Person Motor Company advertised that it was the collection point for scrap rubber—"old tires, garden hose, hot water bottles."

Faculty members at William and Mary were given war-related assignments. George J. Ryan, who taught Latin and Greek, spent thirteen months translating into English four volumes of navigational records of the Greek coastline. Other professors lectured at Fort Eustis and other military posts on such learned matters as the aims of German foreign policy and domestic wartime finances. William and Mary President John E. Pomfret gave talks off campus on the Soviet Union and its role in the war. Dudley W. Woodbridge, dean of jurisprudence, was an air raid warden and Red Cross volunteer.

Academic credit was extended to students who were drafted or enlisted in military service and had to leave campus before they could complete a semester's study. An innovative work-study program, whereby students spent three days in classrooms and three days working in defense-related jobs at the Navy Mine Depot at Yorktown and elsewhere, was initiated.

The Army created a program in 1943 at William and Mary to train military technicians and specialists. Students in the Army Specialized Training Program's Unit 3321 were offered courses in engineering, mathematics, physics, chemistry, and foreign languages. Instruction was also given in camouflage, home nursing, internal combustion engines, map reading, interpretation of aerial photographs, and telegraphy. The students, soldiers who had completed their basic training, lived in Tyler and Brown Halls and in Blow Gymnasium. Every day at dawn they were marched to the dining hall, much to the annoyance of the slumbering residents of Sorority Court. Late one night, the Kappa Kappa Gammas went over to Brown Hall armed with pots, pans, and anything else that would make noise to disturb the

Elizabeth Aurell, left, and Nancy Outland at the piano entertain soldiers convalescing in the Army hospital at Langley Field. The William and Mary coeds were Red Cross volunteers in 1944–1945.

Courtesy, James City County Chapter, American Red Cross

Models on sand tables were used to teach the techniques of camouflage at the Army Specialized Training Program at William and Mary. Here, an industrial site along a railroad, top photo, has been made to appear as a residential area.

Courtesy, University Archives, Swem Library, College of William and Mary

servicemen's sleep. The next morning the men of ASTP Unit 3321 marched down Richmond Road singing, "Lay those pistols down, babes; lay those pistols down. Pistol packing Kappas, lay those pistols down!" The ASTP unit was abruptly withdrawn in March 1944, when the men were urgently needed to replace frontline casualties in Europe. Many of them fought with General George Patton's Third Army in the Battle of the Bulge.

In early 1942, almost as soon as the United States entered the war, the Navy condemned 11,000 acres in York County three miles west of Williamsburg. There, on the York River, the Navy established Camp Peary, named for the naval civil engineer, arctic explorer, and conqueror of the North Pole, Robert E. Peary. The tract included the historic Port Bello plantation on Queens Creek, where Virginia's last royal governor, Lord Dunmore, once had a country home, and the community of Magruder. Some of the displaced families temporarily took up residence in the abandoned Civilian Conservation Corps camp at the edge of the college woods, and others permanently relocated in and about Williamsburg and in the Grove community. At Camp Peary, the U.S. Naval Construction Training Center taught more than 85,000 Seabees how to put up quonset huts, build airstrips and roads, load and unload cargo ships, and use underwater explosives before sending them to combat zones in North Africa, Sicily, and the Pacific, especially to the Solomon Islands.

In the early summer of 1944, Camp Peary's mission changed when it became the site for the U.S. Naval Training and Distribution Center. At this time John D. Rockefeller, Jr., and the officers of Colonial Williamsburg honored Captain James G. Ware, the popular commander of Camp Peary, and his officers at a dinner in the Williamsburg Inn. Rockefeller called Ware, a 1910 graduate of the Naval Academy, "forceful, able, wise…respected, esteemed, trusted…as modest as he is brave; a loyal patriot." Syndicated newspaper columnist Drew Pearson, however, accused Ware of profiteering from the operation of a hog farm at Camp Peary. Ware denied the charges, but a short time later he left the Navy.

In 1942 the USO Club was opened in the Stringfellow Building, one of the new commercial structures in Merchants Square, and was later expanded with Rockefeller's financial assistance. The recreation center became so popular that a wooden addition had to be built and dances held outdoors in the parking lot. A separate USO club was opened for black servicemen in Bruton Heights School. Comedians Bob Hope and Jack Benny put on shows at Camp Peary. Red Skelton, then an Army private stationed at Fort Eustis, staged street

Barracks for sailors in training to be Seabees appear to be rows of Hs in this aerial photograph of Camp Peary. Sawmills were set up in the area known as Magruder, and the camp was built within a few months. Trainees practiced amphibious landings along the York River and, using cranes and cargo nets, practiced unloading ships on a platform along Queens Creek, off the overview to the right. Swimming was taught in more than two dozen swimming pools on post. After the war, Camp Peary became the site for the Armed Forces Experimental Activity.

CAMP PEARY
MAIN ENTRANCEWAY AND HOSTESS HOUSE

Courtesy, Department of Defense,
Camp Peary Archives

The gatehouse pictured in this postcard was located to the far left, out of sight in the aerial overview, on what was then State Route 168 at the end of Airport Road. A prisoner of war camp was established late in the war to the left of the entranceway.

Abby and John D. Rockefeller, Jr., pose with an unidentified soldier, sailor, and marine at the dedication of the USO Club they helped to fund in the Stringfellow Building on Merchants Square. The Rockefellers later provided additional funding to expand the facility. Residents of Williamsburg and the surrounding area, many of them parents of men and women on duty overseas, served as hosts.

Courtesy, John D. Rockefeller, Jr. Library, Colonial Williamsburg Foundation

George Allen, right, a Navy mess steward, swings his partner at a USO dance in the gymnasium of Bruton Heights School. Allen grew up on a farm on Barlow Road in York County and was drafted at age eighteen. He was on leave in early 1945 when this picture was taken by Albert Durant.

Courtesy, John D. Rockefeller, Jr., Library, Colonial Williamsburg Foundation

performances in town. (He later entertained a national television audience with his comic characters Freddie the Freeloader, Clem Kadiddlehopper, and others.) Camp Peary's football team, the Pirates, played home games on William and Mary's Cary Field, and the base's dance band played at dances for teenagers in The Matthew Whaley School.

U.S. Route 60, designated a priority military highway, was widened and improved between Bottoms Bridge east of Richmond and Lee Hall in what was then Warwick County; and the bridge to Jamestown Island was rebuilt. The federal government, in order to ensure an adequate water supply for the booming shipbuilding city of Newport News, laid a pipeline from Walker's Dam, which empounded the Chickahominy River, to the Lee Hall and Harwood's Mill Reservoirs on the lower Peninsula.

To alleviate overcrowding at the Norfolk Naval Base and to help fill empty dormitories on campus, the Naval Training School of Chaplains was moved on 17 March 1943 to William and Mary. The school's purpose was to indoctrinate civilian clergymen who already held naval commissions and some select enlisted personnel in the ways and customs of the Navy. Students were housed in Old Dominion and Monroe halls and attended classes in James Blair Hall, then called Marshall-Wythe Hall. J. Wilfred Lambert, the college's dean of men, was given a commission and assigned to the school's administrative staff. One of the faculty members was Lieutenant Commander Phillip L. Claud, a 1934 William and Mary graduate who had seen action at Guadalcanal. More than 2,700 chaplains received their indoctrination into the Navy before the school closed on 15 November 1945.

During the war, Williamsburg and William and Mary had an especially close affiliation with the Navy. Each October, Navy Day was observed. In 1943, an estimated five thousand people stood along Duke of Gloucester Street to applaud one thousand Seabees from Camp Peary and sailors from Cheatham Annex and the Navy Mine Depot at Yorktown as they marched toward the College Yard. There, from a platform erected in front of the Wren Building, Governor Colgate W. Darden spoke to the commonwealth over WRVA radio.

In June 1941, before America's entry into the war, General George C. Marshall, Chief of Staff of the Army, told 204 William and Mary graduates of the Army's training efforts "to guard against some of the hideous losses of the past caused through poor leadership." A year later, Admiral Ernest J. King, Chief of Naval Operations, assured 190 William and Mary graduates that the United States "would defeat the enemy."

Williamsburg's senior war hero was Rear Admiral John Lesslie Hall, Jr., brother of Mayor Channing M. Hall. Admiral Hall developed and perfected amphibious landing operations in North Africa, Sicily, and Italy; and he commanded a task force of 691 ships that landed elements of the V Corps on Omaha Beach. Still later, Hall commanded a task force invading Okinawa in the Pacific.

The local connection with the Navy was clearly demonstrated in the naming and sponsorship of several vessels. Admiral Hall's wife, Beall Daingerfield Hall, a descendant of a distinguished Alexandria family, was selected by the Navy as the sponsor of the frigate *Alexandria,* launched in September 1943 at a Cleveland boatyard. The Victory ship *William and Mary*—one of about forty named for American colleges—was built in forty-five days and launched 20 April 1945 at Baltimore. Her sponsor was Eleanor Harvey, president of the Women's Student Government Association; Edith Harwood, incoming president of the WSGA, was the maid of honor. Dean of Women Grace Landrum went along as chaperone. Two other wartime cargo ships, both launched in 1943, were named for former William and Mary presidents James Blair and Lyon Gardiner Tyler.

During the war years, most of Williamsburg's tourists wore uniforms. Enlisted men from Fort Eustis were brought to town in truck convoys for indoctrination programs in the Williamsburg Theatre and the Colonial Williamsburg Reception Center to bolster their patriotic fervor. They were encouraged to walk around the historic area and, in lesser numbers, to visit Jamestown. Sailors, too, were given familiarization tours.

Williamsburg was a crowded place. Civilian workers assigned to Cheatham Annex and the Navy Mine Depot (since renamed the Yorktown Naval Weapons Station) and wives and

Admiral John Lesslie Hall, Jr. (1891–1978) on his D-Day command ship. A native of Williamsburg, Hall attended William and Mary and graduated from the U.S. Naval Academy in 1913. (See p. 287.)

Courtesy, U.S. Navy

The Victory cargo ship, James Blair, named for the founder and first president of William and Mary, was launched in the Bethlehem-Fairfield yard in Baltimore on 26 August 1943.

Courtesy, University Archives, Swem Library, College of William and Mary fiancées of military personnel stationed at Fort Eustis and Camp Peary rented every available apartment and room. On weekends, bunks were set up for servicemen in the Presbyterian and Baptist churches—and rented for 50 cents, plus breakfast. By the end of 1942, the population of Williamsburg was estimated to be five thousand, double that of the previous year. Thousands more came in 1943. City officials tracked down reports of rent profiteering; and the Chamber of Commerce, under the leadership of Doctor H. M. Stryker, kept a registry of rental units and served as a clearinghouse. Late in the war, dormitory rooms in Brown and Tyler halls on the William and Mary campus were rented to military families. At The Oaks, the rather substantial home of the Smith family that sat well off Jamestown Road and beside Cary Street, nine bedrooms were rented. Colonial Williamsburg closed the Williamsburg Inn dining room but rented rooms—for $3.50 a night—to officers and their wives. The dining room became an officers club.

For a few days in May 1943, the British General Staff, in Washington for consultations, traveled to Williamsburg and were honored at a convocation at William and Mary. Clementine Churchill, wife of British Prime Minister Winston Churchill, and their daughter Mary, a subaltern in the British army, toured Williamsburg on 8 September 1943. While they were in the Raleigh Tavern, news came that Italy had capitulated. Later that year, Canadian Prime Minister W. Mackenzie King visited the city for a respite.

Williamsburg was the scene of one small flurry of military action. On 13 March 1945, three men—German prisoners of war, who had escaped from a stockade at Camp Peary—attracted attention in the historic area because they were "acting suspiciously." Frank Dobson, director of the Apprentice School for the Newport News Shipyard and a Williamsburg resident, gave chase and cornered them in the shrubbery behind the home of Colonial Wil-

The service and sacrifice of Navy men and women everywhere were recognized and honored by the Williamsburg community on Navy Day, 26 October 1943. After viewing the parade down Duke of Gloucester St., townspeople, William and Mary students, and sailors gathered in the Wren Yard to hear an address by Governor Colgate W. Darden.

Courtesy, Thomas L. Williams archive

"They were always so grateful, so interested," recalls Elizabeth Callis, a longtime guide for Colonial Williamsburg. Callis was one of several hostesses who told soldiers from Fort Eustis of Williamsburg's role in establishing the principles of American democracy. Years later, she said she received more satisfaction from giving these wartime tours than any others.

At the invitation of John D. Rockefeller, Jr., soldiers from Fort Eustis were trucked to Williamsburg for one-day tours of the historic area, which began with an orientation in the Williamsburg Theatre in Merchants Square and included stops, shown here, at the Governor's Palace kitchen and the magazine. Sailors from Camp Peary were sometimes granted liberty in Williamsburg and, as seen in these postcards, visited the courthouse of 1770 and the wigmaker's shop.

No. 205-N   *Official U. S. Navy Photo*
SOLDIERS VISIT OLD COURT HOUSE, WILLIAMSBURG, VA.

No. 204-N   Seabees of Camp Peary Visit Old Williamsburg, Va.   *Official U. S. Navy Photo*

Courtesy, Thomas L. Williams archive and John D. Rockefeller, Jr., Library, Colonial Williamsburg Foundation

liamsburg architect A. Edwin Kendrew. "What I should do," Dobson told the trio, "is to treat you like you'd treat my son if you captured him: knock your brains out." Apparently one of the Germans felt threatened and ran off; but Kendrew, who had come out of his house, ran after him and recaptured him near the home of Doctor A. G. Ryland on Francis Street. The noise of the scuffle attracted Ryland; and Dobson, Kendrew, and Ryland marched their prisoners off to the Williamsburg Inn, where they were met by Police Lieutenant L. N. Smith, who took the Germans into custody. A few days later Dobson learned that his son, Major John W. Dobson, had escaped from a German POW camp in northern Poland and was in friendly hands.

Vernon M. Geddy, executive vice president of Colonial Williamsburg, escorts Clementine Churchill, wife of British Prime Minister Winston Churchill, and their daughter, Army Subaltern Mary Churchill, along the palace green.

Courtesy, Vernon M. Geddy, Jr.

News from abroad about locals filled the pages of the *Virginia Gazette.* Captain Hiram W. Davis of the Army Medical Corps, whose father had been a surgeon in World War I and whose grandfather had been a surgeon in the Civil War, received the Silver Star for gallantry in action in Europe. Navy Lieutenant Alden Hopkins interpreted aerial photographs of Japanese-held islands in the Pacific; John E. Hocutt, assistant dean of men at William and Mary, served as a lieutenant aboard the battle cruiser *Guam* at Okinawa; Frederick W. Hoeing was with the American Field Service in Italy; Anne Ballard Haughwout was a Red Cross worker in North Africa; and WAC Private Emily Y. Wilson, previously employed by Colonial Williamsburg, was stationed in Naples.

Richard Holland wrote to his mother while he was aboard an LST—"a large, slow target," he called it—that participated in the D-Day landing. And First Lieutenant Horace E. "Hunky" Henderson, who landed at dawn at Normandy on 7 June 1944, told Stephen Ambrose, author of *Citizen Soldiers,* that "the beach was covered with debris, sunken craft and wrecked vehicles. We saw many bodies in the water…. We jumped into chest-high water and waded ashore. Then we saw that the beach was literally covered with bodies of American soldiers"; and before they could be removed, "the first religious service was held on Omaha Beach." A few days later Henderson wrote home that he was "comfortably set up in an abandoned Nazi headquarters." He wrote his letter on the same day that Staff Sergeant John T. Blacknall, who had landed with other members of the Virginia National Guard, was killed.

There was other grim news. Economics Professor Albion Guilford Taylor was informed that his son, Lieutenant Robert Guilford Taylor, pilot of a flying fortress, was missing over Germany. He was, it turned out, a prisoner of war. At least two other fliers from the Williamsburg area—Ronald Faison and Garland New—were shot down and held as prisoners of war.

Army Captain James N. Hillman, Jr., was reported killed in a plane crash in California. His father, James N. Hillman, Sr., had been principal of Nicholson School in Williamsburg before he was named president of Emory and Henry College. Williamsburg was particularly saddened when the news came in September 1943 that Second Lieutenant William A. R. Goodwin, Jr., who had left the University of Virginia as a sophomore to volunteer and became a pilot of a P-40, was killed while on a dive-bombing mission near Mount Etna. A few days before, he had written his brother from a base in Sicily: "This is what I've wanted for a year and a half, and I'm not disappointed." He was twenty-two. Goodwin's father was the Episcopal rector of Bruton Parish Church who had been instrumental in the restoration of the eighteenth-century city.

Ellsworth P. Ayers, Jr., Dewey C. Renick, Jr., and Willard Gilley, close boyhood pals who grew up in James City County, had graduated from The Matthew Whaley School in successive years 1937-1939. Each then had gone to Virginia Tech, and, after graduation, went off to war. First Lieutenant Ayers contracted polio while in Italy and died in a Naples hospital in December 1943. First Lieutenant Gilley, an infantry platoon leader, was severely wounded in combat in Italy on 30 March 1945, and spent two years recuperating in an Army hospital. Three days before Gilley was wounded, the plane in which Second Lieutenant Renick was flying crashed in the Luzon Mountains of the Philippines. His body was never located; but his VPI ring, Class of 1942, was recovered and returned to his parents. It was found on a string worn around the neck of a native.

Among the others from Williamsburg and nearby environs who were killed, in addition to Sergeant Blacknall, were James A. Bailey, Philip S. Chess, Jr., Glenn R. Cooley, Robert B. Eubank, Alexander G. Harwood III, Alvin W. Haynes, James G. Heath, W. W. McGee, Howard E. Madison, Walter C. Martin, Jr., Lyon Tyler Miles, Horace G. Munden, Barney Pyle, L. M. Rhodes, John R. Richardson, Edward Rountree, Richard D. Sensel, Sidney A. Vincent, Jr., and Robert G. Whitcomb.

A plaque in The Matthew Whaley School lists the names of 250 former students who served their country in World War II. On a brass tablet in the entranceway of the Goodwin Building are the names of six men associated with Colonial Williamsburg who made the supreme sacrifice.

At William and Mary, the Department of Fine Arts kept a wooden tablet to record the names of the college dead—a marker that, after the war, became a stone memorial placed on an interior wall of the Wren Building. Eighteen faculty members put on the uniform of the armed services and one of them, Murray Eugene Borish of the English Department, was killed when, in January 1943, the transport ship on which he was sailing was sunk. (Through a bequest honoring Professor Borish, since 1979 an endowment fund gives a prize annually to the outstanding senior concentrating in English.) A total of eighty-eight former students were killed or died of wounds.

Post 39 of the American Legion lists 884 men and women from Williamsburg and the surrounding area who served in uniform. After the war, the legionnaires placed a wooden tablet at the intersection of Duke of Gloucester and South Henry streets. This memorial was later transferred to the Williamsburg–James City County Courthouse and stood for many years facing the sidewalk on South England Street.

The sacrifice of servicemen was very much on the minds of everyone in Williamsburg in the late spring of 1944 when preparations were made for a solemn communal outpouring of hope and prayer on the occasion of the invasion of Europe across the English Channel. The exact date of the Invasion Day Assembly was not set, but everyone understood that when the assault began they were to gather in the Wren Yard. And so on the evening of the sixth of June they assembled and sang "Oh, God, Our Help in Ages Past" and "America, the Beautiful." Mayor Channing M. Hall intoned that "the tremendous effort started today" [is]

On 8 March 1946, Winston Churchill fulfilled a desire he had expressed during the dark days of the war—to visit Williamsburg. One day after addressing the Virginia General Assembly and only a few days after delivering his famous "An Iron Curtain Has Fallen" speech, Churchill arrived by train in Williamsburg. He and his wife, Clementine, were accompanied by General of the Army Dwight D. Eisenhower and his wife, Mamie. Responding to the cheers and applause of people lining the streets, Churchill flashed his noted "V for victory" salute.

The wartime leaders spent the day touring the city. Welcomed to the William and Mary campus by President John E. Pomfret, Churchill admired the architecture of the Wren Building. Pausing at the Raleigh Tavern, he and Eisenhower were reportedly entertained "at tea." That evening, Mr. and Mrs. John D. Rockefeller III hosted a dinner in their honor at the Williamsburg Inn; and afterwards, they toured the capitol by candlelight.

The visit was not uneventful; in front of the Governor's Palace, the lead pair of carriage horses, perhaps startled by camera flashbulbs, bucked and reared several times. Churchill grabbed his hat and took a deep puff on his cigar as the coachman brought the horses under control. Rockefeller, chairman of the Colonial Williamsburg board, apologized for the incident; but Churchill, who abandoned the carriage, responded: "Don't mind, old boy. I am having a lot of fun!"

Courtesy, Colonial Studios, Richmond, and John D. Rockefeller, Jr., Library, Colonial Williamsburg Foundation

"a long road [that] stretches out before the forces of evil are overcome." And Delegate Ashton Dovell, the eloquent Speaker of the Virginia House of Delegates, led fellow Williamsburgers in a pledge, swearing "my allegiance, my support and my love to this my country." Black residents gathered at Bruton Heights School for a communal devotional service.

Fourteen months later, on 14 August 1945, the citizenry of Williamsburg assembled to rejoice in the war's end. The next day, stores and the bank were closed, and servicemen dined free at the Lodge, the Travis house, and elsewhere. The exhibition buildings of Colonial Williamsburg stayed closed for two days.

Four clergymen conducted a half-hour ecumenical prayer service of thanksgiving in the Wren Chapel before the regular weekly Wednesday evening community sing-along, held on the lawn in front of the Wren Building. A rain storm, however, abbreviated the singing and served to sober the Surrender Day mood. The next Sunday, the Reverend Van F. Garrett, Jr., rector of St. John's Church in Greenville, Mississippi, who had grown up in Williamsburg, conducted a special service in Bruton Parish Church.

At the POW stockade at Camp Peary, where German and Italian prisoners applauded the announcement of the Allied victory, their chaplain, Navy Lieutenant F. J. Ruetz, preached a sermon: "We should know well by now that the lasting peace can be maintained only when we earnestly and actively seek to do good for others."

Through four trying years, the people of Williams-burg gave their lives, their money, their talent, their energy—their every effort and prayer—to help defeat the Axis powers. Williamsburg was, indeed, a busy and purposeful place.

Detail of an aerial view of Williamsburg taken in 1944 by Robert O. Shaffer, a naval aviator on a training flight from Norfolk Naval Air Station. This photo shows the squares of "victory gardens" planted along Jamestown Road in the area now occupied by Phi Beta Kappa Hall, Morton Hall, and their parking lots.

Courtesy, Colonial Williamsburg Foundation

Selected Sources and Suggested Readings

The author is grateful to the late Thomas L. Williams and his family for making copies of his photographs available. He also wishes to thank the following persons for their valuable interviews: George Bartholomew, Fay Fox, Vernon M. Geddy, Jr., Willard Gilley, Susan Hall Godson, Betty Smith Harris, John Limbeck, Eleanor Mallory Hile, Helen Young Langton, Anne Morledge, Julia Woodbridge Oxrieder, Elizabeth Aurell Schutz, Thomas L. Williams, and Herbert Young.

Ambrose, Stephen E. *Citizen Soldiers: The U.S. Army from the Normandy Beaches to the Bulge to the Surrender of Germany, June 7, 1944 – May 7, 1945* (N. Y.: Simon and Schuster, 1997).

American Legion. Post 39, Archives.

American Red Cross, James City Co. Chapter, Minutes.

Chorley, Kenneth. "The War and Williamsburg," address given 28 April 1943. Colonial Williamsburg Foundation Archives, Pamphlet file.

Daily Press. Newport News.

Ellis, Rex, producer. *Community Remembrances: The World War II Years,* a film documentary made by the Colonial Williamsburg Foundation, 1990.

Godson, Susan H. *Viking of Assault: Admiral John Lesslie Hall, Jr., and Amphibious Warfare* (Washington, D.C.: Univ. Press of America, 1982).

Godson, Susan H., et al. *The College of William & Mary: A History* (Williamsburg: King and Queen, 1993).

Times-Herald. Newport News.

University Archives, Earl Gregg Swem Library, College of William and Mary. Particularly noteworthy are the oral histories given by J. Wilfred Lambert and H. Westcott Cunningham.

Virginia Gazette. Williamsburg.

Wagener, A. Pelzer. "History of Post 39, American Legion." Unpublished manuscript.

Thespis Takes His Bows on the Williamsburg Stage

by: Wilford Kale

In the summer of 1947, a symphonic, historic outdoor drama by playwright Paul Green made its debut at Williamsburg's Lake Matoaka waterside amphitheater. Almost unnoticed among the cast of heroes of the American Revolution was a minor character—Sarah Hallam, who danced for Royal Governor John Murray, Earl of Dunmore.

In his script of *The Common Glory*, Green sought not only to highlight political events during the revolutionary era, but also to present a flavor of the social activities of those years. Miss Hallam was "a Williamsburg beauty and actress," who had settled in the city by the early 1770s and later ran a boarding house and a dancing school.

Historically, her in-laws, Lewis Hallam and his wife, also named Sarah, were an important part of the first professional English touring ensemble of actors and dancers who frequented Williamsburg during the 1750s and acted at the city's second theatre off Waller Street. In fact, Lewis Hallam owned the local theatre for more than three years. But the story of theatrical productions in the city began about 50 years earlier.

The dramatic arts have been presented in Williamsburg almost since its founding. Scholars in the Grammar School of the College of William and Mary are believed to have presented the first theatrical performance as early as 1702. Royal Governor Francis Nicholson, in a letter written to the Archbishop of Canterbury on 22 July 1702, reported the presentation of "a Pastoral Colloquy in English verse, spoken by some of the younger Scholars, in the College hall." The very early student theatrical presentations were performed in the "College"—the structure now known as the Wren Building. By 1718 when the first playhouse in the colonies was built on the palace green, the men of William and Mary performed there, according to published reports.

A New Kent County merchant, dancing master, and producer named William Levingston constructed that first theatre. On 5 November 1716, he purchased a lot east of the palace green and later built "one good Substantall house commodious for Acting Such Plays as shall be thought fitt to be Acted there." Little is known of his playhouse except its location and the fact that according to archaeological investigations the building measured 30 feet, 2 inches wide by 86 feet, 6 inches long and had a brick foundation. Situated just south of where the Brush-Everard house now stands, this playhouse was the first theatrical structure in the English colonies.

Levingston had arrived in the city around March 1716, when he advertised the "lower room at the South End of the College for teaching scholars and others to dance" while his own dancing school was being finished. By the time he had constructed his building, Levingston's interests had, for some unknown reason, shifted from dancing to drama. He apparently sent to England for actors and musicians to supplement his own company of two indentured servants, Charles and Mary Stagg. Theatrical productions were under way at the Levingston Playhouse by May 1718, when Lieutenant Governor Alexander Spotswood, then in residence in Williamsburg, requested that a play be acted at the theatre in honor of the birthday of King George I.

Apparently, the theatre business in Williamsburg was not good, because Levingston was forced to mortgage his property to Archibald Blair, the merchant brother of the Reverend James Blair, president of the college and rector of Bruton Parish Church. In 1724 Archibald Blair became owner of the playhouse site through default.

Apothecary George Gilmer purchased the Levingston-Stagg theatre from Blair on 20 February 1736. The *Virginia Gazette* announced on 20 September that "This evening will be performed at The Theatre by the young gentlemen of the College, [Joseph Addison's] *The Tragedy of Cato*, and on Monday, Wednesday and Friday next week, will be enacted the following comedies, by the Gentlemen and Ladies of this Country, viz [Susannah Centlivre's] *The Busy Body* and [George Farquhar's] *The Recruiting Officer*. " Other student productions then included Addison's *The Drummer; or, The Haunted House* and Farquhar's *The Beaux-Stratagem*. After Charles Stagg died in 1736, the playhouse soon fell dark.

On 4 December 1745, a group of "Gentlemen Subscribers" received a deed to the property, however, and on the same day conveyed the old theatre to "the Mayor, Recorder and Alderman and Common Council" of the city of Williamsburg for use as a hustings' court and common hall for council meetings. The last reference to this building was in 1766 when it was used for what might be thought of as a theatrical purpose, William Johnson's exhibition of experiments "in that curious and entertaining branch of Natural Philosophy called Electricity."

The city's second playhouse was built in 1751 on Waller Street near the site now occupied by Christiana Campbell's Tavern. A subscription drive that entitled the holder "to a

Handbill for a performance (probably in 1770). Although Hallam's theatre had been taken down by 1757, a new one seems to have been built almost immediately; for in 1760 it became the home of the American Company. David Douglass, who had married Hallam's widow and taken on Hallam's troupe, had renamed the troupe the American Company.

Courtesy, Special Collections, John D. Rockefeller, Jr., Library, Colonial Williamsburg Foundation

box ticket for the first night's diversion" helped Alexander Finnie, innkeeper at the Raleigh Tavern on nearby Duke of Gloucester Street, to build his theatre. For a year or so, it was known as the Finnie Theatre. The building was probably a barn-like structure, because records show it was constructed in only two months.

The theatre was built for the first touring troupe to perform in the city, the company of Walter Murray and Thomas Kean, which had acted earlier in Philadelphia, Charleston, and Annapolis and arrived in Williamsburg from New York. These performers have been described by one historian as "mostly stagestruck tradesmen and their wives. They were constantly in financial difficulty."

The next year, Lewis Hallam purchased the Finnie Theatre as a home for his "London Company of Comedians," the first professional troupe in the colonies. The company was outfitted by Hallam's brother, William, in London and had originally intended to go to New York, until several London "gentlemen" persuaded the Hallams to go to Williamsburg. The entire troupe—twelve adults and three children—sailed for Virginia aboard the *Charming Sally*.

On 12 June 1752, Hallam advertised in the *Virginia Gazette*:

THIS IS TO INFORM THE PUBLIC

that Mr. Hallam, from the New theatre in Goodmansfields, is daily expected here with a select Company of Comedians, the Scenes, Cloaths and Decorations are all entirely new, extremely rich, and finished in the highest Taste, the Scenes being painted by the best Hands in London are excell'd by none in Beauty and Elegance, so that the Ladies and Gentlemen may depend on being entertain'd in as polite a Manner as at the Theatres in London, the Company being perfected in all the best Plays, Opera's, Farces and Pantomimes, that have been exhibited in any of the Theatres for these ten years past.

The Finnic Theatre, however, did not fit Hallam's needs. Before any plays were performed, therefore, extensive alterations and remodeling were done to create Hallam's "regular" playhouse, which opened in September with a joint-bill (as was customary in London theatres) of *The Merchant of Venice* and Edward Ravenscroft's *The Anatomist, or, the Sham Doctor*. Later, in November, Hallam's Company presented *Othello* and a pan-

Advertisement in the Virginia Gazette *for the first performance (15 September 1752) at the theatre on Waller St., which Lewis Hallam had purchased and refurbished for his London Company of Comedians, the first professional acting troupe in the colonies.*

Courtesy, Special Collections, John D. Rockefeller, Jr., Library, Colonial Williamsburg Foundation

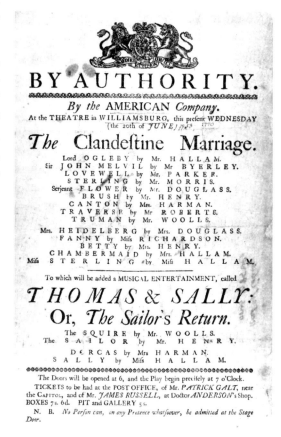

tomime to an audience that included the principal chief of the Cherokee Nation, his wife, and son. Among the other plays produced that season were: *The Recruiting Officer, Richard III, Romeo and Juliet*, and David Garrick's *Miss in Her Teens*.

Hallam's troupe realized they could not survive in Williamsburg producing six new plays a week, however, as the town was "too small to supply new audiences for the old plays." Although it returned to perform several times until Hallam's death in 1756, the troupe, therefore, moved to New York. By 1757, the theatre building in Williamsburg was gone.

Althea Hunt (1890-1971), joined the William & Mary faculty in 1926 and directed and developed support for college theatrical productions in the late '20s and '30s. Her protégé, Howard Scammon (1911-1999), as chair of the Department of Theatre and Speech and Director of the William & Mary Theatre, developed her educational theatre program even further.

Courtesy, Archives, Swem Library, College of William & Mary

In the summer of 1760, actor-producer David Douglass arrived in Williamsburg and by October had married Hallam's widow, Nancy, and changed the name of the troupe to the American Company. They performed at a new theatre, known in its time as the Old Theatre Near the Capitol, which had been built sometime after 1757 across the street from Hallam's theatre. Douglass and his troupe, however, left Williamsburg in May or June of 1772, and the Waller Street theatre would never again be host to a professional troupe. Clouds of revolution were appearing on the horizon. On 4 October 1774, the Continental Congress, meeting in Philadelphia, adopted a resolution to suppress every kind of extravagance, including horse racing, cock fighting, the theatre "and other expensive diversions and entertainments." The theatre building in Williamsburg was apparently left to rot; by 1780 it was in ruins, and by 1787 the remaining bricks from its foundation were sold to a local mason and carpenter.

Along with the government went the city's newspaper, the *Virginia Gazette*, many businesses, and professional men. Enterprises such as theatres now could not survive in Williamsburg. College productions and amateur performances were the town's only dramatic diversions, and it would be the twentieth century before significant theatre would return to Williamsburg.

In the early twentieth century there was a tradition of town-and-gown theatricals, which apparently were efforts of the college's Dramatic Club, formed about 1900. In 1901 the *Colonial Echo*, the William and Mary yearbook, acknowledged the "valuable assistance" of six women of Williamsburg—"Mrs. J. B. C. Spencer, Miss Mary McNair, Miss Rosa Emory, Miss M. L. G. Henley, Miss Lucile Foster, and Miss Virginia B. Braithwaite"—who helped the club. No productions, however, were listed. Although women were not admitted to the college until 1918, Miss Emory and Miss Braithwaite were elected vice-president and secretary, respectively, of the 1901-1902 club. The young gentlemen of the college were no longer "at a loss for a lady," as the *Gazette* of 10 September 1736 had long before said they were. There is no other mention of plays or a dramatic club at William and Mary, however, until after women students were admitted in 1918. Soon thereafter students performed Oscar Wilde's *Lady Windermere's Fan*.

The first formal theater activity in the city in about 150 years came in 1923 with the formation of the Williamsburg Little Theater League, begun primarily by professors from the college. It was originally organized to study plays and the theater, and members often simply read plays together in someone's home. Later, the League sponsored play-writing contests. The first play produced was *Rebellion* by Robert Moses, in 1929.

In 1926 Althea Hunt was appointed to the college faculty as a teacher-director. She initiated a play-production class, and her first show—Lewis Beach's *The Goose Hangs High*—opened on 18 December 1926. The play netted a profit of forty dollars, "in 1926, a good deal of money," enough to pay off the debt from prior play productions and enough to earn President J. A. C. Chandler's enduring support for the theatre. In those early days of "educational theatre," of which William and Mary's was one of the nation's first, Hunt used every means available to develop student, faculty, and also community interest in the theatre.

In 1935 the William and Mary Players, as the group was known then, became firmly established with a full staff—director, designer, technical director. Leslie Cheek, Jr., who later became director of the Virginia Museum of Fine Arts in Richmond, was named chairman of the college's newly formed Department of Fine Arts and from 1935 to 1939 served as designer and technical director of the theatre, which had come under his department.

Later, Howard Scammon, an acknowledged Hunt protégé, built upon her success and, as theater director, tried to select productions over a two- or three-year cycle that would give students the broadest possible theatre experience. Within each cycle, there would be a Shakespeare play, a French farce, a Greek classic, etc. By the mid-1960s, a new Department of Theater and Speech had been created and the by-now legendary, charismatic Scammon became department head while remaining director of the William and Mary Theatre. Supporting him superbly were technical director Albert Haak and designer Roger Sherman. Through Scammon's twenty-year tenure, the college's theatre program produced several outstanding, award-winning, nationally recognized actors, including Linda Lavin ('59), Scott Glenn ('61), and Glenn Close ('74); theatre administrators such as Richard Vos ('66) and Kent Thompson ('76); and entertainment lawyers such as Robert Wachs ('61). From 1957 to 1976, the theatre presented eighty-one productions, involving more than two thousand students.

William and Mary theatre personnel also helped the Colonial Williamsburg Foundation begin a program of eighteenth-century plays. In 1949, at the request of the foundation, Scammon, Roger and Suzanne Sherman, and students initiated a series of plays. The program has become part of the foundation's normal schedule of events.

The 1930s, despite the Depression and its aftermath, saw many theatrical productions in the city—including the annual Lions Club

The William & Mary Theatre trained a number of outstanding performers and theatre administrators from the mid-'50s to the mid-'70s, including Glenn Close (class of '74). Among others, she was in the 1973 production of The House of Bernarda Alba *(rear, second from the rt) and* Anything Goes *in 1974 (second from the rt).*

Courtesy, Archives, Swem Library, College of William & Mary

minstrel show beginning in 1934. By the 1930s, however, "going to the theatre" also meant going to the movies. The Imperial Theatre, initially on Duke of Gloucester Street and later at the corner of North Boundary and Prince George streets, and the Palace Theatre at the south end of the palace green, were opened as the motion picture industry grew. Then, a new movie theatre opened on 12 January 1933—the Colonial Williamsburg Theatre on Duke of Gloucester Street. It was dedicated with a William and Mary Players performance of *The Recruiting Officer*, which had been presented in 1736 by college students. Opening night also featured a Mickey Mouse cartoon, as well as Ann Harding and Richard Dix in the 1932 RKO hit, *The Conquerors*.

A group of Virginia citizens met in Williamsburg during World War II to discuss the production of a patriotic drama. The success of Paul Green's *The Lost Colony* in Manteo, North Carolina, led Virginia Governor Colgate W. Darden, Jr., and others to believe the same kind of commercial success could be achieved in Williamsburg. Encouraged by them and captivated by the history and lore of Williamsburg and the democratic movement that evolved from acts and declarations offered in legislative assembly in the city during the last half of the eighteenth century, Green wrote the second in his series of historic, symphonic, outdoor dramas. The setting of *The Common Glory* was Williamsburg at the time of the American Revolution. The play was successful, and in ways other than just profitable.

In looking back over those "Glory" years, David H. Weston, Jr., believed the drama was successful partly because it pulled Jamestown, Williamsburg, and Yorktown together historically. It also gave visitors something to do in the evenings. "In 1947 (and into the 1970s) Colonial Williamsburg closed at 5:00 p.m. and except for the movie theatres, people had nothing to do," he said.

It also was a boon to actors. There was no training ground for actors in the summer in Virginia, as summer stock was farther north, with the exception of Abingdon's Barter Theatre. A host of actors who had achieved or were later to achieve national prominence per-

In 1949, Colonial Williamsburg asked Howard Scammon and Roger and Susanne Sherman to begin producing 18th-c. plays for tourists. The theatre program has been a feature of the local entertainment schedule ever since. Here a modern playbill on the right announces the revival of a comedy performed in town in 1768.

Courtesy, John D. Rockefeller, Jr., Library, Colonial Williamsburg Foundation

The Lake Matoaka amphitheatre on the campus of William & Mary, where Paul Green's epic-historical melodrama, The Common Glory, A Symphonic Drama with Music and Dance, *was staged in the summers from 1947 through 1976.*

Courtesy, Thomas L. Williams archive

formed in the *Glory*: Goldie Hawn; Harold Gould; "Buck" Ninde, one of Mack Sennett's Keystone Cops; TV's "Alice," Linda Lavin; Jonathan Frakes (later Riker in *Star Trek: The Next Generation*); Glenn Close; TV soap opera star Larry Hugo; and others. But alas, the *Glory* had to close its long run after the 1976 season because of falling attendance and financial problems.

Dr. Thomas A. Graves, Jr., president of William and Mary and a member of Jamestown Corporation's board of directors, was among those who recommended closing the drama. Afterwards, however, he helped encourage and supported the creation of the Virginia Shakespeare Festival, which began at William and Mary in 1978 under the auspices of the Department of Theatre and Speech, with Phi Beta Kappa Memorial Hall as its home. Although on shaky financial footing the first several years, the festival has become financially secure and has staged some outstanding productions, such as director Paige Newmark's *Taming of the Shrew* in 1997.

Earlier, in 1963, a theatrical enterprise had opened in an unusual site—the old tomato cannery in Toano. Although not located within the city limits, the Wedgewood Dinner Theatre

Judging by Scammon's smile and attire and by the grins of Glenn Close [playing Eileen Gordon] (l) and Rachel Lindhart [Martha Jefferson] (rt), rehearsals must have been fun in 1972, the seriousness of Lawrence Greene [William Byrd] and Samuel Heatwole [stage manager] notwithstanding.

Courtesy, Rare Books and Manuscripts, Swem Library, College of William & Mary

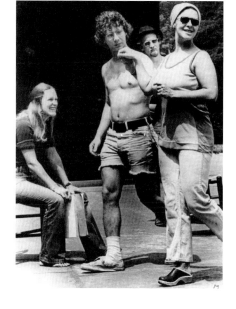

Members of the original 1947 production celebrate the 1000th performance in 1963. Rear (l-rt): Carl Fehr, musical director; Bruce Johnson, assistant technical director; Paul Green, playwright; Albert Haak, technical director; James Bray, actor; and Roger D. Sherman, general manager. Front: Virginia Bray, actress; Susanne Sherman, costume designer; Rachel Hitchens, wardrobe mistress; Benjamin Bray, associate director and stage manager; and Howard Scammon, director.

Courtesy, Rare Books and Manuscripts, Swem Library, College of William & Mary

*Clockwise from top left corner: Jan Noyes &
Richard Thompson (1951), Ann Helms & David
Friedman (1952), Ann Helms & Michael Hauft
(1955), Patricia Ewell & Michael Hauft (1956), and
Ann Helms & David Collins (1953).*

Clockwise from top left corner: Linda Lavin & Rogers Hamilton (1958), Edna Gregory & Rogers Hamilton (1959), Mamie Ruth Hitchens & John Reese (1967), and Edna Gregory & William Hicks, Jr. (1960).

The comedy in the Glory *was supplied by Widow Huzzitt and Cephis Sicklemore. A bumpkin of many words and no money, Cephis was found every summer pleading with the widow for a pastry from her basket, crossing his fingers as he swore to marry her, and absorbing her verbal chastisement while in the stocks for stealing chickens. Because not only locals, but many tourists, returned summer after summer to see the play, the production had to be changed as significantly as possible each year. These nine scenes of the widow and Cephis demonstrate the range of performance variations between 1951 and 1967.*

Souvenir postcard of the Glory: "Scene from the thrilling final battle of the American Revolution. Action revealed by flashes of red and yellow light as American soldiers storm the redoubt. The British flag is being replaced by the Betsy Ross flag of the Revolution. Nightly except Sunday, July and August." Not all performances were so unexceptionally noble, however: one night, Heatwole recalled, as Patrick Henry exhorted a crowd to take up arms against the British, crying out "To arms! To arms," he drew his sword out so fiercely it slipped out of his hand and went flying into the lake.

Courtesy, Will Molineux

was spoken of as "in Williamsburg." It was the brainchild of a quintet of actors and back-stage specialists from the Barksdale Theatre near Richmond. Designed as a dinner theatre, which was in vogue at the time, it was a repertory theatre with fine directors and performers. The theatre's Toano locale and run of sixty-eight plays ended in the spring of 1970 with *A Thurber Carnival*, after which the theatre moved to new quarters in Hampton.

The stage had been set for the Wedgewood experiment by the earlier success of the Williamsburg Players, a local volunteer group of thespians who had set up an interim board in 1956. What now has become an annual season of plays began as play readings in the basement of Orin M. Bullock, Jr.'s home, which is now Shield's Tavern. The Players' organizing group was composed primarily of Colonial Williamsburg employees who wanted to add more culture to the area.

The idea gradually took hold, and the Players started looking for a new home. Patricia Blatt, one of the key participants, said, "We didn't want to look like amateur night on Main Street." Gladys Baras, a Colonial Williamsburg employee and later the Players' president, prevailed on the Foundation to help, and in 1960 the North Ballroom in the Williamsburg Lodge was offered as a theatre with cabaret-style seating. The arrangement was cumbersome, however: a portable stage had to be built, heavy iron stanchions had to be set up to support the lighting, and everything had to be torn down after each weekend performance so that the room could be used during the week.

In its first year (1978) and several following, the Virginia Shakespeare Festival was dependent upon private support. To encourage such support, community leaders Robert and Lois Hornsby, who had already been active in many civic and charitable enterprises, founded the Lord Chamberlain Society and invited actress Helen Hayes to the college to mark the event.

Courtesy, Thomas L. Williams archive

Program cover for the 1963 Wedgwood production of Tobacco Road, *Jack Kirkland's play based on Erskine Caldwell's novel. Frank Staroba of the William & Mary Theatre Department starred as Jeeter.*

Courtesy, Thomas L. Williams archive

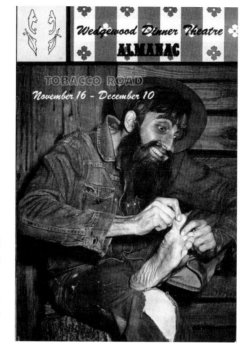

In 1964 and again in 1966 the Players changed their venue; but during that decade, Blatt explained, "Many of the cast were trained professionals and the Players produced one dramatic classic annually, including modern classics from Arthur Miller or Tennessee Williams in addition to popular shows that would make money for us in the box office." And in 1970, the Players "did a very daring thing." Homosexuals were not out of the closet then, but there was a popular play about homosexuality on Broadway—*Boys in the Band*, by Mart Crowley. The Players' director, Gary Battaglia, and president, Susan Gibson, went to New York and got special permission to stage the play in Williamsburg. The production was even mentioned on Johnny Carson's *Tonight Show*, as it was the play's performance outside New York. Blatt said, "we got a standing-room-only response. We advertised that it was somewhat risqué and had foul language, but we had no repercussions." The play was, however, prudently performed in July, outside the normal Players' season so it would not offend the regular members and season ticket holders.

Today, the Players offer a five-production season from September through mid-June with the plays running from four to six weeks. There are about 1,050 subscribers and an average attendance of 1,500 per play. Given their success, the Players are looking in the near future toward the construction of a new theatre building at their Hubbard Lane site. The new facility will double seating to about 250 and increase the size of the new thrust stage. There also will be a new sound and lighting booth and larger lobby to accommodate the larger audience. Rick Hinson, the Players president in 1998, said, "we know we can attract the patrons to fill this larger theatre. Our shows that are well known and our musicals currently could sell out eight weeks in a row."

With its rich history and tradition, theatre in Williamsburg continues to be vibrant, attracts much public attention, and builds upon the successes of its past.

Selected Sources & Suggested Readings

Bush, Charles E. "all the best Plays, Operas, Farces, and Pantomimes—Revival of an old idea; bringing back an 18th-century playhouse in the town where American theater began," *Journal of the Colonial Williamsburg Foundation* 7.3 (Spring 1995): 39-48.

Credle, Harvey B. "Alive and Thriving—18th-Century Theater Continues a Rich Tradition Mirroring Manners and Words of a Society Gently Poking Fun at Itself," *Colonial Williamsburg Today* 5.2 (Winter 1983): 3-7.

Hamant, John. "Debut of Fairbooth Theatre," *Journal of the Colonial Williamsburg Foundation* 11.1 (Autumn 1988): 19-21.

Hunt, Althea, ed. *The William and Mary Theater, A Chronicle* (Richmond: Dietz, 1968).

Jamestown Corporation Papers; Howard Scammon Papers; and Williamsburg Papers, Little Theatre Section, Swem Library, College of William & Mary.

Kale, Wilford. *Hark upon the Gale. An Illustrated History of the College of William and Mary* (Norfolk/Virginia Beach: Donning, 1985).

Kollatz, Harry E., Jr. "A Walking Shadow, A General History of the Colonial Theater in Williamsburg, Virginia." Research Report. Colonial Williamsburg Foundation Research Report, 1988.

Moorehead, S. P. "The Theater of 1716, Williamsburg, Virginia." Architectural Department Report. Colonial Williamsburg Foundation, 1952.

Rankin, Hugh F. *The Colonial Theater, its History and Operations.* 2 vols. (Williamsburg: Colonial Williamsburg Foundation, 1955).

Scammon, Howard. *The William and Mary Theater. 50 Years* (Richmond: Dietz, 1978).

Sherman, Susanne K. *Comedies Useful: Southern Theatre History, 1775-1812* (Williamsburg: Celest, 1998).

Virginia Gazette, Williamsburg.

William & Mary College Monthly, 1890-1915.

A Household Name:
Colonial Williamsburg in the Second Half
of the Twentieth Century

by: Peter A. G. Brown and Hugh DeSamper

Looking back from the end of the twentieth century, we see Williamsburg as a small settlement, important to the English who had colonized it, but far more vital to Americans whose nation began here. We also see the burgeoning popularity and attraction of Colonial Williamsburg since shortly after World War II. What made the Colonial Williamsburg Foundation's historic endeavor to preserve and present an accurate picture of the beginnings of our country so popular?

In the thirties and early forties, John D. Rockefeller, Jr. (see pp. 128, 188, 189, & 196), and the Reverend Dr. W. A. R. Goodwin (see pp. 128, 179, 182, & 184) accomplished an architectural tour de force, *and many hundreds came to see.* After World War II, the foundation focused on an additional dimension: the remarkable assembly here two hundred years ago of great American patriots and heroes — George Washington, Thomas Jefferson, Patrick Henry, George Mason, and their spirited contemporaries— *and many thousands came to see and hear* their stories. Then, beginning in the sixties, to their stories were added those of the common man—the tradesmen, women and children, and black slaves, *and hundreds of thousands came to see, hear, and engage* in an exciting story of our country's beginning.

In 1953 Carlisle H. Humelsine became the president of the Colonial Williamsburg Foundation. He was a stickler for authenticity and research—two activities that ensured quality—and in the fifties and sixties an expanded research staff, encouraged by Humelsine and led by director Ed-

Winthrop Rockefeller, chairman of the boards of Colonial Williamsburg from 1953–1973, and (rt) Carlisle H. Humelsine, president (1958-1977) and later chairman (1977-1985). They were the major figures of the restoration during what are now called "The Golden Years."

Courtesy, John D. Rockefeller, Jr., Library, Colonial Williamsburg Foundation

ward M. Riley and his associate Thad W. Tate, began a new and never-ending search for more details about eighteenth-century Williamsburg.

The DeWitt Wallace Gallery, opened in 1985, is devoted to exhibition and interpretation of an outstanding, growing collection of 17th- and 18th-c. English and American decorative arts.

Courtesy, John D. Rockefeller, Jr., Library, Colonial Williamsburg Foundation

During this period, also, Colonial Williamsburg's second curator, the exuberant John M. Graham II, and his staff crisscrossed North America and Europe to furnish what had been in the early postwar era sparsely furnished exhibition buildings. No major auction of English or American antiques went unattended by a curator or an agent. Private owners of noted collections, won over by the prospect of enhancing the historic buildings, donated special objects or even entire collections. Thousands of items were photographed, measured, indexed, and rotated on and off exhibition as continuing research yielded new clues to more appropriate objects and exhibit sites for them. The restored houses and public buildings did not contain enough space to display the foundation's world-class collection of artifacts, however; and many of them had to be stored in the curators' warehouse, where, unfortunately, they could not be shared with the public. Only more than a decade later could Graham S. Hood, vice-president of Collections and Museums 1971-1997, begin to seek a solution to the problem.

Enter DeWitt and Lila Acheson Wallace, co-founders of *The Reader's Digest* and long-time admirers and supporters of Colonial Williamsburg. The DeWitt Wallace Decorative Arts Gallery, developed in tandem with the reconstruction of the Public Hospital of 1773, was the salutary result of courting the Wallaces. When it opened in 1985, the problem of inadequate exhibition space was solved.

But to return to the 1950s—enhancement of the historic area beyond static presentations became a paramount priority. For example, Ivor Noël-Hume arrived in 1957 and quickly demonstrated the greater encyclopedia of early life that archaeology could reveal.

Archaeological excavation and interpretation of its discoveries has been a continually exciting aspect of Colonial Williamsburg's decades-long program of education. In the 1960 exploration of the Anthony Hay site more than 20,000 objects or fragments were recovered, increasing insight into the life and times of cabinetmaker Hay and his family.

Courtesy, John D. Rockefeller, Jr., Library, Colonial Williamsburg Foundation

Through his efforts the daily life of the past began to come alive. Also, under Humelsine's long-term leadership, the acquisition of greenbelt and protective properties, international recognition, broadened education, and historical interpretation, emergence of the collections to their high state of excellence, increasing development of business properties and hotels, and acquisition and development of additional historical properties contributed to the steady improvement and popularity of Colonial Williamsburg.

As the foundation grew in scope, however, so did expenses. There had been two major sources of support for the foundation—the Rockefeller family and income from museum admissions, hotel and restaurant revenue, and product sales. By the mid-seventies, President Humelsine, the board of trustees, and members of the Rockefeller family all agreed that it was necessary to reach out to all Americans for support. Under the leadership of F. Roger Thaler, Colonial Williamsburg's first development officer, support from the American public was enthusiastic and substantial. In 1976, gifts to the annual fund totaled $50,000 from three hundred donors. Twenty years later, over sixty thousand donors gave more than six million dollars to the annual fund.

During Humelsine's leadership, a score of major building or restoration projects were completed, including The Motor House (now The Woodlands) and Cafeteria (now Commonwealth Hall), the Abby Aldrich Rockefeller Folk Art Collection (now Center), the Public Hospital of 1773, and the renovation of the Information Center and its transition to a Visitor Center. Also, in 1963, a conference center was added to the Williamsburg Lodge: it has attracted hundreds of groups, including such notable ones as the American Institute of Architects, Republican Governors' Conference, Young Presidents Association, Aircraft Industries Association, and the Brookings Institution.

Because of his long association with the Department of State, Humelsine was well equipped to initiate a continuing series of visits to Williamsburg by heads of state and dignitaries from all over the world. The staff came to call this "The King of the Month Club." These visits brought the attention and interest of the world to Williamsburg. The first foreign dignitary to visit in this program was Crown Prince Akihito (now Emperor) of Japan, who embarked on a world tour in 1953 in order to broaden his understanding of history and political science. Twenty-two years after Akihito's visit, his father, the late Emperor Hirohito, making his first trip to America, spent several days in Williamsburg with Empress Nagato (see color plate 20).

After King Paul and Queen Frederika of Greece visited Colonial Williamsburg in 1953, the list of distinguished international leaders grew to include Marshal Tito of Yugoslavia, King Olav V of Norway, King Hussein of Jordan, the Shah of Iran, President Anwar Sadat of Egypt, and Secretary-General of the United Nations Dag Hammarskjold,. At last count, more than 150 international leaders—and every post-WWII president except Kennedy—have walked the streets of Williamsburg.

As more and more visitors came, they began to feel hampered by the constant and insistent encroachment of the additional motor cars; and the foundation began to realize the need to eliminate automobiles from the Duke of Gloucester Street. It took some doing, as

Here being photographed by an enchanted young tourist, Sir Denys Lawson, Lord Mayor of London, visited Williamsburg in September 1951. While here he met with mayors and municipal officers of the colonial cities of America and gave an address at the capitol.

Courtesy, Thomas L. Williams Archive

many Williamsburg citizens were aghast at the notion. Only after town meetings were held and all opinions were aired, was the City Council in the fall of 1962 persuaded to begin a seasonal closure. In 1969, closure became year round.

Early in the evolution of the traffic plan, council approved closure of a South England Street extension that crossed into the market square. Landscape and labor teams moved into instant action "before they change their minds." In a matter of days the street was gone, replaced by soothing, green grass and a gentle path before anyone could say, "Wait a minute!" Tranquility had returned to the space. As time passed, the town became protective of the closed streets. Bicycles, joggers, strollers, and pedestrians enjoyed the change; and visitors became quite intolerant of all incursions by vehicles.

As the number of tourists rose, a much larger and more sophisticated orientation center was required to replace the original one on South England Street, which dated from just after WWII. A major factor in the success of the new Information Center was the orientation film, *Williamsburg: The Story of a Patriot*, filmed in the historic area in 1956. Directed by George Seaton, produced by Paramount Pictures, and now shown in twin theatres, it has been a great favorite of millions of visitors.

Those who worked on the center recall scores of anecdotes. To cite but one—on his first visit to the site, John D. Rockefeller, Jr., walked among the hustle and bustle of construction, and gazed at the piles of materials and all the bricklayers, and bulldozer and crane operators. "Mercy," he exclaimed, "I hope we can afford all this!" Everyone went pale.

From the outset, visitors encountered knowledgeable presentations as they journeyed along their rendezvous with history. This was no accident. Well-researched material and comprehensive training for the men and women who represented Colonial Williamsburg was vital. After World War II, expanding research enriched the interpretive material, and interpreters were able to respond to questions with a broad spectrum of information as well as initiate interesting, accurate narratives. In addition, interpreters heard lectures by the Colonial Williamsburg research staff, William and Mary faculty, scholars at the Institute of Early American History and Culture, and visiting scholars from home and abroad. The curriculum was broad, covering American, English, and European history, social history of the colonial period, trade skills, slavery, furniture and the decorative arts, early American politics, etc.

Visitors responded enthusiastically to the diversely-informed, congenial interpreters— costumed hostesses in the exhibition buildings, tradespeople in the shops, escorts who were assigned primarily to school groups and adult tours, actors on the streets, guides for VIP visitors, carriage drivers, and others. Part of the remarkable, developing reputation of Colonial Williamsburg was the public's confidence in educational information gained during an entertaining visit to Williamsburg. An important dimension of the makeup of the Colonial Williamsburg staff was the inclusion of African Americans among the escorts and interpreters, as well as in other public roles, such as information center desk attendants.

For many years, special events have won the affection of visitors. These include annual celebrations such as fireworks on July 4th, colonial Christmas festivities, the Garden Symposium (started in 1947), and the Antiques Forum (1949). Over the years, Learning Weekends, the History Forum, and archaeology seminars also became popular.

This view of South England St. splitting the market square green is now just a memory.

Courtesy, John D. Rockefeller, Jr., Library, Colonial Williamsburg Foundation

Without automobiles, Duke of Gloucester St. approximates its appearance ca. 1776.

Courtesy, John D. Rockefeller, Jr., Library, Colonial Williamsburg Foundation

The 350th anniversary of Jamestown placed Jamestown, Williamsburg, and Yorktown in world focus. In the festival year, Colonial Williamsburg opened a complex comprising a visitor center with parking for a thousand cars, motel (now known as The Woodlands), cafeteria, and office-registration building.

Courtesy, John D. Rockefeller, Jr., Library, Colonial Williamsburg Foundation

On 15 May 1953, President Eisenhower gave the address at the annual Prelude to Independence.

Courtesy, John D. Rockefeller, Jr., Library, Colonial Williamsburg Foundation

Especially noteworthy, perhaps, is the Prelude to Independence, which celebrates the fifty days from 15 May to July 4th, 1776, when Virginia legislators took the lead in seeking independence from Great Britain. For more than two decades, the annual Prelude address in the capitol attracted national attention. For example, on 15 May 1953, President Eisenhower accepted an honorary degree from William and Mary and gave a Prelude address in which his eloquent words stamped the event as a national forum for renowned speakers. He said, "I wish sincerely that every single man, woman and child that has the proud privilege of calling himself an American, could stand here on this spot and...re-live again [our forefathers'] moments, the problems they met in their own times, and thus regain faith to solve the problems of our day."

Succeeding speakers included secretaries of state John Foster Dulles, Dean Acheson, and Dean Rusk; Vice President Hubert H. Humphrey, United Nations Secretary-General Dag Hammarskjöld, Prime Minister Lester B. Pearson of Canada, and Dr. Charles Malik of Lebanon, former president of the United Nations General Assembly. Malik's address, on 10 June 1960, was widely reported in the national and international press. A Richmond editor wrote that the address "merited a place among the truly great speeches of this century." Another called it "the greatest speech in Williamsburg since Patrick Henry."

Arguably the most noteworthy—and newsworthy—of all events was the ninth Summit of Industrialized Nations. For four days in May 1983, eight world leaders, hosted by President Reagan, discussed international issues in locations known to America's eighteenth-century leaders (see color plate 19). Colonial Williamsburg's president Charles Longsworth wrote in his annual report,

 The eyes of the world were focused upon us, as some 3,000 members of the media transmitted an untold volume of words and pictures around the world.... Behind the scenes toiled a not-so-small army of Colonial Williamsburg workers, from bus boys to vice presidents, all sharing the same concern–that we do a good job. And we did.

The longest running, most comprehensive and most popular of all Colonial Williamsburg's events is the Christmas celebration, begun in 1934, the year President Roosevelt proclaimed Duke of Gloucester Street "the most historic avenue in all America" (see p. 148). The first Christmas event called for nightly illumination of ten evergreen trees in the historic area. It was cheerful and much enjoyed, but cold water was dashed on the idea because the lights were colored, and therefore, not appropriate. In 1935, real lighted candles set in saucers of water glowed from the windows of the historic area buildings, which were guarded against fire by night watchmen, and garlands of natural materials decorated the buildings on the outside. In time, electrified candlesticks were substituted for burning candles and watchmen, but these two early events became the foundation of the holiday activities, and are still mainstays of the "White Lighting" and "Decorating the City" programs.

After World War II, planners structured a broader series of events that would be beneficial at a normally slow time of year—amid cautions to remain within the guidelines of the colonial period. Music, theater, balls, and feasts were ever popular in colonial Williamsburg, so there were precedents for many exciting activities. Gradually, other events were added, including the Yule Log ceremony for guests at the Williamsburg Inn and Lodge, special holiday feasts, lectures on holiday decorations, street caroling, and concerts.

Today's popular season opener, the "Grand Illumination of the City," takes place normally on a Sunday evening early in December. A cannon volley signals residents of the historic area to light their candles, thus commencing the "White Lighting" that continues until New Year's Day. Preceded by fifes and drums and often bagpipes, fireworks erupt at four locations including the Governor's Palace and capitol. Thousands of celebrants descend upon the historic area to view the bombastic display, take in the music and other entertainment, sing carols by flaming cressets, and rejoice with their friends. An annual exhibit of antique toys at the Abby Aldrich Rockefeller Folk Art Center is another popular Christmas attraction. The Christmas season has grown steadily from just a few days to nearly four weeks, and has become so popular that many families return year after year.

What makes Williamsburg's Christmas so different from others is that decorations are limited to natural materials known to the eighteenth century: no plastics, no colored lights, no tinsel, no Santa Claus, no elves, no Rudolph or any other reindeer. The only event permitted because of its grandfathered status—the Christmas Eve Community Tree Lighting Ceremony on the market square—recalls Williamsburg's first documented Christmas tree. In 1842, Dr. Charles Frederick Minnigerode, a professor at the college, planned a holiday party for the children of his friend Judge Nathaniel Beverley Tucker (see p. 75). It resembled those he remembered from his childhood in Germany.

In the 1950s, a militia company was formed by Colonial Williamsburg to represent the citizen soldier and provide pageantry during the daily activities and special events; and in 1963 the Fife and Drum Corps (color plate 24), a group of boys (and as of 1999, girls) from local families, was founded to complement and enhance the militia. Its by-now famous performances total some five hundred each year; and the corps has taken Williamsburg into every state and Canadian province through network television appearances and trips to distant cities. Indeed, it has become a national symbol of Colonial Williamsburg, or as Charles Longsworth often called the corps, "our signature."

Many new programs and activities, ranging from theatre productions, concerts at the palace and capitol, foodways, livestock, expanded craft demonstrations, and even bowling on the green, have been introduced. One of the most dramatic additions to the Colonial Williamsburg program, however, followed the acquisition of Carter's Grove. In 1963, with the aid of the Rockefellers, the foundation acquired this eighteenth-century plantation only six miles from Williamsburg. Surviving in excellent condition, it was opened to the public the following year, thus satisfying a longtime ambition to interpret early Virginia plantation life.

In addition, extensive archaeological exploration revealed portions of a very early English settlement—Wolstenholme—as well as remains of Indian occupancy. These finds enabled researchers to develop an interpretive program telling the story of human activities in the Williamsburg area over a period of four centuries. Presentations of Wolstenholme, an archaeology museum, reconstructed slave quarters, orchards, and a garden completed this important panorama on the James River.

Williamsburg is the headquarters for the oldest and largest system for the production and sale of museum reproductions in the country, with shops adjacent to the Inn and on Merchants Square, and more than 120 "Williamsburg Shops" located in department stores and decorative shops in cities across the nation. These outposts help promote all facets of the

Williamsburg story from cultural history, furnishings, and art to food and gardening. Once several buildings had opened to the public, there was a surge of interest in the gracious, hospitable style of furnishings and decorative arts displayed in Williamsburg. However, antiques were hard to find, and the idea of creating reproductions of antique articles displayed in the historic area buildings led to the formation of Williamsburg Craftsmen, Inc., later retitled WILLIAMSBURG™ Reproductions.

The Craft House opened in 1937 to display and sell those reproductions, whose hallmark has been recognized for decades now as a symbol of integrity and authenticity. From the very few licensed manufacturers before the war, the program has grown steadily to more than fifty licensees and more than two thousand items. In addition to china, silverware, glassware, and furniture, the licensees reproduce rugs, bedding, paints, fabrics, wallpaper, pewter, brass, gardening items, architectural items, gifts, specialty foods, toys, and lighting fixtures.

Carter's Grove has been a landmark on the James River east of Williamsburg since the main section was completed in 1755. It has had a long association with influential Virginians from before the American Revolution to the present.

Courtesy, John D. Rockefeller, Jr., Library, Colonial Williamsburg Foundation

The Jamestown Festival celebration formally opened the reconstructed Jamestown Settlement to commemorate the original landing and colonization of Virginia in 1607. An eight-month program of special events drew visitors by carload, planeload, and busload to view the thatched-roofed reconstructions within James Fort, the three ships that brought the first settlers, the Indian Lodge, and the exhibits in the Old World and New World

This hallmark, symbolic of Colonial Williamsburg reproductions made by licensed manufacturers, adds the letters "C" and "W" to the elongated "4" ending in a double "X." It appeared in 17th- and 18th-c. Virginia as a shipper's or maker's mark, often combined with the initials of planters and merchants. The hallmark assures authenticity, quality, and value.

Courtesy, John D. Rockefeller, Jr., Library, Colonial Williamsburg Foundation

Pavilions. The federal government completed the Jamestown-to-Williamsburg segment of the Colonial National Historical Parkway, finally linking the historic triangle of Jamestown-Williamsburg-Yorktown with a limited-access road through scenic riverside landscapes. The climax of the festival year came in October, when Queen Elizabeth II and Prince Philip visited the fort, the ships, and the pavilions.

According to the foundation's 1957 annual report, the festival year stimulated 1,700,000 persons to visit the historic peninsula and helped spark increases for other nearby attractions. Attendance to Colonial Williamsburg's exhibition buildings jumped nearly fifty percent for the year.

The next major boost to tourism occurred in 1975, when the Anheuser-Busch Company opened The Old Country-Busch Gardens. Starting with 157,020 visitors in the first

In October 1957, Queen Elizabeth II and Prince Philip visited the fort, ships, and pavilions at Jamestown. Aboard the Susan Constant, *one of the organizers mentioned to Her Majesty that the prince was throwing the visit off schedule by lingering too long below decks. "We'll just have to wait. I can't do anything with him when it comes to ships," was her response.*

Courtesy, John D. Rockefeller, Jr., Library, Colonial Williamsburg Foundation

year, Busch Gardens has entertained nearly forty million guests from all over the world. The property also includes a modern brewery, an up-market residential community at Kingsmill-on-the-James, and Busch Corporate Park. The total development has become an anchor for James City County's economy and, indeed, a major economic player in the entire greater Williamsburg area. The Busch corporation also now owns Water Country in York County.

The country's bicentennial loomed large on the horizon as 1976 approached, and the prediction was that Williamsburg would be overwhelmed by visitors thronging to see this cherished bastion of liberty. Surprisingly, the traveling public hit Colonial Williamsburg a year early. Attendance jumped from 923,501 in 1974 to 1,213,403 in 1975; but although 1976 started off fast, and new programs were implemented, the volume suddenly leveled off. Still, 1,250,623 visitors came—the most to date. Despite a gasoline shortage in 1979 and recessional trends in 1982-1983, Williamsburg enjoyed its best decade between 1975 and 1985.

Kenneth Chorley, president of Colonial Williamsburg from 1935 to 1958, wrote in the organization's first annual report in 1951,

 By its activities, Colonial Williamsburg has brought a new way of life to modern Williamsburg. It has created for this county seat a whole new economy based more and more upon the accommodation of visitors.... The quiet community of Williamsburg found itself suddenly the mother of a very large and strange duckling. And yet it does seem possible that seldom has a change of such magnitude taken place in a community with greater good will and under-

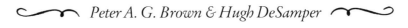

The Rockefellers were often seen about Williamsburg during their regular visits or residence each year. Here they are leaving a community program at Matthew Whaley School.

Courtesy, John D. Rockefeller, Jr., Library, Colonial Williamsburg Foundation

standing. If so, it is a tribute to the good sense, hospitality, and faith of the people of Williamsburg.

Mr. Rockefeller once said, "We are guests in this community," and presidents succeeding Chorley have sought to keep the community aware of the foundation's goals and needs, as well as the importance of the good will of the people, businesses, and fellow institutions. In dedicating his 1988 annual report to the spirit "that has always existed between the city of Williamsburg, the counties of James City and York, and the Foundation," Charles Longsworth added a special insert for employees:

This partnership, strong from the beginning, has been maintained and nurtured through the past 62 years. We have always enjoyed understanding and support from the governing bodies and citizens of this area. The occasional differences—probably inevitable—have been resolved through the spirit of reason and compromise that has been a constant trait of all three municipalities. The past, present, and future of Colonial Williamsburg are welded to this vital partnership.

Williamsburg's residents have always been proud of the astounding events that took place here in the 1770s when the United States was born. The coincidence of history that brought men of great courage and conviction together in this tiny colonial capital has inspired Americans for all time. It is impressive to note the dignity and restraint of our admiration of what happened here. Our visitors are struck by the quiet way in which Colonial Williamsburg communicates the story of the events of 225 years ago. Absent are the loud jangle of band music, rock renditions of the national anthem, or blatant flag-waving extravaganzas.

The reassurance of what it means to be an American today and the overriding confidence of our political independence overcomes many contemporary problems our country faces daily. This immersion in our history seems to make us feel better about ourselves. A quote from an early foundation annual report sums it up: "Americans like to feel their history beneath their feet."

This sensitive treatment of profound emotions, understated, but always present, earned Williamsburg the affections of its visitors in the 1950s and 1960s—and we believe it will continue to do so. In a discussion of this unusual era and the personalities cited, a wise contemporary observer offered the thought that "maybe it was just the times"—and maybe it was simply a gentler couple of decades.

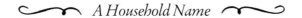

Selected Sources & Suggested Readings

Colonial Williamsburg, quarterly magazine published by the Colonial Williamsburg Foundation.

Colonial Williamsburg Reports, 1951-1990.

Davis, Burke. *A Williamsburg Galaxy* (Williamsburg: Colonial Williamsburg Foundation, 1968).

Goodwin, Rutherfoord. *Williamsburg in Virginia*, 3rd edn. (Richmond: Dietz, 1959).

Kopper, Philip. *Colonial Williamsburg* (N.Y.: Harry N. Abrams, in association with the Colonial Williamsburg Foundation, 1986).

Yetter, George Humphrey. *Before and After: The Rebirth of Virginia's Colonial Capital* (Williamsburg: Colonial Williamsburg Foundation, 1988).

The Whimsical Sixties

Simba the Lion: "Make mine vanilla."

Herman and Anne Dail had kept groundhogs and a water moccasin as pets, but they really loved lions. "They're such pretty animals," said Mrs. Dail. The couple saved their dimes to bring Simba, a male Nubian lion cub, into their Scotland St. home in March 1964. The cub started on a baby bottle but soon graduated to ice cream. Spectators would gather outside High's Ice Cream on Prince George St. to watch Simba, declawed and defanged and affectionate as "a big friendly pup," slurp his cone in the Dails' sedan. He was 325 pounds and still growing when he ran away on Labor Day weekend 1965 and was shot by the police. Ever since, a city code has banned the keeping of "ferae naturae" as pets.

Mayor "Polly" Stryker as a Beatle

After the British rock group, The Beatles, were introduced to America on the Ed Sullivan television show, Beatlemania swept the nation. In 1964, even Williamsburg's mayor, Dr. Henry M. Stryker, was infected by the craze, donned a mop-top wig, and hammed it up with a guitar.

Sisters of Mercy

Walsingham Academy teacher Sister Mary Delphine and principal Sister Stella Maria surge through a snow storm in 1964, when the new Upper School on Jamestown Road opened. From its beginnings in l947, with fifty-eight students at 601 College Terrace, by 1963 Walsingham Academy had increased its enrollment to 789.

*The Society for the Preservation of
Nineteenth-century Williamsburg Antiquities*

*The society posed with great propriety in front of the
Bowden-Armistead house on Duke of Gloucester St. in
1970. Founded in 1968 by Victorian scholar Charles C.
Nickerson, a member of the English Department at the
college, the society was composed almost entirely of his
colleagues. English faculty shown here are: (rear l-rt) Scott
Donaldson, William F. Davis, Jr., Robert Maccubbin, &
Terry Meyers, and (front) Nathaniel Elliott & David Clay
Jenkins. The society served no useful function but did issue a
2-pp. monograph on Oscar Wilde in Williamsburg (he
wasn't). In 1965 Nickerson had formed a more useful
organization, which served the interests of book lovers. The
Botetourt Bibliographical Society, as Nickerson explained,
was named after "a well-known local whose family
wouldn't sue." Lord Botetourt (see color plate 21 and pp.
90, 149, & 152) also was known to have had a good
library, however.*

Master Photographer, Thomas L. Williams

*For fifty years, Tom Williams (1912-1998) captured the city's
events and people on film. While he was stationed at Camp Peary
as a Navy photographer during WWII, Colonial Williamsburg
"borrowed" him to cover important occasions. After the war,
Tom set up and ran Colonial Williamsburg's first photo lab; then
in 1955, he left the foundation to open his own studio and for
some thirty years was the official photographer for William &
Mary and Eastern State Hospital. A beloved local legend, he left a
legacy of thousands of prints, negatives, and transparencies that
tell the story of Williamsburg from 1942 to 1992. Both he and his
daughter Karen generously assisted researchers preparing this book.
This photo shows him still working at age eighty.*

All photographs courtesy, Thomas L. Williams Archive

Williamsburg Traditions

The first Community Christmas Tree dates to 1915, when citizens brought candles and sang around the tree on the palace green. The court house green site (shown here) was first used in 1946. More recently, a Norway Spruce was planted next to the Greenhow Brick Office on the market square, and the Jaycees and Kiwanis have sustained the lighting tradition. In 1843 the German tradition of decorating trees had been adopted in the home of Judge Nathaniel Beverley Tucker.

Courtesy, Thomas L. Williams Archive

Originally called the "White Lighting," the Grand Illumination heralds the holiday season. In 1969, the torch-lit parade was led by Night Watch Ray Townsend. As he called out "Light your candles!" en route from the capitol up Duke of Gloucester Street, white candles were lighted in sequence in windows of homes and public buildings. Colonial Williamsburg has continued the tradition, hosting a colonial-style street party and dazzling fireworks.

Courtesy, *Daily Press*

"An Occasion for the Arts," an annual fall festival, began in 1969, with a visionary ad hoc committee that included Ricks Wilson, George Wright, and Jim Anthony, AOFTA's first producer. This photo from the 1970s shows the display of photographs, paintings, pottery, jewelry, etc. on Duke of Gloucester St.

Courtesy, *Daily Press*

When Colonial Williamsburg added golf to the amenities available at the Williamsburg Inn, Williamsburg's reputation as a world-class golf destination began. Here, Bob Wallace, Bela Norton, Vernon Geddy, and Kenneth Chorley play the nine-hole course, which opened in 1947. The eighteen-hole championship Golden Horseshoe Gold Course opened in 1963.

Courtesy, Thomas L. Williams Archive

The African-American Community
in Williamsburg (1947–1998)

by: Rex M. Ellis

Much of the history of Williamsburg has been written by newcomers or whites; and no history of Williamsburg has been written by African Americans other than the cursory work by Tommy Booger, Wayne Bowman, and Curtis Lassiter. Not only is African-American history integral to an understanding of the area in general, but it is important that the black historical perspective be preserved so that future generations may learn from the challenges blacks have faced, their achievements, and the wisdom they have gained through their struggles.

The black communities of Williamsburg during the last fifty years are: Highland Park, the only black community abutting the historic area; Braxton Court, a small area off Scotland Street; and that along Ironbound, Strawberry Plains, and Longhill roads. Northwest of town is the community at Five Forks; toward the upper end of James City County are communities at Centerville, Lightfoot, Mooretown Road, and Toano; south along York Street is the small community along Pocahontas Street; and toward the west of Williamsburg, along the James River, is Grove, one of the largest black communities in the area. East of the city in York County are the black communities along Penniman and Queens Creek roads and at Springfield Terrace, Carver Gardens, Waller Mill, Carter's Neck, and Croaker. Lower York County includes communities at Lackey, Surrender Road, Grafton, Wolf Trap, and Tabb. Many of these black enclaves continue to have strange boundaries that divide rnunicipalities and discourage black voting blocks. Such areas also challenge efforts to create a comprehensive and cohesive sense of community. For instance, east Williamsburg includes Penniman and Queen's Creek roads; but the west side of Penniman is designated James City County, and the east side, York County.

Beginning about 1928, the restoration of colonial Williamsburg displaced many black families and communities. The Crumps, Parkers, Tuckers, Harrises, Garys, Smiths, Goodalls, Epps, Sheppards, Parillas, Gardners and others lived in and around what is now the historic area. Many who lived on the main street, Duke of Gloucester, still have bitter memories about the circumstances surrounding their displacement. While many white families were allowed to stay, or given top dollar for their properties, the majority of black families received less for their property and in some cases were forced to move. One family even had a huge hole dug around their property, making it difficult for them to get in and out of the house, a hole that wasn't repaired until the family decided to sell the property. Others made out better. When the Reverend L. L. Wales was asked to relocate Mount Ararat Baptist Church on Francis Street, he successfully lobbied for a new church to be built and paid for by the restoration–but only by taking legal action. Also, Allen Jones, who owned almost eighty acres in the area that now borders South Henry and Francis streets, made out well.

W. A. R. Goodwin, the mastermind behind the idea of restoring Williamsburg, related a story of a black man who had approached him about selling his land. He began by announcing he wanted $50,000 for his property. Incredulous, Goodwin replied that it was simply too much money and no one in town had gotten that amount for such a small piece. The man replied, "well what about $5,000?" Goodwin assented and then questioned the man about his reasons for the original price. "Well," said the man, "they told me to start high and come down!" Such was the trust factor of the black community and their faith in being treated fairly.

Further displacement, by eminent domain, occurred during both world wars, which left many African Americans wondering whether they could find new communities that provided them with the same sense of well-being, comfort, and identity that they had come to know in their original homes. The community of Magruder, east of town, was displaced to make room for Camp Peary; along the York River, Cheatham Annex displaced black families; and when the Naval Weapons Station moved in, blacks forced to find new homes populated Grove, Lackey, Grafton, and the Surrender Road corridor of lower York County. Benjamin Smith recalls that the black community raised funds to build a new black school in that area, but when the land on which it was built was condemned, payment for the property was given to the county instead of returned to the people who had paid for the school.

The displacement of predominately black areas like Magruder highlighted the reality that most blacks had few if any resources with which to fight discrimination. Doris Crump Rainey, who has lived in Williamsburg all her life, sums it up:

> If whites wanted anything the blacks could not fight back. The town of Magruder was predominately black. Where Fort Eustis is now, was predominately black; where the Naval Weapons Station is, was predominately black....Blacks could not fight back, they didn't have the resources back then. The lawyers were white, the judges were white. How much money did a lawyer stand to make defending the black community over the U.S. Government, or Colonial Williamsburg, or the state of Virginia?

Making matters worse, although civil service positions were available at the new military installations, initially, few blacks were employed. It was not until President Truman issued Executive Order #9981 and set up the Committee to Study Equality of Treatment and Opportunity in the Armed Services in 1948 that the situation began to improve. Minister, educator, and community leader Junius Moody remembered the challenges of getting a job with the civil service, especially if you were black:

> When the war was imminent...they were hiring people at the Naval Weapons station... Arthur Sasser and I decided to go down...to see if we could get a job....Sasser and I went down at about the same time. And you had to say something about your education. Well, I told them I had finished my junior year at Hampton Institute and I then signed my name. I guess I signed my name too fast. The lady asked me, "Why did you come here?" I told her I came because I wanted a job. Sasser told her he was a graduate of Hampton Institute and he signed his name too fast too. She then said, "You all go and see Mr. Farmer." We found out that Mr. Farmer was head of the railroad. Now this was in February and I had never worked out doors in February in my life. They put us out on the railroad track and I worked for about a week. I

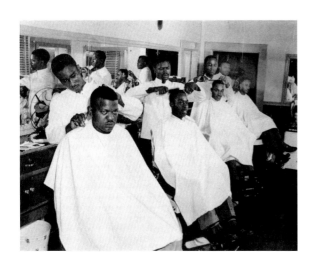

Barbershop, ca. 1950. Tom Crump, George Tabb, and others holding still for that special cut. No electric clippers, just a steady hand and a keen eye.

Courtesy, John D. Rockefeller, Jr., Library,
Colonial Williamsburg Foundation

West End Valet Dry Cleaners, Prince George St., ca. 1950s. Proprietor Charlie Gary with Inelle Hawkins and James Cumber. A double-breasted pin-stripped suit that Charlie made himself. Looking good!

Courtesy, John D. Rockefeller, Jr., Library,
Colonial Williamsburg Foundation

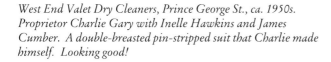

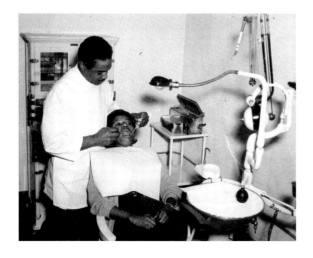

Dentist's office, ca. 1950. Dr. Pegler and Carrie Norcum.

Courtesy, John D. Rockefeller, Jr., Library,
Colonial Williamsburg Foundation

The Triangle block, Prince George St., ca. 1965—where most black folk who went to town hung out during the '60s. The block included James Williams' restaurant, Clarence Web's grocery store, Dr. James Blayton's hospital, and a dentist's office on the second floor.

Courtesy, *Daily Press*

went home and told Mrs. Moody that I couldn't take that job. She said, "Well maybe they're just trying you out, go on out a little longer." I went out there and one day as I was working Sasser says, "Reverend its a damned shame. They found out we been to college and they put our...[hind parts] out here on the railroad tracks." I said, "you can stay out here but I'm not." So I went in and told Mr. Davis, the head of that department, that I had to leave...I couldn't stay out there any longer. He said, "Well preacher, if you leave the railroad you got to go to the Army." I said, "They can't put me in the Army because I didn't register, and I'm too old. Sasser went up there and told the man the same thing. He took me out of the railroad track and put me to work in the warehouse where it was nice and warm. Next time I heard from Sasser, he was over in Luxembourg.

As in much of the south, Williamsburg had both a black and a white aristocracy. In the black community there were families like the Epps, Braxtons, Wallaces, Whites, Tabbs, Alexanders, Redcrosses, Blaytons, and Lees who had long histories with the town. They were all landholders and saw the town through different eyes. They were tow-the-line, hold-your-head up, walk-with-dignity, no-matter-how-badly-you're-treated, don't-sink-to-their-level types of folk. Their standards were higher. They maintained important roles in the civic and religious community. They sent their children to the best schools they could. College was an expectation, not an option. They were a class act without being Uncle Toms. As an example of their kind of behavior, William Pfeifer tells a

James E. Wallace family relaxing in the shade, 1950s. (L-rt) Bernice, Louise, James E. Odessa, Helen, John, James, and Lawrence.

Courtesy, John D. Rockefeller, Jr., Library,
Colonial Williamsburg Foundation

Three generations of the Tabb family celebrate the 50th wedding anniversary of George E. B. and Mary Alice Tabb in 1963. All but two of their children are shown (l-rt): Langford, Cardell, Ruby, Alice, Rev. J. B., Sr., Percell, Russell, Bernice, Oliver, George E., and Leroy. The child in the center is grandson Terry. Like the Palmer, Wallace, Whiting, Blayton, Epps, Lee, Cook, and Moody families, the Tabb family has a long tradition of activism and bridge building in the Williamsburg community. Deacon Tabb set up the first funeral parlor for African Americans, and the family also established a refuse company. Those two businesses are still serving the community.

Courtesy, Oliver Tabb

story about guests at the Williamsburg Inn being intoxicated and obviously out of line in their behavior. Melvin White, who was maître d' in the dining room for many years, was so calm and professional in the face of such behavior that one visitor who observed how professionally he handled the rowdy group said, "I'm beginning to think that the only class act in the dining room is the maître d'!"

After WWII, greater attention had started to be given to American values and concepts relating to democracy. Like other communities around the country, Williamsburg was also to struggle with the testing of those ideals. Perhaps the greatest struggle of the 1950s in Virginia was brought about by the Supreme Court's 1954 *Brown vs. Board of Education* decision, in which Virginia, and particularly Prince Edward County, played a significant role.

NAACP awards chapter meeting at Zion Prospect Baptist Church, Yorktown, ca. 1953. Ezekiel Jones and McKinley Whiting (third & fourth from left) and Professor James Allen (far rt.).

Courtesy, John D. Rockefeller, Jr., Library, Colonial Williamsburg Foundation

On 23 May 1951, Spotswood Robinson of the NAACP filed suit in U.S. District Court asking that the state law validating segregated schools in Virginia be struck down. This was motivated by black students in Farmville, who had gone on strike a week earlier. The court considered only the question of Virginia's compliance with the doctrine of separate-but-equal, not with the question of discrimination and its effect on black children. The *Davis vs. County School Board of Prince Edward County* case was one of four, however, considered in the *Brown* decision that segregation based on color in public schools was a violation of the Fourteenth Amendment. The decision led to the eventual desegregation of schools across America. In Virginia, however, that process would take on a life of its own.

On 6 August, Governor Stanley appointed a Governor's Select Committee on Public Education. No professional educators or blacks were on it, as Stanley was under intense pressure to create a commission that favored the legislature. This pressure was created by his loyalty to Senator Harry Byrd and the Byrd machine, whose support had assured Stanley's election. Then in January 1956 the Byrd juggernaut pressured the General Assembly to pass a referendum supporting tuition grants for private schools, even though on 21 November 1955 the Virginia Supreme Court had declared such grants unconstitutional. Later that year, more than twenty new anti-integration measures were passed, and Byrd was considered the hero of what came to be known as "massive resistance." Then, almost immediately after J. Lindsay Almond succeeded Stanley in 1958—having run on a platform of segregation and contempt for the courts—the General Assembly passed a law closing any school that integrated. In September, Almond closed schools in Warren County, Charlottesville, and Norfolk, in direct opposition to the U.S. Supreme Court's ruling to desegregate those systems.

In 1958 an organized and powerful opposition to massive resistance began to emerge, however. Save-the-schools groups, professional educators, and business leaders publicly opposed massive resistance and white citizens councils. In October, the Virginia Education Association denounced school closings; and in December, twenty-nine Virginia industrial and financial leaders, in a private meeting, urged Governor Almond to abandon his stance on interposition. On 19 January 1959, the Virginia Supreme Court ruled that closing schools and withholding funds was a violation of the State Constitution; and on the same day, Almond received the opinion of the Federal District Court, which held that Virginia was in violation of the U.S. Constitution. Nine days later, Almond announced that he was ending massive resistance.

Meanwhile, in Williamsburg, the black community, especially in James City County, faced challenges of its own, brought about in part by a white community that wanted to see the status quo maintained Lewis Powell, who was general council for Colonial Williamsburg, head of the school board in Richmond, and later Supreme Court justice, took the position that desegregation of schools was long overdue; but he knew that it would take time for many whites to change their way of thinking. At the opposite extreme, the James City County Board of Supervisors had threatened that any black's entering a white school would result in the cutting off of the school's funding. That kind of sentiment was countered, however, by the presence of liberal-minded John D. Rockefeller, Jr., who publicly supported the qualitative improvement of black education and had proven his resolve by providing some of the funding to build Bruton Heights High School and making it a model of education for blacks in the state fourteen years before the *Brown* decision.

One of the reasons for such a peaceful transition in the area was that during those years of "freedom of choice" (roughly 1955-1968), only a small number of black families chose to send their children to previously all-white schools. Most black families continued to enroll their children in Bruton Heights, James Weldon Johnson, and Frederick Douglass. The stance taken by Colonial Williamsburg was, as always, a mitigating influence in the town; and although Rockefeller went to great lengths to placate the local white citizenry, there was never any doubt where he stood on school desegregation: he had insisted from the outset of his financing the town's restoration that facilities operated by Colonial Williamsburg be integrated.

Finally, in September 1968, all schools in the Williamsburg area were desegregated. Unfortunately, that led to the renaming of the two schools that were named for black Americans. James Weldon Johnson became Yorktown Intermediate, and after Frederick Douglass was closed, students attended Magruder Elementary. In James City County, when Bruton Heights was closed, none of the trophies, awards, etc. that were important to blacks were transferred to James Blair. This insensitivity exacerbated the inherently volatile atmosphere, which unsurprisingly erupted in fights. Powell was right: it would take time for attitudes to change.

In February 1950, two black visitors to Colonial Williamsburg received less than satisfactory treatment when seeking lodging or meals. The egalitarian practices of Colonial Williamsburg were unique, because in 1950 section 18.1-356 of the Virginia Code required that the races be lodged separately. Those blacks not fortunate enough to find lodging in the restoration, therefore, had very few options. Mr. George Cohon and his wife were put up in the Willy Baker Tourist Home, which the Bakers (a black family)

Samuel Powell, Leonard Wallace, Virginia Taylor James, and Catherine Wallace stepping out and ready to cut a rug at the Jazz Club, ca. 1950.

Courtesy, John D. Rockefeller, Jr., Library, Colonial Williamsburg Foundation

A night on the town at Wallace and Cook's Beer Garden, ca. 1940. The tavern was located near the present-day Fife and Drum Building on Franklin St.

Courtesy, John D. Rockefeller, Jr., Library, Colonial Williamsburg Foundation

Log Cabin Beach dining room, ca. 1950. It wasn't just a swimming beach, but a place to dine and fellowship (in the black religious community, "fellowship" is a verb) with friends and neighbors.

Courtesy, John D. Rockefeller, Jr., Library, Colonial Williamsburg Foundation

had established to offer some respite to those few black visitors who came to tour Williamsburg and to accommodate the large number of chauffeurs who drove their employers to Colonial Williamsburg. Besides lodging, meals were also not easy to come by. The Cohons wrote, "We really experienced the effect of discrimination the first day when, after trying for an hour in heavy rain, we could not find a place in the Project that would serve us lunch. Since we had failed to arrange with Mrs. Baker for our lunch we went without food from 9am until 6:15pm.

This led Winthrop Rockefeller's black chauffeur, James Hudson, to evaluate the town from his own point of view. Because, his comments are so thoughtful, give an accurate view of the town's black population, and represent one of the few assessments of the black community by a black, they deserve to be quoted in their entirety:

The circumstances under which these observations were made naturally limited the chances of obtaining factually supported information. Reactions seem to differ widely in approach to the real needs. Some of the obviously critical points are:

1. The great need for objective, intelligent *accepted* leadership among the Negro population, in order to organize for unity of purpose. This would have a tremendous effect on the entire citizenry.

2. A major conflict area exists among the newer and younger progressive Negro residents and the older settlers who know only the pattern of gratifying dependency which they have always followed. The latter group are hostile to the attitude of the whites in a passive sort of way, but fearfully refrain from participation in any move or modification they think might jeopardize their 'good relationship' with the white families with whom they have been closely associated thru the years. Problems of advancement and new ideas are handicapped by the confusion the older residents feel when they are faced with giving up their traditional way of thinking and full conformity to "expected behavior." Thru genuine lack of understanding, they avoid any demands for participation in civic betterment, by denying the need for change. Any initiative taken by the more progressive or aggressive few, just seems to thwart their passive need for "dependency" which provokes a state of unwelcomed anxiety as to the outcome.

3. Backwardness, jealousy and lack of courage for self-help are a drawback. The most retarded thinkers have more intimate relationships with the white residents. This makes it difficult for the intelligent Negro to gain the cooperation needed in any forward trend. The net result is a somewhat dispirited majority, who feel that their stability of relationships with members of the other race will be shaken by any changes and they are afraid to become personally involved. The entire population thus suffers by these limitations.

4. For some undetermined reason, there exists an apparent resentment against the Restoration. General statements of feeling on this point are:

a) Loss of choice property locations by the Negroes thru the Restoration and lack of opportunity given to obtain the desirable new locations.

(b) Ideas prevail that as the largest employer, the Restoration has done the group an injustice by not taking more interest in more equal opportunities for all.

(c) By virtue of its holding and position in the community, it should be a part of all city planning areas including the City Council.

5. In further observation: With the exception of two very dilapidated, unhealthy, unwholesome "beer rooms," Negroes actually have no place to which they can go for after-work leisure. The only movie available is at the Bruton Heights High School, and this during the school session. The first movie for the fall did not begin until November 16. The need for opportunities for emotional and social outlet is grave as this condition greatly influences delinquency tendencies.

6. Because of the lack of leadership and the disunity of the Negro group as a whole, I believe it will require a professionally trained person, with organizational ability–a good personality–keen

insight and ability to work with people of both races on all social and economic levels, who could spend the necessary time in careful study and organization of a constructively sound program that will accomplish positive results.

The four citizens listed below have excellent background and represent potentially good leadership but unfortunately do not have the confidence and support of enough Negroes to be effective:

> Dr. Blayton–the only Negro physician
> Reverend Johnson–Pastor of the First Baptist Church (a newcomer)
> Mr. Earl Henderson–Business-man
> Mr. McKinley Whiting–Mortician

To indicate an instance of the lack of unity and understanding among the Negro group in civic affairs–Mr. McKinley Whiting was nominated by members of the white race, as a candidate for the City Council in Williamsburg, and only received 56 Negro votes. An educational program for adults (progressive and otherwise) would certainly help this situation.

Another interesting evidence of the need for leadership, was in regard to the handling of the funds for the movies given at the Bruton Heights High School. The receipts are turned over to the School Superintendent, who in turn gives a percentage to the Parent Teachers Association. Last year the amount turned in by the manager of the movies was $1500.00. The PTA has not called in two years for their checks and no effort has been made to clarify responsibilities. Yet the high school band could not participate with the other high school bands because of lack of adequate uniforms.

As my short contacts were made under circumstances that would not give rise to questions or suspicion, it is difficult to report in other than a general way, the exception being the obvious need for:

1. A city-wide recreational program, with facilities for youth and adults.
2. An education program for adults (all-round)
3. Arrangement for housing and meals for Negroes visiting this National Shrine, who may not be absorbed in the mixed groups.

In conclusion, it is my feeling that the values of the Negroes as a group are not basically different. The older unresponsive citizen who feels the need to conform to tradition and the more progressive group can with proper assistance, overcome the obstacles in achieving a greater sense of pride, security and dignity that will strengthen and preserve any democratic community.

The National Urban League had also written a report concerning Williamsburg, but both Kenneth Chorley, the president of the restoration, and John D. Rockefeller, Jr., were so impressed with Hudson's report that they both wanted him to take on the leadership of the black community. The idea was abandoned on second thought, however.

Next came the startling events of the 1960s, including the Civil Rights Movement. William and Mary enrolled its first black un-

Dr. Martin Luther King, Jr., with (l-rt) two unidentified men, Wyatt Tee Walker, Rev. David Collins, and Deacon Parker at First Baptist Church.

Courtesy, John D. Rockefeller, Jr., Library, Colonial Williamsburg Foundation

dergraduate in 1963, Oscar Blayton, son of Dr. James Bland Blayton, one of the two black doctors in town. Martin Luther King, Jr., visited Williamsburg in the early sixties at the invitation of Reverend David Collins and preached at First Baptist Church. In the mid-sixties Dennis Gardner, Lawrence Gerst, and Allen Clark picketed the local A&P grocery store on the corner of South Henry and Lafayette streets in protest of its discriminatory hiring practices. Also, a few white faculty at William and Mary were involved in efforts to overcome the legacy of segregation and the closing of public schools: Robert Benton and Robert Maccubbin (see p. 229) of the English Department went periodically to Farmville to tutor black students in Prince Edward County; and others, such as David Jones of the Philosophy Department, were involved through the American Civil Liberties Union in a court-monitoring program. The more radical activity that was taking place in other parts of the country did not have a parallel in the Williamsburg area, however; and even the blacks in town did not much support the march organized by John Tabb, Jr., to protest King's assassination.

Because of its national prominence, Colonial Williamsburg also understood the importance of dealing with civil unrest before it became a problem. John Harbour (a former C.W. senior manager) recalled an incident involving a couple of students who had come from Hampton Institute to conduct a sit-in at the Motor House Cafeteria. They got their placards together. They stayed and stayed and stayed and finally after a long while, they left. And their comment was, "They took our money, served us food and we left, but nothing else happened." The system and policy that was in place defused rather than fueled dissension, although among the older local whites there was still tension, largely inseparable from anxiety over nationwide student unrest over U.S. policy in Vietnam. For instance, one of the few William and Mary students to have a beard in this era was arrested by a Williamsburg policeman for "loitering, lingering, and miscegenation": a few minutes after the Corner Greeks had closed at eleven p.m., the student had been harmlessly chatting with an elderly black waitress as she was leaving the restaurant to go home.

Even in the seventies, the lingering issue of segregation and racism was still apparent. In a letter to Carlisle H. Humelsine, president of Colonial Williamsburg, Eugene Vorhies, an African-American businessman from Washington, D.C., complained about the treatment he had received at a private Williamsburg guest house:

 Although we had hoped to be able to stay in the [Williamsburg] Inn or in one of the restored houses, we found this wouldn't be possible because of the heavy bookings of these accommodations long in advance....My wife and I then decided that we'd like to try one of the nearby guest houses, hoping such would be cozier and more in keeping with the spirit of a weekend in Williamsburg than would be a Holiday Inn, etc., etc. I began calling guest houses listed in a Chamber of Commerce flyer that had been sent to us by Colonial Williamsburg, along with some other promotional material. You can imagine that I was more than a little surprised when the operator of the first guest house I called asked me, after considerable hemming and stalling, if I was a Negro, "because we don't take Negroes." At several of the other houses I then called I received the same—what can one call it?—treatment.

Humelsine replied immediately, expressing his chagrin and also assuring Mr. Vorhies that Colonial Williamsburg would make every effort to influence private owners from engaging in discrimination.

One can see why Duncan Cocke, a long-time resident of Williamsburg, was em ployed by Colonial Williamsburg Foundation, in part, to advise upper management about the disposition of the town and its willingness to accept or go along with the ideas and initiatives forwarded by the foundation.

Members of the St. John Baptist Church in East Williamsburg, ca. 1950. (standing, l-rt) John Halcomb, Alene Stephens, Cornelius Roberts, Bertha Jordan, Daisy Brown, Sally Roberts, MayLou Roberts, unidentified, Aline Stephens, & Theodore Roberts; (seated) Gertrude Roberts, Lulabelle Lee, Helen Roberts, unidentified, Nancy Thomas, & Lilly Williams.

Courtesy, John D. Rockefeller, Jr., Library, Colonial Williamsburg Foundation

Ironically, even though there has been a positive change in the interactions be tween blacks and whites in Williamsburg, the atmosphere still separates the races. Churches, social organizations, clubs, and many bars and restaurants, while open to all, are still essentially separate racially–a reality that does not seem to be a major concern to either community.

It is no accident that the nucleus of the area's black community is the church. Just as many white communities marked their identity and maturation in America by build ing institutions of higher education, black communities gauged their legitimacy via the establishment of churches. The black church has historically been the organizer, leader, conscience, and representative of the community. In Williamsburg, churches have rep resented and supported the political and social standards of their people. Now, as then, if you want to know what the black community thinks, what it reveres, and what it hopes for the future, attend its churches. It is a reality that has been accepted by the white community too. Every aspiring politician from George Grayson to Jeanne Zeidler acknowledges the important role the black church has played in the community. It is no accident that ministers such as L.L. Wales, David Collins, Junius Moody, James Tabb, Glenwood Morgan, and Solomon Wesley have been (and are) community leaders, as well as men of God. Finally, and most importantly, the black church in Williamsburg has been a symbol, repository, and nurturer of faith. It is the deep and abiding faith of the area's African-American community that has allowed it to triumph over intolerance,displacement, segregation, miseducation, discrimination,and arginalization.

The Reverend David Collins, shown here giving communion, was minister of the First Baptist Church and an accepted leader in Williamsburg, particularly during the civil rights era.

Courtesy, John D. Rockefeller, Jr., Library, Colonial Williamsburg Foundation

The Reverend M. R. Banks and Deacon Anthony Jones baptize Alice Fay Wallace at Mt. Pleasant Baptist Church, early 1940s.

Courtesy, John D. Rockefeller, Jr., Library, Colonial Williamsburg Foundation

The Williamsburg Quintet, a popular religious singing group, was at its height in the 1940s. The proud artists here with visitor Chandler Cudlip, are (l-rt) Fred Epps, Levi Stephens, Clifton Gardner, Lisbon Gerst, & Archie Rucker.

Courtesy, Gardner family

With a population of 12,000, Williamsburg maintains its small size compared to the neighboring James City County, which has over 43,000 residents. Much of Williamsburg is still seen as elite, however, with most of the communities of color, lying on the periphery or outskirts of the town, and mostly in the same areas they occupied in the fifties and sixties. Many see current problems stemming from the advent of drugs and the disintegration of the black family. The Vietnam war, returning veterans, and an increasingly promiscuous society brought a drug culture into the area, the effects of which have eroded much of the progress of the black community. This is a constant cause of concern and public debate.

Like most others in America, the black community in Williamsburg also struggles to achieve good education for its children. Disparities in SOL and SAT scores, election to the National Honor Society, and other measures of achievement are still problematic. With African Americans such as Barbara Haywood occupying seats on the school board, and a larger number of black principles and administrators in the school system, the black community can advocate more effectively for job equity, curriculum reform, and access; but the road remains difficult. Some still lament the time when black children were taught by black teachers who had a vested interest in their success, and feel that the education offered by schools such as Bruton Heights and James Weldon Johnson during segregation was superior.

The court system still seems unbalanced in the number of blacks convicted and the time they serve. The criminal justice system is still perceived as quick to dole out sentences and punishments that many would argue don't fit the crimes. However,

Like the Williamsburg Human Relations Committee of the 1960s and '70s, All Together, founded in the '90s, is a diverse group of citizens whose goal is to "explore our differences, and encourage human relations in such a way that they become bonds of friendship that will guarantee the common good of all." (Standing, l-rt) David Norman, Tony Conyers, & Buzz Schmidt; (seated) unidentified tax advisor, Lois Hornsby, Jack Charlton, James Baker, Dick Orr, & Ginny Haslett.

Courtesy, Ellen K. Rudolph

Long-time head of Willamsburg's NAACP chapter, Phillip Cooke ran for City Council in 1968, as shown here, and four more times later.

Courtesy, *Daily Press*

the area now has black lawyers, judges, and magistrates who are part of the system. They must take credit for the positive changes as well as responsibility for not championing much needed reform.

Since integration, inter-racial partnerships have been forged to deal with the challenges whites and black have faced as a community. In the sixties and seventies it was the Council on Human Relations, and in the seventies and eighties, Citizens for Community Progress. Today it is the All Together Group, composed of citizens from every sector of the community who see common problems in housing, employment, health, and other areas, and seek solutions that will benefit all.

Finally, the greater Williamsburg area has changed in significant ways. Housing, employment, and political and social interaction have never been better. A large influx of citizens not born in the area (predominately white) have brought about much of the positive and progressive change that has taken place in the community. Although community activism is still present, too few within the black community actively participate. One notable exception was Phillip Cooke, who headed the NAACP for many years and ran for public office five times. He believed that most of his defeats were the result of blacks' not bothering to vote. But like Dennis Gardner, Esterine Moyler, Bobbie Alexander, Anthony Conyers, Eula Radcliffe, Herbert Rainey, Dr. James Baker, and others, most of the area's black community remains vibrant, dynamic, and hopeful. The late Reverend Junius Moody said it best: "This wasn't my home at first, but I've lived here since 1926. When I first came to preach here, one of my members said he didn't like my preaching. He said, 'I'd rather hear a dog bark than Moody preach.' God blessed me to preach over his funeral. I just love my people, and I love this community."

Selected Sources & Suggested Readings

The author is indebted to many people for their informative interviews: Maxine Brown, Phillip Cooke, Dennis Gardner, Jackie Gardner, John Harbour, Reverend Junius Moody, James C. Palmer, William Pfeifer, Doris Rainey, & Benjamin Smith.

Black, Henry Campbell. *Black's Law Dictionary*, ed. Bryan A. Garner. 7th ed. (St. Paul: West Group, 1999).

Boyer, Allston. Letter to George Cohen, 6 March 1950. Rockefeller Archive Center, Tarrytown, N.Y.

Hudson, James E. "Observations on Williamsburg Visit," 26 November 1951. Rockefeller Archive Center, Tarrytown, N.Y.

Rockefeller, John D., Jr. Letter to Kenneth Chorley, 18 Feb. 1952. John D. Rockefeller, Jr., Library, Colonial Williamsburg Foundation.

Vorhies, Eugene, Jr. Letter to Carlisle H. Humelsine, 22 Oct. 1970. John D. Rockefeller, Jr., Library, Colonial Williamsburg Foundation.

Educators

Ever since the founding of the College of William & Mary in 1693, the community has been first and foremost a learning place, distinguished for the quality of its educators. Some of Williamsburg's most beloved school teachers are shown here.

Jeanne Bell Etheridge devoted her career to Matthew Whaley School. A native of Williamsburg, she graduated from William & Mary. She began teaching at Matthew Whaley in 1931 and was principal 1952-1973. She guided the school through the challenging process of racial integration. Her teaching made a lasting impression on her students. Years later, vivid memories enabled one former pupil to write, "Oh marvelous, wonderful 6th grade, where we were taught, loved, cajoled, encouraged, and inspired by the incomparable Miss Etheridge. She inspired in us the love of learning and self-discipline. She understood that we all learned at our own rate when given the freedom to do so. Because of her kindness we learned to be kind, and she built in us self-confidence."

Courtesy, *Daily Press*

Raymond F. Freed, who came to Williamsburg after serving in China and India during WWII to attend William & Mary, began teaching at Matthew Whaley in 1950. He moved in 1955 to James Blair High, where he taught history, social science, and government. This photo was taken in 1973, when he helped move into Lafayette High School, where he was an assistant principal. Returning to the classroom in 1977, Freed estimated he taught some 3,000 high schoolers. A much-admired teacher, Freed died in 1985.

Courtesy, *Daily Press*

Madeline Gee dedicated much of her career to Williamsburg, where she was the first African-American teacher at James Blair High before integration. A graduate of Hampton Institute, she taught at Bruton Heights High, James Blair High, and Berkeley High. After retiring in 1973, she remained active well into her nineties as a leader in Williamsburg's social, cultural, and civic life. Following her initiative, in 1974 the General Assembly enacted the Senior Citizens Higher Education Act, which was amended in 1977 and became a model for the nation. Miss Gee served on Williamsburg's U.S. Bicentennial Committee in 1976 and also on the Advisory Council for Williamsburg's 300th Anniversary in 1999. As Virginia Gazette editor and publisher W. C. O'Donovan noted in an editorial, Miss Gee was so popular that when she was honored as grand marshal for a Christmas parade in the 1990s, "she got more waves than Santa Claus."

Courtesy, Ellen K. Rudolph

Perseverance, Preservation, and Prosperity: The Greek Community of Williamsburg

by: Mia Stratis Spears

Get what you can, and what you get hold,
'Tis the stone that will turn all your lead into gold.

—Benjamin Franklin,
"The Way to Wealth"

Imagine a young man boarding a ship about to set sail for a destination unlike any place he has ever experienced. This young man is wearing his first and only suit and his first and only pair of shoes, and has the name of the person he is to meet when his ship reaches its destination pinned to his jacket. He has little, if any, money in his pocket, does not speak the language of his new country, and has no idea what will happen on the strange, new journey he has decided to take. He promises to be careful and to write as soon as he can. Leaving his village, his country, his parents, and everything he knows behind, he boards the ship to America. Through tears, his mother watches the ship leave port and is overcome with mixed emotions. She prays that God will protect her child in his voyage across the ocean and hopes that America will greet him with kindness and good fortune, yet she fears that perhaps she has made a terrible mistake in allowing her son to go so far away with nothing to protect him from the difficulty he will undoubtedly encounter when he reaches that faraway land. The young man, however, has something more powerful than money and clothing. He has a vision. He comes in search of that "stone" that the notion of "America" promised many immigrants. His strong work ethic, sense of duty to his family, and undying determination enable that young man to persevere, to "turn...lead into gold," and to set an example for the many who would follow him.

This scene depicts the journey of young Greek immigrants who would ultimately settle in Williamsburg. Following family members, friends, or simply an instinct that a promising future might await them, the majority of Greek immigrants who arrived in Williamsburg before the 1960s shared humble beginnings. Few spoke more than a few words of English, few possessed more than the clothing on their backs, and few left their villages in Greece with more than an elementary education. None feared hard work, however, and most brought with them an incredible foresight that would make the presence of the Greek community instrumental in the shaping of a city that would grow to be loved by so many.

Nineteen-year-old Angelo Costas, along with his older brother Nick, arrived in Williamsburg in 1916, where the onset of World War I called for the building of a munitions plant on Penniman Road. The plant generated a population boom that the Costas brothers believed would undoubtedly set the stage for a profitable business. To their surprise, Williamsburg was a village very much like the one they had left behind when they had set sail for America. It had no paved streets, no running water, no electricity, and, to their delight, few restaurants. With $200, the Costas brothers purchased a lot on Duke of Gloucester Street, upon which would be built one of Williamsburg's first public restaurants, the Norfolk Cafe, located across from the Ludwell-Paradise House. Angelo and Nick soon welcomed friends as partners and turned their venture into a successful restaurant that depended on water drawn from a well out back and food cooked on a wood-burning stove by the light of a kerosene lamp.

The William and Mary students who appreciated his good-heartedness, valued his insight, and shared his youth quickly befriended Angelo. It was upon the repeated suggestion of the college students, who feared another restaurant would open closer to the college and hurt business, that the Costas brothers decided to relocate the Norfolk Cafe closer to William and Mary where the Williamsburg Theater is now in Merchants Square. As the college grew in the 1920s, the Costas' business likewise prospered; and the Kandy Kitchen, a bowling alley, pool room, barber shop, and, later, a movie theater, would be added to the restaurant already in place. Angelo and Nick were now successful enough to bring several family members and friends from their village of Enjaykeou to share in their newly found fortune. Although Nick returned to Greece in 1924 to marry, several friends and relatives stayed in Williamsburg and operated the businesses successfully until 1928, when the restoration of Colonial Williamsburg began.

Mike Pete and Tom Baltas came to Williamsburg to join childhood friend Angelo Costas in his business ventures. Pete took over the Kandy Kitchen and then purchased what later became Rose's Trailer Court and Apartments; Baltas entered a partnership with Costas to operate the Capitol Restaurant, one of Williamsburg's most popular restaurants, from 1932 to 1960.

Capitol Restaurant in Merchants Square, ca.1952

Courtesy, Kitsa Kashouty

A stone's throw from the "Middle Greeks," as the Capitol Restaurant was affectionately called, stood the "Corner Greeks." In 1930, Steve Sacalis, a New York flower shop owner, decided to pursue a new interest. He sold his flower shops, traveled to Williamsburg, and opened the Colonial Restaurant (where the bookstore and men's clothing store are now on Merchant's Square). For the first five years there was no kitchen there, so Mrs. Sacalis did all

Dr. Davis Y. Paschall (left) and Steve Sacalis present some of Mrs. Sacalis' baklava to Governor Albertis Harrison (1971).

Courtesy, Mia Stratis Spears

the cooking at her house on S. Boundary St., and Steve took the pots to the restaurant. In 1935 he got permission from Colonial Williamsburg to expand into another portion of the building in order to have a flat-top coal stove. In 1943, having sold the restaurant to his brother, Alex, Steve opened the Williamsburg Restaurant on the southeast corner of "College Corner"; and that restaurant was subsequently sold—to the Belers in 1950. Eventually, the Sacalises opened a somewhat fancier restaurant, The Lafayette Restaurant on Richmond Road. Like his friend Angelo Costas, Steve succeeded in business, amassed a sizable fortune, and won the hearts of the townspeople and college students through his generosity, philanthropy, and goodwill.

Dr. Davis Y. Paschall, a student at the college from 1928 to 1932, fondly recalls spending many nights snacking with his friends at "Middle Greeks" and "Corner Greeks": "Times were difficult in those days, and there were many days when we didn't have money to pay for food, but we were never turned away. The Greeks were hard-working, proud, yet humble people. They had experienced poverty and tough times, and they never forgot what it was like to need. They took care of us, and we were grateful to have them." Dr. Paschall remembers Mr. Sacalis' "big black book." When students didn't have money to pay for their meals, Mr. Sacalis told them to write down in "the book" what they had eaten. He told them to come back and settle their bills when they had graduated and had found jobs. When Dr. Paschall returned to William and Mary in 1960 as its president, Mr. Sacalis amazingly still had his "big black book" and discovered that Paschall had an outstanding bill to pay. Including interest, Dr. Paschall owed Mr. Sacalis $1.32 for a doughnut that had been eaten thirty years before! "Mr. Steve was so pleased that I had gotten a job, however, he waived the debt."

In addition to supporting college students, members of the Greek community never neglected their sense of obligation and responsibility to the city. They believed in the efforts of the college, Colonial Williamsburg, and later, the community hospital, and supported them

Sacalis' smiles and shishkebobs were always on the menu at The Lafayette restaurant in the 1950s.

Courtesy, Thomas L. Williams archives

with sizable contributions. From donating hot meals for hungry students to thousands of dollars for renovation and expansion efforts, several members of the Greek community in Williamsburg were characteristically philanthropic.

By the 1940s, the Greeks had successfully planted roots in Williamsburg, proven themselves shrewd businessmen, and developed a wonderful rapport with both the community and the youth of the college. A cozy atmosphere had emerged from the clamor of Greek kitchens and the warmth of Greek hospitality. Williamsburg was still small enough for everyone to know one another, and the Greeks provided social settings to which students and locals gravitated. During the 1950s, Harriet Beler's famous pecan pie and cinnamon buns and the affordable, home-style cooking, and Chrysa Sacalis ("Mama Steve" as she was affectionately known by the locals), made Greek wives just as popular as their husbands. These businesses were family efforts. Wives worked alongside their husbands, and children followed suit by readily assuming their own positions behind the counters. Together they committed themselves to a service industry that would ultimately cater to millions living in or passing through Williamsburg as students and tourists.

Angelo Mageras in his early days at Ted's Restaurant, ca. 1955

Courtesy, Nickie Mageras

A civil war in Greece in 1947-1948 prompted a second wave of Greek immigration during the 1950s and early 1960s. Many chose to leave their war-torn country, where democracy was threatened by the insurgence of communism and progress and prosperity seemed unattainable. They sought refuge in the democratic safe haven of the United States, some, in Williamsburg. This second stream of immigrants would embrace America very much as had their predecessors: working hard to fulfill a dream. Several began their lives in Williamsburg as dishwashers in Greek-operated restaurants; and upholding the standards set by those before them, this new generation would also achieve success.

In 1951, Angelo Mageras left Karpenisi, a poor village in Greece, and arrived in Newport News. Like Angelo Costas, he arrived when he was only nineteen years old. Mageras moved to Williamsburg in 1953 on a hunch that a poorly run business he noticed driving through town one afternoon had the makings of a sound investment. Mageras purchased Ted's Restaurant on Route 60 with partner Spiros Skarlos, and later, Harry Magus. Together, Mageras, Skarlos, and Magus worked eighteen-hour days cleaning, cooking, dish-washing, and table waiting. Mageras opened his first bank account in the United States with one dollar.

In 1957, Harriet Beler (second from left) poses with nephew Mike Kokolis and nieces Connie Mexis and Nickie Kokolis Mageras, who followed her to Williamsburg.

Courtesy, Nickie Mageras

Over the next forty years, his single dollar would unfold into millions. In 1955, Mageras entered a partnership with his future brother-in-law Mike Kokolis and his friend Lakis Florakis, who had intended to stay in Williamsburg only long enough to have a cup of coffee with Mageras on his way to New Jersey. This partnership, known as the AJ&L Corporation lasted more than thirty years and carried the traditional Greek influence beyond downtown and out Richmond Road, accommodating visitors in its restaurants and hotels.

Friends Angelo Costas (Capitol Restaurant) and Tom Paparis (Yorkshire Restaurant).

Courtesy, Lackey Paparis

Just as Mike Pete was responsible for the arrival of his nephew Tom Paparis and his family, who still operate the Yorkshire Restaurant in Williamsburg, so was Harriet Beler instrumental in arranging for the coming of the Kokolis family. Harriet, along with her husband Pete, operated the Williamsburg Restaurant on the corner of Merchants Square. This "Corner Greek" came from Tarapsa, a tiny village outside of Sparta. When Mrs. Beler met Angelo Mageras, she was impressed with his drive and ambition, and thought that he would make a good husband for her niece, Nickie Kokolis. Nickie met and married Angelo shortly thereafter, in 1958. Over the next several years, six of Nickie Kokolis Mageras' seven siblings gathered in Williamsburg. Mike Kokolis, Kiki Stratis, George Kokolis, Afroditi Sarantakos, John Kokolis, and, later, Connie Mexis, with their spouses, settled in Williamsburg to raise their families and own and operate their own businesses. The Kokolis family continued to grow beyond Tarapsa as sisters Helen Kanelos and Niki Kokolis came with their families to join their cousins in what would become one of Williamsburg's largest extended Greek families. This extended family largely dominated local hotel and restaurant businesses for many years.

According to longtime Greek resident John Baganakis, the Greek community of the 1960s grew to encompass immigrants from several different parts of Greece. While the Baganakis family was originally from Thessaloniki, the Paparis and Manos families came from Thessaly. Like the Kokolis family, the Sarantakos,

The Kokolis family in Greece, before Williamsburg became their home. Parents Katherine and Panayiotis Kololis. and father Marinos Kokolis (back row) stand with their children: siblings Connie Mexis (far right, in back) Kiki Stratis (front center) and Mike, George, and Dimitri Kokolis; Nickie Mageras; and cousins Helen Kanelos and Niki Kokolis.

Courtesy, Nickie Mageras

Papadakos, and Polymenakos families left Sparta for Williamsburg. The Mageras, Florakis, Zaharopoulos, Prassas, Dallas, Tsigaridas, and Lappas families departed from Evritania. The original Greeks in Williamsburg, however—the Costas, Baltas, Pete, Sacalis, and Andrews families—emigrated from former Constantinople. No longer simply in the "middle" or on the "corner," Greek businesses had expanded in two dimensions: one that remained closely connected to the College, and one that existed largely to serve tourists.

Mike Pete greets King Pavlos and Queen Fredericka of Greece at the Williamsburg Inn in 1953.

Courtesy, Lakis Paparis

Both Colonial Williamsburg and William and Mary relied heavily on the Greeks to accommodate their visitors and employ their students. Dr. Paschall described the Greek community as "vital" to the growth of the city. He explained:

> Harriet Baganakis Petrell is an excellent illustration of the interdependence of the college, Colonial Williamsburg, and local Greek businesses. Colonial Williamsburg could not sufficiently accommodate its growing number of visitors in the 1960s. Without the food and lodging provided by the Greeks, our tourists would have had far fewer places to eat or stay during their visits to Williamsburg. Mrs. Petrell not only enticed guests to remain in town with wonderful meals at the Jefferson Inn, but also employed young men from the college as waiters. These waiters, in their interaction with the tourists, shared their enthusiasm and loyalty toward William and Mary and, consequently, generated interest in the college. William and Mary would gain a great deal of support that way—simple word of mouth in a warm and friendly setting. While it is true that the success of Greek businesses largely depended on the traffic generated by the college and Colonial Williamsburg, it is likewise certain that the college and Colonial Williamsburg needed Greek businesses to keep that traffic flowing. Thus, a harmonious balance ensued from the growth of these three dynamic enterprises in the city.

When two cultures meet, a natural apprehension and curiosity result; but, as they explore one another, discovery and acceptance follows. While lack of education and poor command of the language subjected them to prejudice, members of the early Greek community overcame the occasional bias against them, paid their dues as newcomers, and moved forward while they remained true to what they believed in: stability, family, and roots. Because of the generosity and accomplishments of their predecessors, the second wave of Greek immigrants encountered acceptance in a city where they could unite and prosper *in light of* their ethnicity—not *in spite of* it, as the early Greeks had sometimes found necessary.

As the 1960s marked significant changes in Williamsburg, so began a movement within the Greek community itself. Greeks had worked very hard to establish themselves in business and to assimilate successfully into the culture of the larger Williamsburg community. Although the Greek population had grown significantly since the days of Angelo Costas and Steve Sacalis, the nearest place for Greeks to come together and socialize was the Saints Constantine and Helen Greek Orthodox Church in downtown Newport News. In 1964, this gap was filled with the formation of a local chapter of AHEPA. Established in Atlanta in 1922, the American Hellenic Education Progressive Association sought to educate immigrant Greeks in the English language and American culture, help them become better citizens, and help them assimilate into their new communities. AHEPA required chapters to hold English-only meetings to help Greek immigrants broaden their limited vocabularies. Although an AHEPA chapter outside the context of a Greek Orthodox Church is rare in the United States, many local

Greeks would benefit from its presence in Williamsburg. Through its continual contributions to the hospital and local projects, the presence of the AHEPA would likewise benefit the city itself; and through AHEPA the Greek community appropriately donated the city's "Welcome to Williamsburg" signs that presently greet guests.

The AHEPA Hall off of Richmond Road created a place for the Greek community to meet, hold dances, and host dinners; and the hall served the children of immigrants as a Greek school as well. As important as it was for Greek immigrants to learn to speak English, they felt it equally important that their children maintain their Greek culture and heritage. Reliance on business from tourists during the summer and holiday seasons made family visits to Greece difficult. Since Greeks could not leave their businesses during school vacations to take their children to Greece, AHEPA, largely under the direction of John Baganakis, brought Greece to their children. Greek-American children of the 1970s and 1980s thus spent many Saturday mornings in a classroom in the AHEPA Hall, where Julia Ruzecki taught them to read, write, and speak Greek, as well as dance in the tradition of their parents and grandparents.

In addition to the trend of introspection and communal effort to maintain and preserve the culture and heritage of the traditional Greek family, the Greek community of the 1970s also enjoyed economically good years. In the college setting, George Dallas welcomed and entertained scores of college students throughout his years at George's Campus Restaurant on Prince George Street, as did Paul Romeos at the Prince George Delicatessen. The Kerr family at the Green Leafe

Steve Sacalis, Steve Andrews, Angelo Mageras, and John Baganakis celebrate the assembly of the Order of AHEPA in 1964.

Courtesy, John Baganakis

Greek-American children of the AHEPA Greek School observe Greek Independence Day with patriotic poems, songs, and dances (1979).

Courtesy, Mia Stratis Spears

Cafe and the Polymenakos family at the Villa Roma Restaurant, with its basement Cave, provided students with places to eat, drink, and socialize in bar-type atmospheres. The "Holly" was the favorite submarine sandwich at the Colonial Delicatessen on Scotland Street; and brothers-in-law George Stratis and George Kokolis, throughout the 1970s, served thousands of them to William and Mary students. Across the street at the College Delly, James Lappas offered a similar fare, and likewise served thousands of submarine sandwiches to a steady stream of college students.

Greek establishments catering to the tourist industry flourished along Route 60 on Richmond Road as the AJ&L Corporation added more restaurants and hotels to accommodate the ever-rising number of tourists. Nick (Saras) Sarantakos, and later, Steve Manos, arrived in Williamsburg and approached the growing city with a foresight similar to that of the pioneering Greeks before them. For sixty years, Greek businessmen demonstrated an eye for business. They owned and operated popular and profitable businesses, and acquired a great deal of real estate. The value of that property naturally increased with the expansion of the city, and a once otherwise private, ethnic community became highly visible in the 1980s.

Jim Anthony, in a 1985 *Virginia Gazette* editorial, wrote, "We can, each and every one of us take a lesson from these immigrant Greeks as to how to make a fortune—work hard, save, and invest." The AJ&L Corporation of Angelo Mageras, Mike Kokolis, and Lakis Florakis was the second-largest tax payer in the city of Williamsburg in the 1980s. In its prime, AJ&L operated more than thirteen hundred hotel rooms in the area and employed more than twelve hundred people. Besides its business endeavors, AJ&L had become what Anthony called a "major philanthropic force" in the city.

The AJ&L Corporation celebrated its success with continuous and sizable donations to the larger community. In 1984, AJ&L gave $250,000, the largest single gift from a local

George Stratis at the counter of the Colonial Delicatessen in 1979, and menu from 1978.

Courtesy, Mia Stratis Spears

The Green Leafe Cafe and Paul's Deli remain as popular as they were thirty years ago.

Courtesy, Mia Stratis Spears

business, to Colonial Williamsburg for the renovation of the Information Center. The following year, $100,000 aided the expansion of Williamsburg Community Hospital. The partners then formed the Kokolis-Florakis-Mageras Foundation to support educational, cultural, and scientific endeavors.

Similar generosity on the part of other members of the Greek community marked these decades of prosperity. John Baganakis, Nick Sarantakos and the Sacalises particularly supported civic agencies in significant measure. Baganakis made contributions to the Police Department and other organizations. Sarantakos, an avid supporter of the Fire Department, a significant contributor to the American Cancer Society, and a chief donor to the college, was honored by the Pentagon in Washington, D.C., for his good citizenship and humanitarian efforts with an award that recognizes only one in twenty million Americans. The philanthropists within the Greek community, however, are too numerous to mention; their support of local efforts continues in the spirit of generosity and goodwill.

Throughout the 1980s, Greek Americans had successfully built bridges to the larger Williamsburg community through business and philanthropy. However, although their influence had reached far beyond what, perhaps, even they had anticipated, Greeks had yet to venture into politics. They actively supported candidates at the local, state, and national levels; but no one had ever assumed the role of candidate. However, with the arrival of community activist George S. Genakos,

Demetrios and Tony Sarantakos (back row) and Marinos, Nick, and George Kokolis follow in the philanthropic footsteps of their fathers, Nick Sarantakos and John Kokolis, by presenting a contribution to the Children's Hospital of the King's Daughters. WAVY-TV 10 newscaster Barbara Ciara (second from right) looks on.

Courtesy, Nick Sarantakos

Mike Kokolis (front left) and Angelo Mageras pose with Congressman Herb Bateman and President-elect George Bush in 1988.

Courtesy, Mike Kokolis

a retired U.S. Air Force officer with more than twenty-six years' service, that soon changed. To date, the only Greek to be elected to public office in Williamsburg, Genakos added a new facet to the Greek image in Williamsburg.

A first-generation Greek American whose family came from Mani-Laconia, Genakos garnered the most votes of any candidate each time he ran for City Council in 1986, 1992, and 1996. Additionally, his active role in the Greek community as a former president of the Order of AHEPA and his service to the region through work with organizations such as Housing Partnerships, the Salvation Army, the YMCA, the Masonic Order, and various veterans groups, have made George Genakos an outstanding citizen, and an exceptional Greek American.

Benjamin Franklin's advice continues to shape the code by which Williamsburg Greeks have lived. Their perseverance has given their children something that no one had ever been able to give them—a significant head start. The road of opportunity stretches out much further for first-generation Greek Americans than it did for their parents. Language and cultural barriers do not limit this first generation to the kitchen and cash register; and for the first time, most Greek families in Williamsburg can claim a college graduate. Greek-American graduates from colleges and universities throughout the Commonwealth have returned to Williamsburg to contribute to the Williamsburg community in ways and areas their parents could not. While many have followed in the footsteps of their parents and become successful restaurateurs, several have explored other interests, and are making strides in education, law, and medicine.

The far-reaching influence of those first immigrant Greeks who arrived eighty years ago, however, refuses to fade into the bustle of franchise business and outlet traffic that have come into the city. Dean Tsamouras greets the college students with the same smile at the College Delly as Angelo Costas did at the Norfolk Cafe. Across the street at Paul's Deli,

George Genakos takes his oath of office in 1992.

Courtesy, George Genakos

At 1994 Commencement exercises, graduates at William and Mary show appreciation for assistance from their parents and Dean Tsamouras of the College Delly.

Courtesy, Dean Tsamouras

brothers Pete and George Tsipas serve the same "Holly" that George Stratis and George Kokolis served thirty years before. The students have changed, the Greeks have changed, but the sentiment has not.

The evolution of the Greek community has paralleled the growth of the city. Despite finding their "stone" and having turned "lead into gold," however, members of the Greek community have not compromised the values, ideals, and cultural heritage brought from the villages they left behind.

Selected Sources and Suggested Readings

The author wishes to thank the following persons for their valuable interviews: John Baganakis, George Genakos, Kecha Kashouty, Mike Kokolis, Dr. Davis Y. Paschall, Nick Sarantakos, George Stratis, and Dean Tsamouras.

"AJ&L gift is largest ever from area business to CW, "*Virginia Gazette* (11 April 1984).

Belvin, Ed. *Growing Up in Williamsburg: From the Depression to Pearl Harbor* (Williamsburg: Virginia Gazette, 1981).

Costas, Angelo. "The Reminiscences of Angelo Costas," Interview by Wendy Ailor, 1985. John D. Rockefeller, Jr. Library, Colonial Williamsburg Foundation.

"The Greek Influence on Williamsburg," *The Publick Observer* (November 1976).

"Greek restaurateurs dominate the town," *Virginia Gazette* (26 August 1981).

"100 Moments in History: 30 Come Here's," *Virginia Gazette* (17 September 1997).

Rouse, Parke. "Williamsburg has many success stories," *Daily Press* (19 January 1992).

———. "Growth Changes Williamsburg," *Daily Press* (28 July 1996).

From Oligarchy to Democracy: Governing Virginia's First City

by: Jackson C. Tuttle, II

Williamsburg had the first, and for a long time, the only city government in Virginia. One reasonably could have expected that the first city in Virginia, capital of the largest and wealthiest of the American colonies, would emerge one day as a great metropolis. Instead, by the twists of fortune, Williamsburg remains to this day a small town, albeit one with special appeal. Williamsburg can trace the evolution of its government to a time when it stood unique in Virginia—the lone city in a commonwealth divided into counties. This distinction and others led Governor John G. Pollard in 1932, to write, "The establishment of the first city government in Virginia was of primary importance in American political history."

The General Assembly Act of 1699 laid the foundation for Williamsburg's city government. In deciding to move the government of Virginia from Jamestown to Williamsburg, the act envisioned "a new and well-ordered city according to a careful and prepared design." Governor Francis Nicholson and his executive council ensured that the new city would remain under their control by naming in the act a governing board of directors. The original directors included Governor Nicholson himself, Phillip Ludwell, Sr., Phillip Ludwell, Jr., Lewis Burwell, Benjamin Harrison, Jr., Hugh Norwell, Edmond Jennings, Thomas Ballard, and Henry Tyler. A number of these directors, along with James Whaley, Mongo Inglis, and others, also constituted a board of trustees to acquire and transfer land for the new city. Needless to say, all directors and trustees were prominent land-owning gentlemen appointed, not elected, to these positions. Popular election to city office did not occur for another 170 years.

In 1928, John Garland Pollard, professor of government and constitutional law at William and Mary, served as the mayor of Williamsburg. He subsequently served as Virginia's governor.

Courtesy, City of Williamsburg

According to Robert Beverley, writing in 1705,

> Soon after his [Nicholson's] succession to the government, he procured the Assembly and courts of judicature to be removed from Jamestown where there were good accom-

modations for people, to Middle Plantation where there were none, and flattered himself with the fond imagination of being the founder of a new city. He marked out the streets in many places so as that they might represent the figure of a W in memory of his late majesty, King William, after whose name the town was called Williamsburg.

In addition to a lot 475 by 475 feet square for the new capitol building, the Assembly appropriated 220 acres of land for the town proper and 63 acres for two seaports—Queen Mary's Port (Capitol Landing on Queen's Creek leading to the York River) and Princess Anne's Port (College Landing on Archer's Hope Creek accessing the James). On this land, Nicholson engaged in one of the earliest attempts at comprehensive city planning in America.

Williamsburg's first comprehensive plan was no academic exercise, but the basis for immediate action. The central boulevard of the city, a one-hundred-foot wide Duke of Gloucester Street would extend seven-eighths of a mile, along the ridge line dividing the James and York watersheds, from the Capitol Square to the College of William and Mary. To make the grand street straight, four small houses and an oven, all owned by Colonel John Page, had to be moved. While this early example of eminent domain was uncontested (Page supported the new town project and received three pounds in compensation), it may be America's first condemnation proceeding. As always, however, the planner's dreams were not

City Complex in 1930 on South England St. across from the magazine. These buildings were demolished to make way for the Restoration. From left to right, city "barn," sheriff's office and Jail (visible behind fence), firehouse, and city hall. City Council meetings were held in the nearby courthouse of 1770.

Courtesy, John D. Rockefeller, Jr., Library, Colonial Williamsburg Foundation

fully realized: the college was not square on the grand new street; to this day the street itself is not quite straight but meanders in its wide right-of-way; and only traces of Nicholson's original *W* remain. Nonetheless, the attention to such zoning details and design standards as building setbacks, minimum dwelling house sizes, and degree of roof pitch would impress professional city planners today.

City planning in Williamsburg, begun so auspiciously in 1699, was thereafter largely ignored until the mid-twentieth century. The careful grid pattern of streets and the set-aside commons for open space and vistas, gave way to railroad and highway projects bisecting the city as it grew into a confusing and dysfunctional layout that still plagues residents and visitors. City Council created a planning commission in 1930 and adopted increasingly detailed comprehensive plans in 1953, 1968, 1981, 1989, and 1998. Over the years, zoning and subdivision ordinances, urban design standards, and environmental controls have done much to preserve and enhance the physical character of the city. Expansive and visionary planning did not drive the annexations of 1915, 1923, 1941, 1964, or 1984. Rather, through incremental inclusion of newly developed land adjacent to the city, Williamsburg grew from its original one square mile in 1722, when Boundary Street was its western boundary, to today's nine square miles. Since 1987, the Virginia General Assembly has virtually precluded municipal annexations, and Williamsburg will likely remain a small town indefinitely.

Within the street pattern laid out by Nicholson, the city rapidly took shape between 1699 and 1722. The first capitol, palace, jail, courthouse, magazine, and theater were all completed, along with many businesses and private residences. Within two decades, Williamsburg had become the center of political, educational, religious, economic, and cultural life in Virginia.

In 1717, the colony's only city petitioned for a charter to govern itself: a body of "freeholders and inhabitants" appealed for incorporation. The colonial government, like modern state governments, sought to retain control over local affairs. Only when the state finds that control also entails responsibility for solving pesky and endless local problems—such as Williamsburg's hogs' persistently rooting in the public streets—does it find some degree of home rule convenient. Consequently, their appeal languished until 1722, when John Clayton, Archibald Blair, and Thomas Jones succeeded in obtaining a city charter from King George I.

The charter created a self-perpetuating municipal corporation composed of a mayor, six aldermen, and twelve common-councilmen. It named Clayton as recorder and John Holloway as the first mayor. The first aldermen were Blair, Jones, Sir John Randolph (father of Peyton and John), John Curtis, James Bray, and William Robertson. These men selected the twelve common-councilmen, who together constituted the "Common Hall." All officers were to serve "for so long as they shall behave themselves in the respective places," except for the mayor, who was to be elected from the aldermen by the Common Hall annually "on the feast day of St. Andrew." As a closed corporation, the Common Hall filled vacancies caused by death, removal, or resignation. The mayor, recorder, and aldermen acted as justices of the peace and sat monthly as a court of hustings. They were empowered to appoint other officers and make laws to govern the city, provided that local ordinances did not conflict with the laws of the General Assembly.

Extensive legislative, judicial, and administrative powers in the Charter of 1722 were held in check by a severely limited authority to tax, just as today's state legislatures may give localities broad powers and responsibilities, but closely limit their ways and means. The charter gave Williamsburg no power to tax; the city's only revenue came from fines from the exercise of its judicial powers and tolls collected on markets and fairs. The charter stated that markets were to be held each Wednesday and Saturday; semi-annual fairs were scheduled in April and December. Market days and fairs may have added to the economic and social life of the young city, but they were completely inadequate as sources of municipal revenue. The colony granted taxing authority grudgingly and for limited purposes. In 1761, the city was granted power to levy a poll tax to repair streets, which the enabling act described as "in so ruinous a condition as to render it unsafe to pass." In 1764, the power to tax extended to repairing or replacing public buildings, supporting hospitals, purchasing fire engines, sinking wells, hiring watchmen and firemen, repairing streets and lands, and for *no other* purpose.

Williamsburg has struggled with inadequate revenues for nearly all of its history. Not until the latter third of the twentieth century did the city succeed in developing a variety of revenue sources capable of sustaining city operations at an acceptable level. These sources are grounded in the city's tourism economy, namely, taxes on retail sales, hotel rooms, and on the sale of prepared foods.

After the government of Virginia moved to Richmond in 1780, demonstrating the westward shift of political power, Williamsburg's government mirrored the decline of the town itself. The Commonwealth, unable to sell its assets for hard currency, deeded the capitol and the Governor's Palace to the city in 1782. The palace burned in that year, as did the capitol in 1832. The original charter of 1722 and all of the city's antebellum records met the same fate in the great fire of Richmond at the end of the Civil War. Another sign of the city's decline was the failure of local politicians to rise to national prominence. No longer did the roster of the city's governing body include famous names, like Wythe and Randolph.

Only one municipal improvement from this otherwise sad period remains. In 1859, the city acquired four acres of land for a cemetery along the road to College Landing. Expanded over the years to seventeen acres, Cedar Grove Cemetery still serves city residents and is noted as the site of common graves for some 250 Confederate soldiers killed in the Battle of Williamsburg on 5 May 1862.

Local government by closed corporation continued until after the Civil War, when the Reconstruction-era General Assembly ended it through general legislation. In 1884, the city's charter was revised by special legislation. Henceforth, Williamsburg would be governed by a biennially elected mayor, six councilmen, and five other elected officers. For the first time in history, African-Americans served on City Council. Neither the coming of democracy, nor the arrival of the Chesapeake and Ohio Railroad in 1881, did much to reverse the city's ill fortune, however. The proud college, one of only two institutions the city had going for it, suspended classes and closed its doors from 1881 to 1888. Williamsburg entered the twentieth century with little more hope than it had leaving the eighteenth. It is Williamsburg's greatest historic irony that the 150 years in the doldrums allowed many colonial structures to survive into the twentieth century and made the city's rebirth and restoration possible.

A late 1920s' snapshot of conditions for which city government was responsible does not make a pretty picture. In fact, the picture had changed little since colonial times:

- Most of the city streets were unpaved; only Duke of Gloucester and York streets and Jamestown and Richmond roads had concrete surfaces. Streets were poorly lighted, poorly cleaned, and poorly maintained.

- Sewage from the hospital, the college, and the city proper flowed raw and untreated into the ravines surrounding the city and from there to the James and York rivers.

- Drinking water came from wells, pumps, and standpipes—owned variously by the college, hospital, Virginia ElJohn D. Rockefeller, Jr. Library,ectric and Power Company, and the city—operated as a unified system under a cooperative agreement. The water was high in salts, unpleasant in taste, and corrosive.

- Refuse collection dumps and landfills were strictly private affairs. Litter, abandoned cars, and junk were endemic to the town.

- Changes in technology were robbing the town of its remaining dignity. Telephone poles and power lines claimed the center of Duke of Gloucester Street. Gas stations and garages sprang up, which, in Dr. Goodwin's view were "fast spoiling the whole appearance of the old streets and old city."

City government in the 1920s had not been up to the challenge. While the directly elected mayor was the city's chief executive under the charter, he served part time and without pay. He was supposed to supervise all subordinate officers, such as the city sergeant who acted as the chief of police. The city sergeant was also independently elected, but, unlike the mayor, salaried. In practice, the mayor took little administrative authority over numerous independently elected and compensated officials, including the city clerk, the treasurer, the commissioner of revenue, the sheriff, and the city sergeant. For its part, the council divided itself into standing committees such as the committees on streets, health, the cemetery, and the poor. The lack of administrative structure to carry out its wishes and a chronic lack of funds made the council largely ineffective. The total budget was overspent in 1928 and 1929, incurring deficits. Designated sinking funds for payment of outstanding bonds were short by $34,000. The budget did not balance expenditures against revenues; in fact, no formal estimate of revenues was made at the time expenditures were authorized. In short, the city did not have even a rudimentary budgetary accounting system. City government was so casual that in 1912, no one remembered to hold the City Council election.

The existence of such conditions in a small Virginia town in the 1920s was not surprising. The surprise was the force and speed with which a new generation of community leaders recognized and attacked the problems at the height of the Depression. By 1930, the Williamsburg restoration was in full swing. It was apparent to locals and to the newcomers working for Rockefeller's Williamsburg Holding Company that the need to serve thousands of visitors and to protect the re-created town demanded local government action.

Unquestionably, the single most significant motivation for change in city government was the restoration, but the quality of City Council leadership during this critical time cannot be undervalued. Dr. John G. Pollard, professor of constitutional law at William and Mary, became mayor in 1928, only to resign the following year upon his election as governor. Pollard was succeeded as mayor by George P. Coleman, who, as state highway commissioner, had been largely responsible for what street paving had occurred in Williamsburg before the restoration. Local attorney Channing M. Hall served as council president during the early days of the restoration, becoming mayor in 1934 and serving until 1947. He supported the Goodwin-Rockefeller vision and oversaw the modernization of city government during his

The 1949 City Council met in the Municipal Building on North Boundary Street. (L-rt) Vincent McManus, Horace Henderson, Mayor Henry M. Stryker, Lloyd Williams, and Dr. Charles Marsh.

Courtesy, John D. Rockefeller, Jr. Library, Colonial Williamsburg Foundation

City Council changed very little during the Stryker era. In fact, from 1958 to 1966, it didn't change at all. (L-rt) Mayor Polly Stryker, Councilman G. Winston Butts, City Attorney Mary Insman, Councilmen Channing M. Hall, Jr., and Y. O. Kent, Clerk of Council Fannie Nightengale, and Councilman Vincent McManus. McManus had followed Channing M. Hall, Sr., as mayor in 1947, then waited twenty years to again serve as mayor after Stryker's 1968 retirement.

Courtesy, City of Williamsburg

The administrative staff dressed up for a 1955 photo taken in the Municipal Building at 400 North Boundary Street. Seated (l-rt): City Manager Hugh Rice, Secretary Dorothy Parker, City Sergeant William Low, Fire Marshall Elliot Jayne; standing: Sewage Plant Superintendent Stuart Hughes, Commissioner of Revenue William Morecock, Treasurer A. D. Jones, Chief of Police William Kelly, Assistant City Engineer Frank Cox, Filter Plant Superintendent Lewis Jackson, and Public Works Superintendent Paul Angel.

Courtesy, City of Williamsburg

At the end of the Stryker era, former city manager, then finance director, Hugh Rice, Council members Vernon "Bud" Geddy, Jr. (mayor 1970 to 1980), Stella Nieman, (first woman elected to council) Charles Hackett, Mayor Vincent McManus, newly hired City Manager Frank Force, Councilman Robert Hornsby, and Clerk of Council Lois Bodie.

Courtesy, *Daily Press*

With the 1934 water tank (demolished in 1985) behind it, the Stryker Building was used as the Municipal Building from 1967 to 1988. To the left is the building that replaced the City's South England Street complex in the early 1930s. Before the Stryker Building's construction, this modest structure housed all city government administrative functions and the Police Department. It was demolished in 1998 to make way for Municipal Center redevelopment.

Courtesy, City of Williamsburg

A public hearing in April 1970 regarding the location of the Williamsburg Regional Library (see p. 278). Speaking is Roger Leclere, chair of the library board. Other City Council members facing the audience are (l-rt) Robert Hornsby, Mayor Vincent D. McManus, and Vernon M. Geddy, Jr. Seated in the front row (l-rt) are five members of the Planning Commission: Thomas Cutler, manager of the C&P Telephone Co. office; Shirley Low, later elected to the City Council; J. Wilfred Lambert, dean of students at William & Mary; Joe Phillips, who later served as city attorney; and Wilson B. Skinner. Democracy had come to stay.

Courtesy, City of Williamsburg

thirteen years in office. Almost all the civic leaders of the era supported the radical transformation of the town and executed an overhaul of city government.

Early in 1930, the mayor and council took three important steps to address the city's problems: they asked Luther H. Gulick and the Institute of Public Administrators of New York City to make a thorough study of city finances and organization, they circulated for discussion a new draft charter to restructure city government, and they hired A. L. Meisel as full-time city engineer. Meisel later became the city's first city manager.

In 1930s Gulick was a prominent force nationally in the municipal reform movement. As much as anyone, he founded the modern study of public administration, and he served as

A. L. Meisel served as Williamsburg's first city manager from 1932 to 1942.

Courtesy, City of Williamsburg

confidante to New Deal President Franklin D. Roosevelt. Gulick and his Institute team came to town in March 1930. Their extensive study of city government, with particular emphasis on city administrative structure and finances, also included "special engineering reports" on water supply and distribution, fire protection, sewage disposal, city streets, and waste collection and disposal.

In an age before management consultants became commonplace in local government, this work in Williamsburg stands out as thorough and practical. After delivery of the report, Gulick concluded that the study should be published as an example of "present day government and problems of a small American city." The resulting book, *Modern Government in a Colonial City*, opened with a sixty-one-page essay titled, "The Civil History of Williamsburg," written by the Honorable John G. Pollard, governor of Virginia. According to Gulick, Pollard's introduction "would give the reader something of the romance of Williamsburg and an appreciation of the gradual development of its governmental institutions."

In tandem with Gulick's survey, a draft of the first complete revision of the city's charter since 1722 quietly surfaced. It followed closely the model city charter of the National Municipal League, creating a "council-manager" form of government. It also deftly incorporated existing constitutional officers while consolidating authority in the hands of a smaller five-member city council and their appointed city manager. It had the fingerprints of constitutional lawyer Pollard and public administration expert Gulick all over it. The General Assembly approved the new charter on 29 March 1932.

The charter of 1932 provided for the council to appoint the mayor and vice-mayor from its members, rather than requiring direct election of the mayor. The mayor would preside at council meetings and be recognized as the official head of the city for all "ceremonial purposes." Meisel, who had served as city engineer since 1930, now became the "chief executive officer" of the city, chosen "solely on the basis of his executive and administrative qualifications," and "removable at the pleasure of the Council." Meisel, a Richmond native and a 1925 VMI engineering graduate, worked for private engineering firms before coming to Williamsburg in 1928 to work on the Temple Waddill survey for the restoration. When he resigned as city manager in 1942, he returned to the private sector.

Late in 1933, a young dentist named Henry M. Stryker received an appointment to fill a vacancy on City Council. "Polly" Stryker remained at the center of city business for the next thirty-five years, serving as mayor from 1948 to 1968 and representing Williamsburg at home and abroad with style and heart. While technically a "weak" mayor under the council-manager form, by force of personality, Dr. Stryker was in charge. In fact, if there is one dominant figure in Williamsburg city government in the twentieth century, it is Polly Stryker (see p. 228).

Stryker firmly believed that the city's future was now inextricably tied to the success of Colonial Williamsburg. He led the city government through many critical decisions, each designed to uphold the city's side of the partnership despite chronic money shortages. Three notable examples were the purchase of Waller Mill Reservoir, the enactment of land-use zoning, and the reform of the fire department.

During World War II, the federal government dammed Queen's Creek, creating a 1.5-billion-gallon drinking water impoundment to serve Camp Peary. Seeking a more plentiful source of water and to improve the quality of drinking water, the city agreed to buy Waller Mill Reservoir in 1944. By continuing to upgrade and expand the treatment plant, pumps, mains and storage tanks, Williamsburg has become the only jurisdiction on the Virginia Peninsula, other than Newport News, to control its own surface water supply. The reservoir provides the town, college, hospital, and tourist industry with affordable, reliable drinking water. As a significant side benefit, 2,400 acres of watershed property are preserved from development, and Waller Mill Park ranks as a recreational treasure. All this happened because a few farsighted city leaders in the 1940s made it so. Waller Mill is so important to the city that the day in June 1963 when the earthen dam broke and emptied the reservoir is remembered as the city's greatest natural disaster in modern times.

Just as the reservoir divided the town at the time of its purchase—naysayers objected to the cost and to drinking "swamp water"—so enactment of the city's first zoning ordinance in 1947 met stiff opposition. Property owners and business people objected to the imposition of citywide zoning, even though it had been authorized in the charter of 1932. Polly Stryker pushed it through.

Another achievement of the Stryker era was the transformation of the fire department from a well-meaning but ineffective club to a well-trained and well-equipped volunteer and career force. The catalyst for the change was the infamous Brickhouse Tavern fire in 1950 in which one person died. An investigation revealed serious deficiencies in water pressure, fire code enforcement, fire suppression training, and equipment. With funding support and encouragement from Colonial Williamsburg, the city hired Elliot Jayne as fire marshall in 1950. A true professional and no nonsense leader, Jayne created the modern Williamsburg Fire Department

Mayor Henry M. "Polly" Stryker (rt) began his service on the council in 1933 and dominated city government as mayor from 1948 to 1968. Here shown with Kenneth Chorley, Colonial Williamsburg Foundation's president, during a commemorative session of the Virginia General Assembly at the capitol. The picture illustrates the close relationship between the city and Colonial Williamsburg during the Stryker years.

Courtesy, Colonial Williamsburg Foundation

The fire station at 417 Francis Street was an automobile dealership in the 1950s. In 1978, the present fire station was built on Lafayette Street. The 1949 pumper (at far left) is still used for ceremonies and parades.

Courtesy, City of Williamsburg

Fire Chief Elliott Jayne (in white cap) recruited, trained, and molded a spirited cadre of mostly volunteers into a professional fire department with a statewide reputation for excellence. CWF employee volunteers posed with Jayne and the department's dalmatian "Fog" in 1957.

Courtesy, John D. Rockefeller, Jr. Library, Colonial Williamsburg Foundation

with a statewide reputation for excellence in fire prevention, rescue, emergency medicine, and disaster response. The fire department also claims as its heritage an organized fire service dating from at least the 1750s, when the town imported a hand-operated fire pumper and four dozen leather buckets from London. Visitors to Colonial Williamsburg can work the hand pump on a replica of Williamsburg's first fire engine and man the bucket brigade to put out real fires.

In 1968, Mayor Stryker retired from the council. Vincent D. McManus, who had served briefly as mayor before Stryker, returned to the job. That same year, a young attorney, Vernon M. "Bud" Geddy, Jr., whose father had represented the legal interests of Colonial Williamsburg from the earliest days of the Restoration, was elected to council. Stryker had been the senior Geddy's closest friend and the younger Geddy's second father and mentor. In 1970, Geddy took over as mayor and held the office for the next ten years, another long run in the Stryker tradition. Through most of his tenure, Stryker had the support of City Council and nineteen-year veteran City Manager Hugh B. Rice. Before retiring, Stryker over saw the hiring of a new city manager, Frank Force, who remained in the job until 1991. Thus, the Stryker legacy, begun in 1933, is still very much a part of Williamsburg city government.

The 1964 police department: (seated, l-rt) dispatchers Eddie Smith, Bobby Jena Lindsey, J. R. Zepkin, and Dan Waldrup; (middle row) Hamlet Smith, James Glass, Darrel Warren, Llew Smith, Jessie Altigier, Doug Ratcliffe, and Walter Robertson; (rear row) Dan Gardner, Russell Hager, Tom Fisher, Andy Rutherford, Mike Lachly, Chief William Kelly, and Officer Montgomery.

Courtesy, City of Williamsburg

The story of city government since 1970 will be left for another day. Modern times have been full of change and controversy:

- Rapid growth of James City and York counties and the increasingly complex and intense web of joint ventures for schools, library, regional jail, courthouse, and the like.
- Redevelopment of the city's Municipal Center area.
- Creation and work of the Williamsburg Redevelopment and Housing Authority.
- Development of a recreation department and system of city parks.
- Intervention in the lives of citizens in need through an active social service department.

By the mid-1970s, City Council had all new faces. (L-rt): Robert C. Walker (mayor, 1980–1986), James McCord, Shirley Low, Mayor Vernon M. Geddy, Jr. (mayor, 1970–1980), and Gilbert L. Granger (mayor, 1996-1998.

Courtesy, City of Williamsburg

By the late 1980s, the City Council had, again, largely changed over: Stephen D. Harris, Gilbert L. Granger, Mayor John H. Hodges, Vice-Mayor Mary Lee Darling, and George S. Genakos. By 1990, Trist McConnell and Joel Whitley had begun their service, followed by David Kleppinger in 1992. McConnell served as mayor from 1992 to 1996.

Courtesy, City of Williamsburg

By the mid-1990s, both George Genakos and Gil Granger had returned to City Council. The other council members were Vice-Mayor Jeanne Zeidler, Channing M. Hall, III, and Wright B. "Chips" Houghland. In 1998, Jeanne Zeidler became the city's first woman mayor.

Courtesy, City of Williamsburg

- Overhaul of the police department leading to increased professionalism and national accreditation.

- Negotiations and settlement of the "last annexation" into James City County in 1984.

- Acquisition of major tracts of undeveloped property both in the city and in the Waller Mill watershed.

- Completion, by 1999, of an aggressive program of capital improvements, including library expansion, Matthew Whaley School rehabilitation, Municipal Center Parking, Community Building, Williamsburg-James City County Courthouse, and the Waller Mill Water Plant renovation.

Frank Force became Williamsburg's fifth city manager in 1967 and served until his retirement in 1991. He was succeeded by the author.

Courtesy, City of Williamsburg

Through it all Williamsburg city government is has been and still about the business it was created to do in 1699, and striving to realize its vision:

Williamsburg will become an even more safe, beautiful, livable city of historic and academic renown, served by a city government—cohesively led, financially strong, always improving—in full partnership with the people who live, work and visit here (Williamsburg City Council, *Vision Statement, 1995*).

Selected Sources and Suggested Readings

Belvin, Ed. *Growing up in Williamsburg: From the Depression to Pearl Harbor* (Williamsburg: Virginia Gazette, 1981).

City of Williamsburg:

> *Annual Budgets* contain information on city government, including "City Council Goals and Initiatives for the Biennium," Performance Data, and Capital Improvement Program, as well as budgets.

> *Comprehensive Annual Financial Reports* account for all city revenues and expenditures

> *Comprehensive Plans* of 1989 and 1998 provide extensive information related to the physical development and natural environment of the city.

> *Code of the City of Williamsburg* contains the City Charter and the codified ordinances adopted by City Council.

> City Council Minutes of all council meetings and work sessions.

> *Policies and Procedures of City Council* describe rules and guidelines for council operations.

> City of Williamsburg's World Wide Web site is: <www.ci.williamsburg.va.us>

Goodwin, Rutherfoord. *A Brief and True Report Concerning Williamsburg in Virginia* (1940; rep. Williamsburg: Colonial Williamsburg Foundation, 1972).

Luther Gulick. *Modern Government in a Colonial City: A Survey of the City Government and Finances of Williamsburg, Virginia* (N.Y.: Jonathan Cape and Harrison Smith, 1932).

Change and Growth: Williamsburg Begins a Fourth Century

by: Jack Edwards

Colonial Williamsburg's sale of the Kingsmill property "is a truly remarkable example of planning for the long term....It is easy to see how important this development can be not only to the future of Colonial Williamsburg but to the entire area."

With these words, Daniel J. Boorstin, prominent historian and member of the Colonial Williamsburg Board of Trustees, praised the 1969 decision to sell 3,900 acres on the James River to Anheuser-Busch. Not everyone agreed with Boorstin, then or now, but it clearly was a pivotal event in the development of the Williamsburg area, one nearly as important as the 1926 decision of John D. Rockefeller, Jr., to begin purchasing land for the restoration of the colonial city. Rockefeller's decision, combined with vision and hard work, converted Williamsburg into a national treasure; the Kingsmill decision recognized that Colonial Williamsburg had to look beyond the City of Williamsburg to try to protect its national treasure.

The decision to sell was strongly supported by Winthrop Rockefeller, chairman of the board of Colonial Williamsburg. Carlisle H. Humelsine, president of the foundation, articulated the reasons for the sale in a 1969 document called "Planning for the Long Term." Rockefeller and Humelsine (see p. 217) saw Anheuser-Busch as an organization with high standards, great resources, and the ability to develop property in a way preferable to unplanned and piecemeal growth.

Anheuser-Busch purchased the property as the site for a brewery, theme park, and planned residential community. The brewery was constructed within three years, the theme park (Busch Gardens) opened three years after that, and the residential community (named Kingsmill) grew steadily for the next three decades. It is difficult to overstate the importance of these developments. Colonial Williamsburg had long invited Americans to visit Williamsburg; with the planned residential community, Anheuser-Busch invited Americans to live in the area.

Through extensive advertising, the new invitation went out to a substantial part of the nation. A successful Kingsmill having led the way, several other large planned upmarket residential communities followed, including Croffton (later named Powhatan), Middle Plantation (reborn as Ford's Colony), Governor's Land, Greensprings, and Stonehouse. With expensive advertising budgets, most of them joined Kingsmill in telling millions about the joys of living

Anheuser-Busch hosted a ceremonial ground-breaking for its new $40 million Williamsburg brewery in James City Co. on 29 April 1970. Here Colonial Williamsburg President Carlisle H. Humelsine is flanked by Anheuser Busch chairman August A. Busch, Jr. (rt) and his son and vice president, August A. Busch, III. Sale of the Kingsmill property developed through the friendship of August A. Busch, Jr., and Winthrop Rockefeller, Chairman of the Colonial Williamsburg Foundation.

Courtesy, *Daily Press*

Stainless steel tanks used for the thirty-day beechwood-chip aging process at the Anheuser Busch Brewery. The brewery was constructed on a hundred acres of the 4,000-acre property Busch acquired from Colonial Williamsburg and developed near Carter's Grove Plantation. Designed as a prototype brewery to produce two to three million barrels a year in 1972, the Williamsburg brewery by 1998 was the third largest in the Busch system. In addition to augmenting the tax base in James City Co., Busch benefitted the Williamsburg community in many other ways, such as supporting the expansion of the hospital, endowing a professorship at William & Mary, and also providing a soccer field and tennis courts for the college.

Courtesy, *Daily Press*

in the Williamsburg area. Despite some false starts, these planned communities have prospered; and many conventional subdivisions have also emerged, each hoping to profit from the wave of Americans encouraged to move to Williamsburg, and from the substantial increase in job opportunities on the Peninsula over the last twenty years. Since the completion of Interstate 64, many people working on the lower Peninsula have chosen to build or purchase homes in the Williamsburg area.

The residential community at Kingsmill had another effect. Blessed with immense resources ("deep pockets," in the jargon of the day), Anheuser-Busch was able to build much of the infrastructure for the project before it began receiving any substantial revenue from the sale of lots. Kingsmill set new standards for the quality of residential developments. Busch leaders wanted not just a profitable venture, but also a showcase for the corporate name. Consequently, Kingsmill was planned by a nationally-acclaimed consulting firm, and the development included environmental and recreational amenities unknown in Williamsburg to that time. These amenities and other features became standards for subsequent developers, raising the bar of expectations for all who came later.

Busch Gardens Williamsburg theme park was constructed by Anheuser-Busch soon after the brewery, and had its grand opening on 16 May 1975. Former Virginia Governor Mills Godwin and Busch President and Chairman of the Board August Busch III welcomed their first guests "all aboard" an antique steam locomotive for its inaugural ride through Heatherdowns, Festa Italia, and New France.

Courtesy, Thomas L. Williams Archive

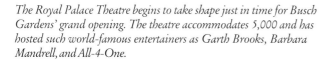

The Royal Palace Theatre begins to take shape just in time for Busch Gardens' grand opening. The theatre accommodates 5,000 and has hosted such world-famous entertainers as Garth Brooks, Barbara Mandrell, and All-4-One.

Courtesy, Busch Gardens Williamsburg

In explaining the sale of the Kingsmill property to Anheuser-Busch, Humelsine also cited the "opportunity for great improvement in the total environment by providing an addition to the James City County tax base, which will greatly assist in meeting the costs of increasing educational demands." He noted that about half of Colonial Williamsburg's employees lived in the county and were, therefore, dependent on county schools.

Since 1955, Williamsburg and James City County had operated a joint school system. By the late 1960s, the system struggled financially because James City had a very limited tax base. To maintain the joint system, the City of Williamsburg in 1969–1970 contributed more than $100,000 in excess of its contractual obligation to the system. The 1969 sale of the Kingsmill property seemed a way to help James City meet its educational obligations.

As predicted, the sale and development of the property had a direct and major impact on the finances of the county. County revenues and expenditures increased rapidly in the early 1970s, especially after Anheuser-Busch built the brewery and theme park. By 1974, James City was able to increase its contribution to the joint school system by thirty-two percent in a single year. Much of that increase came directly from Anheuser-Busch, which soon was paying more than one-sixth of all county taxes. As a result, the rural county that previously had been financially strapped became moderately affluent.

Croffton was one of the first planned communities stimulated by the development of Kingsmill in James City Co. This ambitious 1972 project, projecting 195 single family homes, 500 townhouses, 900 apartments, and a regional shopping center on a 530-acre site off Ironbound Rd., went through delays for water supply, financial hard times, and changes in ownership before it became Powhatan Secondary.

Courtesy, *Daily Press*

To be sure, the area's population growth cannot be attributed entirely to this land sale and the property's subsequent development. Even before Anheuser-Busch came on the scene, population in Williamsburg and James City County had increased, growing more than forty-six percent between 1960 and 1970; and the Newport News–Hampton urban area was growing steadily toward Williamsburg. Although growth may have been inevitable, its type, magnitude, and timing were less certain; but the kind and quality of growth have been greatly affected by the Anheuser-Busch sale, the development of that land, and related projects that have developed as a result. For good or for ill (perhaps both), the sale set in motion many of the changes that have occurred in the community. There is no sign that that motion will slow down.

The most obvious change in the Williamsburg area between 1969 and 1999 has been physical: more homes, more grocery stores, more convenience stores, more fast-food restaurants, more fine restaurants, more parking lots, more churches–more everything. When residential growth occurs, commercial growth almost surely follows to take advantage of new markets, generally with little coordination. A large majority of Americans has always been optimistic about growth and skeptical about land-use controls and planning. This is particularly true in Virginia. Almost inevitably, as the area has grown it has come to look more like the rest of suburbanized America.

In 1969, homebuyers chose from a limited number of small neighborhoods. By 1999, a prospective homebuyer in Williamsburg found many subdivisions, large and small. In 1969, residents shopped at Williamsburg's one shopping center; in 1999, they shop at more than a

Williamsburg Community Hospital opened on 3 April 1961 with sixty-one beds. It served 2,262 patients, including 348 new mothers in its first year. By 1998, the hospital had expanded dramatically: a new wing was opened facing Monticello Ave., there were 139 licensed beds, 6,120 admissions, and 890 babies delivered.

Courtesy, Williamsburg Community Hospital

dozen, as well as several clusters of outlet stores. Although some of the increase in shopping centers reflected changes in American marketing ideas, much of it depended on a growing and more affluent population that made these centers profitable.

When trying to understand growth, a basic place to start is total population. Comparisons prove difficult. The "Williamsburg area" is a mental construct, not a defined jurisdiction. The Census Bureau does not count persons in the "Williamsburg area," but rather counts them in each of the political jurisdictions. Here it is sufficient to define the Williamsburg area as the City of Williamsburg plus eighty percent of James City County (since most of the county except the western part is oriented toward Williamsburg) and that twenty percent of York County adjacent to the city.

The area's population increased moderately through the 1970s and the early 1980s and then jumped, after 1984, as the country emerged from a recession. Population has grown rapidly since that time, except for a slowdown during another recession in the early 1990s.

POPULATION OF THE WILLIAMSBURG AREA

	1970	1980	1990	1998 (est.)
Williamsburg	9,069	10,294	11,409	11,971
James City (80%)	14,282	18,210	27,976	35,386
York (20%)	6, 641	7,093	8,487	11,758
Total	29,992	35,597	47,872	59,115

Increase, 1970-98: 97.1%

The characteristics of the population have changed substantially since 1970, especially racially. In the city, the black and white populations have both grown slowly, so the percentage constituted by each has not changed much. In contrast, the black population of James City County has remained fairly stable, while the white population has increased sharply. As a result, the percentage of the county's population that is black has declined from 35.3 percent in 1970, to 29.6 percent in 1980, to 20.2 percent in 1990. Projections anticipate that the percentage will fall to 13.4 percent by 2000 and to 8.8 percent by 2010.

Another important change is economic. In the last decade, there has been a booming market for expensive housing. It appears that a substantially larger proportion of the population is affluent, though we may have to wait for income statistics from the 2000 census to confirm that change. Increasing affluence is suggested by median family income figures in James City County, which went from 107.0 percent of the state average in 1980 to 112.1 percent of the same average in 1995.

Averages can be misleading, often obscuring as much as they disclose. The James City averages do not help us understand a critical fact about our area: there continues to be a substantial poor population, even though the proportion of very affluent persons is steadily growing. In 1993, almost ten percent of the citizens in Williamsburg and James City County were below the poverty line. At the same time, the proportion of local citizens with annual adjusted gross incomes above $75,000 was above the state average, and it has continued to climb. The Williamsburg–James City schools have long worried about a distribution of students that is "bi-modal" (many poor, many affluent). This problem is apparently getting worse, not better. Growing affluence has obscured poverty, not eliminated it.

In 1973 Les Molineux watched from the cleared roadway on the Kingspoint side of College Creek as a crane was loaded on a construction barge to erect pilings for a bridge on Rte. 199. The 4.4-mile-long stretch of new bypass road connecting routes 5 and 60 cost just over $4 million. Work resumed twenty years later on the remaining 8.5 miles of 199, running north-south between Rte. 64 on the east side of Williamsburg and Rte. 64 on the west, and was completed in 1999. The final section of Rte. 199 cost $57.7 million.

The opening of the Williamsburg Public Library in 1973 fulfilled the dream for a permanent public library. In 1909, a humble fifty-volume rotating collection from the Library of Virginia began to be housed in the St. George Tucker house. Subsequent library services were housed in seven other locations throughout the historic area; and for forty years beginning in 1933, the library called the Nicholas-Tyler Office home, a small building still standing on the corner of Francis and South England streets. In the 1950s and '60s a Friends of the Library organization lobbied for a new, larger building and an improved collection. In 1969 the city incorporated the library as a municipal department. City Council voted to purchase the block bounded by Boundary and Scotland streets and Armistead Ave. for $436,000 (see p. 265). The 1973 construction pictured here was doubled in size during a 1982 renovation that added the children's library and Arts Center wing. A second renovation in 1998 added space to house not only books and other print material but also the infrastructure to access electronic resources.

Eastern State Hospital's last building in downtown Williamsburg was demolished in 1973 to make way for the National Center for State Courts. Built in 1925 as the hospital's diagnostic building, a medical-surgical facility where lobotomies and electro-convulsive therapy were administered, the Brown Building was part of Eastern State's 162-acre downtown site, which was deeded to William & Mary in 1945. Closed in 1968, the building was used by the college as a recycling center and by younger faculty members as a site for candle-light cocktail parties.

All photographs courtesy, *Daily Press*

Prince George St. looked like "Anytown, U.S.A." in 1974, when residents could still get their shoes repaired and their hair cut downtown. That year the city teamed up with property owners to give the street a facelift to improve business: the concrete sidewalks were replaced with exposed aggregate, while around the corner on Boundary St., the city continued laying brick sidewalks from College Corner to the municipal complex.

This plywood shelter on Rte. 143 housed the Society for the Prevention of Cruelty to Animals until 1975, when it was shut down because of bursting pipes. A new concrete building was constructed on Waller Mill Road, using $27,000 from a public fund drive and volunteer labor, notably from the Jaycees and William & Mary. The SPCA closed in 1992, but volunteers created a new organization (now the Heritage Humane Society) incorporated to reopen the facility in '93.

Williamsburg got a new bridge for Capitol Landing Rd. after a Chesapeake and Ohio Railway train derailed in April 1975. Two engines and thirty-six cars of the coal train ran off the tracks next to Lafayette St. To make matters worse, during the clean-up, a work train of flatbed cars loaded high with wreckage and a crane struck the underside of the Capitol Landing auto bridge, and also demolished the adjacent wooden foot bridge. Chessie engineers accepted blame, but it took two years for the railroad to build the concrete replacement bridge.

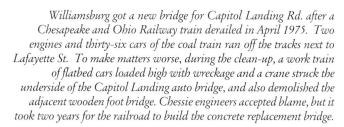

All photographs courtesy, *Daily Press*

Residents have particular concerns about increased traffic. An increase in traffic is often thought to stem solely from an increase in population, but population growth is only one factor. Driving habits constitute another factor of considerable importance. In Virginia, between 1980 and 1990, population increased by sixteen percent, while the number of passenger vehicles rose by thirty-four percent and the total miles traveled jumped by fifty percent. Thus the growth in population directly accounts for only about one-third of the increase in the traffic on Virginia's roads. These figures match the national pattern.

These state and national statistics help explain traffic growth in the Williamsburg area. Although comprehensive and reliable figures are not available for Williamsburg, Virginia Department of Transportation statistics for James City offer some insights. Between 1970 and 1994, the number of vehicle miles traveled on primary highways grew much faster than the population (traffic grew 5.5 percent annually, while population increased only 3.4 percent). Drivers in Williamsburg and James City have many more vehicles available now (.31 per capita in 1970 versus .76 in 1996), and greater affluence enables individuals and families to drive more without worrying about the costs. Also, if a greater proportion of people live farther from places of employment and other destinations–one of the functions of urban sprawl–the number of miles traveled will increase. In the Williamsburg area, as in much of the nation, demands of the automobile and other vehicles are overloading the road capacity.

Williamsburg is an exceptional attraction for the millions of people who visit each year, whether attracted by history, entertainment, or shopping; and, through its preservation and re-creation of our past, it is a wonderful asset for the entire United States. But what makes the Williamsburg area a special place for local citizens? Trying to answer that deceptively simple question is crucial for Williamsburg's future.

A major reason for Williamsburg's special feel is the history embedded in the community. One cannot escape the historical roots of the area. Jamestown Island, Jamestown Settlement, Colonial Williamsburg, the College of William and Mary, and the Colonial Parkway–and Yorktown Battlefield Park just a few miles further away–are also major historical assets. Highly significant recent archaeological finds, especially on Jamestown Island and the William and Mary campus, continue to remind residents of the area's heritage. History runs throughout the community, and its appreciation helps explain recent local controversies over preservation, such as saving "America's oldest continuous working farm" (Mainland Farm) and preserving "America's oldest road" (Greensprings Road).

Residents of Williamsburg, like those in many parts of the nation, believe that the beauty and well-being of the natural environment are critical for the quality of life. There has been a sharp increase in the determination of area citizens to protect the environment. Many local citizens have expressed indignation about damage to the natural environment resulting from rapid development, a determination reflected in the success of the Williamsburg Land Conservancy. In just a few years, the conservancy has worked with landowners to place more than six hundred acres in protective easements; and it is increasingly effective in making owners of key sites as well as the general public aware of its goals and methods. The future of the conservancy is encouraging, indeed.

Two institutions of national stature have shaped the local community for many years—Colonial Williamsburg and the College of William and Mary. Colonial Williamsburg opens many of its facilities, at no charge, to local residents, who have an unparalleled opportunity to

Jimmy Maloney began the Williamsburg Pottery in 1938, along Rte. 60 just west of town. With pots stacked along the curve of Richmond Rd., the Pottery attracted the eye of tourists and soon became a popular stop for Greyhound buses.

The success of the Williamsburg Pottery has fueled commercial development, including outlet malls, in James City Co. northwest of Williamsburg. The Maloney family has also given back to the community, supporting the hospital, Child Development Resources, and William & Mary, among others.

After years of firing his pots with wood-burning kilns, Jimmy built an oil-burning kiln, which he tended from morning until evening. When it reached about 2,300 degrees, he would throw in salt, as shown here, to create his distinctive salt-glaze pottery.

Jimmy decorated slip-ware using a tube filled with the clay and oxide paste, which was squeezed onto the hand-made ceramic forms. His slip-ware was admired by First Lady Mamie Eisenhower, who purchased it for the White House. It is still produced the way Jimmy did it fifty years ago.

experience a wide variety of programs and to enjoy the area's beauty while walking, jogging, or cycling. The college also sponsors many intellectual, theatrical, musical, athletic, and other events and activities. In addition, it has gone to great effort to engage itself in the community through such outreach programs as an adult skills center, which has taught many local residents to read, and the Sir Christopher Wren Association, which attracts many of the area's new retired residents to a very diverse set of mini-courses taught mostly by the college faculty. Even citizens who rarely take advantage of these resources often appreciate their availability and the contributions they make to community well-being.

Many smaller organizations, whose number is remarkable given the modest size of the community, contribute to Williamsburg's specialness. Several provide service to others. For example, Child Development Resources helps challenged children between birth and age three; Housing Partnerships fixes and rebuilds houses for those unable to do so on their own; and Olde Towne Medical Center offers basic medical services, primarily to the uninsured and working poor. These, and the many similar organizations in the area, provide a powerful means for members of the community to help others and to establish connections within the community. Other organizations are designed primarily to enrich the lives of their members. The Parent Pre-school Cooperative, the Wednesday Morning Music Club, and the Williamsburg Bicycle Association have functions that reflect their names.

Williamsburg's size also contributes to its character. Anyone whose experience in Williamsburg goes back to the 1960s has stories to tell about how few traffic lights, stores, and subdivisions there were, or how few cars were on the roads in the tourism off-season. The small numbers permitted the development of the kind of close personal relationships that are difficult to retain in a larger community. Given the flood of people who have chosen to move to Williamsburg in the past fifteen years, some of the advantages of being so small are disappearing. Despite rapid growth over the last three decades, however, it retains much of its small-town feel.

The population of the area will continue to grow. Although many residents (including this author) regret the pace of growth, it is a fact of life because the natural attractiveness of Williamsburg continues to be enhanced by national media advertising and word-of-mouth recommendations.

Some residents prefer to live in Williamsburg even though they must drive to work in Richmond or elsewhere in Hampton Roads. Many choose to retire here. Others have joined the increasing number of Americans who "telecommute" and can, therefore, choose their residence on the basis of the attractiveness of the community rather than the geographical location of jobs. While the actions of citizens and their governments affect the location and quality of growth, as well as its effect on the environment and the economy, these actions probably have little impact on the rate of growth.

If Williamsburg cannot be preserved as a small town, does that mean that all is lost? Certainly not. The feel of a small town is only one factor that defines the quality of Williamsburg. Residents must focus on the other factors that have created its special nature and concentrate on their preservation or development. For example, protecting our historical heritage depends primarily on the priority of our values and a willingness to pay for their preservation even when it is inconvenient or expensive. Similarly, the natural environment is under strong pressure from development forces. Often it is a matter of trying to preserve what exists;

sometimes it is a matter of rebuilding and enhancing the environment in a way that is compatible with sound ecological values. Either course requires a sense of what must be saved, the conviction to make difficult land-use decisions, and a willingness to spend both public and private funds to accomplish the goals.

Although several large organizations call Williamsburg home, Colonial Williamsburg and the College of William and Mary stand apart because of their missions and their not-for-profit status. Both institutions have substantial assets, but each is faced with a challenging environment. Although Colonial Williamsburg enjoys widespread support across the nation, it must contend for tourist dollars in a highly competitive market. In recent years, foundation leaders have begun searching for ways to meet their core preservation and educational responsibilities while staying financially solvent. William and Mary has a widely admired undergraduate program and several highly regarded graduate programs, but it is a public school operating in a state that ranks nationally near the bottom in expenditures for higher education. Both the college and Colonial Williamsburg will prosper (or fail) in their regional and national markets on the basis of institutional merit. Local citizens will have little opportunity to help them directly or programmatically, but the community needs to maintain an environment in which each of them can succeed.

The extent to which Williamsburg will be special in the future will depend partly on whether its residents maintain and enhance the large network of service, intellectual, artistic, and social organizations that characterized Williamsburg even as a small town. Such groups not only enrich the lives of individuals, but also connect citizens to each other and help establish a sense of community. The attractiveness of Williamsburg will be measured in part by the health of organizations mentioned earlier. Government will have little to do with preserving this part of Williamsburg's special character, so citizens must decide if they will simply be consumers of the excellent things Williamsburg has to offer or if they will build and maintain these and other organizations, helping others and the community in the process. If both core institutions and the smaller institutions flourish, Williamsburg will continue to be a special place. If they languish, Williamsburg will gradually become more like many other small American cities with less character.

Williamsburg residents will decide whether they are able and willing to maintain these organizations and connections in ways that are fair and inclusive. For the past three decades, residents of the area have wrestled with the problem of race, with mixed results at best. While demographic changes are making racial problems less visible, they are no less serious. The challenge for future residents of Williamsburg will be to maintain organizations that include all racial and ethnic groups.

Another challenge is economic. The Williamsburg area attracts many affluent persons, who typically are well-educated and successful. Their life experiences have given them confidence about their economic and political influence, but their interests sometimes conflict with those of people with modest incomes and limited expectations for advancement. Again, the challenge will be to create policies and a social fabric that include the participation of all economic segments of the population.

Williamsburg can be proud of its three centuries and its great contributions to the nation. It has been an excellent place to live, to grow, and to raise a family. The area's long history is one of development and change. Williamsburg in 1975 was vastly different from Williamsburg in 1925, just as 2025 will be greatly different from 1975. While it is critically important to preserve the best in our past, it would be a mistake to try to do no more. To keep the values of the past, Williamsburg needs to grasp future opportunities that will enhance those values.

Selected Sources and Suggested Readings

City of Williamsburg and County of James City, Comprehensive Plans. Most recent plans are 1997.

Colonial Williamsburg Foundation, 1969, "...Planning for the Long Term."

Daily Press, Newport News.

Hampton Roads Planning District Commission, Hampton Roads Data Book. Published annually.

U.S. Census Bureau, *Census of Population*. Decennial.

Virginia Employment Commission, Commonwealth of Virginia, Population Estimates. Published periodically.

Virginia Gazette, Williamsburg.

Weldon Cooper Center for Public Service, Charlottesville, Va., Virginia Statistical Abstract. Published biennially.

Williamsburg's 300th Anniversary

Williamsburg hosted a year-long celebration—an array of special exhibits, dances, games, concerts, educational programs, and publications. The highlight was May Day weekend, commemorating the founding of Williamsburg in May of 1699. Events that weekend included a bike ride from Richmond to Williamsburg.

300th-logo Birthday Cake

Bill Barker, interpreter of Thomas Jefferson

Jack Tuttle, City Manager

Jeanne Zeidler, Mayor of Williamsburg

Trist McConnell, Chair of the 300th Anniversary Commission, & assistant Gerry Walton

Mayor Zeidler, Lt. Gov. John Hager, and cyclists after the Bike Month Proclamation Ride from Richmond.

Photos courtesy of Charles C. Troha & Tracy Blevins

1 May 1999 – the Birthday

A commemorative ceremony in front of the Wren Building recalled the historic events of 1 May 1699. William & Mary President Timothy J. Sullivan and five student orators reenacted the role of President James Blair and his scholars, who helped persuade the General Assembly to establish Williamsburg as the capital of Virginia.

City Council dedicated the new community building during a picnic at the municipal center. Colonial Williamsburg opened its innovative exhibition "1699: When Virginia was the Wild West!" at the DeWitt Wallace Gallery, entertained citizens and visitors in "1699-style" games and amusements, and served birthday cake that was happily demolished. (See also color plates 22-24.)

Photos courtesy of Skip Baker,
Charles C. Troha, Bob Leek, &
Martha Hamilton-Phillips

July 4th Independence Day 1999

Reading of the Declaration of Independence

Fife and Drum Corps leading the Children's Parade.

Dr. John Fletcher, Williamsburg's first pediatrician, served as Grand Marshall of the Children's Parade

Local resident Donald T. Regan signing his poster at the Ice Cream Social, which benefitted the Williamsburg Community Hospital Auxiliary.

The U.S.S. John L. Hall, *a Navy missile frigate named in honor of WW II hero and Williamsburg native Adm. John Lesslie Hall, gave public tours. (See p.197)*

Photos courtesy, Ellen K. Rudolph & Charles C. Troha

Celebrating the Arts

Williamsburg began and ended its 300th Anniversary on First Night, the annual celebration of the arts. The National Symphony Orchestra presented a concert for May Day at William and Mary Hall (above). Thanks to Tricentennial arts grants, eighteen local organizations such as the Williamsburg Choral Guild (rt) prepared special exhibits, programs, and performances throughout 1999. Among the free entertainments that brought the community together were the Senior Prom and Senior Follies, organized by Williamsburg's elder citizens (below, l & rt).

Photos courtesy, Martha Hamilton-Phillips, Ralph Patterson, & Charles C. Troha

Genevieve McGiffert celebrated her final year as Williamsburg Choral Guild conductor.

Ernest Proudman and Madeline Gee were crowned King and Queen of the Senior Prom by Dr. James Baker.

Edna Baker (front, rt) leads rehearsals for the Senior Follies.

300th Focus on Youth

Youth Leadership Council at the State Capitol for a visit hosted by Del. George Grayson (kneeling, second from l), and accompanied by Peter Walentisch and City Councilman George Genakos (kneeling, rt).

Rawls Byrd Elementary students Brent Weber and Maura Gilliam read the Virginia Senate Resolution designating Williamsburg "Historic City of the Year."

The Williamsburg Youth Leadership Council expanded their community service projects and educational outreach in 1999. They traveled to Washington and Richmond to meet with legislators; and they helped children by mentoring and with cultural and recreational programs. Fifteen schools were involved in Tricentennial projects, ranging from the award-winning children's garden sponsored by the Williamsburg Garden Club at Matthew Whaley School, to the Fine Arts Festival hosted by Jamestown High.

Photos courtesy, Mary Ann Brendel, Martha Hamilton-Phillips, & Charles C. Troha

Virginia First Lady Roxanne Gilmore (lower rt) helps dig at the tricentennial archaeological excavation on Nassau St.

"Mattey's Garden" was beautifully planted by May Day.

A Legacy for the Future

Looking beyond the 300th and planning for Williamsburg's next century, community leaders took steps to protect our heritage and encourage philanthropy. Renowned rock and jazz musician Bruce Hornsby (above) performed three piano concerts to benefit the Williamsburg Land Conservancy. Acoustic musician Tim Seaman (above, rt) recorded the CD Celebration of Centuries *and brought 300 years of musical traditions to children at local libraries and schools. The December Gala Dinner Dance benefitted the newly founded Greater Williamsburg Community Trust, a community foundation that creates endowment funds for the future.*

Photos courtesy, Ellen K. Rudolph

Mrs. Carlisle Humelsine, Chair of the 300th Gala, and her daughter Mrs. Tommy Norment

Mayor Zeidler dances with guest of honor Sir Angus Stirling, a descendant of 18th-c. royal governor Lord Dunmore

Sen. and Mrs. Charles S. Robb (rt) with 300th executive director Martha Hamilton-Phillips at the Gala

Chronology of the City of Williamsburg

Compiled by: Susan H. Godson

17th Century

1607	Colonists arrive at Jamestown
1610-11	Colonists' attacks force the Paspaheghs from their land near Jamestown
1619	First representative assembly meets at Jamestown
	First African slaves arrive in Virginia
1622	Opechancanough leads Indians in attack that kills 347 settlers
1624	With withdrawal of London Company charter, Virginia becomes first royal colony
1633	Middle Plantation established
1634	Colony divided into eight counties or shires
1658	Middletowne Parish established and united with Marston Parish
1644-46	After second attack led by Opechancanough, Indians are defeated, making the whole Peninsula English territory
1674	Bruton Parish formed from Middletowne and Marston parishes at Middle Plantation; new church building completed in 1683
1676	Nathaniel Bacon's Rebellion–first major uprising against royal authority; Bacon burns Jamestown and holds large encampment at Middle Plantation
1677	The General Assembly temporarily meets at Middle Plantation
1693	College of William & Mary founded at Middle Plantation by royal charter
1698	Statehouse at Jamestown burns

1699	General Assembly votes to build capitol and City of Williamsburg at Middle Plantation
	Governor Nicholson lays out the city, with Duke of Gloucester, Francis, and Nicholson streets. Area of city: ca. one square mile

18th Century

1705	Continuing Act names trustees for Williamsburg land transfers and appoints Board of Directors
	Matthew Whaley dies and a schoolhouse on his parents' plantation is named for him
	College burns: rebuilt between 1710 and 1721
	Capitol completed
	Burgesses and Governor's Council enact Slave Code
1714	Powder magazine built
	James City Co. seat moved to Williamsburg
1715	Courthouse built at corner of Francis and England streets
	Bruton Parish Church nave and chancel completed and opened for services
1716-18	Theatre built–first in colonial America
1717	Postal system carries mail from Williamsburg to Philadelphia
1718	Blackbeard's pirates executed in Williamsburg
1720	Governor's Palace built

1722	Charter by governor incorporates City of Williamsburg, provides for a seal and local government by mayor, recorder, six aldermen, and twelve-member common council. Called "Common Hall," this corporation is a self-perpetuating closed corporation. City may send one member to House of Burgesses
	John Holloway named first mayor
1723	Mayor, recorder, and aldermen sit monthly as Hustings Court
	Williamsburg becomes a separate militia district
	Brafferton building for educating Indians constructed at the college
1732	College chapel opened and foundations laid for the President's House
1736	*Virginia Gazette* newspaper founded
1739	Reverend George Whitefield, evangelist, preaches at Bruton Parish Church
1743	In memory of her son Matthew, Mary Whaley bequeathes to Bruton Parish Church land in York Co. and funds for a school
1744	City builds its own jail
1745	First playhouse given to city to be fitted out as a courthouse
1747	Capitol burns
1748	Smallpox epidemic sweeps the city
	Population: 885
	Public Records Office built near capitol
1750	City mace created
1751	Alexander Finnie's theatre built on Waller St. on site of present Christiana Campbell's Tavern
1752	Lewis Hallam remodels the new playhouse and his professional company of London actors presents its first play. Building is gone by 1757

1753	First fire department established–manned by volunteers
	Rebuilding of the capitol completed
1754	Burgesses order one fire engine and 48 leather buckets for use in the city
1756	Lots east of Waller St. along York St. are added to the city
1757	Common Council approves building a market house on the market square
1758	More James City Co. land added to the city
1758-59	York Co. land added to the city
1760	First known performance (by David Douglass' American Company) in the town's third theatre, called the "Old Theatre Near the Capitol": building gone by 1780
1761	Common Hall levies poll tax to repair roads
1762	Common Hall can levy poll tax to sink wells, fix pumps
1765	Presbyterians successfully petition for right to meet in Williamsburg
	Patrick Henry's speech against Stamp Act incites Williamsburg mob into forcing local stamp agent's resignation
1768	Another smallpox epidemic sweeps the city
1770	Williamsburg/James City Co. build common courthouse
1772	Council approves four night watchmen (forerunners of police)
	Council prohibits dogs' running loose without collars
1773	Public Hospital for Persons of Insane and Disordered Minds opens as first hospital in colonial America devoted entirely to such patients
	Society for the Promotion of Useful Knowledge established

Race course built

Masonic Temple built

1774 Virginians protest the closing of the port of Boston with a day of fasting and prayer: local citizens attend a service at Bruton Parish Church

1775 Population: 1,880–52% black and 48% white

Governor Dunmore removes fifteen barrels of gunpowder from the powder magazine; residents protest and governor flees

Governor issues proclamation freeing slaves

1776 Williamsburg's greatest moments in history occur at the capitol with passage of the "Virginia Resolution for Independence" (15 May), the "Virginia Declaration of Rights" (12 June), and a new state constitution (29 June)

First Baptist Church (black) organized

Phi Beta Kappa founded at William & Mary

1779 Pulaski Club founded

1780 Virginia capital moved to Richmond in April

1781 Lord Cornwallis' troops occupy and plunder the city; college closes for a year;

Governor's Palace and interior of President's House at college burn

General George Washington and the Marquis de Lafayette gather troops here for siege of Yorktown

Soldiers introduce another smallpox epidemic to the city

1783 City celebrates Treaty of Paris and end of the Revolution

1784 Court of Hustings also becomes a Court of Record

1790 Court of Hustings can impanel grand juries

Population: 1,344

1793 First Baptist Church officially recognized by membership in the Dover Baptist Association

East Wing of the capitol torn down

19th Century

1805 Williamsburg Female Academy opens

1818 By now First Baptist Church has a meeting house on Nassau St.

1820 Population: 1,402

1824 The Marquis de Lafayette returns to the city and is made an honorary citizen

1828 Racially mixed Baptist congregation formed and meets in the powder magazine; in 1832 becomes Zion Baptist Church

1832 West wing of the capitol burns; completing its destruction

Common Hall given taxing power for expenses

1833 The capitol square given to the city

1834 Governor, not Common Council, to name new aldermen

Tornado causes extensive damage

1835 Sir Charles Augustus Murray, grandson of Governor Dunmore, visits

1840 Town clock installed in steeple of Bruton Parish Church

1841 Mental hospital now called "Eastern Asylum." Dr. John Minson Galt, II, initiates humane treatment of patients

Mayor can serve successive terms

1842 First Christmas tree in Williamsburg displayed at St. George Tucker house

Methodists build brick church near the powder magazine

1849 Williamsburg Female Academy acquires property on the capitol site

1850 Population: 877

1853 Zion Baptist Church begins to build a new church on Duke of Gloucester St.: completed in 1857, it becomes Williamsburg Baptist

1856 First Baptist Church dedicates new brick church on Nassau St.

1859 Main Building at college burns and is rebuilt

  City buys four acres on South Henry St. for Cedar Grove Cemetery

  Raleigh Tavern burns

1860 Population: 1,111

1861 Eastern Asylum is renamed "Eastern Lunatic Asylum"

1861-65 College closes during the Civil War

1862 Battle of Williamsburg, 5 May

  Main building at college burned by Union troops, 8 September

1862-65 Union forces occupy city

1865 Original city charter destroyed in fire at Richmond

1866 City requests replacement charter from London

1867 Awarded proceeds of Mary Whaley's estate, the college renames the grammar school "Grammar and Mattey School"

1870 College builds Mattey School on the palace grounds

  Popular election of mayor, twelve councilmen, four J.P.s, city sergeant, city treasurer, commissioner of revenue, collector, overseer of poor, and street commissioner

  First school board organized

  Population: 1,392

1871 Free (public) schools start, using rooms rented in houses and other buildings

1873 School Board leases Mattey School to improve facilities for white pupils

1880 Population: 1,480

1881-88 College closed for lack of both funds and students

1881 C&O Railway puts temporary track down Duke of Gloucester St. for the Yorktown Centennial

1882 Permanent track from Williamsburg to Newport News and Richmond laid outside city

1884 Revised Williamsburg Charter: election every two years for mayor, six councilmen, city sergant, and commissioner of revenue. City and James City Co. to elect treasurer

  School Board moves classes to Mount Ararat Baptist Church to improve facilities for black pupils

  Mattey School for white boys opens; white girls attend Saunders House School

  First electricity in Williamsburg at Eastern Lunatic Asylum

1885 Eastern Lunatic Asylum burns

  Presbyterians buy lot on the palace green for sanctuary

  Public school for blacks opens on Francis St.

1888 King's Daughters organized

1889 Association for the Preservation of Virginia Antiquities chartered. It soon acquires the powder magazine, the site of the capitol, and the church and churchyard at Jamestown

1890 Population: 1,831

1892 Organization of city government provides committees for finance, streets, markets, fire, cemetery, poor, sanitary, and ordinances

1894	Eastern Lunatic Asylum renamed "Eastern State Hospital"
1897	Peninsula Bank established
	Nicholson St. School (white) opens
	Offices of Fire Commissioner and Police Justice established
1898	Street lights installed
	West Williamsburg starts to develop
1899	Williamsburg Businessmen's Association established
1895-1900	Industry comes to Williamsburg: planing mill (1895), Denmead Ice Factory (1898), steam laundry (1899), Williamsburg Canning Company (1899), and knitting mill (1900)

20th Century

1900	Population: 2,044
1901	Williamsburg goes dry
	Telephone service begins
1903	First automobile in Williamsburg
	Woman's Christian Temperance Union established
1903-09	Rev. Dr. W.A.R. Goodwin rector of Bruton Parish Church
1907	Williamsburg Civic League founded
	Jamestown Exposition attracts many tourists to Williamsburg
1908	Confederate monument erected on palace green
	Williamsburg Female Institute opens (closes 1916)
1910	Population: 2,714
	First movie theatre opens
	Williamsburg Creamery established
	President William Howard Taft's visit begins custom of U.S. presidents' coming to Williamsburg

	Williamsburg Ice Cream factory opens
1911	Williamsburg League for Woman's Suffrage organized
1912	City officials forgot to hold election in June
1913	Palace Theater opens
	Council refuses to pay to have town clock wound
1914	Town library opens
1915	Citizens enjoy first community Christmas tree
	Odd Fellows' Hall begins showing movies for blacks
	City annexes college lands
1916	President Woodrow Wilson visits Williamsburg
	E.I. duPont deNemours builds ammunition plant at nearby Penniman
	Modern well-water system installed
1917	Williamsburg Power Company built to supply electricity to city
1918	Women admitted to William & Mary
1919	Mayor and City Council can issue bonds for schools, streets, and utilities
	Home mail delivery begins
1920	Population: 2,462
1921	Williamsburg High School (white) opens on the palace green
	President Warren G. Harding visits
	Duke of Gloucester St. paved
1924	James City County Training School (black) built at Nicholson and Botetourt streets
1926	First private hospital opens
	President Calvin Coolidge visits
	City Zoning Commission established

1926-27   Rev. Dr. W.A.R. Goodwin, once again rector of Bruton, persuades John D. Rockefeller, Jr., to restore Williamsburg

1930   Matthew Whaley School (white) built on Scotland St.

Council appoints first City Engineer (retitled "City Manager" in 1932)

Council creates City Planning Commission

Population: 3,778

Bell Hospital opens on Cary St.

1931   New Post Office begins operating

New Casey's store opens

Work on Colonial Parkway begins

Business block on Duke of Gloucester St. to be rebuilt

President Herbert Hoover visits

1932   New City charter: council to consist of five elected members who choose mayor and vice mayor from among themselves and appoint City Manager

New courthouse built on South England St.

A&P grocery store begins operating

St. Bede's Catholic Church opens

Raleigh Tavern opens as Colonial Williamsburg's first exhibition building

1933   Williamsburg Theatre opens—the first building in town with air conditioning

City annexes more college land

1934   New City Charter goes into effect: government reorganized

President Franklin D. Roosevelt officially opens Duke of Gloucester St.

First phase of the restoration of Colonial Williamsburg is substantially completed

1937   Williamsburg Inn admits first guests

1938   Williamsburg Pottery Factory opens

1939   Williamsburg Lodge opens

1940   Bruton Heights School (black) opens

Population: 3,942

1941   Bruton Heights auditorium equipped to serve as move theatre for blacks

1942   Colonial Parkway tunnel under the market square completed

1944   City acquires Waller Mill Reservoir

1946   Prime Minister Winston Churchill and General Dwight D. Eisenhower visit

1947   *The Common Glory* opens at Lake Matoaka amphitheatre

City adopts first zoning ordinance

1948   President Harry S. Truman visits

1950   First paid Fire Marshal hired

Population: 6,735

1953   Williamsburg/James City Co. school systems merge

City has its first modern comprehensive plan

President Eisenhower visits

1954   The Queen Mother Elizabeth visits

1955   First Baptist Church moves to Scotland St.

1956   Williamsburg Players founded

1957   Her Majesty Queen Elizabeth II and Prince Phillip visit

1958   Christian Science Church built on Jamestown Rd.

1959   Temple Beth El founded

King Hussein of Jordan pays his first of several visits

1960   Population: 6,832

1961   Williamsburg Community Hospital opens

1963   St. Stephen's Lutheran Church opens on Jamestown Rd.

Colonial Williamsburg acquires Carter's Grove

Wedgwood Dinner Theatre opens in Toano–closes in 1970

President Tito of Yugoslavia visits

First black undergraduate enrolls at William & Mary

1966   Prime Minister Indira Gandhi of India and King Faisal of Saudi Arabia visit

1967   President Lyndon B. Johnson visits

1968   New courthouse built on Court St.

Williamsburg/James City Co. schools desegregated

1969   Royal visitors include King Hussein of Jordan, King Baudouin I of Belgium, andthe Shah of Iran

An Occasion for the Arts begins

Walnut Hills Baptist Church built on Jamestown Rd.

1970   Population: 9,069

1971   President Richard M. Nixon visits

1973   National Center for State Courts headquartered here

Anheuser-Busch brewery built

1975   Japanese Emperor Hirohito and Egyptian President Anwar Sadat visit

Busch Gardens Williamsburg, a theme amusement park, opens

1976   Gerald Ford/Jimmy Carter presidential debate held at William & Mary

1978   Virginia Shakespeare Festival begins

1980   Population: 9,870

1981   H.R.H. Prince Charles, President François Mitterand of France, and President Ronald Reagan visit

1983   Economic Summit of Industrialized Nations meets here

1984   Most recent city annexation of adjacent county land: area of city now nine square miles

1985   DeWitt Wallace Decorative Arts Gallery opens

1990   Population: 11,409

Fire Marshall upgraded to Fire Chief

1993   William & Mary celebrates its 300th anniversary

1995   President William J. Clinton visits

1997   Chinese President Jiang Zemin visits

1999   New courthouse built on Monticello Ave.

Community Center and municipal complex open

Williamsburg's 300th Birthday

The 300th Birthday is over and the road signs come down in January 2000.

Courtesy, Charles C. Troha

Mayors of Williamsburg from 1722, The Date of the City's Incorporation

1772-23 John Holloway

(Record Incomplete)

1735-36 Abraham Nicholas

1736-37 Edward Barradall

1737-38 John Harmer

1738-39 Dr. Robert Davidson

(Record Incomplete)

1745-46 John Harmer

1746- ? George Gilmer

(Record Incomplete)

1748- ? John Anson

(Record Incomplete)

1751-52 John Blair, Jr.

1752-54 John Holt

1754-55 George Gilmer

1755-56 John Randolph

(Record Incomplete)

1757-58 Robert Carter Nicholas

(Record Incomplete)

1759-60 John Prentis

(Record Incomplete)

1765-66 John Randolph

1766-67 Thomas Everard

1767-68 James Cocke

1768-69 George Wythe

1769-70 John Blair, Jr.

1770-71 John Randolph

1771-72 Thomas Everard

1772-73 Thomas Cocke

1773-74 John Blair, Jr.

1774-75 John Dixon

1775-76 Dr. William Pasteur

1776- ? Edmund Randolph

(Record Incomplete)

1779-80 Samuel Griffin

(Record Incomplete)

1782-83 William Holt

1783- ? William Finnie

(Record Incomplete)

1787- ? Philip Barraud

(Record Incomplete)

1796-97 John Bracken

(Record Incomplete)

1800-01 John Bracken

1801- ? John Henderson

(Record Incomplete)

1805-06 Richard Greenhow

(Record Incomplete)

1812- ? Robert Anderson

(Record Incomplete)

1817- ? Robert Carr

(Record Incomplete)

1820- ? Robert Anderson

(Record Incomplete)

1822- ? William T. Banks

(Record Incomplete)

1828-29 Robert Anderson

1829-30 W. W. Webb

1830-31	Thomas Coleman	1888-90	T. M. Southall
1831- ?	Thomas G. Peachy	1890-96	John A. Henley
	(Record Incomplete)	1896-1904	John L. Mercer
1838-39	Beverley Tucker	1904-1916	E. W. Warburton
1839- ?	Robert Saunders	1917-28	Dr. John M. Henderson
	(Record Incomplete)	1928-29	John Garland Pollard
1850- ?	John W. Maupin	1929-34	George Preston Coleman
	(Record Incomplete)	1934-47	Channing M. Hall
1863-64	W. R. C. Douglas	1947-48	Vincent D. McManus
1864-68	John H. Barlow	1948-68	Dr. Henry M. Stryker
	(Record Incomplete)	1968-70	Vincent D. McManus
1869- ?	William A. Durfey	1970-80	Vernon Geddy
	(Record Incomplete)	1980-86	Robert Walker
1879-82	John A. Henley	1986-92	John Hodges
1882-83	E. H. Lively	1992-96	Trist McConnell
1883-84	Parke Slater	1996-98	Gilbert Granger
1884-86	T. M. Southall	1998-	Jeanne Zeidler
1886-88	John W. Davis		

Five men served as mayor or filled in unofficially during emergency situations for periods of six months or less: Lemuel Bowden in 1862, Robert Saunders and Robert F. Cole in 1868, John D. Munford in 1869, and L. W. Lane in 1904.

Compiled by Julia Woodbridge Oxrieder from City Council
minutes at the Library of Virginia, Richmond.

Williamsburg was not incorporated until 1722, during Alexander Spotswood's administration as lieutenant governor. The charter then granted read in part as follows:

GEORGE [I] by the Grace of God…KNOW YEE that we being willing to encourage all our good and faithfull Subjects…within the said Town of Williamsburg…HAVE constituted and erected, and by these our Letters Patents, do constitute and erect, the said Town of Williamsburg, and the said Ports…by the Name of the CITY OF WILLIAMSBURG:…the said City shall be a City incorporate, consisting of a Mayor, one Person learned in the Law stiled and bearing the Office of Recorder of the said City, six Aldermen, and twelve other Persons to be Common Council Men…AND we…appoint *John Holloway*, Esquire, to be Mayor of the said City for the Year ensuing, and afterwards, untill the Day for the Electing a Mayor herein after appointed….

Further on in this charter, the "Feast Day of Saint Andrew [30 November] in every Year" was named as the day on which the mayor, recorder, aldermen, and common council were to gather to elect a mayor, "by major Vote of such of them as shall be then present" from "one other of the Aldermen of the said City," to serve for the ensuing year.

Leaders of Williamsburg's Historically-Important Institutions

Presidents of the College of William & Mary

James Blair, 1693 – 1743

William Dawson, 1743 – 1752

William Stith, 1752 – 1755

Thomas Dawson, 1755 – 1760

William Yates, 1761 – 1764

James Horrocks, 1764 – 1771

John Camm, 1771 – 1777

James Madison, 1777 – 1812

John Bracken, 1812 – 1814

John Augustine Smith, 1814 – 1826

William H. Wilmer, 1826 – 1827

Adam Empie, 1827 – 1836

Thomas Roderick Dew, 1836 – 1846

Robert Saunders, 1846 – 1848

John Johns, 1849 – 1854

Benjamin S. Ewell, 1854 – 1888

Lyon G. Tyler, 1888 – 1919

Julian A. C. Chandler, 1919 – 1934

John Stewart Bryan, 1934 – 1942

John Edwin Pomfret, 1942 – 1951

Alvin Duke Chandler, 1951 – 1960

Davis Young Paschall, 1960 – 1971

Thomas Ashley Graves, Jr., 1971 – 1985

Paul R. Verkuil, 1985 – 1992

Timothy J. Sullivan, 1992 –

Chancellors of the College of William & Mary

Henry Compton, *Bishop of London*, 1693 – 1700

Thomas Tenison, *Archbishop of Canterbury*, 1700 – 1707

Henry Compton, *Bishop of London*, 1707 – 1713

John Robinson, *Bishop of London*, 1714 – 1721

William Wake, *Archbishop of Canterbury*, 1721 – 1729

Edmund Gibson, *Bishop of London*, 1729 – 1736

William Wake, *Archbishop of Canterbury*, 1736 – 1737

Edmund Gibson, *Bishop of London*, 1737 – 1748

Thomas Sherlock, *Bishop of London*, 1749 – 1761

Thomas Hayter, *Bishop of London*, 1762

Charles Wyndham, *Earl of Egremont*, 1762 – 1763

Philip Yorke, *Earl of Hardwicke*, 1764

Richard Terrick, *Bishop of London*, 1764 – 1776

George Washington, *First President of the United States*, 1788 – 1799

John Tyler, *Tenth President of the United States*, 1859 – 1862

Hugh Blair Grigsby, *Historian*, 1871 – 1881

John Stewart Bryan, *20th President of the College of William and Mary*, 1942 – 1944

Colgate W. Darden, Jr., *Governor of Virginia*, 1946 – 1947

Alvin Duke Chandler, *22nd President of the College of William and Mary*, 1962 – 1974

Warren E. Burger, *15th Chief Justice of the United States*, 1986 – 1993

Margaret, The Lady Thatcher, *Former Prime Minister of Great Britain*, 1994 – 2000

Directors of Eastern State Hospital

James Galt, 1773 – 1800

William T. Galt, 1800 – 1826

Jesse Cole, 1826

Dickie Galt, 1826 – 1836

Henry Edloe, 1837

Philip I. Barziza, 1837 – 1841

Alexander D. Galt, M.D., 1841

John Minson Galt II, M.D., 1841 – 1862

Peter Wagner, M.D., 1862 - 1865

5th PA. Cavalry, U.S. Army Occupation

Leonard Henley, M.D., 1865 – 1866

Robert M. Garrett, M.D., 1866 - 1868

A. E. Peticolas, M.D., 1868

F. Camm, M.D., 1868 – 1869

D. R. Brower, M.D., 1869 – 1876

Harvey Black, M.D., 1876 – 1882

Richard A. Wise, M.D., 1882 – 1884

James D. Moncure, M.D., 1884 – 1898

John W. Nash, M.D., 1898 - 1899

L. S. Foster, M.D., 1899 – 1907

O. C. Brunk, M.D., 1907 – 1911

George W. Brown, M.D., 1911 – 1943

Joseph E. Barrett, M.D., 1943 – 1946

Granville L. Jones, M.D., 1946 – 1956

Joseph E. Barrett, M.D., 1957 – 1959

James B. Funkhouser, M.D., 1959 – 1960

Howard H. Ashbury, M.D., 1960 – 1972

Kurt T. Schmidt, M.D., 1972 – 1979

David C. Pribble, 1979 – 1991

John M. Favret, 1992 –

Chairmen of the Board(s) & Presidents of the Colonial Williamsburg Foundation

CHAIRMEN

No official position, only acting chairmen, 1928 –1934

Arthur Woods, 1935 – 1939

John D. Rockefeller, 3rd, 1939 – 1953

Winthrop Rockefeller, 1953 – 1973

Lewis F. Powell, Jr., 1973 – 1977

Carlisle H. Humelsine, 1977 – 1985

Charles L. Brown, 1985 – 1991

Charles R. Longsworth, 1991 – 1994

George B. Beitzel, 1994 – 1998

Colin G. Campbell, 1998 –

PRESIDENTS

Vernon M. Geddy, Sr., 1928 – 1928

Arthur Woods, 1928 – 1935

Kenneth Chorley, 1935 – 1958

Carlisle H. Humelsine, 1958 – 1977

Charles R. Longsworth, 1977 – 1992

Robert C. Wilburn, 1992 – 1999

Frederick C. Nahm (Acting) , 1999 –

Sponsors

Sean and Lauren Allburn
Margaret and Robert Birney
Chambrel at Williamsburg
Nan and Pete Cruikshank
Jamestown-Yorktown Foundation
Jamestown Settlement & Yorktown Victory Center Museums
Helen and Trist McConnell
Sheila and Terry Meyers
Newport News - Williamsburg Airport
Prime Outlets - Williamsburg
Thaddeus W. Tate, Jr.

❊❊❊

In Honor of the Sarantos George Genakos Family
given by George S. and Jean M. Genakos
In Honor of Kathy, Russell, Keith and Bruce Hornsby
given by Ann and Jim Yankovich
In Honor of Lois S. Hornsby
given by 300th Anniversary Commission
In Honor of Vernon L. and Elizabeth K. Nunn
given by Joyce and John McKnight

❊❊❊

In Memory of the Honorable Russell M. Carneal
In Memory of Channing M. Hall, Sr.
by Mrs. Channing M. Hall, Jr., Channing M. Hall, III and John Lesslie Hall, III
In Memory of Channing M. Hall, Jr.
by Mrs. Channing M. Hall, Jr., Channing M. Hall, III and John Lesslie Hall, III
In Memory of Robert S. Hornsby
In Memory of S. Dean Olson
In Memory of the Honorable A. B. Smith, Jr.

Joshua Cobb in the 1999 Chamber of Commerce Christmas Parade.

Courtesy, Charles C. Troha